Tracing the Earliest Recorded Concepts of International Law

Legal History Library

VOLUME 8

Studies in the History of International Law

VOLUME 4

The titles published in this series are listed at brill.nl/lhl

Tracing the Earliest Recorded Concepts of International Law

The Ancient Near East (2500–330 BCE)

By

Amnon Altman

MARTINUS NIJHOFF PUBLISHERS

LEIDEN · BOSTON
2012

Cover illustration: The Assyrian king Shalmaneser III shaking hand with a Babylonian king, very likely Marduk-zakir-shumi, beneath a canopy. The picture is taken by permission from M.E.L. Mallowan, *Nimrud and its Remains* (1966), Vol. 2, p. 447, fig. 371d. Photograph by courtesy of the British Institute for the Study of Iraq.

Library of Congress Cataloging-in-Publication Data

Altman, Amnon, 1935–
Tracing the earliest recorded concepts of international law : the ancient Near East (2500–330 BCE) / By Amnon Altman.
p. cm.—(Legal history library ; 8) (Studies in the history of international law)
Includes bibliographical references and index.
ISBN 978-90-04-22252-6 (hardback : alk. paper)
1. International law—History. 2. Law—Middle East—History. 3. Law, Ancient. I. Title.

KZ1242.A44 2012
341.0935—dc23

2012007324

This publication has been typeset in the multilingual "Brill" typeface. With over 5,100 characters covering Latin, IPA, Greek, and Cyrillic, this typeface is especially suitable for use in the humanities. For more information, please see www.brill.nl/brill-typeface.

ISSN 1874-1793
ISBN 978 90 04 22252 6 (hardback)
ISBN 978 90 04 22253 3 (e-book)

This book is printed on acid-free paper.

Dedicated to the memory of
Prof. Pinḥas Artzi
(23.5.1923—8.4.2007)

CONTENTS

GENERAL EDITOR'S PREFACE

Within the grand narrative of the history of international law as it appears from Western historiography, the Ancient Near East holds its place, if only at the fringe. As the civilisations of the Ancient Near East and pre-Hellenistic Greece are considered the cradles of Western civilisation, historians of international law have time and again asked themselves if modern international law has roots in ideas and practices stemming from this remote past. But this interest has induced very few historians of international law to study the laws and rules governing the international relations of the Ancient Near East in depth and in their own right. The discourse of international legal historians on the Ancient Near East and by extension on classical Antiquity is by and large dictated by the concern about their place in the overall history of (Western) international law.

In fact, much of the debate on ancient international law among historians of international law focuses on two questions. First, did 'international law' exist in Antiquity, and if so, in what periods from Antiquity? This question is looked at from two perspectives. On the one hand, there is the question whether the necessary conditions were fulfilled for an 'international law' to emerge. For most authors, this would mean the existence of regular relations between mutually independent powers, or by extension, the existence of an international community of independent powers. On the other hand, there are the related questions whether the rules governing these relations qualify as law and as 'international' in the sense that they are based on international consent. Second, did the 'international law' of Antiquity have any impact on later, medieval and modern, international law? Can we speak of a continuous development, and if so, how did it come about?

But as Carlo Focarelli explains in a paper to be published in one of the next volumes in this series,[1] even a negative answer to both questions would not make the study of Antiquity obsolete for the understanding of modern international law. Regardless whether 'international law'

[1] Carlo Focarelli, 'The Early Doctrine of International Law as a Bridge from Antiquity to Modernity and Diplomatic Inviolability in 16th- and 17th-Century European Practice', in Randa ll Lesaffer (ed.), *The Twelve Years Truce (1609–1621): Peace, truce, war and law in the Low Countries at the turn of the 17th Century* (Studies in the History of International Law, Leyden/Boston: Martinus Nijhoff, forthcoming).

existed in Antiquity and regardless whether it had any real impact on later developments, to the writers from the Early Modern Age it did and it had. Many of the practices and doctrines of the law of nations of the Late Middle Ages that survived into the Early Modern Age and from there on found their way into modern international law, had been informed by the late-medieval jurisprudence of Roman and canon law, which in turn was influenced by ancient Roman law. Moreover, under the influence of humanism, the great writers on the law of nations from the 16th and 17th centuries made ample use of historical examples which they drew from historical, religious and rhetorical sources from Antiquity, most of these referring to classical history but some also to pre-classical—in particular biblical—history. To them, the impact of Antiquity was a given. This in itself should give the study of 'international law' in Antiquity an impetus, as it raises the question to what extent the views on ancient 'international law' of the early-modern writers was formed by their own concerns and to what extent it rested on a correct understanding of ancient practices and ideas.

But all this hardly led to a sustained effort in modern scholarship to study the history of international relations and law in the Ancient Near East. Apart from an interest which is too much determined by the continuity debate, this also has its causes in the linguistic and other demands the historiography of the periods imposes upon the scholar. Altman's book goes quite a way in filling the gap in our knowledge which has been left by international legal history-writing. Professor Amnon Altman from the Bar-Ilan University in Ramat Gan (Israel) is an accomplished historian of the Ancient Near East. For four decades, he has researched and published about the international relations of the powers of the Middle East, mostly from the second half of the 2nd millennium BC. Over time, he has built up a vast knowledge of and insight in the international relations of the period. He is, as few are, acquainted with the sources and modern scholarship relating to the period and the subject.

With this book, Altman discloses a lot of the knowledge historians and archaeologists of the Ancient Near East have to offer relevant to the history of international law. Altman does not concern himself neither with the question about the existence of a pre-classical 'international law', nor with the continuity debate. As he explains himself, he browses 'through the available sources looking for interstate affairs in order to glean from them practices that might have been regulated by some accepted rule.' While this might leave the reader looking for the grand narrative of ancient international law somewhat disoriented, this approach makes

Altman's book into a treasure-trove of information on the ideas and practices of international relations and the rules that guided them from the Ancient Near East, many of which are for the first time disclosed to non-specialists of the era. As such, Altman's book will offer a steadier ground to stand on for international legal historians looking for the oldest roots of international law.

Randall Lesaffer

ACKNOWLEDGEMENTS

The writer is indebted to Dr. Joan Goodnick Westenholz, chief curator at the Bible Lands Museum, Jerusalem, for her comments on the first draft of Chapter 2; to Prof. Jack M. Sasson, of Vanderbilt University, Nashville TN, for his comments on the first draft of Chapter 3; and to Prof. Israel Eph'al and Prof. Mordechai Cogan, both of the Hebrew University, Jerusalem, for their comments on the first draft of Chapter 5. Gratitude is also due Mrs. Bella Barneah, and to my former students and friends Mr. Jacques I. Offen and Mr. Joseph Ra'anan, for their help in processing the materials. Finally, thanks are due to Mr. Raphael Rosenbaum, my copy-editor, for rendering this book more readable.

The writer thanks the following publishers for granting him permission to quote from their books:

Helsinki University Press, for quoting passages from Ivan Starr, *Queries to the Sungod—Divination and Politic in Sargonid Assyria* (SAA IV), 1990.

The Netherlands Institute for the Near East, for quoting from S. Greengus, *Old Babylonian Tablets from Ishchali and Vicinity* (PIHANS 44), 1979.

University of California Press, for quoting from Miriam Lichtheim, *Ancient Egyptian Literature*, Vol. II: *The New Kingdom*, © 1979 by the Regents of the University of California, Published by the University of California Press.

Princeton University Press, for quoting from James B. Pritchard (ed.), *Ancient Near Eastern Texts Relating to the Old Testament*, 3rd edition with supplement © 1950, 1955, 1969, renewed 1978 by Princeton University Press.

The Society of Biblical Literature, for quoting from—

Gary Beckman, *Hittite Diplomatic Texts*, 2nd edition 1999;

Harry A. Hoffner Jr., *Letters from the Hittite Kingdom*. 2009;

Martti Nissinen, *Prophets and Prophecy*, 2003.

University of Toronto Press, for quoting from—

Douglas R. Frayne, *Presargonic Period (2700–2350 BC)* The Royal Inscriptions of Mesopotamia, Early Periods Vol. 1 (RIME 1), © University of Toronto Press, 2008.

Douglas R. Frayne, *Sargonic and Gutian Periods (2334–2113 BC)*, The Royal Inscriptions of Mesopotamia, Early Periods Vol. 2 (RIME 2), © University of Toronto Press, 1993.

Douglas R. Frayne, *Ur III Period (2112–2004 BC)*, The Royal Inscriptions of Mesopotamia, Early Periods Vol. 3/2 (RIME 3/2), © University of Toronto Press, 1997.

Kirk A. Grayson, *Assyrian Rulers of the Third and Second Millennia*, Vol. I (*To 1115 BC*), and Vol. 2 (*1114–859 BC*), The Royal Inscriptions of Mesopotamia, Assyrian Periods Vols. 1–2 (RIMA 1–2), © University of Toronto Press, 1987 and 1991.

The book is dedicated to the memory of my former teacher and later friend and colleague, Prof. Pinhas Artzi of Bar-Ilan University Departments of History and Hebrew and Semitic Languages who, back in 1959, introduced me to the world of Assyriology, and later to the specific field of interstate relations in the Ancient Near East.

PREFACE

The object of this study is to collect, present and discuss attested conduct and proclaimed statements pertaining to the realm of international relations, which seem to disclose accepted concepts and in certain cases customary rules of international law practiced in the Ancient Near East. It is intended primarily for scholars engaged in the history of international law, this in order to close what seems to the present writer a wide gap between what is known today about this field of study among historians of the Ancient Near East and among historians of international law with regard to the Ancient Near East. As a second objective, it was written with students of Biblical and Ancient Near Eastern studies in mind, hoping that this book will contribute to the meager collection of Ancient Near Eastern studies in the field of international law and promote further research.

The chapters of this book were published originally as a series of articles under the same title in the *Journal of the History of International Law*, Vols. 6/2 (2004), 153–172; 7/2 (2005), 115–136; 10/1 (2008), 1–33; 11/1 (2009), 125–186; 11/2 (2009), 333–356; 12/1 (2010), 101–153. It was at the suggestion of the present publisher that these articles be compiled into a book. While retaining these articles mostly unchanged, some modifications were needed in order to accommodate them to a book format, as well as updating mainly in the references.

ABBREVIATIONS AND SYMBOLS

Bibliographic Abbreviations

A	Registration number of texts found at Mari.
ABL	R.F. Harper, *Assyrian and Babylonian Letters belonging to the Kouyounjik Collection of the British Museum*, 14 vols., London and Chicago 1892–1914.
AbB	F.R. Kraus (ed., later edited by K.R. Veenhof), *Altbabylonische Briefe*, 14 Vols., Leiden 1964–.
AfO	*Archiv für Orientforschung*, Berlin 1926–.
AHw	W. Von Soden, *Akkadisches Handwörterbuch*, I–III, Wiesbaden 1965–1981.
ANET^{3}	J. Pritchard (ed.), *Ancient Near Eastern Texts*, 3rd edition, Princeton, Princeton University Press 1969.
ARAB	D.D. Luckenbill, *Ancient Records of Assyria and Babylonia* Vols. I–II, Chicago 1927.
ARM	Archives royals de Mari, Paris 1946–.
ARMT	Archives royals de Mari, Traductions, Paris 1950–.
AT	Alalakh Tablets, edited by Wiseman 1953.
ATHE	B. Kienast, *Die altassyrischen Texte des Orientalischen Seminars des Universität Heidelberg und der Sammlung Erlenmeyer*, Berlin 1960.
BBSt	L.W. King, *Babylonian Boundary-Stones and Memorial Tablets in the British Museum*, London 1912.
BIN 6	Babylonian inscriptions in the collection of J.B. Nies, Vol. 6: *Old Assyrian Letters and Business Documents*, by F.J. Stephens, New Haven 1944.
BM	Objects at the British Museum, London.
Bo	Inventory numbers of Boğazköy tablets excavated 1906–12.
Borger *Ash*	R. Borger, *Die Inschriften Asarhaddons Königs von Assyrien* (*AfO* Beiheft 9) 1956.
Borger *BIWA*	R. Borger, *Beiträge zum Inschriftenwerk Assurbanipals. Die Prismenklassen A, B, C = K, D, E, F, G, H, J und T sowie andere Inschriften, Mit einem Beitrag von A. Fuchs*, Wiesbaden: Harrassowitz Verlag 1996.
CAD	*The Assyrian Dictionary of the Oriental Institute of the University of Chicago*, Chicago 1956–.

CAH^2	J. Boardman *et al.* (eds.), *The Cambridge Ancient History*, 2nd edition.
Vol. III/1	*The Prehistory of the Balkans; and the Middle East and the Aegean world, tenth to eighth centuries B.C.*, Cambridge 1982.
Vol. III/2	*The Assyrian and Babylonian Empires and other States of the Near East, from the Eighth to the Sixth Centuries B.C.*, Cambridge 1991.
Vol. IV	*Persia, Greece and the Western Mediterranean c. 525 to 479 B.C.*, Cambridge 1988.
CHD	*The Hittite Dictionary of the Oriental Institute of the University of Chicago*, edited by Hans G. Güterbock, and Harry A. Hoffner, Jr., Chicago 1980–.
CTH	E. Laroche, *Catalogue des textes hittites*, Paris 1971 (Suppl. in *RHA* 30, 1972).
EA	El-Amarna tablets according to the edition of Knudtzon 1915 and Rainey 1978.
ETCSL	J.A. Black, *et al.*, *The Electronic Text Corpus of Sumerian Literature* (http://etcsl.orinst.ox.ac.uk/), Oxford 1998–.
HKM	S. Alp, *Hethitische Keilschrifttafeln aus Maşat-Höyük*, Ankara 1991.
HSM	Harvard Semitic Museum Monographs, Cambridge (Mass.).
JAOS	*Journal of the American Oriental Society*, New Haven 1843–.
JCS	*Journal of Cuneiform Studies*, New Haven, Connecticut 1947–.
JHIL	*Journal of the History of International Law*, Leiden 1999–.
JNES	*Journal of Near Eastern Studies*, Chicago 1942–.
K	Tablets in the Kouyunjik collection of the British Museum.
KBo	Keilschrifttexte aus Boghazköi, Leipzig/Berlin 1916–.
Kt	Sigla of texts from Kültepe.
KUB	Keilschrifturkunden aus Boghazköi, Berlin 1921–.
LAPO	Littératures anciennes du Proche-Orient, Paris.
16–18	J.-M. Durand, *Les documents épistolaires du palais de Mari*, I–III, Paris 1997, 1998, 2000.
M	Registration number of texts found at Mari.
MARI	*Mari. Annales de Recherches Interdisciplinaires.* Paris 1982–.
MDOG	*Mitteilungen der Deutschen Orient-Gesellschaft*, Berlin 1898–.
MVAeG	*Mitteilungen der Vorderasiatisch-Ägyptischen Gesellschaft*, Leipzig 1896–1947.
NABU	*Nouvelles Assyriologiques Breves et Utilitaires.* Paris 1987–.

ND	Objects excavated in the British excavation at Nimrud, Iraq.
PRU	*Le palais royal d'Ugarit*, Paris.
PRU III	J. Nougayrol, *Textes accadiens et hourrites des archives est, oust et centralles*, Paris 1955.
PRU IV	J. Nougayrol, *Textes accadiens des archives sud.* Paris 1956.
RA	*Revue d'Assyriologie et d'Archéologie*, Paris 1884–.
RHA	*Revue Hittite et asianique.* Paris 1930–1978.
RIDA	*Revue internationale des droits de l'antiquité*, 3e série, Bruxelles 1954–.
RIMA	The Royal Inscriptions of Mesopotamia. Assyrian Periods.
RIMA 1	A.K. Grayson, *Assyrian Rulers of the Third and Second Millennia BC (to 1115 BC)*, with the assistance of G. Frame and D. Frayne, and a contribution of M. Maidman, Toronto-Buffalo-London 1987.
RIMA 2	A.K. Grayson, *Assyrian Rulers of the Early First Millennium BC*, I (*1114–859 BC*), Toronto – Buffalo – London, 1991.
RIMA 3	A.K. Grayson, *Assyrian Rulers of the Early First Millennium BC*, II (*858–745 BC*), Toronto – Buffalo – London, 1996.
RIME	The Royal Inscriptions of Mesopotamia. Early Periods.
RIME 1	D. Frayne, *Pre-Sargonic Period* (*2700–2350 BC*), Toronto – Buffalo – London, 2008.
RIME 2	D. Frayne, *Sargonic and Gutian Periods* (*2334–2113 BC*), Toronto – Buffalo – London, 1993.
RIME 3/1	D.O. Edzard, *Gudea and His Dynasty*, Toronto – Buffalo – London, 1997.
RIME 3/2	D. Frayne, *Ur III Period* (*2112–2004 BC*), Toronto – Buffalo – London, 1997.
RIME 4	D. Frayne, *Old Babylonian Period* (*2003–1595 BC*), Toronto – Buffalo – London, 1990.
RlA	*Reallexikon der Assyriologie und vorderasiatischen Archäologie*, Berlin – New York 1932–.
RS	Tablets excavated at Ras Shamra, Syria.
SAA	State Archives of Assyria, Helsinki.
SAA 1	S. Parpola, *The Correspondence of Sargon II, Part I: Letters from Assyria and the West*, 1987.
SAA 2	S. Parpola and K. Watanabe, *Neo-Assyrian Treaties and Loyalty Oaths*, 1988.
SAA 4	I. Starr, *Queries to the Sungod. Divination and Politics in Sargonid Assyria*, 1990.

SAA 5	G.B. Lanfranchi and S. Parpola, *The Correspondence of Sargon II*, Part II: *Letters from the Northern and Northeastern Provinces*, 1990.
SAA 18	F. Reynolds, *The Babylonian Correspondence of Esarhaddon and Letters to Assurbanipal and Sin-šarru-iškun from Northern and Central Babylonia*, 2003.
SAAS	State Archives of Assyria Studies, Helsinki.
StBoT	Studien zu den Boğazköy-Texten, Wiesbaden.
StBoT Beih.1	H. Otten, *Die Bronzetafel aus Boğazköy—Ein Staatsvertrag Tuthalijas IV.*, Wiesbaden: Otto Harrassowitz. 1988.
Streck, Asb.	M. Streck, *Assurbanipal und die letzten assyrischen Könige bis zum Untergang Niniveh's*, I–III (Vorderasiatische Bibliothek 7), Leipzig: J.C. Hinrichs 1916.
TCL	Textes Cunéiformes du Louve, Paris.
TCL III	F. Thureau-Dangin, *Une relation de la huitième campagne de Sargon, Paris: P. Geuthner 1912.*
THeth	Texte der Hethiter, Heidelberg.
Urk IV	K. Sethe, *Urkunden der 18. Dynastie* (*Urkunden des ägyptischen Altertums*, IV. Abt.). Translations: fasc. 1–4 (Urk. IV 1–313) by K. Sethe, Leipzig 1914 (reprinted: Berlin 1984); fasc. 5–16 (Urk. IV 315–1225) by A. Burkhardt et al., Berlin 1984; fasc. 17–22 (Urk. IV 1227–2179), by W. Helck, Berlin 1961.
YBC	Yale Babylonian Collection.
ZA	*Zeitschrift für Assyriologie und verwandte Gebiete*, Leipzig. 1886–.
ZAR	*Zeitschrift für Altorientalische und Biblische Rechtsgeschichte*, Wiesbaden 1995–.

Other Abbreviations and Symbols

obv.	obverse
rev.	reverse
[ ]	encloses restorations of lacunae
⌜ ⌝	partial restoration
< >	encloses text assumed to be omitted by scribal error
( )	encloses clarification additions in translations
[...]	indicates a break in the text
...	indicates omission by the present writer in translations
+	a joint

INTRODUCTION

We do not know, and will very likely never know, when and under what circumstances the first rules of behavior, designated to regulate the relations between two or more human groups, were created. Hidden deep in the mists of the very long prehistoric era, they are far beyond our reach. We may speculate about the circumstances of their first appearance, but it is only with the invention of writing, and when echoes of these early rules were given in writing, that we can speak more confidently about this issue.

Writing first appeared in the Near East during the late fourth millennium BCE with the earliest written documents from the site of Warka, ancient Uruk (biblical Erech), in the southernmost part of Mesopotamia (ca. 3100 BCE). Yet, for the next six hundred years or so the employment of writing was restricted to economic and administrative records, and to sign-lists for the use of the scribal schools.[1] It is only from around 2500 BCE that we have the first royal inscriptions reporting political events, and it is only from this date on that our research could start.

The period covered by the present study extends from 2500 BCE up to the fall of the Achaemenid Persian Empire in 330 BCE and the conquests of Alexander the Great that introduced the Hellenistic Period. During this long period, the geographic horizon of the available documents gradually changed. While the earliest documentation, that of the years 2500–2350 BCE, is confined to only southern Mesopotamia, at the last phase of this long period it reached its furthest extension with its arena stretching from the Hellespont to Egypt and as far as northern India. At the same time, the ethnic and cultural makeup of this changing arena had also gradually changed with the influx of new ethnic groups. This, in turn, poses a question as to whether it is proper to speak about one uniform set of interstate conduct rules and to what extent we may maintain that there was a continuity of these rules throughout this long period. We may assume, indeed, that the necessity of co-existence sooner or later should have brought the diverse peoples to come to terms with each other and to create a unified international community following one set of accepted

[1] See for these Englund 1998. Toward the end of this stage, ca. 2600–2500 BCE, also literary compositions started to be written. For these, see Krebernik 1998: pp. 317–335.

rules. For that matter, the Akkadian language and its cuneiform writing system, that during the second millennium BCE was adapted as the *lingua franca* of international relations throughout western Asia, should have made a significant contribution. Nevertheless, we must bear in mind that we do not have information covering all the peoples living in the region during this entire period; nor can we ever be sure that the same set of rules was acceptable by all. In order to avoid this limitation, as well as to avoid of what may emerge as a false impression of the continuation of one set of rules throughout this long period, I preferred to divide this period into five separate spans of time in order to spotlight the changing geographic horizon at each stage illuminated by the documents, as well as the appearance of new peoples.

Of the hundreds of thousands of documents exposed from this period, including a number of law collections found in Mesopotamia and Asia Minor,[2] not one single document recording either statutory or customary law pertaining to interstate relations has been so far discovered. This is not to speak about a theoretical treatise, which not only was not recovered so far, but also most likely was never written. Moreover, in order to consider a certain conduct as reflecting accepted rules of international law, more than one reference to that conduct involving more than one country needs to be discovered, but such cases are still quite rare.

These facts necessarily had, and still have, an impact on the research in this field. In sharp contrast to the many studies devoted to the civil laws of the Ancient Near East, there was, and still is, hardly any significant research on the international law of this period and region, with the exception of two areas: treaties and diplomacy. Interest in diplomacy evolved shortly after the discovery of the el-Amarna tablets in 1887,[3] and strengthened with the publication, starting in 1946, of the first volumes of letters from the rich archives of Mari,[4] and the diplomatic archives in Ugarit in 1956.[5] As with diplomacy, interest in treaties followed their discovery. Up to 1906 only one treaty was known, the Egyptian version of the treaty concluded between the Hittite king Hattušili III and the Egyptian king Ramesses II. It was only after the first seven Hittite treaties discovered in 1906 were published—first in 1916 with only cuneiform copies (KBo I),

[2] For which see more recently Martha T. Roth 1995.
[3] Bezold 1893.
[4] Munn-Rankin 1956.
[5] Nougayrol 1956.

and later with their transliterations and translations[6]—that they could be available to the wide scholar commuity. A further impetus to the study of Ancient Near Eastern treaties was given in an article by G.E. Mendenhall in 1954, where he pointed out the affinity between the Hittite treaties and the Biblical covenant, a claim that drew many Biblical scholars to a deeper study of the treaties.

Apart from the study of diplomacy and treaties, hardly any more comprehensive study of Ancient Near Eastern international law was attempted. Of the few attempts made by Assyriologists, one should mention the dissertation of J.R. Ziskind (1967), the article of R. Westbrook in Cohen and Westbrook 2000: pp. 28–41, 239–242, and the articles of R. Westbrook, J. Cooper, J. Eidem, G. Beckman and S. Parpola in Westbrook (ed.) 2003: Vol. I, pp. 82–85, 241–251; 745–752; 753–774; Vol. II, pp. 1047–1066. Of studies made by non-Assyriologists, an article of W. Prieser (1954), and the book of D.J. Bederman (2001) should be mentioned. In view of the very meager number of comprehensive studies by Assyriologists, it is no wonder that historians of international law seem to have no interest in Ancient Near Eastern materials.

This apparent ignorance by non-Assyriologists has its roots in the objection declared by many legal historians against associating "international law" with "antiquity", not to say with the "Ancient Near East". While the very idea of "international law" was debated by some juristic thinkers,[7] many more have rejected the idea that we may refer to international law before modern times.[8] It was not before 1911 that the first serious work to review the Greek and Roman concepts and rules of international law appeared,[9] and not before the end of World War II that the first advocate

[6] In 1916 the first volume of KBo (by H.H. Figulla and E.F. Weidner) appeared, including cuneiform copies of seven Hittite treaties (*CTH* 41.I, 51, 52, 53, 75, 91, 92). The first (English) translation of the Hittite-Egyptian treaty (*CTH* 91) was done by S. Langdon and A.H. Gardiner in 1920, and the first (English) translation of the seven treaties, whose cuneiform copies were published in KBo I, was provided by D.D. Luckenbill in 1921. In 1922, E.F. Weidner published KUB III, including copies of new treaties, as well as some duplicates of the older ones. In 1923, Weidner published a transliteration and improved German translation of all the Hittite treaties drawn up in Akkadian whose cuneiform copies were published in KBo I and KUB III. The major source-book for Hittite treaties drawn up in the Hittite language was published by J. Friedrich 1926 and 1930. In 1931, appeared V. Korošec's dissertation on the Hittite treaties, a study that still serves as the basis for any discussion of them.

[7] Most prominent among them is John Austin, the founder of the so-called analytical school of jurisprudence, whose book, containing a criticism of the idea that "international law" may be considered as "law", appeared in 1832.

[8] For a short review, see Bederman 2001: pp. 11–13.

[9] Phillipson 1911; cf. there his assertions on p. viif.

in favor of including the Ancient Near East in the history of international law voiced his arguments.[10] Only then, some references to Ancient Near Eastern diplomacy and treaties started to appear in the histories of international law.[11] Yet, even then, not the entire span of time covered by the present discourse was considered as contributing to its history. Setting down the existence of an international legal order as the essential criteria for the examination of the question whether a law of nations existed in Antiquity,[12] it was asserted that only two spans of time, each case for only about two hundred and fifty years, may be taken into account for the existence of such an order in the Ancient Near East.[13] However, if it is accepted that "an international legal order can only be assumed to exist if there is a plurality of relatively independent (although not necessarily equal-ranking) bodies politic which are linked to each other in political, economic and cultural relationships and which are not subject to a superimposed authority having comprehensive law-making jurisdiction and executive competence" and that "in their mutual relations these bodies politic must observe norms which are deemed to be binding on the basis of a legal consciousness rooted in religious, cultural and other common values",[14] then more and enlarged spans of time, particularly the 19th and 18th centuries BCE, should be taken into account for the Ancient Near East.

There is still another question involved here, one that at the present state of our knowledge cannot be answered, and that is whether we may consider the rules of the Ancient Near East as of the basis for modern European international law. For apart from the difficulty of proving an uninterrupted continuity of principles and practice of international law from the Classical period to the late Middle Ages, there is a serious obstacle in establishing continuity from the Ancient Near East to the Greek-

[10] Preiser 1954.

[11] E.g. Nussbaum 1954: pp. 1–2; see also Stadtmüller 1951 who started dealing with the history of international law with the ancient orient (the book was not available to me; the reference is taken from Hueck 2001: p. 195 with note 3).

[12] Grewe 2000: p. 7.

[13] According to Preiser (1984b: p. 133f.), we may speak about an international legal system in the Ancient Near East only from about 1450 to 1200 BCE and from 600 to around 540 BCE with the establishment of the Achaemenid Empire; Grewe (2000: p. 10) delimited these two spans of time from 1450 to 1200 BCE, and from 600 to 338 BCE; Bederman (2001: p. 16) found state system and international relations to have existed in the Ancient Near East from 1400 to 1150 BCE and from 966 to 700 BCE.

[14] Grewe 2000: p. 7.

Roman world. Trade between the Aegean and the Near East existed at least as early as the second Millennium BCE. Those contacts and the later Greek settlements in the Levant, as well as Phoenician trade with the Greek and Roman world, might have served as channels through which Ancient Near Eastern cultural elements, including the tenets of international law, might have become known to the Greek world and later also to the Romans.[15] Other possible channels that might have transferred the legacy of the Ancient Near Eastern tenets of international law to the Romans and then, either via them or directly, to the late Middle Ages are the fathers of the early Christian church on the one hand, and the Seleucids, the Parthians, the Sasanians, and their later successor—Islam, on the other hand. However, while this question still remains to be solved, I rather adhere to the opinion that "general legal history is, for good reasons, concernd with all legal developments of the past regardless both of where or when they appeared, and also of whether or not they prevailed over the longer term. The history of international law has no reason for proceeding otherwise."[16]

In the following pages I will ignore the question whether the norms discussed in this study had some influence over other peoples beyond those of the Ancient Near East. I will also ignore the question whether in each of the five spans of time, into which the long period of the history of the Ancient Near East was divided here, there existed an international legal order, and whether in each of those spans the attested relations between the various bodies politic were indeed stable enough so that an international legal system could progress beyond an early stage.[17] Assuming that in many cases the lack of evidence for the existence of the conditions needed for the creation of such a system is but a result of the chances of finding the relevant documentation, I will concentrate on browsing through the available sources looking for interstate affairs in order to glean from them practices that might have been regulated by some accepted rule. Yet, by

---

[15] Indeed, some similarities in the formulation of treaties have been pointed out, indicating possible Ancient Near Eastern influence on the West; see e.g. Weinfeld 1973; Barré 1983 (see in particular his conclusions on pp. 100–103); Karavites 1992. However, at the same time findings in recent decades in the Ancient Near East, as will be presented here, reveal some clear differences in the practice of treaty-making as well as in diplomacy and other fields of international law between the East and the West.

[16] Preiser 1984a: p. 128.

[17] See the criteria set down by Preiser 1984a: p. 133 in justification of his denial of the relations between the Sumerian city-states as sufficient for the creation of a real international legal system.

no means does the present study claim to exhaust the available documentation. Moreover, one has to keep in mind that there is a steady flow of new documentation and each day may bring up new information. Thus, whatever might be the shortcomings of this study, in view of this steady flow it may sooner or later necessitate a revision.

Unless otherwise stated, all the dates given in this book are Before the Common Era (BCE). Quotations from the Bible are according to the new English translation of the Holy Scriptures according to the Masoretic text by the Jewish Publication Society of America, Second Edition, Philadelphia 1999.

CHAPTER ONE

THE EARLY DYNASTIC PERIOD IN SOUTHERN MESOPOTAMIA (2900–2350)[1]

1. The Geo-Political Scene, the Actors and the Sources

From around 2900 on, the alluvial plain of southern Mesopotamia, which much later became known by the name Babylonia, seems to have been populated by two distinct ethnic groups who divided it into roughly two equal halves. The southern half was occupied by Sumerians, whose language cannot be affiliated to any of the known language families, while the northern part was occupied by Semitic Akkadians, whose language constitutes the eastern branch of the Semitic language family. Recent studies have suggested that there was a striking difference between the political organizations of these two groups. While the Sumerians developed a system of independent city-states, the Akkadians seem never to have developed such a system, and there are strong reasons to believe that during most of the 27th–24th centuries the northern part had the form of a single political configuration. The paramount position in it was held by the city of Kiš, while two other secondary power-centers, Akšak and Mari, seem to have competed with Kiš for the control of that configuration.[2] The much later "*Sumerian King List*",[3] and some Sumerian literary works commemorating the struggles of the southern city of Uruk with the

[1] For a more recent review of the chronological question regarding the different phases of the so-called "Early Dynastic Period" (c. 2900–2350), see Frayne 2008: pp. 3–5. For a recent detailed survey of the documents of this period and the information they provide about the history of southern Mesopotamia at this period, as well as about religion, military aspects, economy, administration, and private life, followed by a quite detailed bibliography, see Bauer 1998. For more concise surveys, see Edzard 2002a; Steinkeller 1992: pp. 724–726; Kuhrt 1995: I, pp. 27–44.

[2] See more recently Steinkeller 1993: pp. 116ff.

[3] For which see Jacobsen 1939, and there pp. 77–85 for the role of Kiš in this list. The list records the fact that Enmebaragesi of Kiš "carried away as spoil the weapons of the land of Elam" (col. ii, 35–37), A more recent composite text of this list may be seen at the website of the ETCSL project: <http://etcsl.orinst.ox.ac.uk/cgi-bin/etcsl.cgi?text= t.2.1.1 & charenc=j#>.

Kišite kings Enmebaragesi and Akka,[4] suggest that Kiš exercised considerable influence in the south sometime during the 28th–27th centuries, and may even have succeeded in gaining some kind of suzerainty over it.[5] From around 2500, we have documents found at the site of Fāra, ancient Šuruppak, hinting at some kind of military cooperation between six Sumerian city-states in the southern part of the alluvial plain. The evidence we have suggests that that organization was created as a response to a threat posed by the northern power of Akkadian Kiš.[6] Further echoes of military struggles from this remote past are found in some later literary works, which are associated with the names of some early kings of Uruk.[7]

More reliable and dateable information starts to become available, however, only from when the written word was adopted by the scribes for royal inscriptions,[8] from which we also get our earliest concepts of interstate law. Unfortunately, however, the great majority of these early royal inscriptions, and particularly those reporting political events, came from one state, that of Lagaš (from the sites of Girsu [Tello] and Lagaš

[4] See particularly the literary composition *"Gilgameš and Akka"*. Recent edition: Katz 1993. ETCSL edition: <http://etcsl.orinst.ox.ac.uk/cgi-bin/etcsl.cgi?text=t.1.8.1.1#>. For another composition see the hymn "*Šulgi O*", lines 53–60, edited by Klein 1976; ETCSL edition: <http://etcsl.orinst.ox.ac.uk/cgi-bin/etcsl.cgi?text=t.2.4.2.15#>.

[5] Cf. Jacobsen 1957: p. 116f. with notes 55–56; Steinkeller 1993: pp. 118–119, 128. Two label inscriptions of (En)mebaragesi, king of Kiš, dated to c. 2600 (RIME 1, pp. 55–7: E1.7.22.1–2), which are the earliest royal inscriptions found so far, have turned this legendary king into a historical figure. One of these two inscriptions was found in modern Hāfāji, a fact which may indicate that Kiš controlled in that time at least portions of the Diyala region: cf. Steinkeller 1993: p. 119.

[6] Pomponio 1994. The Sumerian cities are: Uruk, Adab, Nippur, Lagaš, Šuruppak and Umma.

[7] See particularly the epic *"Enmerkar and the Lord of Aratta"*, for which see Vanstiphout, 2003: pp. 49–96; ETCSL edition: <http://etcsl.orinst.ox.ac.uk/cgi-bin/etcsl.cgi?text=t.1.8.2.3#>.

[8] For a more recent edition of these inscriptions, including both transliteration and translation, see Frayne 2008 [=RIME 1]. Please note that all the inscriptions mentioned in this chapter whose number starts with E1 refer to this publication, and the same is true for the page numbers which follow in parentheses. As for the system of numbering the texts, E stands for Earlier Periods (=RIME), a sub-series of the RIM (=The Royal Inscriptions of Mesopotamia) series; 1 for the first volume of this sub-series. The next number stands for the number given to a certain dynasty in this volume by its editor (e.g., the number 9 in E1.9.3.2 stands for the dynasty of the city-state of Lagaš), and it followed by the number of the ruler in that dynasty; the final number (2 in the example of E1.9.3.2) stands for the specific text of this ruler in the order assigned by the editor. The reading of the rulers' names whose inscriptions are referred to follows Frayne's reading. Note that the writing of some names with components written in capital letters, as e.g. URU-KA-gina, indicates that the reading of these components is not certain (in this specific case, the reading Uruinimgina was suggested, replacing the previous reading Urukagina).

[al-Hibā]). Only very few inscriptions found in other cities, such as Nippur, Uruk and Ur, contribute any significant information beyond the names of the rulers in whose names they were written. What we have from some other sites are only very short votive inscriptions that do not contribute anything of significance to the issue under consideration here. The information we have is, therefore, very partial and one-sided.[9]

There is yet another fact pertaining to the nature of these inscriptions—called in the jargon of Assyriology "Early Dynastic IIIb Inscriptions" or "Pre-Sargonic Inscriptions"—that should be noted. Save for some seals and seal impressions, as well as some scribal practice pieces, the vast majority of these early royal inscriptions are essentially dedicatory inscriptions that commemorate the dedication of a structure or object by the ruler to a specific god. With the possible exception of a few free-standing sculpted and inscribed steles, inscriptions that commemorate the building of a structure were usually inserted into the walls of that structure, impressed on its bricks, or ceremonially buried in its foundations or under its floors, while dedicated objects were put inside the temple.[10] To most if not all of these inscriptions, common people had no access. The accounts of political and military affairs described in these inscriptions should, therefore, be taken as reports addressed not to the people but rather to the gods, relating to them the achievements of the king, their delegated official, or—most rarely—about affairs that affected their terrestrial property.[11]

When, around 2500, the curtain is fully raised above the historical stage of southern Mesopotamia, we encounter a scene of military struggles between half a dozen city-states. These armed struggles were fought both locally and countrywide. On the local plane, they were between neighboring cities over water and sown lands that could be irrigated. The documents attesting to these struggles also refer to arbitration awards made by a third party and non-aggression agreements concluded between two rival city-states, as well as to repeated violations of these agreements.[12] In

---

[9] For a recent review of the problems involved in a reconstruction based on these inscriptions of the political history of southern Mesopotamia during the Early Dynastic period, see Frayne 2008: pp. 5–15.

[10] For the nature, materials, shape, structure and content of these inscriptions, see Cooper 1986: pp. 4–13.

[11] Such is the inscription of URU-KA-gina, which laments the destruction of temples in Lagaš carried out by the ruler of Umma: E1.9.9.5 (RIME 1, pp. 276–9).

[12] See particularly the cone inscription of Enmetena (a name previously read Entemena), ruler of Lagaš (E1.9.5.1 [pp.194–199]), which reviews the dispute between the neighboring cities of Lagaš and Umma, the previous agreements reached, and their violations by the rulers of Umma (written from the viewpoint of Lagaš). For another inscription from

the countrywide conflicts, some of the prominent city-states in southern Mesopotamia took part, as well as some other city-states such as Elam on the east, and Mari, on the Middle Euphrates, to the north-west.[13] The main object of these latter struggles was to gain control over other city-states, and we may see in them the earliest historical sprouts of imperialism. These struggles brought about the temporary supremacy of one city-state king over the others, which gave rise to what we may call the 'hegemonic king'.[14] The full extent of powers such a king had is still unknown. What we do know is that he was able to mobilize the troops of the city-states under his authority against an enemy foreigner;[15] that he was entitled to conscript their laborers;[16] and that he had the authority to intervene and act as arbitrator in border-disputes between city-states.[17] In all probabil-

Lagaš, which records the oath and ritual by which the ruler of Lagaš swore in the ruler of Umma, see the inscription of the "*Stele of Vulture*" of Eanatum: E1.9.3.1 (pp. 126–140). For a more recent discussion of the documents related to the conflict between these two city-states, see Cooper 1983a.

[13] We have clear echoes of those struggles in the inscriptions of Ennail (of Kiš?; E1.8.3.1 [p. 75]), Enšakušana of Uruk (E1.14.17.1–2 [pp. 429–430]), and of the Lagašite kings Urnanše (E1.9.1.6b [p. 89f.]), Eanatum (E1.9.3.5–6,7a–10 [pp. 145–159]), Enanatum I (E1.9.4.4 and 9 [pp. 174–175, 180–181]), and unknown king from Lagaš (E1.9.10.2 [pp. 290–291]). Note particularly the involvement of Mari in these struggles as echoes in the inscription of Eanatum E1.9.3.5, and the involvement of Elam in the inscriptions of Ennail E1.8.3.1, and of Eanatum E1.9.3.1, 5–7a, 8–9.

[14] On this term and its institution see Jacobsen 1957: pp. 129–136. According to Jacobsen the title "King of Kiš" claimed by some southern kings (Mesanepada of Ur, Lugalkiginedudu of Uruk, Eanatum of Lagaš, and Lugalsilasi whose city is not certain) actually implied hegemony over both southern and northern Babylonia. This view was challenged by Maeda 1981: pp. 1–17, who believes that when the title was used by Sumerian rulers it denoted the rule over only the city of Kiš. Cooper (1983: p. 25, and 1986: pp. 18 and 42 note 3) argued that it denoted hegemony over northern Babylonia. While Steinkeller (1993: p. 120) suggested that in its southern application, the title was a generic term that described a particular form of kingship, namely, an autocratic and hegemonic type that was associated with the Kišite kingdom.

[15] This may be inferred from two of the inscriptions of Sargon, king of Agade (Akkad), which refers to the fact that Lugalzagesi, on his march to battle with Sargon, was followed by 50 city rulers. For these inscriptions, see RIME 2: pp. 13–17, inscriptions E2.1.1.2–3.

[16] See Enmetena's inscription, E1.9.5.1 (pp. 202–204), which declares that Enmetena "cancelled obligations for the citizens of Uruk, Larsa and Patibira. He restored (the first) to the goddess Inanna's control at Uruk, he restored (the second) to the god Utu's control at Larsa, he restored (the third) to the god Lugalemuš's control in the (temple) Emuš (in Patibira)" (v 4–vi 6). These laborers, who were conscripted by Enmetena of Lagaš from these three cities subordinated to him, were apparently released following a weakening of Lagaš's military power in favor of Uruk. It was very likely this weakening that brought about the concluding of a "brotherhood" agreement between Lagaš and Uruk, an agreement referred to in E1.9.5.3 (p. 201f.); see the discussion in Cooper 1983a: p. 31f.

[17] Cf. the role of Mesilim as arbitrator in the border dispute between Lagaš and Umma in the inscriptions of Eanatum and Enmetena kings of Lagaš: E1.9.3.2–3 (pp. 140–41), and

ity, he also had to assume responsibility for the welfare of the local major gods in the cities under his hegemony.[18] The authority of such a king, backed by the military power under his control, did not remain long in the hands of one city-state ruler, but rather passed from one city-state to another, reflecting thereby their struggles to achieve hegemony.[19]

These documents indicate that already at this early documented period, interstate relations were conceived by the people of the Ancient Near East to be under the supervision and sanction of the gods. Accordingly, the "hegemonic king" was presented as acting under the authorization given

---

E1.9.5.1 (pp. 194ff.; quoted below). We, however, do not have any clear evidence that such an arbitrator ever exercised his power and authority to punish any violator of an arbitration award made by either he or any previous arbitrator. It may, however, be that the violations of such awards occurred particularly when the power and authority of such hegemonic king were in decline, while no other king replaced him yet in the office. See, however, in the "*Stele of Vulture*" of Eanatum (E1.9.3.1 [pp. 126ff.]), where the god Ningirsu declared angrily that "Kiš itself must abandon$^?$ Umma!", which seems to refer to military help expected by Umma from Kiš. It may also be that the wide attack against Eanatum and Lagaš referred to by Eanatum (E1.9.3.5–6 [pp. 145ff.]), which included Kiš, Akšak, Mari and Elam, with some other city-states in the south such as Ur, Uruk and Umma, was connected with the border dispute he had with Umma. If this is indeed the case, then we may see in this attack a reaction of a hegemonic king to punish Eanatum for transgressing the border of Umma.

18 This may be inferred from the three inscriptions of Mesilim "King of Kiš" found in Girsu (Lagaš) and Adab (E1.8.1.1–3 [pp. 69–71]). These inscriptions record him as building a temple for Ningirsu in Girsu and performing some rite in the temple Esar in Adab, dedicating there something (the inscription is damaged), probably to the goddess Ninḫursag. See also Enmetena's inscription found in Tell al-Madā' (ancient Patibira) (E1.9.5.3 [pp. 200–202]), recording his building of the Emuš, the temple of the gods Inanna and Lugalemuš in that city (cf. also his inscription E1.9.5.4 [pp. 202–204], recording the building of that temple). Although Enmetena did not have the standing of hegemonic king, he still had at that time hegemony over some Sumerian cities: see the discussion by Cooper 1983a: pp. 30ff.

19 The rulers who seem to have achieved some degree of hegemony over other city-states, whether or not it included the hegemony of both the southern and the northern parts of Babylonia, are as follows: (1) Mesilim (of Kiš?), whose hegemonic rule is attested in his own three inscriptions found in Girsu (Lagaš) and Adab (E1.8.1.1–3 [pp. 69–71]), and by the testimonies of Eanatum and Enmetena of Lagaš (E1.9.3.2–3 [pp. 140–44], and E1.9.5.1 [pp. 194–199]); (2) Mesanepada of Ur (E1.13.5.2 [p. 392]); (3–4) Eanatum and Enanatum I of Lagaš (E1.9.3.5 [pp. 145–149], and E1.9.4.9 [pp. 180–181]); (5–7) The kings of Uruk Lugalkiginedudu and Urzage who are both titled "King of Kiš" (E1.14.14.2 [p. 415], and E1.14.16.1 [pp. 427–8]), Enšakušana who is titled "lord of the land of Sumer and king of the nation" (E1.14.17.1, and E1.14.17.3 [pp. 430 and 432]), and perhaps also Lugalkisalsi whose inscription was found in Nippur (E1.14.15.1 [p. 422]); (8) Lugalzagesi of Umma and Uruk (E1.14.20.1 [p. 433–37]). To this list we may perhaps add also Enna'il whose city is not known but whose inscription was found in Nippur (E1.8.3.1). For the political importance of Nippur for claiming hegemonic rule over the country, see Jacobsen 1957: pp. 104–106.

to him by the gods,[20] and his success in gaining the "hegemonic" office and status was presented as deriving from his having been elected to this office by the gods.[21]

These early royal inscriptions also reveal something about the religious concepts of the people of southern Mesopotamia at that time—concepts that should have largely dominated and regulated interstate relations. The scanty information provided by these inscriptions is supplemented by literary compositions such as myths, hymns, and epics. These literary works, which have come down to us in later copies, in all probability originated in much earlier periods,[22] since they reflect a type of political organization which should have predated the monarchic regimes of the so-called Early Dynastic IIIb period (ca. 2500–2335) with their well-established institutions of kingship.[23] From this combined information it appears that according to the official ideology, the city-state—a territorial entity, comprising a major city and the surrounding countryside, with its towns and villages—was the property of an extended divine family. The senior god, as the head of that family, was regarded as the owner of the whole state, who, at the same time, held—together with his spouse and children—the major city as his private domain. Junior deities, belonging to his household, owned smaller domains, comprising towns and villages. The king of the city-state was regarded as having been elected by the city-god to serve as his earthly representative to take care of his estate. The divine families of all the city-states were united into one super-extended

[20] See the inscriptions E1.9.3.2 (pp. 140–142; of Eanatum), and E1.9.5.1 (pp. 194–199; of Enmetena, quoted below), which open with a reference to the authorization Mesilim got from the god Enlil to demarcate the border between Lagaš and Umma. In reality, such an authorization was obtained most likely through omens following a deliberate ritual in the course of which the god was invoked to give his answer in the entrails of an animal. The use of divination to obtain the approval of the gods for a certain intended act is attested for that period in an inscription of Urnanše, ruler of Lagaš: E1.9.1.17: iii, 3–6 (p. 103f.).

[21] See the inscriptions E1.9.3.5 of Eanatum, E1.9.4.9 of Enanatum I, and E1.12.7.1 of Lugalzagesi (RIME 1, pp. 145ff., 181–2, 375–6 respectively), which declare that the victory over the foreign lands was granted to these rulers by some deity. See also the inscription E1.14.17.1 of Enšakušana, which declares that his attack on Kiš was according to the command he got from the gods (p. 429f.).

[22] Duplicate manuscripts of some Sumerian myths and hymns have been found in Fāra and Abu Salabikh, dated to ca. 2600–2500: see Krebernik 1998: pp. 317–335. But their (oral) origin should have been still much earlier.

[23] For these see Jacobsen 1957: pp. 99–109. It should be taken into account that religious concepts are usually much more conservative and not easily given to rapid changes, and once put in writing they tend to become fossil.

family, with Enlil, the chief god of Nippur, occupying the position of the *paterfamilias.*[24]

It may be noted, however, that in these early royal inscriptions, while Enlil bears the title "father of all the gods",[25] which alludes to a patriarchal-tribal organization, he is more often referred to as the "king of all lands",[26] or as "king of heaven and earth".[27] These latter titles reflect the accommodation of the image of the divine world organization to the more recent political development of human society and the emergence of kingship.[28] Accordingly, Enlil is presented as the one who fixed the boundaries of the lands, namely the terrestrial estate of each of the more prominent gods, and his decisions are presented as final without the review and consent of any divine assembly.

2. War

2.1. *Basic Concepts*

The most basic concept that dominated interstate relations throughout the long history of the Ancient Near East was the notion that countries are the private domains of the gods who fixed their borders and continuously kept them under observation. An early clear expression of this concept is found in the Sumerian myth "*Enki and World Order*".[29] According

24 See Steinkeller 1993: p. 116f. It may be noted, however, that in the myths, which seem to represent an older tradition, the god An, the god of Heaven, is usually presented as the one who preceded the divine assembly, while Enlil occupied a somewhat secondary position. Note also, that in one inscription of Lugalzagesi of Umma and Uruk (E1.14.20.1.), while Enlil is again and again referred to as the "king of all lands", the god An is also referred to as "king of all lands" (line i, 14), and Enlil is invoked to supplicate An (who is presented as his father) on Lugalzagesi's behalf. For further occurrences of An as "king of all lands" see note 26 below.

25 In an Inscription of Enmetena: E1.9.5.1 (pp. 194–199).

26 See E1.9.5.1 (pp. 194–199; Enmetena); E1.12.7.1 (p. 375f.; Lugalzagesi); E1.14.14.1 (p. 413f.; Lugalkiginedudu); E1.14.15.1 (p. 421f.; Lugalkisalsi); E1.14.16.1 (p. 427f.; Ur-zage); E1.14.17.1 (p. 429f.; Enšakušana). Note, that in some royal inscriptions of the kings of Umma and Uruk, also the god An is titled as "king of all lands": E1.12.7.1 (p. 375f.; Lugalzagesi); E1.14.13.1 (p. 411f.; Lugalsilasi); E1.14.14.2 (p. 414f.; Lugalkiginedudu, dedicated in Nippur, the cultic center of Enlil). In one Lagašite inscription (E1.9.4.5 [p. 176f.] of Enanatum I) the goddess Inanna of Uruk is titled as "queen of all the lands".

27 "*Stele of the Vultures*": xvii (E1.9.3.1 [pp. 128–140]).

28 Cf. Jacobsen 1970: p. 43f., and notes 18–23 on pages 327–331.

29 See Benito 1969: pp. 77–160 (translation, composite text, commentary). For a more recent translation of ETCSL see <http://etcsl.orinst.ox.ac.uk/cgi-bin/etcsl.cgi?text=t.1.1.38#>.

to this myth, the god Enki, after demarcating the borders and fixing boundaries (line 369), appointed Utu, the Sun-god, as a supreme judge in charge of the entire heaven and earth (lines 373–379), and charged the goddess Nisaba, the patroness of scribes, to measure and mark the borders (line 415). Appointing the Sun-god Utu (Šamaš in Akkadian literature) as supreme judge over the universe meant that the entire universe, including gods and humans alike, were under *one law* and must behave accordingly.[30] Charging the goddess Nisaba with measuring and marking the borders meant that the borders of the countries were the creation of the gods and under their authority. This implied that any trespass of these borders, all the more so the subjugation of one country by another was regarded as a violation of the divine established order, and thus, a grave offense liable to be severely punished by the gods if not properly justified.

Indeed, this Sumerian myth reached us in copies from the end of the third millennium or the beginning of the second, and there is no certainty that it already existed in the Pre-Sargonic Period (i.e., before 2350). Yet the concept that the borders of city-states are the creation of the gods is attested already in the Early Dynastic IIIb inscriptions of Eanatum and Enmetena of Lagaš.[31] One of its best expressions is found in the opening lines of one of the inscriptions of Enmetena, the king of Lagaš (ca. 2450). Since this inscription will dominate much of the discussion in this chapter, the quotation extends beyond the opening lines of the inscription (RIME 1, pp. 195–199: E1.9.5.1: cols. i–iv):

> The god Enlil, king of the lands, father of the gods, by his authoritative command, demarcated the border between the gods Ningirsu and Šara. Mesilim, king of Kiš, at the command of the god Ištaran stretched the measuring rope on the field and erected a monument there.
>
> Uš, ruler of Umma, acted arrogantly; he ripped out (or smashed) that monument and marched on the Eden district of Lagaš. The god Ningirsu, warrior of the god Enlil, at his (Enlil's) just command, did battle with Umma. At the god Enlil's command, he cast the great battle-net upon it, and set up its burial tumuli (honoring his dead) in the Eden (district).
>
> Eanatum, ruler of Lagash, uncle of Enmetena ruler of Lagaš, demarcated the border with Enakale, ruler of Umma. He led off the (boundary) channel from the Nun canal to the Gu'edena district, leaving a 215 *nindan* (1290 m.) (strip) of Ningirsu's land under the control of Umma and establishing a no-man's land there. He inscribed (and erected) monuments at that (boundary)

[30] Jacobsen 1976: p. 85.
[31] The inscriptions E1.9.3.2 and E1.9.5.1 (pp. 141–2, 195–9), discussed below.

> dike and restored the monument of Mesilim, but did not cross into the Eden (district) of Umma....
>
> The leader of Umma could exploit 1 *gur* (5184 hl.) of the barley of the goddess Nanše and the barley of the god Ningirsu as an (interest-) bearing loan. It bore interest, and 8,640,000 *guru* (44,789,760,000 hl.) accrued. Since he was unable to *repay* that barley, Urluma, ruler of Umma, diverted water from the boundary dike of the god Ningirsu and the boundary dike of the goddess Nanše. He set fire to their monuments and ripped them out (or smashed them) and destroyed the dedicated(?) chapels of the gods that were built on the (boundary-levee called) Namnunda-kigara. He hired the (people) of the foreign lands (as mercenaries) and transgressed the boundary dike of the god Ningirsu from above (i.e., from the north). Enanatum, ruler of Lagaš, fought with him in the Ugiga-field, the field of the god Ningirsu. Enmetena, beloved son of Enanatum, defeated him. Urluma escaped, but was killed in Umma itself....
>
> At that time, Il...took the rulership of Umma for himself. He diverted water from the boundary dike of the god Ningirsu and the boundary dike of the goddess Nanše.... He repaid(?) (only) 3600 *guru* (IX.662,400 hl.) of Lagaš's barley. When, because of those (boundary-) channels, Enmetena, ruler of Lagaš, sent envoys to Il, ruler of Umma. Il, ruler of Umma, the field thief, speaking hostilely, said: "The boundary dike of the god Ningirsu and the boundary dike of the goddess Nanše are mine! I will dry them up from (the town of) Antasur (as far as) the temple of Dimgal-abzu", he said. But the god Enlil and the goddess Ninḫursag did not allow him (to do) this....

The historical review of the relations between the two states opens with an ancient arbitration award made by Mesilim, "King of Kiš", in the dispute between these two city-states. Mesilim—either actually ruling that northern city-state or only bearing that title as an hegemonic title[32]—in his capacity of "hegemonic king" demarcated and fixed the borders between the two states. We are not told what the situation was before Mesilim interfered in this border dispute, nor whether Mesilim was indeed the first to demarcate that border. Mesilim's act is presented here as the actual mortal rendering of a divine decision made by the god Enlil, "the king of all lands", in the border dispute between Ningirsu, the titular god of Lagaš, and Šara, the titular god of Umma, over the extent of their

32 For this title as hegemonic title, see note 14 above. Mesilim is not known from any other source to have belonged to Kiš, and not even one inscription of his has been found in Kiš. The title "King of Kiš" alone cannot bear on it. Cf. the inscription of Mesanepada E1.13.5.1 where this king is titled only as "King of Kiš". Had we no other documents that proved him as the king of Ur, we could have been mistaken in taking him as belonging to the city of Kiš.

terrestrial estates.[33] Yet, Enlil, as befitting a king, did not himself demarcate the (new) boundary, but rather entrusted that to the god Ištaran,[34] who in turn entrusted it to the mortal Mesilim.

Such a concept, quite obviously, should have sanctified the demarcation of the borders of the city-states as being a part of the divine world order, and in turn, made their violator not only a transgressor against human order but also a sinner in the eyes of the gods. Particularly, such a violator was conceived to offend the titular god of the city he attacked and turn him into his enemy.[35]

It is in this light that we have to see the emphasis repeatedly put by Enmetena on the fact that each time the border was violated, it was rather the ruler of Umma who trespassed it, violating the extant agreements. Note also the Enmetena's assertion that his uncle Eanatum, despite his victory over Umma, did not enter its territory. The same assertion is found also at the end of one of Eanatum's own inscriptions, E1.9.3.2 (RIME 1, p. 141f.):

> Eanatum, ruler of Lagaš, . . . restored to the god Ningirsu's control his beloved field(s). Eanatum did not pass beyond the point where Mesilim had erected the (boundary) monument, and (even) restored that (boundary) monument (iv 2–21).

While these assertions reflect the concept that the borders of the city-states were sacrosanct and should not be violated, in two of Eanatum inscriptions we find a statement that appears to be a justification for the very act of waging a war against another city-state (E1.9.3.5: iv, 25–v, 8; E1.9.3.6: v, 10–vi, 5):

---

33 Note, however, that the inscription does not mention any dispute between these two gods over the extent of their estates, and the impression the reader gets is that this was the original border between these two estates.

34 The status and role of this god here is not entirely clear. His cult center was in the city of Dēr (see Lambert 1976–80), but it is not clear if this city was also Mesilim's city, and whether Ištaran's involvement in the border dispute between Lagaš and Umma was made in capacity of his being the god of the hegemonic city, or in another capacity. Note that the reference in Giša-kidu's inscription E1.12.6.2 to the involvement of this god in this dispute for the second time, as he who gave the command to Giša-kidu to erect a (new) monument (lines 79–82), does not prove or disprove anything. The appealing of Giša-kidu to this god for approval for this act could have simply stemmed from the fact that the original monument, set by Mesilim, was set by command of that god.

35 See the accusation raised by URU-KA-gina against Lugalzagesi: "The leader of Umma, hav[ing] sacked L[ag]aš, has committed a sin against the god Ningirsu" (E1.9.9.5: vii, 10–ix, 3 [pp. 276–9]).

> In the year of the offensive of Akšak,[36] Eanatum, nominated by the god Ningirsu, crushed Zuzu, king of Akšak, (all the way) from Antasura of Ningirsu to Akšak, and killed him.

By asserting that Eanatum "crushed Zuzu ... from the Antasura of Ningirsu to Akšak" these inscriptions made clear that the war started in Eanatum's own territory, a fact rendering the act to be defensive. This, in turn, may be seen as reflecting the concept that waging a war against another city was forbidden, unless it was an act of defense or redressing a wrong. The same concern of Eanatum to clarify the fact that the war was fought in his own territory—the territory of Lagaš—is found in another passage where he refers to defeating a coalition of countries (E1.9.3.5: vi, 6–vii, 2):

> Elam trembled before Eanatum (and) he drove the Elamite back to his own land. Kiš trembled before Eanatum. He drove the king of Akšak back to his own land. Eanatum, ruler of Lagaš, ... defeated Elam, Subartu and Arawa at Asuḫur(-canal). He defeated Kiš, Akšak and Mari at Antasur of the god Ningirsu.

We may, however, wonder, if this was truly a defensive war as these inscriptions attempt to show, or that this wording was dictated by a concept that attacking without having been attacked is a transgression or even a sin, and should not be admitted.[37]

On reading these assertions, one should note that neither the god Enlil nor the god Ištaran are supposed to punish the offender for violating an agreement or arbitration award. According to the above quoted inscription of Enmetena, when Uš, the king of Umma, infringed the arbitration award of Enlil, made through Mesilim, it was the wronged god and his human delegate, the king of Lagaš, who had to redress it by their own

[36] Cooper (1986: p. 42, note 1) reads instead "Because the king of Akšak attacked." Yet, even if we follow the translation "In the year of the offensive of Akšak", still the sentence asserts that the king of Akšak initiated the fight.

[37] Cf. Vanstiphout 1970: p. 27f. for a similar opinion. However, Vanstipout ascribed to this idea what he finds to be a "lack of aggressive policy, this aversion to the idea of conquest, this restriction of war to raids with purely temporary aims." I would ascribe to this idea only the limiting of the *boasting* and admitting openly the committing of such actions in the statements addressed to the gods. I doubt, therefore, whether Steinkeller (1993: p. 118 note 20) is right in arguing that "the fact that, by Eanatum's own admission, the war was fought *in the territory of Lagaš* ... assures that Eanatum's success did not amount to much more than repulsing the enemy and saving his kingdom." Cf. Cooper's doubts regarding the veracity of Eanatum's declaration that he only "restored" Ningirsu's Gu'edena to Lagash: Cooper 1983a: p. 28. See further the observation of Westenholz (A.) 1993: p. 160 where he regards the Sumerians as "a people of law and order".

force.[38] The role of Enlil in the punishment of the offender is limited here only to granting the wronged god the authorization to punish him.[39] At the same time, however, it also reflects the concept that even where the wronged king had the right to redress that wrong, he was still required to first obtain authorization from the supreme god.

The concept reflected here is no doubt quite old, and very likely goes back to the time when human society only started to expand beyond the boundaries within which order was secured merely through the power of public opinion and religious *taboos*.[40] At this stage of social development, when new institutions suitable to cope with the expanding society had not yet evolved, and society still lacked the tools to impose its law on its members, the burden to redress a wrong should have been left to the wronged party. Under such circumstances, the only gesture to rule of law was the need for the wronged person to get an authorization in advance to act against the offender.[41]

As a matter of fact, such a procedure may not have accorded any longer with the political reality of the city-states of southern Mesopotamia in the 25th–24th centuries, when their kings were able to muster troops in order to act against external and internal offenders. It is, therefore, very likely an ancient practice that was projected on the divine world, and as for any other conservative religious concept, continued to prevail long after the social human conditions that brought it about had changed. Yet, it is still remarkable that also the "hegemonic king" is not mentioned here as having been involved in redressing the wrong and punishing the offender; nor even as one who authorized the kings of Lagaš to act against the offenders. This fact may be taken as an indication that not always was the status and power of the "hegemonic king" sufficient to intervene successfully in the dispute between two city-states, and not always could the wronged

---

[38] See also in Eanatum's inscription E1.9.3.3 (p. 143): ii', 1–5: "[The god Ningirsu] ordered Eanatum, and he destroyed Umma."

[39] An authorization gained very likely through divination; see note 30 above.

[40] For a society whose order is secured by these means, see e.g. the classic book of Malinowski 1926.

[41] Cf. in general Rheinstein 1960, particularly pp. 407–412. Note there (p. 411f.) Rheinstein's reference to Roman law of the early republic that illustrates a stage of development "which may be typical of a government which has grown to sufficient strength to suppress the feud but has not yet developed the technical means effectively to enforce law on behalf of the individual citizen. At this stage it is still left to the person injured ... to size the debtor or adversary and to take vengeance on him.... But, before he is allowed to take such measures, the creditor must obtain the permission of the community as represented, in Rome, by the praetor and judex."

party rely on him.[42] Under such circumstances, where there was no stable supreme human authority to impose order in interstate relations, there was also no inducement for that conservative religious concept to be changed.

Realizing the limited power of the "hegemonic king" to maintain order in the land, and since no ruler could be sure that whenever his territory would be attacked he alone would have sufficient power to punish the offender, the rulers had to resort to the power of curses and to enlist them as means to secure compliance to agreements. Thus we find in a concluding passage in an inscription of Giša-kidu king of Umma, which defines the course of its border (E1.12.6.2: 83–93 [RIME 1, p. 374]):

> If another leader destroys it (the new boundary monument) there, or takes it away and makes off (with it), may [his] city, like a place (infested) with harmful snakes, not allow him to hold his head erect! May poisonous fangs bite that ruler in his ruined palace!

And at the end of an inscription of Eanatum there is the following (damaged) passage (E1.9.3.3: ii, 18–iii 16 [RIME 1, p. 143f.]):

> If [a leader of] Um[ma cros]ses the canal in order to take away the fields, may the god Ningirsu be a (hostile) dragon to him! May the god Enlil make salt come up in his furrows! May the deity ŠU.KAL [... not give him life!] ... May (the people) rebel against him in his (very) own city!

A similar curse-prayer addressed to the god Enlil to punish any future ruler of Umma who would trespass the border ended the above-quoted inscription of Enmetena (E1.9.5.1: vi, 9–29 [RIME 1, p. 199]):

> If the leader of Umma crosses over the boundary dike of the god Ningirsu and the boundary dike of the goddess Nanše, to take away fields by force—whether he be the leader of Umma or any other leader—may the god Enlil destroy him! May the god Ningirsu, after casting his battle-net upon him, bring down upon him his giant hands and feet! May the people of his own city, after rising up against him, kill him there within his (own) city!

The last-quoted passage of the Enmetena inscription raises two questions. The first concerns the god Ningirsu, the wrong god of Lagaš who is invoked to punish the transgressor. Why was he, the one who under such circumstances would have been the first to be injured, needed to be invoked to punish the transgressor? Was it not self-evident that this god would participate in any event? The available royal inscriptions of this

42 See note 17 above.

period do not bear on this question. Yet, from later documents we know that the titular god was conceived as one who is likely to abandon his city to its fate if he is enraged against the ruler of that city or its people. An alternative answer, or rather a complimentary one, is to take into account that at this period and stage of cultural development the gods were still conceived as capable of acting unpredictably and capriciously. It was only later, in the second millennium, that the gods became to be conceived as acting more carefully and predictably according to the rules of justice.[43] In any event, the above invocation of Enmetena to Ningirsu indicates that a ruler could by no means take for granted the help of the titular god of his city.

The second question pertains to the titular god of the *offending* city. We may note that while Enmetena invoked the gods Enlil and Ningirsu to punish any future ruler of Umma who would transgress the border of Lagaš, he said nothing about any sanction against Šara, the titular god of Umma. This becomes more apparent in an accusation inscription of a later ruler of Lagaš, URU-KA-gina, who accused Lugalzagesi, the ruler of Umma, for the destruction he brought upon Lagaš and its temples (E1.9.9.5 [RIME 1, pp. 277–279]).[44] The inscription ended with the following words (vii 10–ix 3):

> The leader of Umma, hav[ing] sacked L[ag]aš, has committed a sin against the god Ningirsu. The hand which he has raised against him will be cut off! It is not a sin of URU-KA-gina, king of Girsu! May Nissaba, the god of Lugalzagesi, ruler of Umma, make him (Lugalzagesi) bear the sin![45]

URU-KA-gina is careful to declare himself as innocent, namely that he did not provoke the ruler of Umma and did not cause the attack. But again, Šara, the god of Umma, is not accused of having any role in this offense. This, despite the fact that the titular god was supposed to gain, if not from

---

[43] See Jacobsen 1976: pp. 147–164.

[44] This document very likely may be regarded as the earliest available example of an indictment presented to a divine tribunal in an interstate issue of law; cf. Wilcke 2007: p. 162.

[45] There is a much debate regarding the proper translation of the last sentence. The interpretation of this sentence as demanding the goddess Nisaba to punish Lugalzagesi was argued by Kramer 1963: p. 323; Hirsch 1967: pp. 101–106; Vanstiphout 1970: p. 28, note 93; and was adopted by Steible 1982: 337 and Cooper 1986: p. 79 in their translations of these royal inscriptions. A different interpretation of this sentence, as demanding Nisaba to carry the sin on her own shoulders, was argued by Thureau-Dangin 1907: p. 59; Barton 1929: p. 91; Sollberger and Kupper 1971: p. 81f., No. IC11m; Jacobsen 1976: p. 157; and more recently by Wilcke 2007: p. 162 and note 5 on p. 167. A different translation was given by Frayne 2008: p. 279: "May Nissaba . . . make them (the people of Umma) bear the sin."

the booty taken in a plunder raid,[46] at least from the profits provided when the victor subjugated another city-state.[47] It is also not certain that URU-KA-gina accused of this offense the personal god of Lugalzagesi,[48] a god, who, according to the belief known from later periods, was perceived as the one responsible for the success or failure of his protégé.[49]

It would seem, therefore, that a concept, which would have ascribed to the titular god of one city-state the encroachment on territory belonging to another god, contradicted the Sumerians' concepts about their pantheon. They obviously could not tolerate the idea that in such a close family, to which their gods were thought to belong, one of its members would try to take property belonging to another member of the extended family. As long as that view dominated, the only way left to the Sumerians to understand such an encroachment was to ascribe it to the human ruler of the offending city alone, who in such a case, acted sinfully not only against the titular god of the attacked city but also against the god of his own city.

Some of Eanatum's inscriptions include, however, a statement that does not seem to fully accord with the above conclusion. It presents Eanatum as one "who subjugates foreign lands for Ningirsu" (E1.9.3.1–2, 4–5, 10, 14),[50] or, more specifically, as one "who sub[jugates foreign lands]

---

46 The only instance of an explicit dedication to a god of the booty taken in the course of an attack is in two inscriptions of Enšakušana of Uruk, E1.14.17.1–2 (pp. 428–431). But in these cases the dedication was made not to the titular god of Uruk but to Enlil, "king of all lands". It is remarkable that in the inscriptions which contain a detailed battle narrative, such as that of Ur-Nanše (E1.9.1.6b), some of Eanatum's inscriptions (E1.9.3.1–6, 8), and of Enanatum I (E1.9.4.2, 9), no mention is made of such a dedication. This is more apparent in inscriptions which ascribe the victory to either the help or the decision made by some god: E1.9.3.5 (Inanna gave Eanatum the kingship of Kiš); E1.9.4.2 ([Enlil?] turned over the control of Umma to [Nin]g[ir]s[u], who, in turn, put it in Enanatum I's control); E1.9.4.10 ([Lu]galurub put all foreign lands in Enanatum I's control, and [set?] the rebellious lands at his feet); E1.14.20.1 (Enlil, king of all lands, gave to Lugalzagesi the kingship of the nation). While we may assume that at least part of the booty taken in such battle was dedicated to the gods, it is remarkable that no mention is made of it, and one is left to wonder whether references to such a deed were tactfully omitted.

47 See the inscriptions of Eanatum of Lagaš, which present him as one "who subjugates foreign lands for Ningirsu" (E1.9.3.1–2, 4–5, 10), or, more specifically, as one "who sub[jugates foreign lands] for Ningirsu, subjugated [Elam] and Subartu to him." (E1.9.3.7a). For the right of the subduer to conscript laborers from the subordinate lands, see note 16 above.

48 See note 45 above for a different translation, according to which the goddess Nisaba is required to be responsible for the offense.

49 See Jacobsen 1976: pp. 155–157.

50 It recurs also in Enanatum I's inscription E1.9.4.4.

for Ningirsu, subjugated [Elam] and Subartu to him." (E1.9.3.7a).[51] This statement renders the god Ningirsu as an imperialist and the war as a "holy war" intended to expand his territory at the expense of the national gods of these "foreign lands". Had it referred only to countries outside the Sumerian orbit, such as Elam and Subartu, we would have taken it to indicate that the solidarity which the Sumerians ascribed to the divine world was in fact limited only to the Sumerian pantheon. But, at least the inscription E1.9.3.5 (RIME 1, pp. 146–49) mentions some Sumerian city-states like Uruk and Ur among the "foreign lands" defeated by Eanatum. I cannot avoid therefore the feeling that we have here a substratum of contradictory attitudes to war. This feeling is reinforced by the fact that there are some inscriptions that openly declare the launching of an attack on some foreign rulers without giving any justification,[52] or, when providing a justification, it was ascribed to a divine command with no further justification for that command. Such is the justification that appears in an inscription of Enšakušana, ruler of Uruk (E1.14.17.1 [RIME 1, p. 430]: 6–7): "When the gods commanded him, he sacked Kiš and captured Enbi-Ištar, the king of Kiš." This statement, which later recurs in many royal inscriptions throughout the history of the Ancient Near East, may be taken as a forerunner of similar later imperialistic statements.[53]

An imperialistic attitude certainly contradicts the concept that the borders of countries, having been fixed by the gods, were sanctified as part of the divine world order, and under perpetual divine control. This leads us to ask how the Sumerians in that period explained the fact that one city succeeded to subordinate another. The above-mentioned accusation inscription of URU-KA-gina (E1.9.9.5), is the only inscription we have from that period that represents the view of the offended party but contributes nothing to resolve our question. Yet, we do have some inscriptions that present the views of the victors. Thus we find that "to Eanatum, ruler of Lagaš, the goddess Inanna, because she loves him so, gave him the king-

---

[51] See also lines ii 7–iii 5: "Eanatum, who is commissioned by [the god Nin]gir[su], because of the strength given by the god Ningirsu (when he rages) against the foreign lands, nobody is able to resist him."

[52] Thus we find Ennail, whose city is not certain, presenting himself as "who smote Elam with weapons" (E1.8.3.1: 5–6 [p. 75]), and Urnanše, Eanatum's grandfather, declaring that he "went to war against the leader of Ur and the leader of Umma" and defeated them (E1.9.1.6b: rev. i, 1—ii, 2 [pp. 89ff.]). No justification is given there for those acts.

[53] Cf. Cooper 1983: p. 11: "This theological rationale of all Mesopotamian imperialism—making war in the name of a god for territory claimed by a god or given to the warring ruler by a god—was thus presented at the beginning of recorded Babylonian history." Such a "command" was obtained no doubt through divination; see note 20 above.

ship of Kiš in addition to the rulership[54] of Lagaš" (E1.9.3.5: v, 23–vi, 5). In one inscription of his brother, Enanatum I, we find that "[the god Lu]gal-URUxKAR granted the kingship of Lagaš to Enanatum, put all foreign lands under his control, and [set?] the rebellious lands at his feet (E1.9.4.9: ii, 13–iii, 8). Then, in one of the inscriptions of Lugalzagesi, king of Uruk and Umma, there is the following statement:

> When the god Enlil, king of all lands, gave to Lugalzagesi the kingship of the land, directed (all) the eyes of the land (obediently) toward him, put all the lands at his feet, and from east to west made them subject to him (E1.14.20.1: i 36–ii 2 [p. 436]).

In these and similar statements,[55] no legal reason is attached to the decision of the divinity to grant the rule of the entire land to a certain king at the expense of others, including their patron gods. Such a seemingly arbitrary decision accords, in fact, with what we find in some later literary works. Thus, the "*Sumerian king list*" portrays the transfer of the "hegemonic" kingship from one city-state to another as the result of a divine arbitrary decision.[56] From about the same period, the beginning of the second millennium, we have "*The Lamentation over the Destruction of Sumer and Ur*", which laments the fall of the so-called 'Ur III' dynasty that ruled over the lands of Sumer and Akkad and beyond in the last century of the third millennium.[57] In lines 363–370, we find the following response of the god Enlil to the pleading of Nanna-Sin, the titular god of Ur, that his city would not be destroyed:

---

[54] Note that the term "rulership" by itself does not necessarily designate any inferior status or position to "kingship". During this early period, the terms used to designate the king varied from one city to another. The term "ruler" came to be used by modern scholars as a translation of the term *ensik* practiced in Lagaš, while the term "king" is employed for the term *lugal* (literally "Great Man"), that was practiced in cities like Kiš and Ur. A third term *en*, practiced in Uruk, is translated by the term "lord", while occasionally we find the designation *lú* "man" in the sense of king, translated as "leader".

[55] See e.g. E1.9.4.2, an inscription of Enanatum I, which states that "[the god Enlil?], for the god [Nin]g[[ir]s[u], took [Gu'edena] from the hands of Umma and filled Enanatum's hands with it" (vii 1–6); E1.14.14.1 of Lugalkiginedudu of Uruk, which states that "when the god Enlil truly summoned him and combined (both) lordship and kingship for him, he (Lugalkiginedudu) exercised lordship in Uruk and exercised kingship in Ur" (4–14). In another inscription of Lugalkiginedudu, E1.14.14.2: 5–14, the same is ascribed to the goddess Inanna.

[56] For this composition, see note 3 above.

[57] Michalowski 1989; ETCSL translation: <http://etcsl.orinst.ox.ac.uk/cgi-bin/etcsl.cgi?text=t.2.2.3#>.

> Oh Nanna, the noble son . . ., why do you concern yourself with crying? The judgment uttered by the assembly cannot be reversed. The word of An and Enlil knows no overturning. Urim was indeed given kingship but it was not given an eternal reign. From time immemorial, since the Land was founded, until people multiplied, who has ever seen a reign of kingship that would take precedence for ever? The reign of its kingship had been long indeed but had to exhaust itself. O my Nanna, do not exert yourself in vain, abandon your city.[58]

No legal or ethical reasoning is provided by Enlil to cut off the reign of Ur. The decision is presented as an arbitrary one whose only justification is that it follows a very old practice. The presentation of the gods' decision as arbitrary is found also in other later literary works, which nevertheless reflect an early stage in the evolution of the concepts of interstate law.[59] In order to find another kind of reasoning, one which refers to justice and legal judgment, we have to wait for the Sargonic and Ur III periods that mark the next stage of the development of interstate law. It may be noted, however, that the above-quoted statement made by Eanatum to the effect that "Inanna, because she loves him so, gave him the kingship of Kiš" (E1.9.3.5: v, 23–vi, 5), presents a reasoning alluding to divine reward for devotion to the deity. Such reasoning prevailed indeed throughout all the periods of the Ancient Near East, side by side with that referring to divine justice and legal judgment.

2.2. *Declaration of War*

In a much damaged inscription found in Girsu, E1.9.10.1 (p. 289f.), most probably of a Lagašite ruler whose name was not preserved, we read as follows:

> [He s]ent [envoys to . . .]: "Be it known that your city will be completely destroyed! Surrender! Be it kno[wn] that Umma[60] will be completely destroyed! Surre[nder!]" (lines iv' 2'–9').

---

58 ETCSL translation.

59 See e.g. the *"Lamentation over the destruction of Ur"*, lines 155–164 (translated by Kramer 1969b; ETCSL translation: <http://etcsl.orinst.ox.ac.uk/cgi-bin/etcsl.cgi?text=t.2.2.2#>), and the Sumerian version of the Deluge (translated by Kramer 1969a; ETCSL translation: <http://etcsl.orinst.ox.ac.uk/cgi-bin/etcsl.cgi?text=t.1.7.4#>), as well as its Babylonian version attached as Tablet XI to the *"Epic of Gilgameš"* (translated by Speiser 1969: pp. 93–97). In the latter two versions of the Flood story, no justification is provided for the decision of the gods to destroy humankind.

60 Omitted in Frayne's translation but preserved in his transliteration (iv' 5': ^{giš}KUŠU.KI).

What make this inscription so interesting is not its reference to diplomatic messengers and messages; they are mentioned also in some other inscriptions.[61] It is rather the content of the message that makes this inscription so important. For here we have the earliest dated reference to a declaration of war sent in advance to the opponent, a well-known practice from later periods.

2.3. *Treatment of the Enemy's Dead Soldiers*

A repeated phrase in the Lagaš inscriptions states that the victorious ruler made burial mounds of the enemy's dead soldiers.[62] This phrase is illustrated by one of the scenes engraved on the so-called "*Stele of the Vultures*", on which Eanatum's inscription E1.9.3.1 was also engraved. The stele was so named because of the scene that accompanied the text: vultures hovering over presumably the corpses of dead Ummaite soldiers (not preserved) and carrying away in their beaks and claws the heads and an arm of the slain. The main scene on the obverse shows the god Ningirsu holding a large net filled with enemy soldiers, illustrating the battle-net of this god that figures in the curses. The main scenes preserved on the reverse side show Eanatum leading a Lagašite phalanx and Eanatum in a chariot at the head of a detachment of spear-bearers. At the lower left, there is a scene of the construction of two burial mounds.[63] The latter scene clearly show two piles of corpses, and two men with baskets for carrying earth on their heads making their way up the second pile, intending very likely to cover the corpses with earth. This reinforces the interpretation of the expression "he made a burial mound for them" not as just heaping the corpses in a mound without covering them, but rather as constructing for them some kind of tumulus. This, in turn, suggests that we have here an early attestation of the victor's obligation to bury the dead soldiers of the defeated enemy.

---

[61] See the above-quoted long inscription of Enmetena, E1.9.5.1: iv 13–18 (p. 197), referring to the envoys he sent to Il, ruler of Umma, and the inscription of URU-KA-gina E1.9.9.3: col. iv (p. 274), referring to the envoys sent by Enanatum I to (Urluma) the ruler of Umma. The dispatch of messengers is also a well-known topos in Sumerian literary texts, as was noted by Cooper 1983: p. 40 with note 9.

[62] For the Lagašite inscriptions referring to the construction of burial mounds, see e.g. E1.9.1.6b (pp. 89–93; Urnanše); E1.9.3.5–6, 8 (pp. 145–152, 154–156; Eanatum); E1.9.5.1 (pp. 194–199; Enmetena). The issue of burial of dead enemies has been dealt with by Westenholz (A.) 1970.

[63] For pictures of the stele, see Pritchard 1954: p. 94f., figs. 298–301; Strommenger 1964: pp. 66–69; Moortgat 1969: pp. 118–121. For a discussion of the stele and its scenes see particularly Winter 1985.

3. Treaties

The earliest available record of an interstate agreement is the one inscribed on the above-mentioned so-called "*Stele of the Vultures*" of Eanatum, king of Lagaš, (RIME I, pp. 126–140: E1.9.3.1). The document is not a treaty per se, but rather a monumental royal building inscription, written on the occasion of the recovery of disputed territory from the city-state of Umma. It commemorates the oath that Eanatum forced on the defeated ruler of Umma. Nevertheless, it may give us some idea about the treaties of this period, reflecting the utmost importance that was attached at the time (24th cent.) to the curses accompanied by ritual acts as elements of concluding an interstate agreement. The administration of the oath is described in great detail, including the undertakings of the ruler of Umma quoted in first person singular. It is coupled with a self-curse clause and the performance of a magical ritual, repeated six times, each time evoking a different deity. To each oath and self-curse uttered by the ruler of Umma is attached a complementary curse made in the third person. The king of Umma promises to exploit a certain area (the "field of Ningirsu") as an interest-bearing loan; not to transgress that territory; not to shift the course of its irrigation canals; and not to smash its monuments. The terms of the agreement, including the interest rate, are however omitted, suggesting that what mattered to the scribes who composed it were not the terms, but rather the oath, the curse and the ritual. Following is an excerpt taken from that inscription (obv. xvi, 12–40):

> Eanatum gave the great battle-net of the god Enlil to the leader of Umma, and made him swear to him by it. The leader of Umma swore to Eanatum: "By the life of the god Enlil, king of heaven and earth! I may exploit the field of the god Ningirsu as a(n interest-bearing) loan. A dike was dug to spring. F[orever and evermore, I shall not transgress the territory of the god Ningirsu!] I shall not shift (the course of) its irrigation channels and canals! [I shall not rip out its monument!] [Whenever I do transgress, may the great battle-net of Enlil, king of heaven and earth, by which I have sworn, descend upon Umma!]"

These oaths and curses were repeated six times, each time evoking a different great god.[64] Yet, Eanatum, not content with this repeated self-

[64] A fact which enabled the restoration of the damaged lines. In the following oaths and curses, the names of Enlil and the Ekur, his temple in Nippur, were replaced with the names Ninḫursag (in Keš), Enki (temple: the Abzu in Eridu), Su'en (temple: the Ekišnugal? in Ur), Utu (temple: the Ebabbar in Larsa), and Ninki.

cursing, added the following complementary curse, made in the third person and attached to each self-cursing made by the ruler of Umma (xvi, 41–xvii, 20):

> Eanatum was very clever indeed and he made up the eyes of two doves with kohl, and anointed their heads with cedar (resin). He released them to Enlil, king of heaven and earth, to the E-kur? in Nippur: "After what he has declared] and has reiterated [to my master the god Enlil], if any leader in Umma reneges against the agreement, when he opposes or contests the agreement, whenever he violates this agreement, may the great battle-net of Enlil, by which he has sworn, descend upon Umma!"

Regarding the scenes of this stele, described above (p. 19), it may be noted that while all its scenes may have been intended to serve only as a memorial to commemorate Eanatum's victory, still the scene on the obverse, presenting the god Ningirsu holding a large net filled with enemy soldiers, may have been intended to illustrate the curses, and to function as some kind of magic means to realize them.

While the "*Stele of the Vultures*" does not disclose the full terms of the agreement reached between Eanatum, ruler of Lagaš, and Enakale, ruler of Umma, further details are given in the inscription of Enmetena, Eanatum's nephew, E1.9.5.1. According to that inscription, Eanatum, despite his victory over Umma, left a strip of land over one km. deep, belonging to Lagaš, along the border under Umma's control, According to Eanatum's inscription on his "*Stele of the Vultures*" (E1.9.3.1), the ruler of Umma was obligated under oath to "exploit the field of Ningirsu as a(n interest-bearing) loan." According to Enmetena's inscription, the amount of land Umma could use was stipulated by the acreage needed to produce 1 *guru* (5184 hl.) of grain, at the current annual rate of 33⅓%.[65]

Apart from the above-mentioned "*Stele of the Vultures*", we do not have any document that fully records an interstate agreement. Nevertheless, there is one reference to such an agreement, which appears in one of

---

[65] Or 50%. See the discussion of Cooper 1983a: p. 28f., whose interpretation is followed here. According to the interpretation of the above Enmetena's inscription by G. Steiner (Steiner 1986: pp. 239–246), the renewal of the conflict between Lagaš and Umma in the days of Enanatum I was because Enanatum, the ruler of Lagaš, refused to continue the above arrangement reached in the previous generation. According to Steiner, Enanatum did not want it to last more than 40 years, lest it would constitute a basis for an Ummaite claim to the right of possession over the territory considered. If this interpretation is correct, we have here the earliest indication of a claim to the right of possession in the realm of interstate relations, a claim attested later in the Hittite documents and in the Bible for which see Altman 2001.

Enmetena's inscriptions, E1.9.5.3 (p. 202), and is worthy of special attention (ii, 4–10):

> At that time Enmetena ruler of Lagaš, and Lugalkiginedudu, ruler of Uruk, established a brotherhood (pact) (between themselves).[66]

Apart from the fact that in the diplomatic parlance known from the second millennium, such a 'brotherhood' denotes the conclusion of a parity treaty, it also signified a higher degree of diplomatic relations, one that required a special agreement between the would-be "brothers" to such a promotion of their relations.[67] From slightly later than the conclusion of the above "brotherhood" between Enmetena and Lugalkiginedudu, we have from Ebla in northern Syria a letter sent by the steward of the palace of the king of Ebla to his "brother", the envoy of the ruler of Hamazi, which includes a reference to such a "brotherhood" and gives us some further idea what it actually meant:[68]

> I am (your) brother and you are (my) brother. What is (appropriate) to brother(s): whatever desire you express, I shall grant and you, (whatever) desire (I express), you shall grant.

---

66 For the background of the conclusion of that "brotherhood", see Cooper 1983a: p. 31f.

67 For the most recent discussion of such a "brotherhood", as pertaining to the first half of the second millennium, see B. Lafont 2001: pp. 232–238.

68 Michalowski 1993: pp. 13–14, No. 2. Note that the two rulers are also referred there (col. iv, 6– vi 1) as "brothers".

CHAPTER TWO

THE OLD AKKADIAN AND UR III PERIODS IN MESOPOTAMIA (2350–2004 BCE)

I. The Old Akkadian Period

1. The Expanded Geographic Scene and Its Political Regime

In the previous chapter, the royal inscriptions of the Mesopotamian Early Dynastic Period served as the main and actually the only source for any significant information pertaining to international law of that period. Yet, while there are quite a number of these inscriptions, only few contain more or less significant information about the concepts of interstate relations and law. Moreover, that information is actually confined to the concepts of the Sumerians who populated the southern half of the Mesopotamian alluvial plain. The ideas of the Akkadians, who lived in the northern half, are hardly expressed in these records. The more informative Sumerian inscriptions tell us that interstate relations were already conceived as being under the control of the gods, but the gods mentioned are only of the Sumerian pantheon, reflecting the fact that the geographic horizon of these inscriptions is also very limited. While some powerful city-states outside the Sumerian region are mentioned as taking part in the playoff to gain hegemony over the alluvial plain, the actual orbit of these inscriptions was limited to the southern Sumerian city-states.

Things began to change with the onset of the Sargonic Period (2334–2113),[1] which introduced the Eastern Semitic Akkadians to the historical scene. With it, a new phase in the development of ideas and practices of interstate relations in the Ancient Near East may be discerned in the Mesopotamian documents of that period.[2]

[1] The dates, which include the 40 years of Gutian rule, follow Brinkman 1977's chronology. For a more recent discussion of the various opinions, see Boese 1982 and Foster 1982a: pp. 152–156 (who advocates the dates 2310–2160 for the dynasty of Akkade).

[2] For a survey of the available documents of the Sargonic Period with references to relevant studies and literature, see most recently Westenholz (A.) 1999. For more concise surveys, see Edzard 2002b; Steinkeller 1992: pp. 726–732). A very important collection of papers discussing some main aspects and questions pertaining to the Sargonic period and

The most conspicuous innovation of the Sargonic Period was the creation of the Akkadian empire by Sargon (2334–2279), the first empire in the recorded world history.[3] This new political system replaced the former "hegemonic" looser form of control over subordinate states by a centralist system that abolished the autonomous standings of the Sumerian city-states. Under the new system they were rendered into mere provinces with Akkadian officials, replacing their local kings. Political submission was expressed by the destruction of defensive walls, payment of tribute, quartering and supplying members of the crown household and military, erection of royal stelae in conquered areas, forfeiture of certain lands to the crown for redistribution to royal retainers, sporadic use of royal year names in dating, acceptance on the local level of royal administrators, and, in the later Sargonic period, imposition of a cult of deified kings, acceptance of royal family members for high priesthood in important sanctuaries, and ceremonial expressions of fealty in the form of greeting gifts, visits to the capital, oaths using the royal name, and use of a specific type of seal.[4]

The driving forces behind this empire were the Semitic speaking Akkadians who populated the northern part of southern Mesopotamia already as early as ca. 2900 if not earlier.[5] It was recently suggested that many of the attributes of this new system—namely, autocratic monarchy, centralized government, land-tenure practices, and ideology of conquest—were already characteristic of the region populated by the Akkadians long before Sargon.[6] According to this opinion, the greatness of Sargon and his successors lay in their ability "to forge these traits into the instruments of total power".[7]

---

empire is Liverani (ed.) 1993, which includes also a very detailed bibliographic essay (pp. 171–182, by B.R. Foster).

[3] Cf. Foster 1993a: p. 36: "If by empire is meant a large, multinational state with a heartland and provinces, presided over by a ruler who presents himself as larger than life, with a consistent, centralized pattern of administration throughout its domains, then the Sargonic political achievement can certainly be called an empire."

[4] Foster 1993a: p. 28 with note 29. To these we may also add royal progress of the kings visiting their realm, as was pointed out to me by Dr. Joan Goodnick Westenholz.

[5] The name Akkadian, for both the people and their Eastern Semitic language, is derived from Akkade, the name of the city which Sargon, the founder of the Sargonic dynasty, chose to be his capital. Note that the name of the city is also spelled as Agade or Aggade.

[6] Steinkeller 1993: pp. 116ff.

[7] Steinkeller, op. cit. p. 129. This is the place to provide the uninformed reader with the warning issued by Westenholz (A.) 1999: p. 18, that "almost everything pertaining to the Sargonic period is a matter of controversy", and that "current scholarship on Sargonic his-

Be that as it may, the achievements of the early Sargonic kings—as far as we can judge from the declarations found in their inscriptions,[8] that can only partly be verified[9]—are quite impressive. The Sargonic Empire, at its height, included southern and most of northern Mesopotamia, at least parts of northern Syria, parts of western Iran, and its campaigns in the south reached the coast of Arabia. These achievements, as well as the new imperial drive and the system of dominion they introduced, that endowed the Sargonic kings with enduring fame and lasting traditions for more than two millennia. Fame, which turned two of them—Sargon, the founder of the dynasty, and Naram-Sin, his grandson—into models of a ruler, for better or for worse.[10]

The empire reached its zenith with Naram-Sin (2254–2218), and with him we also find the appearance of a royal title claiming universal rule[11] and disclosing a clear imperialistic aspiration: "King of the Four Quarters

---

tory, society and culture is ... still the preserve of a limited number of people who disagree profoundly with each other, even on basic facts." Historians, such as the present writer, who are not experts in this particular period, have, therefore, to carefully navigate their way between the various opinions expressed by those experts. Since, however, this book is devoted to the issue of international law, I will refrain from referring to controversies which are not directly concerned with this issue.

[8] For their royal inscriptions, see more recently Gelb and Kienast 1990; Frayne 1993 (=RIME 2). The numeration of these inscriptions here referred to, as well as their quoted translation, will follow those of Frayne. To this period belong also the Sumerian royal inscriptions published in RIME 3/1. All inscriptions, whose number starts with E2 as well as their page numbers which follow in parentheses, refer to the RIME 2 edition; inscriptions whose number starts with E3/1 refer to the RIME 3/1. It may be noted that only a small part of the Sargonic inscriptions is original. Yet we are lucky to have many reliable copies made in the scribal schools of the Old Babylonian Period (20th–16th centuries) which are an invaluable source for the reconstruction of the history of this period. The majority of these inscriptions are recorded in the Old Akkadian dialect; a minority is both in Sumerian and Akkadian versions, and a handful is in Sumerian alone. For discussion of the nature of these inscriptions, see Westenholz (J.) 1998.

[9] To a certain extent these declarations can be verified through the list of sites where their original inscriptions have been found, or cities that employed the Akkadian dating formulae (for which see below note 21) invoking a Sargonic king, as well as by seal impressions and dedication inscriptions of royal officials found in various locations throughout the empire.

[10] For a recent annotated edition of almost all of the known legends of the Sargonic dynasty with references to the very few that were not included, see Westenholz (J.) 1997.

[11] His grandfather, Sargon, revived indeed the prestigious title "King of Kiš" used by some Early Dynastic IIIb's Sumerian rulers as a claim to some hegemonic rule (see in Chapter One, note 14). D. Frayne, in his edition of the Sargonic inscriptions, translated the title as "king of the world" (RIME 2, p. 7). However, this translation, based on the much later attested usage where KIŠ stands for the Akkadian word *Kiššati* "totality", "world", is not widely accepted. Objections to such a translation were raised already by Hallo 1957: pp. 21–29, and most recently by Westenholz (A.) 1999: p. 37f.

(of the world)".[12] Naram-Sin was also the first Mesopotamian king to be deified, rendering him as the patron god of the capital Akkade, starting thereby a practice that lasted for about two hundred years.[13] This event had its immediate effect upon Naram-Sin's royal inscriptions, where we find that his name started to be prefixed with a divine determinative, or to be also followed by the title "god (of the city) Akkade" as an apposition.[14] In addition, he presented himself as "the spouse of the goddess Aštar-Annunitum".[15] His son and successor, Šar-kali-šarī, went a step further: not only was his name prefixed with a divine determinative,[16] but he was also titled as the "beloved son of the god Enlil".[17]

2. War

2.1. *The Akkadian Official Attitude to War*

The creation of the empire did not pass without opposition. Time and again we find in the inscriptions of Sargon's successors—Rimuš, Man-ištušu, Naram-Sin and Šar-kali-šarri[18]—repeated references to rebellions and battles fought in Sumer and Iran, attesting to the stubborn opposition posed by these regions. The scribes who formulated these inscriptions

---

[12] For a discussion of the title, see Hallo 1957: pp. 49–56. It may be noted that such an aspiration is already echoed in the inscriptions of Lugalzagesi, the king of Uruk and Umma, who was the last to hold the "hegemonic" office before his defeat by Sargon. In one of his inscriptions (E1.14.20.1; RIME 1, pp. 433–437) we find the following declaration: "When the god Enlil, king of all lands, gave to Lugalzagesi the kingship of the land, directed (all) the eyes of the land (obediently) toward him, put all the lands at his feet, and from east to west made them subject to him" (i, 36–ii, 2).

[13] In one of his inscriptions there is a unique declaration made to this effect: "In view of the fact that he protected the foundations of his city from danger, (the citizens of) his city requested from (the great gods) Aštar in Eanna, Enlil in Nippur, Dagan in Tuttul, Ninḫursag in Keš, Ea in Eridu, Sin in Ur, Šamaš in Sippar, (and) Nergal in Kutha, that (Naram-Sin) be (made) the god of their city, and they built within Akkade a temple (dedicated) to him." E2.1.4.10: 20–57 (RIME 2, p. 113f.).

[14] See Hallo 1957: pp. 56–65. In the latter case, which is attested in many seal impressions, it has the format: "GOD Naram-Sin GOD (of the city) Akkade". See e.g., inscriptions E2.1.4.2003, 2007, 2008, 2009, 2018 (pp. 165–170, 176).

[15] E2.1.4.1: ii 8'–9' (p. 88). For the appellation "spouse of the goddess 'Aštar/Inanna", see Westenholz (J.) 2000: p. 81f.

[16] E2.1.5.2: 1; E2.1.5.4: 3; E2.1.5.6: 4; E2.1.5.10: 1; E2.1.5.2001: 1; E2.1.5.2010: 1; E2.1.5.2012: 1; E2.1.5.2015 (pp. 188, 191, 194, 197, 198, 205, 206, 208).

[17] E2.1.5.2: 1–2; E2.1.5.6: i, 4–5 (pp. 188, 194). Note, however, that already Naram-Sin presented Enlil as his father: E2.1.4.8: v 2–6; E2.1.4.23: 18–19 (p. 110, 127).

[18] Regarding Šar-kali-šari, see his date-formulae that refer to his military campaigns in RIME 2, pp. 183 and 186.

(save those of Naram-Sin) would not admit to such opposition and generally avoided the explicit mention of rebellion.[19] Yet they did not refrain from providing repeated descriptions of the military campaigns launched by the Sargonic kings. Moreover, they did not limit the publication of these campaigns to the royal inscriptions, some of which were incised on steles erected in conquered areas,[20] but rather publicized them through year names.[21] It is this bellicose spirit, in the first place, that separates these inscriptions from those of the older Early Dynastic IIIb period.

Indeed, also in the older group of inscriptions one finds here and there references to hostilities and descriptions of battles. Yet, they also include assertions reflecting the concept that the borders of the city-states were sacrosanct and may not be violated, and in case of war against another city-state there was a need for a justification, either explicit or at least implied.[22] The relative rarity of belligerent descriptions in those inscriptions may in turn be understood as reflecting reluctance to openly declare an aggressive act. Accordingly, we also hardly find in those inscriptions any references to dedications made to the gods from the booty taken in a warlike act.[23] The Sargonic year names and royal inscriptions, in striking contrast, exhibit an approach entirely free of such a reservation. These inscriptions openly declare waging war on, and conquering of, both neighboring and distant lands, generally without providing any justification.[24] In accordance with this bellicose spirit, we find that the Sargonic kings did

[19] Although, apart from the explicit reference to the Great Revolt against Naram-Sin in his inscriptions, one may also find an occasional mention of a rebellion in the inscriptions of other Sargonic kings; see e.g., Rimuš E2.1.2.4: 44–47 (p. 48).

[20] See, e.g., Naram-Sin E2.1.4.10 (p. 113f.), incised on a statue base from Bāsetkī, a village located on the road between Mosul and Dohuk, about 70 kms northwest of Mosul.

[21] Year names (or date-formulae) is a system of dating the years by giving each year a name after a major event that occurred in the previous year; e.g. "The year Sargon destroyed Elam." As a system of dating, being in everyday use by all the people throughout the empire, these year names enjoyed maximum publicity. For the year names of the Sargonic period see RIME 2, pp. 8, 40, 85–87, 182–84.

[22] See above in Chapter One, pp. 10–11 with note 37; see there, however, also note 52 for inscriptions that lack such justification.

[23] See Chapter One, note 46.

[24] The absence of any justification is particularly conspicuous in Rimuš' inscriptions where the inscriptions refer to campaigns launched against rebellious cities and lands, namely cases where the rebellion could have served as a justification. There, instead of referring to these rebellions, the scribes chose to ignore them altogether, obviously in order not to reveal the opposition posed by Sumer and Elam to the Sargonic dynasty.

not abstain from dedicating to the gods samples from the booty taken on their campaigns, declaring openly that these objects were taken as booty.[25]

Instead of apologizing, the Sargonic kings boasted of their victories, and some of them even took care to declare the veracity of their statements: "By the gods Šamaš and Ilaba I swear that (these) are not falsehoods, (but) are indeed true",[26] reflecting at the same time the originality of these impressive acts.[27] Some of the Sargonic royal inscriptions acknowledge the divine help granted to the Sargonic kings in their conquests, following a claim found already in the Sumerian Early Dynastic royal inscriptions.[28] Thus we find that the god granted them the conquered lands,[29] or that their conquests were achieved "through the love which the goddess Aštar showed" them.[30] Yet, in some cases the inscriptions ascribe to the gods more active involvement in the battles on the side of the Sargonic kings. Thus, "the god Enlil instructed (Sargon) and he (the king) showed mercy to no one."[31] Rimuš declares that "the god Enlil showed him (the way)",[32] and Sargon and Naram-Sin assert that the god helped them with his divine weapon.[33] Moreover, some of the Sargonic kings claimed that their campaigns were fought "for the god Enlil",[34] or that they conducted them on a mission

[25] Rimuš: E2.1.2.11: 11–13; E2.1.2.13: 11–13; E2.1.2.14: 11–13; E2.1.2.15: 11–13 (pp. 62–65); Naram-Sin: E2.1.4.4: 5–7 (p. 100); Dudu: E2.1.10.2 (p. 211). I did not include the many references to dedications not explicitly marked as booty.

[26] Rimuš: E2.1.2.4: 73–78; E2.1.2.6: 78–83; E2.1.2.7: 37–42; E2.1.2.8: 29–31 (pp. 49, 54, 57, 58); Man-ištušu: E2.1.3.1: 47–52 (p. 76). A similar declaration appears also in Naram-Sin E2.1.4.2: vii 28–29, viii 4–15 (p. 94).

[27] See also the declarations made in Naram-Sin E2.1.4.25: 17–32 (p. 131): "[Wh]en he (=Naram-Sin) went [t]o Talḫadum—no king (previously) had gone on such a campaign—Naram-Sin, king of Akkade, went there and the goddess 'Aštar gave him no rival"; and in Naram-Sin E2.1.4.26: i, 1–20 (p. 132f.): "Whereas, for all time since the creation of mankind, no king whosoever had destroyed Amānum and Ebla, the god Nergal... opened the way for Naram-Sin..."

[28] See Chapter One, pp. 16–17.

[29] Sargon: E2.1.1.1: 73–78; E2.1.1.2: 77–81 (the god Enlil); E2.1.1.11: 20–28; E2.1.1.12: 13'–21' (Dagan); E2.1.1.13: 18–22 (Enlil); Rimuš: E2.1.2.9: 1–7; Naram-Sin: E2.1.4.26: i 11–29 (Nergal), ii 14–19, iii 17–31 (Dagan) (pp. 11, 14, 28, 30, 32, 59, 133–4). Man-ištušu E2.1.3.2: 5–12 does not state clearly that Enlil had granted him the lands he conquered. I did not count the statements to the effect that the supreme god allowed no rival to the king.

[30] Naram-Sin: E2.1.4.10: 10–12 (p. 113). For the goddess 'Aštar as identified with the Sumerian goddess Inanna of Uruk, and the role she played, see Westenholz (J.) 2000.

[31] Sargon E2.1.1.13: 12–17; E2.1.1.15: 26–29 (pp. 32, 34); although we do not know what exactly is concealed behind this expression. See also Rimuš E2.1.2.7: 35–36 (p. 56); Naram-Sin E2.1.4.28: 34–43 (p. 138), and Šar-kali-šari E2.1.5.5: 35–44 (p. 193).

[32] Rimuš E2.1.2.6: 66–67; E2.1.2.8: 28 (pp. 53, 58).

[33] Sargon E2.1.1.2: 17–18; 3: caption 1'–6'; Naram-Sin E2.1.4.26: i 11–20, 30–ii 1 (pp. 13, 17, 133).

[34] Rimuš E2.1.2.9: 8–17; Naram-Sin E2.1.4.28: 14–27; Šar-kali-šari E2.1.5.5: 15–28 (pp. 59, 138, 192).

"for the goddess 'Aštar",[35] rendering these deities into imperialistic warriors, eager to enlarge their domain at the expense of foreign gods. This Sargonic concept stands thus in sharp contrast to the Sumerian concepts about their gods as reflected in the Early Dynastic royal inscriptions.[36]

2.2. *The Emerging Principle of Divine Judgment in Interstate Relations*

Much the same as in the preceding Early Dynastic Sumerian royal inscriptions, nowhere in the Sargonic royal inscriptions were the above assertions followed by any explanation why the gods helped the Sargonic kings or showed their love for them. It seems, therefore, that these assertions were but the logical deduction from their victories in view of the general belief that no battle could be won without the consent and help of the gods. And since the gods own the lands, they may grant them to whomever they like; their decisions are arbitrary, and there is not much point to look for their motives.[37]

Nevertheless, something new does appear in the Sargonic royal inscriptions regarding the decision of the gods to grant the foreign countries to the Sargonic kings. These inscriptions introduce for the first time the idea that such a divine grant resulted from a verdict rendered by the supreme god or goddess following legal proceedings. Thus we find the following statement: "When the god Enlil rendered a verdict for him and (Sargon) conquered Uruk..." (Sargon E2.1.1.6: 10–16 [RIME 2, p. 19]). Similar statements figure in Naram-Sin's inscriptions: "By the verdict of the goddess Aštar... Naram-Sin, the mighty was victorious in battle over... at Bašar, the Amorite mountain" (Naram-Sin E2.1.4.2: iii 14–6 [RIME 2, p. 92]); "By the verdict of the goddess Annunitum and the god Anum, Naram-Sin, the mighty, was victorious over the Kišite in battle at Kiš" (Naram-Sin E2.1.4.6: iii 26'–35' [RIME 2, p. 106]).[38] In none of these cases, however, was the background, which would explain the verdict, provided or preserved.[39]

---

35 Naram-Sin E2.1.4.3: rev. ii 16–20, iii 22–26, iv 33–36 (pp. 96–97).

36 See, however, above in Chapter One, pp. 15–16 for what seems to be a substratum of contradictory expressions.

37 For a reflection of this idea in the literary works of the end of the third and the beginning of the second millennium, see in Chapter One, pp. 17–18.

38 See further Naram-Sin E2.1.4.3: rev iv 3–7, 37–v 8 (Enlil's verdict); E2.1.4.6: ii 14'–22'; v 39' (Aštar-Annunitum); E2.1.4.26: ii 29–iii 1 (Dagan), (pp. 97, 105, 108, 133–4 respectively).

39 In Naram-Sin E2.1.4.6: i 12"–22" (p. 105) we read (following Westenholz [A.] 1999: p. 52, note 184): "Naram-Sin, the Mighty, his army mustered, made his stand in Akkade; that done, he brought his case for Šamaš: 'Oh, Šamaš, the Kišite [(*broken*)]'." The text seems to have narrated here Naram-Sin's appeal to the Sun-god for divine judgment. Later tradition, which might have preserved an original appeal, ascribed to Naram-Sin the following

This innovation reflects the development of the machinery of justice that took place in the city-states of southern Mesopotamia, which became more efficient in the course of the second half of the third millennium. This development was followed gradually by the growing notion that justice is something that man may anticipate not as an act of grace but rather as something to which he is entitled as his basic right. Moreover, he is entitled to demand justice from the gods much the same as from mortal rulers and judges.[40] This development was accompanied by the development in the way the people of southern Mesopotamia perceived their gods, who now become more "human" and less arbitrary in their decisions.[41] The human demand for a just world found its expression in the Sumerian myth "*Enki and World Order*", with its idea that the entire universe, gods and humans alike, were under *one law* and must behave accordingly.[42]

2.3. *The Encounter with Foreign Pantheons and Its Implications*

In contrast to the Sumerian Early Dynastic royal inscriptions, the Sargonic royal inscriptions never refer to the god Enlil as the "king of all the lands" (lugal kur.kur.ra). The verdicts referred above as handed down by Enlil to Sargon, and by Anum and Annunitum to Naram-Sin, are confined to the cities of Uruk (Sargon) and Kiš (Naram-Sin), namely, to the Sumerian-Akkadian homeland.[43] The most we have in the Sargonic royal inscriptions regarding a grant made by Enlil, is the claim that Enlil granted

words, which render the case as one of ingratitude (Westenholz [J.] 1997: p 234/5: 5–11; cf. pp. 240–43: lines 16–20): "My (fore)father Sargon conquered the city of Uruk and established [fre]edom for the Kišite (people), [and] had their [slavemarks] shaved off... and (yet)... [they reb]elled against me."

[40] For this development, see Jacobsen 1949: pp. 223–231.

[41] For this gradual change, see Jacobsen 1976: Chapters 2–5. Cf. Lambert 1960: pp. 1–20.

[42] See above Chapter One, p. 7 with note 29. Note that this composition, as it reached us, was composed or at least inscribed very likely toward the end of the third or the beginning of the second millennium, but its basic ideas might have been much older. Thus we find that the idea of a goddess who is in charge of states' borders is attested as early as the 22nd century in the Sumerian inscriptions of Gudea, king of Lagaš, and a bit later in those of Utu-ḫegal, king of Uruk (2119–2113): Gudea E3/1.1.7.25–27, 29 (RIME 3/1, pp. 126–9); Utu-ḫegal E2.13.6.1 (RIME 2, p. 281). The goddess referred to in these inscriptions as invested with this charge is Nanše.

[43] Sargon: E2.1.1.6: 10–16; Naram-Sin: E2.1.4.6: ii 14'–22', iii 26'–35' (pp. 19, 105–6). The only exception is Naram-Sin E2.1.4.2: iii 14–6 (p. 92), which claims that Naram-Sin was victorious in battle at Bašar (Bišri Mountain in the Syrian steppe) by the verdict of the goddess 'Aštar.

Sargon the rule over the Upper Sea and the Lower Sea.[44] However, Enlil is never referred to as granting the region of the Upper Land, namely Mari, Iarmuti, and Ebla (i.e. the Middle Euphrates and northern Syria), as far as the Cedar Forest and the Silver Mountain. In this sense, the Sargonic inscriptions are consistent. When it came to these latter regions, it was the local god Dagan who granted them to Sargon:

> Sargon, the king, bowed down to the god Dagan in Tuttul (and) he gave to him the Upper Land: Mari, Iarmuti, and Ebla, as far as the Cedar Forest and the Silver Mountain.[45]

Likewise, we find Naram-Sin declaring that the god Dagan had given him the people of the Middle Euphrates.[46] Furthermore, the inscription Naram-Sin E2.1.4.10: 24–53 (RIME 2, p. 113f.), quoted above (note 13), includes the god Dagan among the great gods to whom the citizens of Akkade turned to request that Naram-Sin be made the god of their city.[47]

It seems, then, that as long as the Sargonic campaigns were confined to southern Mesopotamia, their victories were ascribed mainly to the god Enlil. But once they overran the borders of this region, new gods came onto the scene. Marching up the Euphrates River, the Sargonic kings felt that they entered a region that was outside Enlil's jurisdiction and control.

The Sargonic kings, campaigning far beyond the borders of southern Mesopotamia, should still have been faced with a much more serious theological question than the need to pay homage to the foreign gods who were the divine owners of the newly conquered territories. Believing that interstate relations are controlled by the gods, and having encountered foreign peoples who had their own pantheons, they should have raised the question how the various pantheons would interact and behave

---

44 Sargon E2.1.1.1: 73–78; E2.1.1.2: 77–81; E2.1.1.13:18–22 (pp. 11, 14, 32). Apart from this we have the claims that Enlil granted Rimuš with the kingship (Rimuš E2.1.2.4: 1–7 [p. 47]), and gave him all "the land" (kalam.ma.ki = the land of Sumer; Rimuš E2.1.2.9: 1–7 [p. 59]); and that he made Man-ištušu great and granted to him the scepter of kingship (Man-ištušu E2.1.3.2: 5–12 [p. 77]). We also find that Rimuš "holds the Upper Sea and the Lower (Sea) and the mountain (lands) for the god Enlil" (Rimuš E2.1.2.9: 8–17 [p. 59]).

45 Sargon E2.1.1.11: 14–28; E2.1.1.12: 6'–21' (pp. 28, 30).

46 Naram-Sin E2.1.4.26: ii 14–23 (p. 133).

47 Dagan was originally apparently an Old Amorite god, or at least West Semitic, who was adopted into the Akkadian pantheon (Cf. Roberts 1972: p. 60). In personal names he is attested in Ebla (northern Syria) already in the Pre-Sargonic Period, and few occurrences from this period are known from Mesopotamia as well: cf. Di Vito 1993: pp. 128 (Ebla), 134 (Nippur), 136 (Kiš); Pettinato and Waetzoldt 1985.

toward each other. This question was particularly critical when the idea of a divine trial, which controlled interstate relations, began to prevail. The question bears particularly on the conclusion of treaties, over which the gods were called to be supervisors. One solution was to identify foreign gods with their own gods according to their role and status in their respective pantheons. This was evidently done by the Akkadians with their own gods when they first encountered the Sumerian pantheon.[48] But as we know from other periods and regions of the Ancient Near East, this was not always so, and their peoples seem to believe that the world is controlled by more than one pantheon, not necessarily with collaboration.[49] Unfortunately, the Sargonic kings, in their inscriptions, do not refer to any other foreign god, save Dagan, so we cannot be sure about their attitude to those other gods. But their presentation of their own gods as warrior gods, eager to expand their domain, suggests that they believed that in the divine arena, much like in the human world, the various pantheons fight each other. To this question, the treaty that Naram-Sin concluded with an Elamite king, to be discussed below, is relevant.

2.4. *The Treatment of Conquered Communities and Cities*

Putting aside the theological question and turning to the rules of war, the Sargonic inscriptions also provide us for the first time some information on how the conquered cities and communities were treated. While Sargon, on conquering a city for the first time, contented himself with only the destruction of its walls and taking its ruler into captivity,[50] Sargon's successors treated the rebellious countries more harshly. Here we find another precedent. In the few references to battles in the Early Dynastic IIIb inscriptions, reference is made only to the thousands of enemy corpses piled up in heaps[51] with no mention of captives taken. With Rimuš, Sargon's immediate successor, we hear for the first time about people taken as captives. Thus we read in one of Rimuš' inscriptions (E2.1.2.3: lines 1–36 [RIME 2, p. 45f.]) that—

---

[48] Westenholz (A.) 1999: pp. 78–84.

[49] See e.g., the Hittite "*Ritual before Battle*", in *ANET*³, p. 354f. (translated by A. Goetze; discussed below in Chapter Four, §2.1.2) where the Hittites request their gods to summon the gods of the Kaškeans to appear before the divine assembly for a trial.

[50] See e.g., Sargon E2.1.1.1: 12–17, 32–48; E2.1.1.11: 1–8 (pp. 10–11, 28).

[51] See in RIME 1 the inscriptions E1.9.1.6b (pp. 91–3; Ur-Nanše); E1.9.3.5–6, 8 (pp. 146–152, 154–156; Eanatum); E1.9.5.1 (pp. 195–199; Enmetena).

> Rimuš...was victorious over Ur and [Lagaš] in battle and struck down 8,040 men. He took 5,460 captives. Further, he captured KA-ku, king of Ur, and Krituš-id, governor of Lagaš. Further, he conquered their two cities and destroyed the walls of both of them. Further, he expelled 5,985 men from their two cities and annihilated them.

Indeed, the translation "he annihilated them" is still in debate, the alternative and more common is "he placed them in a forced labor camp."[52] In any case, those who were taken either to be killed or to be placed in labor camps are mentioned separately from those who were taken into captivity.[53] We are not informed, however, whether the captives were males or rather females and children, namely non-combatants, nor what was done with those captives and how they were treated. But since those who were killed in battle, and those taken afterwards to be killed (or taken to labor camp) are explicitly designated as males, we may presume that the captives taken included non-combatants. Only in one case is Rīmuš a bit more informative about these questions: he declares that he dedicated male and female slaves, taken from Elam and Parahšum, to the (temple of the) god Enlil.[54] Also Naram-Sin mentions taking captives,[55] but again—without specifying what was done with them.

As for the enemy soldiers killed in battle, we find here again the statement we previously encountered in the Lagašite inscriptions of the preceding period: "he heaped up over them a burial mound",[56] which seems to indicate a fulfillment of an accepted rule of war, to pay last respects to the dead enemies by taking care to bury them.[57] Yet, after defeating the armies of the rebellious cities on the occasion of the "Great Revolt",

52 For the debate of the correct translation of the expression *ana karasim iškun* with reference to previous literature and preference of the former translation, see D. Frayne, RIME 2, page 41 (in commentary); for a preference of the latter translation, see more recently Westenholz (A.) 1999: p. 41, note 130. Should this latter translation be proved to be correct, we will have here the earliest dateable reference to a forced labor camp in human history.

53 These three categories—struck down, captives, and expelled—are also mentioned with varied numbers regarding different cities and regions in Rimuš E2.1.2.1, 2, 4–6 (pp. 41–55).

54 Rimuš E2.1.2.6: 131–144 (p. 55). If I understand this statement correctly, it seems to refer to people that were already slaves when Elam and Paraḫšum were conquered. The fact that no free citizen is mentioned to be dedicated to the temples, or else to be sold as a slave, raises in turn the question what was done with the numerous captives that were taken.

55 Naram-Sin E2.1.4.2: vi 13–25 (p. 93); E2.1.4.6: iii 1'–12', iv 1'–24' (p. 106).

56 Rimuš E2.1.2.6: 43–47 (p. 53); E2.1.2.7: 19–23 (p. 56); E2.1.2.8: 19–24 (p. 58); Naram-Sin E2.1.4.24: iii 2–4 (p. 129). For the preceding period, see note 51 above.

57 Westenholz (A.) 1970.

Naram-Sin declared that he "filled the Euphrates River with their (bodies)." On that occasion he also treated harshly the city of Kiš, the leader of the rebellious cities: he "made the river/canal go forth in its (the city's) midst and struck down 2,525 men within the city."[58]

One royal document, "*the Sargonic victory stele*" found in Girsu (Telloh) in the province of Lagaš, sheds some further light on the way at least one Sargonic king punished rebellious provinces.[59] Its inscription records the allocation of enormous tracts of land in the Lagaš province to named individuals. It would seem that the Sargonic king confiscated those vast areas in this province,[60] and bestowed them on his retainers.[61] This created a new category of land, which lasted in the Near East up to the 19th century CE: the crown's lands, granted to royal dependents in exchange for service.

3. Treaties

Two treaties from this period are known today. One is a treaty concluded by Naram-Sin with an Elamite king of Awan.[62] The treaty, which was found in the debris of the temple of the Elamite god Inšušinak in the city of Susa, is written in Old Elamite, of which our knowledge is unfortunately very poor. In addition, it reached us in rather poor state of preservation, which made it even more difficult to decipher. Yet, two facts led scholars to identify the document as a treaty: the text calls on a series of Elamite and some Akkadian gods to "listen" to the words of the document (columns i–ii), and there is a repeated phrase that can be translated: "The enemy of Naram-Sin is my enemy, the friend of Naram-Sin is my friend!"

---

[58] Naram-Sin E2.1.4.6: iv 26'–44' (p. 107). This seems, however, to be an exceptional treatment, reflecting his wrath.

[59] For its inscription see Foster 1985: pp. 15–30; Gelb *et al.* 1991: pp. 88–90 (No. 24; see also p. 115f., No. 22). Its exact date is not certain; while Foster, and more recently Westenholz (A.) 1999: p. 42, ascribe it to the reign of Rimuš, Gelb and others would ascribe it to Naram-Sin or even later.

[60] According to Foster's calculation (p. 26f.) the total area is about 133,960 hectares, which, if square and contiguous, would be about 36 km by 36 km.

[61] For a detailed study based on administrative and economic documents, see Foster 1982b.

[62] Publication: Scheil 1911: Pl. I; König 1926: No. 3. Translations: König 1965: pp. 29–34 (No. 2); Hinz 1967; Koch 2005; cf. Kammenhuber 1976: pp. 172–175, 210–213. Discussion: Hinz 1971: pp. 651–3, 663–70; Korošec 1983: pp. 63–69, 74–76. For Elam in this period, see Stolper 1984: pp. 10–16.

(cols. iii, iv), a typical formula of subordination treaties known from the second millennium.

The text of the treaty is formulated as a declaration made by the Elamite king. It consists of three parts: (1) An appeal to the gods to listen to the words of the treaty followed by an oath formula (cols. i–ii); (2) unilateral undertaking of the Elamite king to Naram-Sin (cols. iii–vii); (3) declarations of the Elamite king (cols. viii–xii). The appeal to the gods enumerates more than 35 deities who constitute almost all the deities of the Elamite pantheon, among whom four Akkadian deities are also mentioned. Yet the fact that the latter were not called upon as a separate, distinct group, but were rather mixed in among the Elamite deities, and the fact that save for one, the god Ninurta, the other three are not reckoned among the senior deities of the Sumerian-Akkadian pantheon, raises the possibility that these four deities were adopted by the Elamites into their pantheon, and that the Elamite king took an oath before Elamite deities only.[63] At any rate, instead of swearing to Sumerian-Akkadian gods, Naram-Sin was satisfied that the Elamite king swore to the Elamite deities, who have the responsibility to punish him should he violate his oath and promises.

There is no consensus whether this is a parity or a subordination treaty, where the Elamite king is the subordinate party. Those in favor of the former bring up as support a reference in the text, which in their opinion alludes to a marital alliance, according to which Naram-Sin probably took the daughter of the Elamite king in marriage.[64] Those favoring the latter refer to the inscriptions of Sargon, Rīmuš and Man-ištūšu that declare Elam was conquered by them, while from Akkadian documents discovered in Susa it is clear that this city was under Naram-Sin overrule.[65] Also the formula "Your friend is my friend, your enemy is my enemy", which means subordinating and adapting one king's foreign policy to the foreign policy of another king, seems to me to favor a subordination treaty.[66]

63 The oath formula, which repeats six more times through the text, is not so clear.

64 In column x: 13–26, the Elamite king seems to bless Naram-Sin's wife that she would give birth to a crown prince. Hinz (p. 85) raised the possibility of diplomatic marriage, in which he was followed by Korošec 1983: p. 66f., who took it as a decisive fact indicating the parity nature of the treaty.

65 See Stolper 1984: p. 14; Westenholz (A.) 1999: p. 93.

66 I am unaware of any other Ancient Near Eastern parity treaty that employs this formula, which is characteristic of subordination treaties. But taking into account that this treaty is one of the two earliest examples available, this reasoning can not be taken as conclusive.

In connection with this question, it may be noted that this is the earliest known document written in (Old) Elamite, whereas all the known Elamite documents of the Sargonic Period up to the days of Naram-Sin are written in Akkadian.[67] This may suggest that this is an Elamite translation made for the Elamite court from an original Akkadian text. Moreover, it was recently pointed out that "the superb writing and the careful spelling of the Elamite mark the tablet as a product of the royal chancellery at Akkade, and no doubt an Akkadian version is waiting to be excavated there."[68] If this observation is correct, we may have here a case similar to the customary practice of the first half of the second millennium. According to that practice, the parties exchanged tablets that included a unilateral undertaking on which the addressee was supposed to take an oath before his (and the symbols of the other party's) gods in the presence of the messenger of the other party who brought the tablet.[69] In such a case, the Elamite treaty might have been part of a parity, or almost parity, transaction, whereby its two parties exchanged unilateral undertakings.

The fact that the treaty was found in the temple of Inšušinak, the chief god of the city of Susa, presents the earliest evidence of the well attested practice to keep copies of the treaty in the sanctuaries of the main gods, so that they could ensure the fulfillment of its terms by the party who was under their jurisdiction.[70]

From the general span of time extending from ca. 2400 to about 2250, and possibly preceding the Elamite treaty, we have another treaty that was found in the rich archives of Ebla in northern Syria.[71] This treaty, as other documents in the archives, is written in a Semitic language dubbed "Eblaite", in cuneiform script, employing many so-called Sumerograms and perhaps also Akkadograms (i.e. words spelled in Sumerian or Akkadian). Both the language and the correct reading of the Sumerograms are not entirely known, so that there are various translations of the treaty, differing considerably from each other, and even the name of the city or

[67] Hinz 1971: p. 651.

[68] Westenholz (A.) 1999: p. 92.

[69] See in the next chapter under §3.

[70] Although Inšušinak is listed only as the sixth in the list of the deities invoked in the treaty, still according to Hinz 1971: p. 667, Inšušinak was the god of oaths for all Elam, and this may account for the fact that the treaty was deposited in his temple.

[71] About Ebla and its archives see Pettinato 1991. The exact date of the treaty is unknown, and the only date that can be given is that of the end of the archives which is ascribed to the conquest of Naram-Sin. I am indebted to the late Prof. P. Artzi for his comments on this treaty.

country with which it was concluded is not in consensus.[72] Some of its stipulations, which are formulated as laws legislated by the state for its citizens, even evoke the question whether this is a treaty at all. Yet, it is now widely accepted that it is indeed a treaty, whatever would be the explanations given to those formulations. The copy we have of this treaty was no doubt composed for Ebla, and most likely in Ebla, since it reflects Ebla's interests. We may assume that a parallel version, written by the second party and safeguarding its interests, was drafted as well.

The treaty has three parts: introduction, stipulations, and a formula of a malediction for those who violate the pact. The introduction, divided into two sections, provides a detailed list of cities and their forts belonging to Ebla. Each one of the sections ends with the clarification that all the localities that are in the hands of the king of Ebla belong to him, and all the localities in the hands of the second party belong to that party. Eblaite citizens staying there are under the jurisdiction of the king of Ebla whereas the citizens of the other party are under their sovereign's jurisdiction. If this is indeed the correct meaning of the text, then it seems to grant the foreign merchants staying in Eblaite territory extraterritorial rights. Following this, there are 21 clauses concerning such questions as taxing foreign citizens, emissaries' movement, interstate trade, corporeal damages, theft, damages to commodities, adultery, enticement, etc. The treaty ends with a curse on the one who would break the treaty: the Sun-goddess, the Storm-god (Adda, spelled 'À-da), and the deity "Star" (MUL= Ištar$^{?}$), in their capacities as the gods of judgment, would punish him. Although most provisions of the treaty are formulated unilaterally, ensuring Eblaite interests, it is in all probability a parity treaty, and we have to assume that a parallel text was written safeguarding the interests of the other party.

Two further points pertaining to this treaty should be noted. One, the parties are identified only by the names of their respective city-states and not by their personal names. Also, in at least one article, the city-state appears as an active party.[73] This would seem to indicate, that the real

---

72 For translations see Sollberger 1980; Lambert 1987; Kienast 1988; Pettinato 1991; Edzard 1992; Fronzaroli 2003, and Neuman 2005.

73 Lines 112–132 (obv. vi, 6–20–vii, 1–12), following the translation of Lambert, read as follow: "If a man opposes *ab-ar*-QA^{ki} [= the other city], Ebla shall/may arrest him. If a man opposed *ab-ar*-QA^{ki}, *ab-ar*-QA^{ki} [shall/may kill him]. [If a man opposes Ebla], *ab-ar*-QA^{ki} shall/may arrest him. If a man opposed Ebla, Ebla shall/may kill him." See further rev. iv 9–14, and vi 4–vii 7.

parties were the city-states, while their rulers acted as their organs and representatives only. Second, many clauses open with the word *su-ma* to be identified with the Akkadian *šumma* "if",[74] which opens a conditional clause that is characteristic of later treaties as well as law collections. This latter feature seems to indicate the beginning of a new tradition in treaty formulation.

II. The Ur III Period

1. Ur III Political Scene

The breakup of the Sargonic Empire began during the reign of Naram-Sin's son, Šar-kali-šarī (2217–2193). By the end of his reign the empire shrank to a small territory around the city of Akkade.[75] From his reign we also have the first reports about the Gutians, a people whose home was in the Zagros Mountains.[76] Taking advantage of the weakness of Šar-kali-šarī's reign, they descended from the highlands northeast of the lower Tigris River and eventually won control over at least the southern part of the alluvial plain of southern Mesopotamia for about forty to fifty years. In 2113 they were expelled from Mesopotamia by Utu-ḫegal, king of Uruk (2119–2113), who evidently managed to achieve hegemony over the Sumerian cities in southern Babylonia.[77] With his death, Ur-Nammu (2112–2095), the military governor of Ur and the founder of the so-called "Third Dynasty of Ur" (= Ur III), took the lead. But it was his son and successor Šulgi (2094–2047) who built it and transformed Babylonia into a highly centralized bureaucratic state which lasted to 2004.[78]

[74] For the writing *su-ma* for *šumma*, see Gelb 1957: p. 255, and see Artzi 1988: especially p. 14.

[75] For the decline and fall of the empire, see the summary of Westenholz (A.) 1999: pp. 55–59.

[76] For the Gutians, see Hallo 1957–71: pp. 708–720.

[77] This may be inferred from his three inscriptions commemorating his act as arbitrator in a border dispute between Lagaš and Ur (RIME 2, pp. 283), and from two dedicatory inscriptions for his life found in Ur, testifying to the control he had over this city: RIME 2, pp. 295–6.

[78] For its organization, see Steinkeller 1987. For a survey of the available documents of the period with references to relevant studies, see most recently Sallaberger 1999. For the royal inscriptions, see Steible 1991; Frayne 1997 (= RIME 3/2).

2. War

2.1. *Theological Concepts of War*

Turning to ideas and practices pertaining to international law we note something new in Utu-ḫegal's inscriptions. We have already noted the references to divine judgment in the Sargonic inscriptions, but these were given without any explanation about what brought the divine judges to render a verdict in favor of Sargon and Naram-Sin and to the detriment of the conquered lands. Such explanation appears (or is preserved) in the Mesopotamian royal inscriptions for the first time in the inscriptions of Utu-ḫegal. In one of his inscriptions, Utu-ḫegal provides the following explanation for his success in expelling the Gutians:

> The god Enlil—(as for) Gutium, the fanged serpent of the mountain, who acted with violence against the gods, who carried off the kingship of the land of Sumer to the mountain land, who filled the land of Sumer with wickedness, who took away the wife from the one who had a wife, who took away the child from the one who had a child, who put wickedness and evil in the land (of Sumer)—the god Enlil, king of all the lands, commissioned Utu-ḫegal, the mighty man, king of Uruk, king of the four quarters, the king whose utterance cannot be countermanded, to destroy their name (RIME 2, E2.13.6.4: 1–23 [pp. 284–5]).

It may be noted that the Gutian offenses against the Sumerian population are considered as offenses against the Sumerian gods.[79] Indeed, the very idea that an offense against the gods is liable to bring disaster upon the offender is undoubtedly much older.[80] But an explicit accusation of crimes against humanity as a basis for divine punishment and the connection made here between these crimes and sins against the gods appears here for the first time.

From this period, we also have the first literary work that employed the idea that collapse of a kingdom indicates divine punishment for sins: "*The Curse of Akkade*".[81] It is a kind of historiographic work about the fall

---

[79] In lines 33–45 there are further accusations against Tirigan, the king of Gutium: he had blocked water from the fields, and had closed off the roads.

[80] It already appears in an Early Dynastic inscription of URU-KA-gina, the ruler of Lagaš, E1.9.9.5 (RIME 1, pp. 277–279), accusing the ruler of Umma for the destruction of Lagaš and its temples.

[81] Edition and study: Cooper 1983b. For its date of composition—no later than the end of Ur III Period (ca. 2000)—see there p. 10f.

of the Sargonic Empire, a tendentious composition written by Sumerians and reflecting their resentment against the Sargonic kings. It interprets the destruction as a divine punishment brought about because of Naram-Sin's sin against the god Enlil by attacking and plundering his temple in Nippur. Henceforth, the interpretation of defeat in battle and collapse of kingdoms as a divine punishment for sins continued to be widely employed in the Ancient Near East down to the Achaemenid Empire, mainly by the victor,[82] but occasionally also by the defeated party.[83]

Returning to the above inscription of Utu-ḫegal, it may be noted that although Enlil, as the supreme god and the "king of all the lands", authorized Utu-ḫegal to launch a military campaign to deliver Sumer, he himself was not supposed to take any part in it. And similar to the Sumerian Pre-Sargonic inscriptions, in order for his mission to succeed Utu-ḫegal had to enlist the support of the divine patrons of his main cities. Thus we find in the following lines (not quoted here) that Utu-ḫegal prayed to the gods Inanna, Iškur and Utu,[84] and claiming that he got the authorization of Enlil, he asked for their support (lines 24–32, 83–89, 90–97). Also, in accordance with the presentation of his war of liberation against the Gutians as divine judgment, Utu-ḫegal was presented (lines 59–64) as having been given a divine "deputy" (maškim) to accompany him, "just as the plaintiff in a law case was given an official 'deputy' to look into his complaint."[85]

Another point to be noted in the above inscription of Utu-ḫegal is the designation of Enlil as the 'king of all the lands', namely as one whose jurisdiction also includes the land of Gutium. This designation, used already in Early Dynastic IIIb royal inscriptions,[86] but not in the Sargonic inscriptions, in its re-appearance in the inscriptions of Utu-ḫegal, Ur-Nammu, and Amar-Sin (2046–2038),[87] seems to challenge the Sargonic concept suggested above that limited the jurisdiction of Enlil to the Akkadian-Sumerian homeland only. In line with this Sumerian concept, the inscrip-

---

82 See the inscription of "*Cyrus Cylinder*" in *ANET*³, p. 315f. (translated by A.L. Oppenheim).

83 See, e.g., the so-called "*Second Plague Prayer*" of Mursili II in Singer 2002: pp. 57–61.

84 Whose respective cultic centers were in the Sumerian cities of Uruk, Ur and Larsa.

85 Jacobsen 1976: p. 86.

86 See RIME 1, pp. 195–199: E1.9.5.1 (Enmetena); p. 375f.: E1.12.7.1 (Lugalzagesi); p. 413f.: E1.14.14.1 (Lugalkiginedudu); p. 421f.: E1.14.15.1 (Lugalkisalsi); p. 427f.: E1.14.16.1 (Urzage); p. 429f.: E1.14.17.1 (Enšakušana).

87 Ur-Nammu E3/2.1.1.38 and 39 (RIME 3/2, pp. 75–77); Amar-Sin E3/2.1.3.3, 5 and 6 (RIME 3/2, pp. 248, 250–51).

tions of Šu-Sin (2037–2029) ascribe to Enlil the granting of the eastern foreign lands of Simaški to Šu-Sin.[88]

Turning to the descriptions of battles in Ur III royal inscriptions, the reign of Šulgi was one of territorial expansion with many military engagements, and also those of Ur-Nammu and Amar-Sin involved some military activities.[89] Yet, it is only with Šu-Sin that we find more detailed and informative descriptions about his campaigns. Here again we find an accusation of the enemy provided as an explanation for the supreme god's decision to severely punish the sinner. And here again we find the gods Enlil and ('Aštar/)Inanna playing the same roles as in the above inscription of Utu-ḫegal. Thus we read in one of Šu-Sin inscriptions that "the god Enlil made Inanna … as the helper for Šu-Sin, mighty king, king of Ur, king of the four quarters."[90]

2.2. *Imperialistic Aspirations*

In matters of titles and political propaganda, and in their ideology of conquest, the Ur III monarchs followed the path of the Sargonic kings. Already Utu-ḫegal bore the title 'king of the four quarters', and later so did Šulgi, Amar-Sin, Šu-Sin and Ibbi-Sin. These latter kings were also deified, as testified by the divine determinative that prefixes their names.[91] Following the Sargonic example, the kings of Ur III referred proudly to their military campaigns and victories in their year names,[92] and in their inscriptions they present the gods as taking part in the fighting or aiding them in their conquests.[93]

The kings of Ur III also adopted another medium of propaganda, the royal hymns, addressed to the gods, courtiers, and students of scribal schools, where the next generation of royal officials were educated.[94] One of Šulgi's hymns, designated as "*Šulgi F*", which seems to reflect one of

---

[88] E3/2.1.4.5: 1–14 (RIME 3/2, p. 309).

[89] See Sallaberger 1999: pp. 132–34 (Ur-Nammu), 140–44, 156–9 (Šulgi), 163–4 (Amar-Sin).

[90] Šu-Sin E3/2.1.4.1: i 40–ii 13 (RIME 3/2, p. 296).

[91] Note that Šu-Sin also presents himself as the god of the town he built for the captives: E3/2.1.4.1: iv, 44–6 (RIME 3/2, p. 298), quoted below.

[92] For these and the correlated royal hymns, see RIME 3/2, pp. 10–20, 92–110, 236–41, 285–94, 361–66.

[93] Ur-Nammu E3/2.1.1.20: 131–34; Šu-Sin E3/2.1.4.1: i, 37–ii, 16; E3/2.1.4.3: III 6–11; Ibbi-Sin E3/2.1.5.3: 17–19 (RIME 3/2, pp. 48, 296, 303, 372).

[94] This medium was first introduced by Gudea of Lagaš; see Klein, 1989.

his coronation rites, and describes the proceedings that led the gods to elect him to kingship, has a special bearing here. After Nanna, the titulary deity of Ur, chose Šulgi for the office, Nanna had to travel to Nippur to obtain the approval of Enlil, the supreme god. Upon pleading for Šulgi, his protégé, Nanna ended with the following request: "Confer upon him a good blessing! May he subjugate the foreign land for me!" (line 83). To this request Enlil responded as follows (lines 85–87): "He whom you have chosen in (your) heart, with his war (campaigns) let him bend the foreign land like…, in (the whole extent of) heaven and earth!…destroy the rebellious land!"[95] In other words, one of the main duties of an Ur III king was to "subjugate the foreign land for the god", following, thus, the Sargonic views, by rendering their patron gods as imperialistic warriors, eager to enlarge their domain at the expense of other gods.

2.3. *The Treatment of Rebellious Communities*

Šu-Sin's inscriptions also provide us with information about how he treated the rebellious communities and the fate of the captive enemy soldiers and the civilian population. In one of his inscriptions we read:[96]

> He killed both strong and weak. He sowed the heads of the just and the iniquitous (alike) like seeds. He piled up the corpses of the people into a heap.
>
> The [me]n who had evaded battle and who, like birds, saved their lives (by fleeing) to their cities, did not escape his hand. Against [their] cities he himself screeched like the Anzu bird. He turned their established cities and villages into (ruin) heaps. He destroyed their walls. He blinded the men of these cities, whom he had overtaken, and established them as domestic (servants) in the orchards of the god Enlil, the goddess Ninlil and the great gods. And the [wom]en of [those cities], whom he had overtaken, he offered as a present to the weaving mills of the god Enlil, the goddess Ninlil and of the great gods.
>
> (As for) the [pe]ople of Ḫa[būra] and [Mar]daman, Šu-Sin…raised servitude for them (and) co[vered] (them with it) as with garment. In order to mine silver (and) gold he set them (to work) there (in Zabašali) from there (Bulma [=a site in the land of Simaški]).

---

95 Klein 1981: pp. 11–2, 25.

96 E3/2.1.4.3: iii 16–21, iv 2–31, and vi 8–18 (RIME 3/2, pp. 303–5).

And in Šu-Sin E3/2.1.4.1: iv 34–v 23 (RIME 3/2, p. 298f.) we read:

> He settled the enemy people, his booty, (namely) Simānum, for the god Enlil and to the goddess Ninlil, on the frontier of Nippur,[97] (and) built for them [a town]. He set (them) apart for them (Enlil and Ninlil). The god of their town was Šu-Sin. Since the days decreeing the fates, no king has established a town for the god Enlil and the goddess Ninlil on the frontier of Nippur, with the people he had captured, (but) Šu-Sin, mighty king, king of Ur, king of the four quarters, [established] Simānum........... [for] the god En[lil] (and) [the goddess Ninlil] on the fron[tier] of Nipp[ur] established Simānum.

This statement is the earliest record we have about settlement of a captured and expelled foreign population in the Near East, a practice that was adopted and followed by various peoples in the Ancient Near East during the second and first millennia.[98]

Further information about the fate of the captives taken by Amar-Sin and Šu-Sin is provided by some administrative documents from their reigns examined by I.J. Gelb.[99] From the reign of Amar-Sin we have two sets of three texts each. The three texts of the first set, dated to the fifth regnal year of Amar-Sin, months 2, 5, and 7 respectively, deal with the distribution of barley rations (in the first text) or flour and beer (in the two other texts) to women and children war captives staying in the city of Umma, all listed by name. The first text names 167 women, of whom 121 are alive (but of whom 23 are denoted as sick) and 46 dead, plus 28 children, of whom five are alive and 23 dead, plus two old women (of whom one is sick), all of whom are under the supervision of six foremen. The two other texts of this set are identical with regard to the details they provide. They list the names of 39 women and 10 children, almost all of whom appear also in the first text, with no sick or dead mentioned. Of the 23 women listed in the first text as sick, only five re-appear in the two other lists, suggesting that only they survived the sickness. On the other hand, Gelb observed that the rations received by the women and children were sufficient in quantity and represent the standard rations received by women and children of all classes. The sharp reduction in the number

97 The most sacred Sumerian city, where the temples of Enlil and his spouse Ninlil were located.

98 Cf. Gelb 1973, especially p. 91f. Better documented are the settlement of deportees by the Hittites, the Egyptians and the Assyrians for which see below in Chapter Four, §2.3.2, and for the Assyrian also Chapter Five, §2.3.1.2.

99 Gelb 1973: pp. 74–77.

of the captive women and children in three months, from 128 in the first list to 49 in the two other texts, might therefore be understood as due to sickness, the difficulties of transport, or the hunger they endured before they started to receive the rations due to logistic difficulties.

The three documents of the second set are dated to the 9th regnal year of Amar-Sin and are almost identical in content. These are receipts issued by the governor of Umma for 172 slaves, consisting of 113 women and 59 children, who are said to be the booty of Šariphum which was offered ex-voto to the temple of the god Šara at Umma. In addition, we have records concerning the fate of male captives from the sixth and eighth regnal years of Šu-Sin. They list captives taken from Šimanum who are engaged in agricultural activities together with a number of native workers, or replacing native workers (or soldiers) who were called to service.

Based on the available Sargonic and Ur III evidence, Gelb concluded that prisoners of war, immediately after having been captured, belonged to the state and most of them probably remained under the permanent control of the state, though many of them, mainly women and children, were offered to temples. No records are known about captives distributed to individuals, although that cannot be excluded.[100]

2.4. *Organization of Conquered Territories*[101]

The empire system of the Ur III state consisted of three different forms of control applied to three different zones: (1) the core zone, which comprised the alluvial plain of southern Mesopotamia and the lower section of the Diyala region; (2) a peripheral zone extending from Urbilum (modern Erbil) and Aššur on the left bank of the Tigris and running southeast parallel to the Zagros range as far as the Persian Gulf; (3) an outer belt of client states extending to the north and east of the peripheral zone, whose degree of dependence on the kings of Ur varied from place to place and from one region to another.

The territories of both the core and peripheral zones were annexed and incorporated into the Ur III state, but these two zones differ from each other in the way they were organized and managed. The core zone was subdivided into over twenty provinces that in terms of their number and

---

100 Gelb 1973: p. 81.

101 The basic study is that of Steinkeller 1987, briefly summarized in Steinkeller 1992: pp. 729–731. For more recent studies and critics, see the brief review of Sallaberger 1999: pp. 190–199.

territorial extent corresponded very closely to the former city-states of Sumer and Akkad. Each included the main city with its surrounding hinterland of towns, villages and hamlets. The provinces were administered by governors who were royal appointees and could in theory be removed from office or transferred to other posts, although in practice their office tended to be hereditary. As a rule, these governors were selected from among the local population, probably from the descendants of the local ruling dynasties of the former individual city-states. Yet their power was counterbalanced and checked by district military commanders who, like the governors, resided in the province's capital. These commanders were predominantly outsiders, very often foreigners, who earned their positions through their service to the king, and many were related to the royal family, either by birth or through marriage. They enjoyed full independence from the governors and, like the governors, remained under the direct orders of the chancellor and of the king. The lines of authority between the governor and the commander are not entirely clear, but it seems that the former controlled the temple households and their employees, while the latter were in charge of military personnel and other types of royal dependents settled in the province on crown land.

Regarding the economic organization, the core provinces compromised three basic sectors: temple domain, royal domain, and private sector—the least known—whose lands were privately held. In his 21st regnal year, Šulgi reorganized the system of the provincial temple households, which were the most important contributors to the central government. These temple households now became de facto property of the state under the control of the provincial governors who ensured that all the surplus revenues of the temple households were delivered to the central government. Reviving a policy first introduced by the Sargonic kings, Šulgi also created a new category of land—crown land—which was distributed in the form of allotments among the members of the military organization and other types of royal dependents in exchange for service. Taking advantage of controlling a vast and ecologically diversified territory, Šulgi also created huge industrial complexes based on a policy of regional specialization for highly specialized commodity production, with each major region concentrating on the production of different staples and goods, and run directly by the central government. Under this policy, a central redistribution system was imposed on each province, depending on its size and economic capabilities and its specific types of contributions and services. The collection and distribution of these contributions was done through centrally located establishments.

The peripheral zone differed from the core zone in that all its land and other resources were apparently considered the property of the crown. Its territories were subdivided into autonomous provinces, with each having a major settlement that served as the province administrative center, and a number of smaller, subordinate settlements under the charge of junior commanders. Most larger settlements were administrated by high ranking military commanders ("general"), although some of them had governors. In any case, the one in charge was vested with both military and civilian authority. Those officials were royal appointees who could be dismissed or transferred to other positions. These peripheral provinces served primarily for defense, to check the nomadic Amorites from the west, and to secure access to the Iranian plateau to the east.

3. Dynastic Marriage Alliances

Another "first recorded" to be found in the Ur III documents are references to diplomatic (or dynastic) marriages. The king of Marḫaši took the daughter of Šulgi in marriage, and another daughter of Šulgi was given to the governor of Anšan. Šu-Sin also gave his daughter to the governor of Anšan, and his son Ibbi-Sin gave his daughter to the governor of Zabašali.[102] Although this practice belongs rather to the realm of interstate relations, it had some important bearing on interstate law. For when Simanum, Ḫabura, and the surrounding districts "chased his daughter away from her residence", Šu-Sin had a *casus belli*, and after "he smote the heads of Simanum, Ḫabura, and the surrounding districts, he returned his daughter to her residence, (and) he assigned to her service Simanum, Ḫabura, and the surrounding districts."[103] Diplomatic marriage was regarded in the Ancient Near East as an alliance, which when violated entitled the father or brother of the bride to intervene in the affairs of her husband's country.[104]

---

[102] For references, see Röllig 1972–75: pp. 282–87. Note that the references under Nos. 1–5 can hardly be regarded as diplomatic marriages. See further Sallaberger 1999: pp. 159–61.

[103] Šu-Sin E3/2.1.4.1: iv, 4'–10', 21–33 (RIME 3/2, p. 298). For the episode, see Michalowski 1975.

[104] For a much later similar case see below in Chapter Four, §4, regarding the case of the Assyrian king Aššur-uballiṭ I who gave his daughter to the Babylonian king in marriage.

4. The Legal Obligation of Gratitude

Finally, attention should be given to the literary composition "*Gilgameš and Akka*".[105] This short composition deals with a conflict between the city-states of Kiš, in northern Babylonia, and the Sumerian Uruk, in the south, that resulted in the liberation of Uruk from the overrule of Kiš. The conflict is ascribed to the days of two legendary figures: Akka, the king of Kiš, and Gilgameš, the king of Uruk, namely to the transition to the Early Dynastic II Period, around 2700. All the manuscripts and copies we have of this work are dated to the first half of the second millennium. Yet, the work is generally considered as narrating an event that has a historical kernel,[106] and its composition is generally ascribed to the Ur III Period, or shortly after, though evidently employing an older tradition. According to the plot, Akka sent a demand to Gilgameš that Uruk provide Kiš with some irrigation works, reflecting Uruk's subordination status. Gilgameš rejected the demand, and when the army of Kiš arrived at the gates of Uruk, he attacked and defeated that army.

While this story seems to quite credibly reflect a fairly common event in the interrelations of the city-states of Babylonia in the Early Dynastic Period, what is of special interest are lines 100–112 at the end of the plot. After the description of Gilgameš's successful attack on the army of Kiš and the capturing of Akka, the king of Kiš, we read:[107]

> Gilgameš, the lord of Kulaba, said to Akka: "Akka my lieutenant, Akka my captain, Akka my governor, Akka my general, Akka you have given me breath, Akka you have given me life, Akka, you have taken the refugee on your lap, Akka you have nourished the fleeing bird with grain.... By (the god) Utu, I now repay you the former favour!" He set Akka free (to go) to Kiš.

While we have no information to clarify the statement made on lines 103–104, these lines do suggest that Gilgameš was forced at one time to run for his life from Uruk, and found refuge with the king of Kiš. This, in turn, suggests the possibility that the king of Kiš might have helped Gilgameš to gain (back?) the throne of Uruk, by virtue of which Akka claimed suzerainty over Uruk. If this suggestion is acceptable, then whether or not this

---

105 For a recent edition, see Katz 1993; ETCSL translation: <http://etcsl.orinst.ox.ac.uk/cgi-bin/etcsl.cgi?text=t.1.8.1.1#>.

106 Katz 1993: pp. 11–14 with the literature mentioned there.

107 Katz' translation (p. 45) is followed.

story narrates a historical event, we would have here the earliest recorded reflection of a well attested legal concept, according to which saving someone's life entitles the savior to enslave that person, a concept which was adopted into the Ancient Near East interstate law.[108] However, if one would have deemed that such saved person is obliged to be loyal to his savior to the end of his life, this composition does not seem to share this view. For once Gilgameš revolted against his savior, all that was requested of him was to remunerate the savior for his favor, and that was done by releasing Akka and allowing him to return to his city.

[108] See Altman 2004a: pp. 229–236, and see there pp. 207–210 for evidence that ingratitude was considered as a just case for declaring war; see also note 39 above.

CHAPTER THREE

THE NEAR EAST IN THE OLD BABYLONIAN PERIOD (2003–1595 BCE)

1. The Political and Cultural Scene

The collapse of the Sumerian Ur III kingdom in 2004 ushered in the so-called Old Babylonian Period (2003–1595) in Mesopotamia.[1] The period took its name from the earliest known stage of the Babylonian dialect of Akkadian that developed in southern Mesopotamia. It replaced there the Old Akkadian and the Sumerian spoken languages, but left Sumerian to flourish as a written language for royal, ritual, and scholarly texts. The Babylonian dialect, which dominated the available documentation of this period, was, in turn, influenced by the so-called West-Semitic Amorite dialect of the semi-nomad tribes that toward the end of the third millennium flowed into Babylonia from the Syrian Desert. Apart from their linguistic contribution, these tribes contributed also their own political, social, legal, and religious traditions to the Mesopotamian cultural melting pot. Another branch of these semi-nomads, which settled along the Middle Tigris in the region known later as Assyria, brought about the development of the Assyrian dialect of Akkadian, the earliest stage of which is called "Old Assyrian".

This period is one of the richest periods of the Ancient Near East in an ever-growing documentation.[2] Of this documentation, most important for us here is the very extensive epistolary material,[3] which includes diplomatic correspondence that sheds light on the diplomatic relations and practices,[4] as well as a number of treaties. Of no less importance is the fact

[1] The most recent and detailed survey of the period is that of Charpin, Edzard and Stol 2004. For the political history, see there pp. 25–480 (by D. Charpin). For a summary of international law of the period see: J. Eidem, 2003. The dates given here are according to the so-called "Middle Chronology".

[2] For a detailed bibliography, see Charpin, Edzard and Stol 2004: pp. 403–480 (political history), 616–640 (literature and religion), and in the footnotes accompanying the text of Stol 2004.

[3] See particularly the following collections: *AbB*; ARMT, Vols. I–VI, X, XIII–XIV, XX, XXVI/1–2, XXVII–XXVIII (for new translations and notes see: Durand 1997–2000); Eidem and Læssøe 2001; Michel 2001.

[4] For a detailed discussion, see Lafont 2001a; see further LAPO 16, pp. 383–639. It should be noted, that while royal inscriptions of this period are much more numerous than those

that this rich documentation came from numerous and culturally diverging sites, stretching over a much wider arena than ever before.

The cultural makeup of this arena was composed of both indigenous cultures and the cultures and practices that accompanied the influx of new peoples. In addition to the immigrating West-Semitic Amorites, some other major ethnic groups entered Mesopotamia, northern Syria and Anatolia. One such major group were the Hurrians who descended from the north or the east into northern Mesopotamia toward the end of the third millennium. By the 18th century they were already settled there and in northern Syria, and a century later they reached the Mediterranean littoral. The Kassites, another ethnic group, migrated apparently from Iran over the Zagros Mountains into southern Mesopotamia no later than 1740. In the early 16th century, a Kassite dynasty gained control of northern Babylonia and around 1475 conquered southern Babylonia. In Anatolia, special attention must be accorded to the Hittites, whose language is related to the Indo-European group of languages, and who about 1650 founded a kingdom with Ḫattuša (modern Boğazköy) as its capital within the great loop of the Kizil Irmak River. Nevertheless, despite this wide cultural diversity, these various ethnic groups, both the indigenous and the immigrated populations, came to accept certain rules of coexistence and to share some basic concepts related to interstate relations and law.[5]

The empire system of the latter part of the third millennium was replaced in this period by a multi-pole system, headed by some half dozen relatively powerful kings, each controlled a cluster of small satellite city-states ruled by petty kings or tribal chiefs who were bound to him by a loyalty oath. The subservient kings had some defined obligations toward their overlord. The more significant of these were the military obligation to provide him with troops upon request, to render yearly tribute, pay yearly homage, and to subordinate their foreign policy to that of their overlord. The overlord on his part had the obligation to protect them.[6]

---

of the earlier periods, still their contribution to the issues under consideration here is relatively meager, since most of them deal with local achievements, and the few that do refer to foreign affairs do it mostly only in very general terms. For the royal inscriptions, see Frayne 1990 (=RIME 4).

[5] For the Amorites, see Whiting 1995. For the Hurrians, see Wilhelm 1989 and 1995. For the Kassites, see Sommerfeld 1995. For the Hittites, see Bryce 1998; Klengel 1999.

[6] The best recent discussion of this system is by B. Lafont 2001a: pp. 232–261.

2. War

Preliminaries to war in the Ancient Near East—apart from the military preparations and the cultic rites to ensure the safety of the army[7]—included a declaration of war sent to the adversary ruler and an appeal to the gods for authorization to set out on a military campaign and for divine help.[8]

2.1. *Opening Hostilities*

2.1.1. *Declaration of War and Its Justification*

As pointed out in Chapter One (§2.2), a declaration of war preceding the opening of hostilities was in all probability already known in southern Mesopotamia in the Early Dynastic Period IIIb (2500 2335). From the end of the third millennium or the beginning of the second, we have indications that such a declaration of war might have been preceded or accompanied by a kind of ultimatum demanding redress or fulfillment of certain demands, which only upon having been rejected justified such a declaration. This fact is reflected in two Sumerian literary compositions, "*Gilgameš and Akka*"[9] and "*Enmerkar and the Lord of Aratta*",[10] dated to the 21st century or the beginning of the second millennium. In a collection of celestial omens—"*The Venus Tablet of Ammisaduqa*"—found in a Neo-Assyrian edition of the 1st millennium, but stemming no doubt from the Old Babylonian Period, there is the following warning: "king will send messages of war to king."[11] From about the same time (the late

---

[7] For these cultic rites—known from the first millennium but no doubt go back to the second millennium if not earlier—see Elat 1982, and more recently Schwemer 2007 and the references cited there to further studies.

[8] Logically, one may take the appeal to the gods to precede the declaration of war. However, at least in some cases the declaration of war was accompanied by an ultimatum demanding redress, which only after having been rejected justified launching the campaign.

[9] For this composition, see note 105 in the previous chapter. According to the plot, Akka, the king of Kiš sent a demand to Gilgameš, the king of Uruk, that Uruk would provide Kiš with some irrigation works, reflecting Uruk's subordination status. Gilgameš rejected the demand, and the army of Kiš arrived at the gates of Uruk.

[10] Vanstiphout 2003: pp. 49–96. For the ultimatums, see lines 106–133, 175–206. This composition may be accessed through the internet: http://etcsl.orinst.ox.ac.uk/cgi-bin/etcsl.cgi?text=t.1.8.2.3#.

[11] Reiner 1975: p. 13f. (sub 21) and p. 34: line 11; variant: lines 37, 56 (pp. 49 and 58); cf. lines 22b, 25b: "messages of hostility." The collection, which reached us as Tablet 63 of the

17th century), we have a summons to war in an Old Hittite literary or historiographic text dealing with a Hittite campaign in northern Syria,[12] which refers to an attack on the city of Ḫaššu(wa). According to the narrative, the attack was preceded by an oral message sent to the ruler of the city: "I am coming against you; come on! [But if] you would not come, I will attack you like (attacking) a bear, and you will die by strangulation!"

An attack without a declaration of war in advance was considered a violation of an accepted ethical behaveor. This fact is reflected in an Egyptian literary composition, "*The Instruction of King Merikare*", composed evidently toward the end of the third millennium.[13] There, in a paragraph characterizing the Asiatic nomad as barbaric, we find as follows (lines 91–94): "He does not announce the day of combat, like a thief who darts about a group."

That such behavior was considered also an offense against divine norms is pronounced in a Hittite autobiographic composition, the "Apology" of the king Ḫattušili III, from the 13th century. There, in a passage describing Ḫattušili's rebellion against his nephew Urḫi-Teššub (iii 66–71) we read as follows:

> But when I made war upon him, I did not do it (as) defilement, as to rebel against him in the chariot, or to rebel against him within the house. In a manly manner I sent him a declaration (of war, saying): "You have begun strife with me... Come on! And we shall let (the goddess) Ištar of Samuḫa and the Weather-god of Nerikka decide the lawsuit!"[14]

In this passage, Ḫattušili is not worried lest the very rebellion against the legitimate king be considered an act of "defilement"; he had already presented justification for that act in a previous passage (iii 54–64). Here, he is more concerned that the *manner* of his rebellion should not be considered as such. He, therefore, takes care to assert that it was a fair revolt, preceded by a proper declaration of war. Being considered a "defiling" act, attacking without a declaration of war would accordingly be regarded as

canonical corpus of celestial omens "*enūma Anu Enlil*", was ascribed to the Old Babylonian king Ammisaduqa (1646–1626).

[12] Otten 1953: pp. 60ff.

[13] The composition is preserved in three fragmentary papyri, dating to the 14th century: Papyrus Leningrad 116A; P. Moscow 4568, and P. Carlsberg 6. Its composition, however, in all probability goes back to the last centuries of the third millennium. For bibliography, see Lichtheim 1975: p. 98, whose translation (on p. 104) is followed here.

[14] Otten 1981: pp. 22/23.

an offense against the norms of world order as determined by the gods,[15] what was considered to arouse the rage of the gods.

The same view is found also in the biblical commandment in Deuteronomy 25, 17–18:

> Remember what Amalek did to you on your journey, after you left Egypt—how, undeterred by fear of God, he surprised you on the march, when you were famished and weary, and cut down all the stragglers in your rear.

Here the condemnation is not only for the fact that Amalek failed to declare war in advance, but, emphatically, also for the fact that the Children of Israel were then "faint and weary", which rendered the attack as unfair, a transgression against divine ethic. Below, upon discussing the letter of Anum-Ḫirbi of the 18th century, we shall find a similar condemnation.

However, in order to be legitimate, war needed not only to be properly declared in advance but also to have a justifiable case. A good example of an Old Babylonian declaration of war accompanied by an accusation, which constitutes the justification of that declaration, is a letter sent by Yarim-Lim, king of Yamḫad, to Yašub-Yaḫad, king of Dēr (A.1314):[16]

> Tell Yašub-Yaḫad; Yarim-Lim, your brother,[17] says: (the god) Šamaš ought to investigate and decide on your conduct and mine. I have acted as father and brother to you; toward me, you have acted as a villain and enemy. What good was it that, by means of the weapons of (the god) Addu and Yarim-Lim, I saved the city of Babylon and gave life to your land and to you? Were it not for (god) Addu and Yarim-Lim, 15 years ago, the city of Dēr could have been windblown (matter?); as if it were chaff, one would never have found it. Would you then have been able to treat me like this? Certainly, Sin-gamil, king of Diniktum, very much like you would repeatedly respond to me by means of lies and provocation. Having docked 500 boats in Diniktum's quay, I "sank" his land as well as him for 12 years! Now, as to you being like him: you are continually responding to me with lies and provocation. I swear to

[15] See Moyer 1969: pp. 17–20, who refers to Douglas 1966.

[16] For the text, see Sasson 1985: pp. 237–256, whose translation is followed here. As a matter of fact, Sasson is inclined to take it as "a fictitious letter, involving living personalities, which was drafted in Mari, the city from whose soil it was ultimately recovered.... The fact that this letter was found in Mari would... betray it as a literary school exercise..." (p. 251). Sasson has more recently repeated this opinion in the Appendix to his forthcoming paper (Sasson Forthcoming). However, even if his opinion is accepted, still this document should have reflected some known practice in order to be used as a school exercise. Cf. Charpin's comment on this document in Charpin 2004: p. 285f.

[17] It was customary for rulers in the Ancient Near East to address their peers as "brothers". Yet, such an address was conditioned on a mutual consent of the parties in advance, which was usually followed by concluding a "brotherhood" treaty.

> you by Addu, my city's god, and by Sin, my own god: [may I be punished] should I ever go away before annihilating your land and you! Now, therefore, I shall come at springtime and shall pitch camp at your city's gate. I shall have you witness the galling weapons of Addu and Yarim-Lim.

We do not know what were the "lies and provocation" that Yašub-Yaḫad had sent to Yarim-Lim, but the argumentation is clear. Yarim-Lim had saved Yašub-Yaḫad and his country in the past, but Yašub-Yaḫad paid him back ungratefully. It may be noted, that although the writer and the addressee were most probably bound to each other by a treaty, there is no mention of such a treaty, and no accusation is brought against the addressee for its violation. The accusation of ungrateful behavior seems to provide a sufficient justified *casus belli.*

A similar accusation of ungrateful behavior is found in a letter sent by the king Anum-ḫirbi of Mama to Waršama, the king of Kaniš,[18] both of them Anatolian overlords (*rubā'u*) to whom the lesser kings (*šarru*) of Taišama and Sibuḫa were subordinated.[19] It reads as follows:[20]

> 1–2Thus says Anum-ḫirbi, the Mamean *rubā'u.* 3–4To Waršama, the Kanišean *rubā'u* say: You wrote me as follows: 5–7"The Taišamean is my slave (=subservient); I shall take care of him. But do you take care of the Sibuḫean, your slave?" 8–12Since the Taišamean is your dog, why does he argue with other *šarrus*? 13–15Does the Sibuḫean, my dog, argue with other *šarrus*? 15–16Is the Taišamean *rubā'u* to become the third *rubā'u* with us? 17–23When my enemy defeated me, the Taišamean invaded my country and twelve of my settlements he destroyed and their cattle and sheep he carried away. 23–25He said thus: "the *rubā'u* is 'dead' (=politically finished), so I have taken (my) fowlers snare." 25–29Instead of protecting my country and encouraging me, he burned up my country and made the smoke to stink. 29–34While your father Inar was besieging for nine years the city of Ḫarsamna, did my land invade your land and did it kill an ox or a sheep? 34–36Today you wrote me as follows: "Why do you not free the road for me?" 36–37I will free the road. 37–49(*too much damaged for translation*). 49–50[........... you wrote] to me as follows: "Let us take an oath." 51Is the former oath insufficient? 52–55Let your messenger come to me and let my messenger come regularly to you. 56–57Tarikutana (evidently the messenger of Waršama), instead of silver, sealed stone (he

---

18 Balkan 1957. Both sites are in Anatolia. The letter is dated to the 18th century.

19 The acknowledged title of such an overlord in the later part of this period was "the Great King" (*šarru rabû*). When this letter was written, however, there was not yet a common, accepted title, and the writer used the more regular Old Assyrian title for king—*rubā'u* ("nobleman, prince") to designate an overlord, while the other title for king, *šarru,* served to denote petit, subordinate king. Note that the expressions "slave" and "dog", ascribed here to the subordinate kings, are not to be taken as humiliating ones; they, and particularly "slave", were ordinary designations of political subordination.

20 Balkan's translation was followed here with only few very minor changes.

> brought) and deposited (them here). Are these (things) good to (=in the sight of) the gods?

In this letter, Anum-ḫirbi, king of Mama, responds to three requests of Waršama, the king of Kaniš: (1) that the former would restrain his subservient king, the king of Sibuḫa, who apparently went on committing some hostile acts in the territory under the suzerainty of Waršama; (2) that Anum-ḫirbi would open the commercial road passing through his territory for Waršama's emissaries and merchants, which Anum-ḫirbi had closed as a sanction against Waršama; and (3) that the two overlords would conclude a treaty ("taking an oath") in order to resume the good relations between them. No mention is made of any reparation and indemnity, but this might have been mentioned in the damaged lines 38–49. Anum-ḫirbi's answer discloses that the hostilities of the Sibuḫean king were in fact a sanction imposed by him in retaliation for the hostile actions of the king of Taišama, which brought about also the closing of the road and the severance of all diplomatic relations. Anum-ḫirbi blames Waršama for allowing his subservient king to conduct an independent foreign policy (lines 13–16), including military actions (17–23). Moreover, these acts were carried out at the rear, when Anum-ḫirbi was weakened in the wake of a recent defeat by another enemy, and very likely were carried out without having been preceded by a formal declaration of war. While we may assume that such acts were very likely quite common, the letter clearly reflects that they were considered reprehensible.[21]

The letter also clearly discloses that the people of this period already acknowledged the responsibility of an overlord for hostile actions carried out by his subservient kings. I am not sure whether the acts referred to in the concluding sentence of the letter (lines 56–57), as might have provoked the gods' anger, included also the above hostile acts of the king of Taišama and his overlord (lines 17–29).[22] But for sure these latter acts were a clear violation of any alliance treaty, even if carried out by a subordinate king and not by the signatory king himself. Even if such acts were not explicitly prohibited in an existing treaty, such a prohibition was self-evident since it goes to the root of any alliance treaty.

---

21 For a further text condemning such behavior, see the prologue of the Šunaššura treaty of the 15th century quoted in the next chapter (p. 93).

22 Balkan provides the following explanation of the episode related in lines 56–57 (p. 30): In order to make Anum-ḫirbi sure that the diplomatic relations will continue, the envoy of Waršama, Tarikutana, left a bag with Anum-ḫirbi, allegedly full of silver; but when it was eventually opened, there were stones instead of silver.

Now, while we may agree that the Old Babylonian people did acknowledge the idea that war required a justifiable case and a formal declaration in advance—even if perhaps more often they did not adhere to it—there are still some further questions to be asked. Did these peoples, when launching an attack against an enemy, ask the question whether the above requirements should or should not be applied? Did they ever make any distinction in this regard between a rival country headed by a king, a tribal semi-nomad group headed by an acknowledged chief, or a gang of brigands?[23] Also, did the peoples of that period consider it as essential to either precede or accompany a declaration of war by a kind of ultimatum demanding redress, which only upon having been rejected justified a declaration of war? While this may be the case, and occasionally one may indeed find a reference to an ultimatum sent in advance to the opponent,[24] the extreme rarity of available references to such a declaration of war[25] precludes taking a stand about these questions. It is only from the Hittites, some hundreds years later, that we have clearer indications for distinguishing between a 'civilized' and a "barbarian" country with regard to addressing the former with a declaration of war, preceded by a request for redress.

Another question is whether the peoples of the Ancient Near East drew any distinction between a real war, in which the attacker mobilized its entire army with the intention to conquer and occupy foreign territory, and a raid into a neighboring territory with a limited number of soldiers with the intention to only plunder and take captives? As far as I am aware, there seems to be no distinction in the available documentation between a real war and a mere raid. Both were considered as a *casus belli* and as acts that offend the gods and their cosmic order. Yet, not every raid necessarily was countered by opening a war; it much depended on the military situation of the victim.

2.1.2. *War as an Ordeal and the Need for Divine Authorization*

The above letter of Yarim-Lim and the quoted passage from Ḫattušili's "Apology", disclose yet another basic concept about war: it was regarded

[23] For such a distinction by the Romans, see Cicero, *Philippics* 4, vi/14 and *De officiis* III, 29, 107; references are taken from Grewe 1995: Vol. I, p. 191.

[24] E.g., ARMT XXVI/2, 479, referring to an ultimatum sent by an Ešnunnakean commander.

[25] Cf. Sasson Forthcoming.

as an ordeal by battle, and its results as a verdict by the divine judges.[26] According to the above letter of Yarim-Lim, the writer is convinced that the major gods Šamaš and Addu will vindicate his case and aid him in his campaign; Šamaš, the sun god, in his capacity as the supreme divine judge of the entire universe and the guardian of the borders of states, and Addu, as the patron-god of his city. Yet, the god Šamaš was only supposed to investigate the case and render a verdict, while the god Addu was the one who was supposed to help Yarim-Lim on the battlefield. What we have here, then, is actually a reflection of the same concept we have previously encountered in dealing with the inscriptions of the kings of Lagaš in the Early Dynastic Period IIIb,[27] according to which the one who was supposed to punish the offender was not Enlil, the supreme god, but rather the patron god of the wronged city. The role of the supreme god was confined to granting the wronged god the authorization to punish the offender. For even where the wronged god (not to say his human delegate) had the right to redress the wrong, he was still required to obtain authorization from the supreme god before launching his campaign. The same concept is reflected here in the letter of Yarim-Lim, the only difference being that here the supreme divine judge, Šamaš, replaced the role of Enlil. Šamaš, after investigating the case, was supposed to grant authorization to Addu, the wronged god, to redress the wrong, while Addu on his part was supposed to authorize his human delegate, Yarim-Lim, and help him to carry it out.

Since the supreme god of the state was considered its real owner and its king his human agent, it was mandatory for the king to obtain the confirmation of his god for opening war before either declaring war or launching an attack,[28] much the same as before concluding a peace treaty with an enemy.[29] This was done by a supplication addressed to the god, whose response might have been obtained through different kinds of divination,[30] such as extispicy[31] or prophecy.[32] Thus, we find in a

---

[26] Cf. Fensham 1971.

[27] See Chapter One, p. 11f.; see also Chapter Two, p. 40.

[28] Cf. Guichard 1999: p. 35f.

[29] See, e.g., ARMT XXVI/1, 199, delivering to the king the prophetic message warning him not to commit himself to a peace treaty without consulting the god.

[30] For the systems employed in ancient Mesopotamia for communication between kings and gods throughout the 2nd and the 1st millennium, see more recently Pongratz-Leisten 1999. For the genre of divination texts, see Starr 1990: pp. xvi–lv.

[31] For which see Starr 1990: pp. xxxvi–xxxix.

[32] For the available collection of prophecies of the Ancient Near East, as well as for recent discussion of this genre, see Nissinen 2003.

prophetic oracle delivered to king Zimri-Lim of Mari the following warning of the god Addu of Aleppo:[33]

> If you go [off] to the war, never do so [wi]thout consulting an oracle. [W]hen I become manifest in [my] oracle, go to the war. If it does [not] happen, do [not] go out of the city gate.

A letter sent by Baḫdi-Lim, the governor of Mari, to his king Zimri-Lim, has a similar warning:[34]

> As long as my lord cares for the wishes of (the gods) Dagan, Šamaš, and Addu, my lord should not hurry to do battle.... [When] Dagan, Šamaš, and Addu, these gods, have answered you with yes and [your] extispicies [are sound], in that very day my lord [should do] battle!

The need to achieve a divine authorization in advance is clearly reflected in the case of the reaction of Ḫammurabi, king of Babylon, to a series of pillaging raids launched by Rim-Sin, king of Larsa, his southern neighbor.[35] Ḫammurabi's first reaction was to cut off diplomatic relations with Rim-Sin. Then he sent messages to his allies requesting military support. Yet, before he finally launched his counterattack, he carefully consulted the gods as to whether they would certify it. We learn this from a report sent to Zimri-Lim, king of Mari, by an unknown functionary on a mission to the Babylonian court, quoting Ḫammurabi's address:[36]

> The man (=king) of Larsa harried my land with repeated pillage attacks.... I have granted the man of Larsa many favors but he did not reward me (even) for one favor. Now, I complained to the gods Šamaš and Marduk,[37] and they answered me with "Yes!"[38] I would not have launched this attack without the (consent of the) god!

The beginning of the letter is unfortunately broken, but in all probability these words of Ḫammurabi were addressed to the writer of the letter to be conveyed to Zimri-Lim. If this is so, we may conclude that it was in Ḫammurabi's interests to convince not only the gods, but also his mortal allies, that he had a justifiable cause to wage a war against Larsa, and that he received divine authorization in advance. This is a significant point, for

[33] A.1968: 12'–17'. Recent translation by Nissinen 2003: p. 21f. No. 2.
[34] ARMT XXVI/1, 176 (=LAPO 17, No. 620): 10–16.
[35] For these events, see Charpin 2004: p. 317f. (§ 9.1.1).
[36] ARMT XXVI/2, 385: 8'–15', following Charpin's translation; cf. Heimpel 2003: p. 333.
[37] I.e., the supreme divine judge (Šamaš) and the divine patron of Babylon (Marduk).
[38] I.e., that he has a justifiable case to launch a counter-attack and that they would stand by his side.

it demonstrates the need of the kings in this period to take into account, upon launching an attack, the negative effect it would bear upon public opinion in the neighboring countries, and particularly on their allies. If until now we had only indications that the fear of divine judgment might have restrained the kings to some extent in attacking their neighbors, we have here an indication that public opinion might have also played a role; particularly when the agenda called for the establishment of a coalition against some common enemy or lending military support.

An appeal to the god included necessarily also a request for the god's help, since it was inconceivable for a battle to be won without the support of the gods, let alone against their will.[39] This, however, would mean that the forthcoming battle would turn to be not only a battle between two adversary rulers but also between their national gods. This might have led the rulers involved to appeal to divinities above and beyond those of their respective states, such as the god Šamaš, the Sun-god who was acknowledged as supreme judge of the universe. Alternatively, they might have appealed to their national gods to summon the gods of the adversary state before the general assembly of the gods in order to pass judgment against them as well as against their human protégés.[40]

In order for the divine judges to investigate the case and render their verdict, the wronged party needed to appeal to them verbally and to accompany its appeal with a written accusation.[41] On the other hand,

---

[39] Cf. e.g. Deuteronomy 1: 42. As a matter of fact, divine judgment was believed in every case to determine the fate of both the individual and the nation. This concept is well attested for the second millennium (see for references *CAD* D, p. 152, s.v, *dīnu*, *sub*. mng. 1a3'), and is traceable to the third millennium (Jacobsen 1976: p. 85f.). It is from this basic conception that the perception of war as a form of divine judgment was derived (see in general Fensham 1971), and this was also the basis for the formulation both of prayers to the gods for recovery and help, and prayers for divine oracles, as appeals for a divine judgment. For the former, see in general the material in Gamper 1966, pp. 82–92, and for the Hittite prayers, see Laroche 1964/5, particularly pp. 13–20; Houwink ten Cate 1969; for the latter (prayers for divine oracles), see e.g. Goetze 1968 (YBC 5023); Starr 1983, pp. 30ff. (HSM 7494). For Hittite concepts of war as a lawsuit to be decided by the gods, see in Muršili II's *Annals* (*CTH* 61), KBo 3.4: ii 14 (Goetze 1933: p. 46); KUB 14.17: iii 17–19 (Goetze 1933: p. 98); and in Ḫattušili III's "Apology" (*CTH* 81): iii 71–72 (Otten 1981: p. 22f.). For the same concept in the Bible, see Judges 11: 27.

[40] See the Hittite so-called "*Ritual before Battle*", partly quoted and discussed below in Chapter Four, p. 97 with note 41.

[41] The earliest available examples of a written accusation are the Early Dynastic inscriptions E1.9.5.1 (RIME 1, pp. 194–199) of Enmetena king of Lagaš, and E1.9.9.5 (RIME 1, pp. 276–9) of URU-KA-gina king of Lagaš, discussed in Chapter One. The very need for such an appeal in case of interstate disputes is reflected by a number of Late Bronze Age documents. One such document is the Hittite "*Ritual before Battle*" (*CTH* 422; von Schuler 1965: pp. 168–173; Goetze 1969: p. 354f.), which contains the ritual of an appeal to the

the offender, in anticipating an appeal of the wronged party to the gods, would have to provide the same tribunal with his own version of the events that brought the wronged party to request divine judgment. As far as I am aware, we do not have so far an Old Babylonian example of a written accusation submitted by a wronged party to the gods. But we are fortunate to have the apology of the other party (the offender or the victorious one) written to the god to justify its conquests. This seems to be found in ARMT I, No. 3, a letter written by Yasmaḫ-Addu, the ruler of Mari, to the god Nergal. It relates the events that eventually brought about the removal of the offspring of Yagid-Lim from the throne of Mari, replacing him with the writer (Yasmaḫ-Addu), the offspring of Ila-kabkabu:[42]

> [To Ner]gal, the fearful (and) exalted, my lord,[43] [sa]y, [thus (says)] Yasmaḫ-Addu, your servant and your worshipper: There was no one from my lineage[44] who (ever) sinned against a god; everyone adhered to the norms of the god. Previously, Ila-kabkabu and Yagid-Lim swore a grave oath between them. (Ever since,) Ila-kabkabu against Yagid-Lim did not sin; (but) Yagid-Lim against Ila-kabkabu did sin. (Then) you undertook (the matter) and interrogated it, and (as a result—) at the side of Ila-kabkabu you went (to help him), and Ila-kabkabu demolished his (Yagid-Lim's) fortress and defeated [his son] Yaḫdun-Lim.

---

gods to pass judgment against the Kaška people. Another Hittite document, which very likely contains an actual appeal to the gods with an accusation of treaty violation, is the Madduwatta text (*CTH* 147; Beckman 1999: pp. 153–160). In the Šunaššura treaty (*CTH* 41.I; Beckman 1999: pp. 17–25): A iv 5–10, we find a statement made by the Hittite king that he would by no means accede to the request of the Hurrian king to return Hurrian subjects, and the statement concludes with the sarcastic remark: "Let the Hurrian invoke the gods of the oaths" (cf. the translation of Goetze 1940: p. 42). When Šuppiluliuma I heard that his son was murdered by the Egyptins, we find him to turn to the gods with an accusation about this act as well as of attacking the border of his country (Güterbock 1956: p. 107f. fragment 31, 8'–11'). As for the need to read aloud the relevant documents in the presence of the (images of the) gods, we learn it from the Hittite letter KBo 18.24 (Hagenbuchner 1989: I, No. 188), and from the "*Epic of Tukulti-Ninurta I*", obv. iii 9' (Machinist 1978: p. 88f.; cf. Foster 1993: I, p. 218), where the Assyrian king declares: "I raised the tablet with the treaty (made) between us and read it out to the lord of heaven."

[42] For its new collation, see Charpin and Durand 1985: pp. 339–342; for a new translation, see Durand, LAPO 18, pp. 72–74 (No. 931) with his comments on pp. 69–72, which I found hard to follow.

[43] Durand reads here instead: "Dis à Nergal, la vénéré, qui m'a ainsi parlé." Although it would not effect the following interpretation of the letter, it does not seem likely that the writer would fail to designate the god as his "lord"; cf. e.g., the opening of ARMT XXVI/1, 192.

[44] Or: "since my birth", although the reference to his grandfather would make "lineage" more likely.

At this point and in the following eleven lines or so, the letter becomes unreadable because of severe damage. But as can be inferred from the words that survived in these lines, and from the latter part of the letter, the story repeats itself concerning the next generation: Šamši-Adad, the son of Ila-kabkabu, and Yaḫdun-Lim, Yagid-Lim's son, took an oath, which Yaḫdun-Lim soon violated. The writer emphasizes here once again the fact that this latter offense was against the one "who adhered to the norms of the god" (rev. 4'). The story turns then to the son of the sinner, to Sûmû-Yamam, who in turn also sinned against the god by demolishing his temple and replacing it with a palace for his own wife (rev. 7'–10'). This, according to the letter, moved the god to interfere once again and he punished Sûmû-Yamam by causing his death by the hands of his servants, and by turning over the banks of the (Middle) Euphrates, including the city of Mari, into the hands of Šamši-Adad, (rev. 11'–19'). At the end of the letter, the writer seems to complain that the god killed his son, and this misfortune seems to be what had motivated the writer to claim his innocence in order not to be punished further.

The letter was addressed not to the patron-god of Mari, the capital city of Yasmaḫ-Addu, nor to Šamaš, the supreme divine judge. It was addressed rather to Nergal, apparently in his capacity as the titular god of the city of Ṣuprum, the cradle site of the opponent, defeated dynasty of Yagid-Lim.[45] This would accord with the concept cited above, according to which the injured god was the one who was expected to redress the wrong. By addressing this letter to him, the writer very likely intended to win over this opponent god, and to neutralize any anticipated accusations raised by the defeated dynasty in an endeavor to move its patron god to take action.

2.2. *During the War*

ARMT XXVI/2, 385: 16'–20' relate Ḫammurabi's instructions to his army upon opening the campaign against Maškan-šapir, a city of the kingdom of Larsa:

> He spoke to his troops as follows: "Go! May the gods go in front of you! If, (when) you arrive, the city will open (its gates) to you—accept its peace! (Although) [it] despised the oath by the gods Šamaš and Marduk, to this [city] no [harm would you do]!"

[45] See LAPO 18, p. 72.

The second part of these instructions is damaged and we do not know what they were regarding the case if the city refused to surrender. Anyhow, the merciful attitude of Ḫammurabi toward Maškim-šapir, whatever the reasons behind it, is by no means a unique case; Mari letters contain some other examples of a similar attitude, where the rationalization for such a policy is also given.[46] Some months later Ḫammurabi treated Larsa itself mercifully, having been content to only demolish the city walls, exiling its king and family to Babylon, and confiscating the latter's royal domains. He then installed himself on the throne of Larsa, trying to create a "Personal Union", but a few months later he seems to have abandoned the idea and annexed this kingdom.[47]

Merciful treatment might have been demonstrated also some time after the war was over, as we find in one royal inscription of Ḫammurabi's successor Samsu-iluna, where he boasted of his forgiving attitude: Two months after he conquered the land of Idamaraz and demolished all the fortresses of the land of Warûm, he set free and gave life to the captives and troops he had taken, and "he (re)built the various fortresses of the land of Warûm which he had destroyed (and) regathered and resettled its scattered people."[48]

A refrainment from punishment of a defeated community is also declared in the Hittite text of Anitta, king of Kuššar (in central Anatolia, *ca.* 1750):

> (Anitta,) the king of Kuššar, ca[me] down out of the city (of Kuššar) with large numbers and to[ok] (the city of) Neša during the night by storm. He captured the king of Neša but did no harm to any of the citizens of Neša. He treated [them] (all) as mothers and fathers.[49]

Whatever were the reasons for these cases of merciful attitude, and notwithstanding the fact that by emphasizing this attitude these texts disclosed its exceptionality, these texts at the same time also reveal that such an attitude was appreciated by the people.

[46] See LAPO 17, p. 312, and the letters Nos. 474, 475, and 500 on pp. 51–55, 92–93.

[47] For references, see Charpin 2004: p. 323, § 9.1.1.3. It is one of the earliest (if not the earliest) clear attestation of this kind of political arrangement, whereby two states share—either voluntarily or by force—a single head of state, while each of them retains its separate legal personality, and remains a separate administrative unit.

[48] RIME 4, p. 389f. (E4.3.7.8): 1, 25–56.

[49] *CTH* 1: §2, A 5–9; Edition: Neu 1984; more recent translations are Hoffner 1997a, whose translation was adopted here, and Beckman 2006a. According to line 33, the above lines were part of the inscription (A 1–35) that Anitta inscribed on a tablet posted on his city gate.

Usually, however, conquered cities were thoroughly plundered, and might have been burned to the ground and their people enslaved;[50] in extreme cases, all males were executed.[51] Alternatively, in some cases the entire community was exiled to another locality where it was mixed with another, more loyal community.[52] Regarding the plunder and the enslaved captives, it seems that there were some rules controlling how they were divided. First, the king's share was separated, as well as that designated for the main temples of the conquerors;[53] then the officers drew lots and received their share, and finally the ordinary soldiers took their share;[54] in case allied troops were engaged in the same campaign, they also took their share.[55]

2.3. *After the War is Over*

Having conquered a city-state, the conqueror might have annexed it, replacing the local dynasty by one of his officials as a governor. Alternatively, he might have allowed the local king to retain his position after he had been sworn in a loyalty oath as a subordinate king ("vassal").[56] Whether he had voluntarily accepted political subordination or was forced into it, the subservient king had the same defined obligations toward his overlord; the more significant of these were the military obligation to provide the overlord with troops upon request, to render yearly tribute, to pay yearly homage, and to subordinate his foreign policy to that of the overlord.[57] His overlord on his part also had to take an oath in behalf of the subservient king[58] and had the obligation to protect him. In certain

50 See LAPO 17, pp. 311–325.

51 E.g., ARMT IV, 24 = LAPO 17, No. 506 with note c on p. 100.

52 See LAPO 17, p. 312 and the letter No. 624 on p. 315f. (ARMT I, 33).

53 Regarding the share of the temples, see particularly ARMT XXVI/1, 194: 13–18, as well as the list of the gifts given to the gods in the document M.6765+, edited by Guichard 1997: p. 332.

54 See LAPO 17, pp. 405–409, and particularly the letter No. 457 (ARMT II, 13) on pp. 31–33. See also Elgavish 2002: pp. 242–273.

55 See ARMT XXVI/2, 408: 21–26; cf. Elgavish 2002: pp. 255–260.

56 Although the conventional use of the term 'vassal' in the context of the political life of the Ancient Near East had become commonly accepted, I refrain from using it since it is borrowed from a different cultural environment, and its legal definition, as well as the rights and obligations associated with it, only partly correspond to that of the subordinated kings in the Ancient Near East.

57 Cf. B. Lafont 2001a: pp. 247–251.

58 See e.g. the Shemshara letter No. 1 (Eidem and Læssøe 2001: pp. 70–2). When a new governor or a subordinate king was imposed on a conquered city both parties—the local citizens and the new ruler—might as well have exchanged oaths: see ARMT XXVI/2 409,

case, when the subordinate king was suspected of his loyalty, the overlord might have forbidden him to accept foreign messengers without an official of the overlord attending.[59] In case the subordinate king passed away, the suzerain was entitled to intervene in the hereditary succession by either approving or denying the heir apparent.[60]

At the end of the war, the rulers of both sides might have entered negotiations to exchange war captives.[61] It seems, however, that usually it was up to the families of the captives to ransom them, either by offering other people as their substitutes,[62] or by paying ransom money,[63] while the palace might have been involved only as a last recourse.[64] Provision §32 of the Laws of Ḫammurabi illustrate this well:

> If there is either a soldier or a fisherman who is taken captive while on a royal campaign, a merchant redeems him and helps him to get back to his city—if there are sufficient means in his own estate for the redeeming, he himself shall redeem himself; if there are not sufficient means in his estate to redeem him, he shall be redeemed by his city's temple; if there are not sufficient means in his city's temple to redeem him, the palace shall redeem him; but his field, orchard, or house will not be given for his redemption.[65]

The bodies of the defeated soldiers killed in battle might have been granted in some cases a burial, a practice attested already in earlier periods.[66] More usually, however, they seem to have been left unburied.[67] There is no evidence so far for arranging a truce during the war to bury the dead, such

---

where the inhabitants of the city Šuḫpad swore loyalty to Atmarum, their new lord, and he as well took an oath not to hunt, kill or deport them.

59 See ARMT XXVI/2, 307 and 308.

60 See ARMT XXVI/2, 356 and 359.

61 See e.g., Whiting 1987: p. 102f., No. 46: lines 16–27.

62 See ARMT XXVII, 85; XXVIII, 173: 17–33.

63 For examples and discussion, see Villard 1984.

64 Nevertheless, there are some letters that attest to the intervention of the ruler in behalf of a certain captive of war, presumably on occasion when more influential persons interceded in his behalf. See, e.g., Stol 1981: p. 22/23, No. 32, where Ḫammurabi of Babylon orders to give money taken from the temple of Sin to ransom a captive. Another example is the letter ARMT XXVIII, [illegible] written by Sammetar, the ruler of Ašnakkum, to Zimri Lim of Mari, sending him 11 shekels of silver as redemption money in order that he would release a certain captive. A further example is very likely ARMT XXII, 263 (cf. Villard 1984: p. 478, note 59).

65 Roth 1995: p. 87. See also Frankena 1966: p. 28/9, No. 46, a letter sent by two captives of war asking the addressee to intercede on their behalf with their "fathers" to redeem them.

66 See A. Westenholz 1970; for Old Babylonian references, see there Nos. 7 ("You will defeat the enemy and heap a burial mound upon their corpses") and 10 ("He smote Rim-Sin ... and heaped a burial mound upon him").

67 See the references cited by Guichard 1999: p. 45f. In any case, the evidence we have for either case is very meager.

as was known in Classical Greece,[68] nor of a rule according to which the bodies of enemy soldiers were returned to their families. Yet, there is one letter, which reports that a corpse of some enemy person was redeemed and recovered by its family.[69]

2.4. *The Attitude to Temples and Gods' Images of the Enemy*

The basic concept that underlaid the attitude of the peoples of the Ancient Near East to their gods was that mortal humans were created in order to serve the gods by providing them with all their needs. In return, the gods were expected to provide the people with protection and prosperity. These relations were based on the principle of *do ut des*, "I give in order that you give", and the gods were expected to remove their protection once the people failed to fulfill their duty to them, even if it was not the people's guilt. This latter case seems to stand behind the vague statement in the above-mentioned Anitta text[70] that when the city of Ḫattuša "suffered from famine, their deity Ḫalmašuitt deliver it up, and I (Anitta) took it by storm at night."[71] Such a statement, which ascribes the abandonment of the city divine patron to the deity's selfish interests, not associated with any moral failure of his protégés, is, however, very rare and more often it is ascribed to some sin committed by the people.[72]

These concepts necessarily should have had their impact felt on the battlefield before, during, and after the war. Already before the battle had started, the contending parties might have tried to win the gods of the enemy to their side by offering them tempting offers.[73] On the other hand, whenever a weaker party felt that there was a danger that his gods' images might fall into the hands of the enemy, he would have gathered them all into a safe shelter.[74] Having gained victory, the victorious party would remove the cult images of the defeated enemy and bring them to its own

68 See e.g., Bederman, 2001: p. 258f.

69 LAPO 17, No. 456 (=A.3552); cf. Guichard 1999: p. 46.

70 See above p. 62 with note 49.

71 Inscription B: §11, A 38–48 (Beckman 2006a: p. 218).

72 Another occasion where the abandonment of the divine patron was ascribed—this time rather by his worshippers—to his own interests is found in the Babylonian literary composition so-called "*Marduk prophecy*" (Foster 1993: I, pp. 304–307), where the fact that his statue was carried out by the Hittites, then by the Assyrians, and finally by the Elamites, is explained in his drive to traverse the universe.

73 For Hittite documents testifying to this practice, see in the next chapter at the end of §2.1.2 with note 52.

74 Thus e.g. we find in Tiglath-pileser I's inscriptions that the inhabitants of the city Urraṭinaš in order "to save their lives they took their gods (and) possessions and flew like birds to ledges on high mountains." (RIMA 2, p. 15 [A.0.87.1]: ii, 39–42).

territory where they would be welcomed and provided for as honored guests. This would deprive the defeated enemy of any hope to appease their divine patrons and to get their help.[75] The idea was that since these cult images served as the medium through which the gods who embodied them could be worshiped, preventing the defeated people from worshipping their gods would cause these gods to abandon their former protégés and transfer their favors to their new providers.[76]

But there are records of a different attitude that reflect a different concept. According to that other concept, the terrestrial war is also a war between the patron gods of the combating human parties, and just as the defeated army is taken into captivity, also the defeated gods (i.e. their divine statues) may be taken as captives together with cultic items of their temples. Such an attitude we find in the *Annals* of the Hittite king Ḫattušili I (*ca.* 1650):

> [A i 9–14][Thereafter] I went to (the city of) Zalpa and destroy it. I took its deities and three palanquins and carried them off for the sun-goddess of (the city of) Arinna. I carried off one golden ox and one golden rhyton in the shape of a fist to the temple of the storm-god. I carried off the deities that remained to the temple of (the goddess) Mezzulla.
> [A i 36–41]I destroyed Ulma and sowed [cress] on its territory. And I carried off seven deities to the temple of the sun-goddess of Arinna, ... I carried off the deities that remained to the temple of Mezzulla.[77]

---

[75] Thus we find in the Anitta text, §15 (A 57–58), that some time after the patron goddess of Ḫattuša delivered up that city to Anitta, he took care to furnished her temple with goods he brought back from campaign. See also the account in II Chronicles 25: 14–16, about Amaziah, king of Judah, who after defeating the Edomites took their gods, set them up as his gods, and offered up sacrifices to them. In certain cases, when the subjugated party was proved a loyal subordinate, his suzerain might have granted him back his captive cult images; see the examples collected in Cogen 1974: pp. 35–39.

[76] A passage in an Old Hittite text, the so-called "*Puḫanu Chronicle*" (recent edition: Soysal 1987), which seems to deal with the necessity to first win over the Storm-god of Ḫalab (Aleppo) in order to be able to conquer that city, is quite revealing in this regard: "... as long as(?) the Storm-god of Ḫalab runs at our side. As soon as [we have entreated(?)] him, he (i.e. the god of Ḫalab) will come to us and he will be the one who will begin to run in front of us. The male gods of the Storm-god of Ḫalab sent me to the King (saying): 'Go (and) find the Great Ones and let the Great Ones say to the King: You have shown me respect, (therefore) I have come'." (KBo 3.40: rev. 7'–11'; see Singer 1994: p. 87, whose translation and interpretation are followed; cf. Houwink Ten Cate 1984: p. 71).

[77] *CTH* 4. The document is a Hittite-Akkadian bilingual. For most recent translation (based primarily upon the Hittite version), see Beckman 2006b, and there also §§11–12, 15 and 17. It should be noted, however, that nowhere in the Hittite texts do we find an explicit statement that clarifies the status granted to these captive gods. Nevertheless, from the context, and particularly from their association with the other items of spoil taken and

3. Treaties

We currently have from this period one treaty from the Diyala region,[78] four treaties from Mari (Middle Euphrates),[79] five from Tell Leilan (northern Mesopotamia),[80] three from Kültepe (ancient Kaniš, about 20 km. northeast of Kayseri, in Anatolia),[81] and one from Alalah (northern Syria),[82] as well as two very small fragments of a further two treaties.[83] The earliest of these treaties is the treaty between the city-states of Šadlaš and Nērebtum, both in the Diyala region, which dated to the first half of the 19th century.[84] The treaty, written in the wake of the war between the two cities, is devoted mainly to solving the problem of those of their citizens who, due to the war or because of other reasons, were cut off from their homeland and found themselves in the other country. Yet, it also addresses a few other problems which are typical of two neighboring city-states, such as murder, cattle robbery, and bad treatment of merchants, which might cause a deterioration of their interrelationship. The treaty concludes with a note to the time when the provisions would become applicable, and the date (composed of month, day, and year-formula) when it was concluded.

---

brought into the temples of the conquerors, we may conclude that these gods were given to the main Hittite temples in order to be employed there as servants and workers; cf. Schwemer 2008: pp. 140–147 who discussed the issue in detail.

78 See note 84 below.

79 (1) The treaty between Zimri-Lim of Mari and Ḫammurabi of Babylon: Durand 1986; (2) the treaty between Zimrî-Lim of Mari and Ibâl-pî-El II of Ešnunna: Charpin 1991; (3) the subordination treaty of Atamrum of Andarig to Zimri-Lim of Mari: Joannès 1991; (4) a small fragment of a treaty between Zimri-Lim of Mari and the king of Kurda, for which see Joannès 1991: p. 176f.

80 Of these, only one has been fully published so far, the one concluded between the king of Apum (Tell Leilan) and the city of Aššur: Eidem 1991. Another treaty, between the king of Apum and the king of Razamā, was published only in translation: Eidem 2008: pp. 316–321. This latter treaty and the two other unpublished treaties are due to be published in Eidem Forthcoming.

81 These are commercial treaties concluded by the city of Aššur with the kings of Kaniš, Ḫaḫḫum, and of a city whose name was not preserved. For these treaties, see Çeçen and Hecker 1995; Günbatti 2004.

82 A(lalakh) T(ablets) 456, for which see Wiseman 1958b; Draffkorn 1959; Klengel 1965: pp. 137–139. More recently: Dietrich and Loretz 1985; Hess 2000b.

83 (1) Between Ilum-gāmil king of Uruk and unknown king: Falkenstein 1963: p. 54f. (cf. Kraus 1984: p. 289); (2) between Bêlakum king of Ešnunna and unknown king (unpublished so far; it was reported by Jacobsen 1940: p. 198, No. 98.

84 Greengus 1979: pp. 74–77, No. 326. For comments and corrections, see Kraus 1984: p. 91, note 204; Greengus 1988: p. 154f.; Stol 1991: p. 864. For a discussion of its provisions, see Yuhong 1994: pp. 53–61.

[1–3]The treaty of Šadlaš and Nērebtum.
[4]A free man (his rate is) $^{1}/_{3}$ mina of silver; [5]a slave of a free man (his rate is) 15 shekels of silver; [6]a female slave—10 shekels of silver; [7]an old man, an old woman, [8][a child] or a baby—<. . .> (their) rate. [9](A free resident) of the land of Šadlaš and its outlying pasture land [10](or) of the land of Nērebtum and its outlying pasture land [11]who has fled from (his country) because of the war [12](and) was cut off (from his home)—his master shall not hold him. [13]If (his removal from his land resulted from) a kidnapping or *brigandage*[?] [14]he shall be investigated: if (he was) not (originally) a foreigner (in his land)—he may go back (home); [15]if (he was) a foreigner—he may be seized. [16–17]As one household [to] (other) households....... [18]If (the unlawfully removed person is) the son of a free man, he (=his present master) shall return the son of a free man [19](and) he will pay 1 mina silver; [20]if (the removed person is) a slave of a free man, he (the present master) shall return the slave of a free man (to the former master, and) [21]he will pay ½ mina silver. [22]If it would be established to be a capital crime, [23]if one (person did it)—he shall die; [24]if as many as two, three, five [25]or more (did it)—they shall be seized for capital crimes, [26](and) the one whom *they convict* shall die, [27]and . . . all of them shall pay 1 and 2/3 mina. [28]If (it is a case of) *brigandage*[?], and an enemy had seized him—[29](it would be handled) according to the treaty (as has been stated for the case of kidnapping). [30]A citizen of (the city of) Šadlaš and its outlying pasture land [31](or) a citizen of (the city of) Nērebtum and its outlying pasture land [32]who, before the war, for purpose of profit [33]went (to the other city) and was held, shall be set free; [34](if) a slave of a free man (went to the other city) either before the war [35]or after the peace-treaty was concluded [36](and) was imprisoned—may return (home). [37]If there has occurred a robbery of cattle or sheep, [38](and) if it is under the reach and authority of the judges, [39](then) if he (the accused) is a citizen of Nērebtum, [40](he shall take) the oath of a citizen of Nērebtum, [41](namely) by the god Sin of Kamanum; [42]the oath of a citizen of Šadlaš [43](will be) by the god Sin of Ur-Iškur. [44]Silver (belonging) to a merchant—(either) new or old (debts)—shall be paid back. [45](The goods in) a repository and (grain) in a granary belonging to a free man (of the other city) [46]should not be consumed at his expense; (if) consumed, it must be replaced. [47]A soldier of Sumu-numhim (king of Šadlaš) [48]Ḫammi-dušur (king of Nērebtum) shall not enlist; [49]a soldier of Ḫammi-dušur [50]Sumu-numḫim shall not enlist.
(*Empty space of several lines*)
[51]When the [wa]r has passed, [52]ever after, this treaty of [53]Sumu-numḫim [54]and Ḫammi-dušur (will be binding).
(*Empty space*)
[55]The month of Simanum (= III), day 15, the year after Yarim-Lim died.

According to this treaty, if a person was forced to leave his home because of the war and find refuge in the other country, the one who granted him refuge has no right to enslave him or to prevent him from leaving whenever he wishes. If, however, the refugee did not willingly come to his present place of refuge, but was brought there by force, his former citizenship would determine his fate. If he was a citizen of either Šadlaš or Nērebtum, the parties to this treaty, he should be free to leave; but if he was a citizen of another city-state, the man who granted him refuge may hold him. The treaty, thus, gives protection only to citizens of the cities involved. On the other hand, in order to safeguard the interests of the respective rulers, the treaty prohibited enlisting soldiers of the other party who on their own deserted and sought another master (lines 47–50).[85] A remarkable feature is the treaty opening (lines 4–8) where tariffs for different people are listed, as a basis for calculating indemnities.

Noteworthy is the fact that the treaty is presented as an agreement between the two cities and not between their kings who are only first mentioned in lines 47–49, and only in lines 52–54 is the treaty ascribed to them. The treaty is not signed by the parties, although two empty spaces, between lines 50 and 51 and between 54 and 55, were left open, very likely for the signatures. This suggests that this is merely a first draft, what may also account for the absence of divine witnesses and for the fact that no curse is included as was customary in treaty-making during this period. These might have been intended to be added in the final version.[86]

What we have here is a parity treaty that was drawn bilaterally, namely— it contains the obligations of both parties. In this respect, this treaty stands alone, since the other known treaties of this period (save the one from Alalah) were drawn unilaterally, so that the obligations undertaken by one party were drafted by the other. In the recent 20 years, following the works of J.-M. Durand, D. Charpin, B. Lafont and J. Eidem, it became clear that at least in Mesopotamia during the 18th century there existed two other different practices regarding concluding a treaty.[87] The simple practice brought the concerned heads of political entities together to a summit meeting where they discussed the terms of the treaty. When an agreement was reached, a ritual took place, in which an animal (a donkey

85 Similar provision appeared already in the treaty between Naram-Sin, king of Akkad and the king of Elam (the 23rd century), for which see above in Chapter Two pp. 34–6. There (obv. iv, 15–16), according to the recent reading and translation of Koch 2005, we read: "[a deserter] I will not take to me", namely, the Elamite king undertook not to enroll deserters who run away from Agade. It also appeared later in the treaty between Ramesses II of Egypt and Ḫattušili III of Ḫatti, for which see below on p. 159f.

86 Cf. Greengus 1979: p. 77.

87 See Durand 1986 and 1997: pp. 429–458; Charpin 1988: p. 144f., and the letter ARMT XXVI/2, 372 on pp. 179–182; Eidem 1991, 2003: pp. 747–749, and 2008: pp.311–321; Lafont 2001a: pp. 262–293.

is usually attested) was slaughtered, and the parties smeared its(?) blood. The parties then exchanged oaths regarding the terms of the agreement in front of the divine statues or symbols brought to the meeting for this purpose. A festive drinking (of the blood?) and exchange of gifts concluded the ceremony. On certain occasions, the parties had some subordinated chiefs who were also presented as well as many representatives of both city-states and envoys from the major powers. Usually, such an agreement was concluded orally, and we learn about it only from the preserved letters that described the ceremony.[88] Upon concluding a subordinate treaty, the subordinate ruler or chief was expected to appear personally before his would-be suzerain.

Yet, a summit meeting between two independent kings, while still possible between lesser kings, was most uncommon among more powerful ones. For concluding a treaty between them, another practice was followed. According to this practice, the parties first exchanged what was called a "small tablet" (*ṭuppum ṣeḫrum*; also called *ṭuppî lipit napištim* "tablets of touching the throat"). It constituted a proposal sent by one party to the other for agreement, and included a limited list of obligations that the other party was supposed to undertake under oath, although it might have sometimes included quite detailed terms.[89] The addressee on his part, having assented to the proposal, took an oath over it while performing a ritualistic act of "touching the throat", symbolizing the sanction of death that would befall him should he violate the oath. Then he sent back to the proposer a similar "small tablet" over which the latter was supposed to take an oath and to perform the ritual of "touching the throat". Having accomplished these initial steps, the parties went on with exchanging messages discussing the terms, in which the emissaries of the parties involved played an important role. Having reached an agreement, each party sent to the other a "large tablet" (*ṭuppum rabûm*; called *nīš ilim* "[an oath by] the deity's life"), which contained the full specification of the obligations and promises that the other party was supposed to take upon himself.[90] This was formulated unilaterally even when it was a parity treaty, so that each party took an oath over, and undertook the obli

[88] See particularly ARMT XXVI/2, 404. For further references, see B. Lafont 2001a: pp. 263–271.

[89] An example in point is the one sent by Ibâl-pī-El II of Ešnunna to Zimri-Lim of Mari (A.1289+M.13103+M.18136): Charpin 1991: pp. 147–157.

[90] See particularly the letter ARMT XXVI/2, 372, and page 144f. for the discussion by D. Charpin.

gations specified in, the version drafted for him by the other party. The oath was taken in front of the statues (or symbols) of the gods of the local party and of those brought to the ceremony by the emissaries of the other party, and in the presence of those emissaries who took care to ensure the proper swearing in of the local party. The same ceremony was repeated by the other party either simultaneously or afterward. In case where the discussion over the terms of the agreement was simple and relatively short, the oath ceremony included, besides the swearing, the symbolic ritual of "touching the throat".[91]

Accordingly, a treaty thus concluded would have created two sets of parallel tablets: two parallel "small tablets" and two parallel "large tablets". As for the structure of the unilateral agreements, as far as we may infer from the available published treaties, a "small tablet" might have contained only the version of the oath, composed of the name of one or two gods by whom the oath was taken, and of the promise made in only very general terms. A good example of a "small tablet" of an ad hoc treaty between two kings on equal standing, is the treaty between Ḫammurabi, king of Babylon and Zimri-Lim king of Mari, in which they undertook a common policy toward their enemy, the Elamite king:[92]

> [1]Šamaš of the sky, lord of the land, [2]Adad of the sky, lord of the ve[rdicts]—[3](by) these gods Ḫammurabi, [4]son of Sin-Muballiṭ, king of [Babylon], [swore]: [5]"From this day, as long as [I] li[ve], [6]against Ṣiwa-Palar-Ḫuḫpak [7]I indeed will be at war. [8–9][My servants, my messengers, I will not (allow) taking the road with his servants, (and) them (my messengers)] [10]I will not dispatch to [him]. [11]Without (the consent of) [Zimri-Lim], [12]king of Mari and [the land of the Ḫana], [13–14]I will not make peace with Ṣiwa-Pala[r-Ḫuḫpak]. [15–16][If] in order to make peace with Ṣiwa-Palar-[Ḫuḫpak] I will set my face, [17]with Zimri-Lim, son of Yaḫdun-Lim, [18]king of Mari and the land of the Ḫana [19]I will consult indeed. If [. . .] (there is a decision) to make peace [21]with Ṣiwa-Pala[r-Ḫuḫpak], [22]together [23]we shall make pea[ce]. [24]My oath by the god Šamaš and the god [Adad], [25–26]that was s[worn] to Zimri-L[im, son] of Yaḫ[dun-Lim], [26]king of Mari and the la[nd of Ḫana], [27–28]with good sentiments and wholeheartedly I will take ca[re of it]. [. . .].

[91] For such a case, see the letter mentioned in the previous note. The reservation made by J. Eidem (2003: p. 750) is in place here: "In principle we must therefore assume a system with two parallel documents. . . . It must be emphasized, however, that extant evidence does not support entirely clear patterns for the use of treaty documents. No parallel set of documents relating to the same treaty has yet been found. . . . Similarly, the exact nature of the 'small tablet', used in the *lipit napištim* ceremony, remains to be elucidated."

[92] M.6435+ M.8987. Edited by Durand 1986: pp. 111–115. Cf. LAPO 16: No. 290; Anbar 1991; Sasson 1992; Heimpel 1983: p. 512f. and p. 58f. for discussion. Lines 8–9 are damaged and the restoration suggested here is circumstantial.

A "large tablet", on the other hand, opened with a much longer list of gods by whom the oath was taken. This list was followed by a detailed list of the obligations undertaken by the one who was taking the oath, and concluded by quite a detailed curse, which would fall upon him, should he fail to fulfill his obligations. An example of such a treaty, which though damaged still contains these three components, is the one concluded between Ibâl-pī-El II of Ešnunna and Zimri-Lim of Mari (A.361).[93] It was composed of four columns, which opened with a long list, enumerating at least 16 divinities (beginning and end are missing), and ended (on column iv) with at least 12 lines of curses (again, the beginning and end are missing). Of the provisions preserved (cols. II–III), all are devoted to issues of military co-operation, which seems to be the goal of this treaty, and are formulated as undertakings made in the first person. They are all concerned with the proper behavior of the king of Mari toward the troops of Ešnunna: not to betray those troops, not to disclose their plans to the enemy, and not to incite his or other troops against them.

Quite obviously, in view of the technologically inability to ensure the simultaneously performing of the swearing in of the both parties, such a procedure was very problematic. For it means that while one party would undertake certain obligations under oath, the other party had not yet obligated himself by an oath and could have entirely retreated from the agreement.[94] Moreover, in such a system, the two parallel versions may not have to refer to the same rights and obligations; the rights of one party, which appear in the version drawn up by him, might not appear as acknowledged in the version drafted by the other party. For under such a system, each party was likely to take care and to formulate for the other party only the rights and obligations that were within his own interests, although with due respect to the other party's reservations as were agreed upon. In any event, the very fact that these agreements were formulated unilaterally meant that the undertakings of one party were not conditioned by the fulfillment of the other party's obligations. In such a case, the failure of one party to fulfill his obligations, or to acknowledge the other party's rights, did not entitle the other party to consider himself as discharged of his own undertakings. Such a system was thus only liable to

[93] See note 79 above, sub (2).

[94] Cf. the very instructive letter ARMT XXVI/2, 469, and the remarks of S. Lackenbacher on p. 395 (note h), as well as LAPO 16, 287 (p. 448f.). The writers warn their king, Zimri-Lim, not to take the final oath before they bring him the final version upon which Ḫammurabi took an oath. See also A.4626 (LAPO 16, 286 [p. 447]).

raise problems in the future. It is no wonder, therefore, that the bilateral format of agreements, such as the treaty between Šadlaš and Nērebtum quoted above, was preferred and followed later in the Late Bronze Age.

All the available treaties of this period, similar to the treaty between Šadlaš and Nērebtum, were not sealed. This may be interpreted as reflecting the fact that they were only drafts or secondary copies. Another explanation recently given for lack of seals is that these treaties might have been encased in sealed envelopes.[95] Yet, it is still reasonable to take it as reflecting a different concept regarding the written document of the treaty, according to which such a document was not required to be sealed in order to prove its authenticity. It may be noted that the sealing of a legal document in this period had quite a different significance from the one it has today. The modern written contract creates a legal agreement; the signatures of the parties acknowledge and create obligations they must fulfill. The Ancient Near Eastern contract, on the other hand, having been drafted as a protocol written from the viewpoint of the witnesses, only attested the fact that an agreement was reached by the parties over the transaction.[96] Sealing such a document only acknowledged its accuracy and authenticity as an evidence instrument. But according to Mesopotamian private law, while the presence of witnesses was prerequisite to the validation of the transaction, sealing a legal document was not necessary to attest its authenticity.[97]

Still a fourth, different tradition of treaty-making seems to be reflected in an agreement from Alalaḫ in northern Syria, AT 456, dated to the later part of the 18th century.[98] This document recorded an exchange of settlements agreed upon between Abba-El,[99] king of Yamḫad/Ḫalap (Aleppo), and his brother, Yarim-Lim, who held the city of Irride together with some other settlements situated on the eastern border of the kingdom as his appanage domain that was granted to him by their father, the previous king of Yamḫad. Following a revolt of the other brothers against Abba-El,

[95] Eidem 2008: p. 321. Eidem (there, in note 125) also drew attention to ARMT XVIII 94 where the sender asks Zimri-Lim, the king of Mari, to send him a seal to be imprinted on a "tablet of (an oath by the) god's life", namely a treaty. For the custom to enclose legal documents in an envelope on which the text was repeated and the obligated party and some of the witnesses impressed their seals, cf. recently Westbrook 2003b: p. 374 (§3.3.2). For an example in point, see the document AT 7 in Wiseman 1953: pp. 34–36.

[96] Renger 1977: pp. 75–87.

[97] San Nicolò 1931: p. 138.

[98] See note 82 above.

[99] The name, written Abba-AN, may perhaps be read Abba-Il.

in the course of which Irride suffered heavy damage, and in the wake of which Abba-El reorganized the kingdom, he offered Yarim-Lim the city of Alalaḫ as a compensation for Irride. AT 456 records thus the agreement between the two brothers about this exchange of settlements.

The document opens with a list of the localities that changed hands as part of this agreement (lines 1–18). Quite a long explanation then follows about the circumstances why Yarim-Lim had to surrender the city of Irride, his former domain, in exchange for the cities of Alalaḫ and Murar: There was a revolt in the city of Irride, which Abba-El had to suppress by military force, resulting in the destruction of the city (lines 19–39). Following this is a reference to an oath and some ritual performed by Abba-El, followed by his promising not to take back these cities (39–42). This latter declaration is made, however, with some reservations, stipulated on lines 43–67, under which circumstances Yarim-Lim or his descendants might forfeit their new princedom. The document ends with a list of human witnesses, before whom Yarim-Lim took an oath of loyalty to Abba-El and his descendants.

We hardly know anything about the actual status of the princedom of Alalaḫ and the extent of autonomy its ruler had at that stage. There is, therefore, some uncertainty whether we should regard this document as a treaty or just a contract. But it certainly differs from the known treaties of this period. While it is a unilateral document, being a clear dictation of the suzerain, it also contains besides the obligations of the subordinate that of the suzerain (line 42), and the oaths of both parties (Abba-El: 39–42; Yarim-Lim: 74–76). In addition, while the treaties from Mari and Tell Leilan open with a reference to the gods in whose presence the parties took their oaths, the AT 456 document does not have such a list of gods.

However, the feature that seems the most striking in its novelty in this document is the apology of the suzerain for taking over Irride from Yarim-Lim (lines 19–39):

> [19–21]Zitra-Addu, the mayor of [Irride], went against(?) Yarim-Lim, and then he [accepted] the leadership of Mušna-Addu, the robber. [22]He (Zitra-Addu) brought him (Mušna-Addu) into Irride, his city, and [23] [24]he made the whole country hostile toward Abba-El, the(ir) king, and in/with . . . [. . .]. [25]And the mighty weapon [of . . . .] [26]with silver, gold, lapis-lazuli, crystal(?), and the great weapon of the god Addu, [27]the city of Irrite he (Abba-El) captured and [28–29]destroyed, and he seized Mušna-Addu, his enemy. [30]To Ḫalap (Aleppo) he (Abba-El) returned safely (saying): [31–32]"Would I give Irride, the smashed city to my brother?! [33–34](So,) in exchange for Irride [which] rebelled [against] him (Yarim-Lim), [35]and which [I capture]d and de[stroyed], [36–39][the city of Alal]aḫ [. . .] I shall give to Yarim-Lim, and the city of Murar over and above his share I shall add to it!"

The only reason I can think of for attaching this apology in this written *legal* document is the fact that Yarim-Lim was supposed to take an oath on this document, thereby confirming his acceptance of the apology. This, in turn, was in all probability intended to thwart in advance any counter-allegation by Yarim-Lim to the effect that Irride was taken from him illegally, which in turn would have entitled him to contravene the agreement. Similar legal sensitivity of the drafters to the need, in certain cases, to include in the prologue of the treaty an apology and justification for acts done by the suzerain, is one of the most pronounced features of the Hittite subordination treaties of the 15th–13th centuries.[100] The apology of the present document may therefore very likely be taken as a forerunner of the so-called "historical prologue" section of these later Hittite treaties.

4. Commercial Treaties and the Status of Traveling Merchants

Commercial treaties fall into a category of their own. Four such treaties belonging to the Old Babylonian period are known at present: one from Tell Leilan and three from Kültepe.[101] These treaties were concluded by the city of Aššur with North Mesopotamian and Anatolian kings. As far as can be judged, based on their preserved sections, these treaties share the same features and structure with the abovementioned treaties found in Mari. All are parity treaties designed to safeguard both the common and different interests of the Assyrian merchants as well as those of the kings who harbored them or allowed them to pass through their territories.[102] The survived part of the treaty Kt. n/k 794 from Kültepe may give the present reader some idea of these treaties. It was concluded by the city of Aššur with an unknown ruler. The text presents the version upon which that ruler and his dignitaries took an oath, namely the version that safeguarded Assyrian interests:[103]

---

100 For the Hittite treaties, see Beckman 1999: pp. 1–4, 11–124. For prologues presenting an apology, see there e.g. the treaties of Šunaššura (No. 2: §§ 2–8), Niqmaddu (No. 4: §§ 1–2), and Šattiwaza (No. 6A: § 1). For the role of this apology in these treaties, see Altman 2004b, and in more detailed discussion, Altman 2004a.

101 See above notes 80 and 81 respectively.

102 For the commercial activities of the Assyrians during the first quarter of the second millennium, their colonies and institutions see Garelli 1963; Orlin 1970; Larsen 1976; Dercksen 2004 and 2008; Veenhof and Eidem 2008.

103 The English translation adopted here is that of J.G. Dercksen, as was given in his "editor's note" in the article of Günbatti 1994: p. 250, note 8.

> $^{1-3}$There shall be no loss (of property belonging) to an Assyrian in your country, rope, peg or anything. $^{4-7}$If there occurs a loss in your country you shall search (the lost object) and you shall return it to us. $^{7-11}$If there occurs blood(shed) in your country you shall hand over the killers to us and we shall kill (them). $^{11-15}$You shall not make Akkadians come (to your country). If they travel overland to your country you shall hand (them) over to us and we shall kill (them). $^{15-16}$You shall not demand anything from us. $^{17-20}$Just like your father you may take 12 shekels of tin per (donkey) from a caravan on its way to Kaniš. $^{20-23}$You may consume, like your father, $1^1/_4$ shekels of silver per donkey from a return caravan. $^{24-25}$You shall not take anything in excess (of this). $^{25-28}$If there is a war so that the caravan is unable to come to you, they will send you 5 minas from (the colony of) Ḫaḫum. $^{29-32}$He raised his hand towards (the gods) Aššur and Adad, to the Netherworld and to the spirits of his ancestors, $^{32-35}$he . . . his table and his chair . . . and he filled his cup and then emptied it; $^{35-38}$the ruler said: . . . $^{39-42}$And they (i.e. his dignitaries) said: "If we reject your (pl.) sworn treaty our blood shall be shed like (the contents of) the cup!"

The other two treaties from Kültepe (Kt.00/k 6 and 10) add some further provisions: the moveable and immoveable properties of the Assyrian should not be taken by force or in payment at a lower price (k 6: 17–18, 64–68); if an Assyrian is killed, the local ruler shall pay the fixed amount of the blood-money besides handing over the murderer to the Assyrians (k 6: 39–44); in case a local citizen and an Assyrian citizen go to court, the local ruler shall pass honest judgment on them (k 6: 46–49; k 10: ii, 1–5); the business activities of an Assyrian who has a debt owed to a local citizen should not be restricted, and if that Assyrian went to another locality, no other Assyrian could be held responsible for him (k 6: 50–53, 72–76);[104] the local ruler is responsible for the security of the caravan road passing through his territory as well as for the security of the water routes in the regions where river transportation was carried out, and he shall pay the full amount for any loss of Assyrian freight on these routes (k 10: 11–18); and Assyrians shall be exempt from the local state service (k 6: 78–81).

These rights and guarantees granted to the Assyrian merchants clearly reflect the profits the Anatolian rulers earned from the trade between Anatolia and Aššur.[105] These rights went so far, at least in one treaty, as to enable the Assyrian to dictate a provision denying access to the Akkadians (=North Babylonians) merchants, their competitors (Kt. n/k 794: 11–15).

104 For Mari letters illustrating such a practice, see Durand 1990: pp. 62–64.

105 Cf. the remark of Günbatti 2004: p. 255.

Rich documentation about the activities of the Assyrian traders in Anatolia was found in the archives of these traders in their colony at the foot of the modern site of Kültepe. This colony was the administrative capital of a network of Assyrian commercial colonies and trading stations, stretching from central and southern Anatolia to northern Syria and the western part of northern Mesopotamia that flourished between the 20th and 18th centuries.[106] From the hundreds of texts recording commercial or diplomatic contacts with local rulers that were discovered there, additional information can be gleaned about the agreed terms which enabled the Assyrian merchants to conduct their commercial activity with relatively little risk in these foreign countries.[107] The local kings guaranteed the Assyrians the following rights: (1) residence rights in the Assyrian colonies and presumably some kind of protection there; (2) full extraterritorial rights so that the colonies were in a sense political and juridical extensions of the city government of Ashur (Aššur); (3) protection of the roads and guarantees against losses due to robbery and brigandage in the territory controlled by the local king. The Assyrians in turn had to acknowledge the following points: (1) to pay taxes to the local palaces on caravans: the basic tax amounted to 5% on textiles and approximately 3% on tin; (2) the palaces retained the right to buy (against reduced prices) up to 10% of all shipments of quality textiles; (3) the palaces had a monopoly on the trade in certain luxury commodities, first of all meteoric iron and certain precious stones. Assyrians violating their obligations, such as smuggling goods, were tried and punished by the local kings who could throw the offender into jail to make others fear for their lives.[108]

As long as the traveling merchants did not violate customs obligations, they could easily cross foreign borders, and except for cases where their passage was blocked as an act of sanction against their or a neighboring king,[109] they were also able to enter and cross enemy territory.[110] In certain

---

[106] For references, see above note 102.

[107] Summarized by Larsen 1976: p. 245f.

[108] See e.g. the letter ATHE 62, cited by Larsen 1976: p. 244, note 53: "The son of Irraja had his smuggled goods conducted to Pušu-ken but his smuggled goods were seized, and the palace seized Pušu-ken and put him in prison. The guards are vigilant. The queen (of Kanish) wrote to (the Anatolian kingdoms of) Luḫusaddija, Ḫurama, Šalaḫšuwa and to her own country with respect to the smuggling, and scouts have been posted. Urgent! Do not smuggle anything!"

[109] For such a case, see lines 34–37 of the above quoted letter of the king Anum-ḫirbi of Mama (p. 54 above).

[110] See Charpin and Durand 1997: pp. 377ff. ("2.2. Marchands et diplomats").

cases, when they traded with royal merchandise, we may find them provided by a letter of requesting the foreign authorities not to impose a tax on their merchandise.[111]

5. Managing Conflicts

While a war would have served as a means for settling disputes by force of arms, believing its outcome to be the verdict of the divine judges, Ancient Near Eastern people still employed two peaceful ways to settle controversies between disputing states—negotiation and arbitration.[112] Summit meetings between two heads of political entities were very rare phenomena in the Ancient Near East, and the role of negotiation was assumed by competent emissaries of both sides who traveled between the two royal courts. They were authorized to reach an acceptable formula, but the final decision to accept or reject rested with the two sovereigns.[113]

Turning to arbitration, in contrast to the well-known practice of such an institution in ancient Greece,[114] the recourse to arbitration or mediation of some third party in disputes between states not dependent on him is hardly known in the Ancient Near East. What we do have in the Ancient Near East is the intervention and arbitration of a suzerain king in interstate disputes between two countries subordinated to him.[115] When the arbitrator was a suzerain, exercising his authority and power to settle a dispute between two of his subordinate kings, his award was in fact more like a verdict issued by a judge with whom the contending parties had to comply. In such a case, it would seem that it was sufficient that one of

[111] An example of such a letter is ARMT V, No. 11, sent by Aplaḫanda, king of Carchemish to Yasmaḫ-Addu, king of Mari: "Say to Yasmaḫ-Addu: thus speaks Aplaḫanda, your brother. This transport is mine; so do not bother my servitors with a story of taxes." Cf. LAPO 17, p. 36, No. 461.

[112] For arbitration in the realm of international law in the Ancient Near East, see S. Lafont 2000: pp. 564–578.

[113] A good, detailed example of such negotiation is provided by two letters found in Mari: ARMT XXVI/2, Nos. 449 & 450. They concern a border dispute between Zimri-Lim of Mari and Ḫammurabi of Babylon over the control of certain cities located along the Middle Euphrates. While Ḫammurabi was ready to waive his claim on most of these cities, he insisted on maintaining his control over the city of Hīt. The most he was ready to suggest is that both Zimri-Lim and he would hold the city and that both would station garrisons there.

[114] Tod 1913; Ager 1996.

[115] Cf. S. Lafont 2000: pp. 564–578.

the contending parties would have recourse to the suzerain to make him intervene, without getting the other party's consent in advance.[116]

Yet, also some cases of the other kind of arbitration seems to be attested in this period, in which recourse was made to a third party on whom the contending parties were not dependent. Two such cases are known.[117] The first case brings us back to the abovementioned dispute between Zimri-Lim and Ḫammurabi over the city of Hit. In the two letters mentioned above (note 113) ARMT XXVI/2 Nos. 449 and 450, we find a reference to the *sukkal* (emperor) of Elam, which hints at his involvement in the case. According to letter 449, the region of Hit was first conquered by Šamši-Adad who granted it to Ḫammurabi, allowing him to station soldiers there; later on, the king of Elam conquered the region and granted it to Zimri-Lim. It would seem that following the refusal of Ḫammurabi to acknowledge the right of Zimri-Lim to hold this region, the latter appealed to the king of Elam to intervene. In the same letter, there is a reference to Elamite messengers who seem to have been presented while the emissaries of Zimri-Lim negotiated the matter with Ḫammurabi, a fact that would support the assumption about the involvement of the Elamite king. Yet, toward the end of this letter, Zimri-Lim's messengers cited Ḫammurabi's request: "do not speak to the *sukkal* of Elam", which hints at his rejection of the king of Elam as arbitrator in the matter.[118]

Some years later, another letter returned to the issue of the yet unsolved dispute over Hit.[119] It was sent to Zimri-Lim by another official, reporting about his negotiation with Ḫammurabi with regard to concluding a pact for conducting a joint policy against Elam. There, on lines 6'–9' of the reverse side of the tablet, we find the following interesting suggestion made by Ḫammurabi:[120]

> Remove Hit from the treaty tablet, and I shall commit myself! Then take the lead of the troops and get underway! After every single objective has been accomplished—afterwards, the kings, our brothers, must sit down. They must give us direction on the case and I will heed the judgment they render.

[116] See e.g., ARMT X, 5; XXVI/2, 389; XXVIII, 34. For much earlier examples of this kind of arbitration, see Chapter One, p. 4 with note 17; Chapter Two, p. 38 note 77.

[117] For both cases, see S. Lafont 2000: pp. 570–574.

[118] For a discussion of the status and influence of the Elamite king at that time, see Charpin and Durand 1991.

[119] ARMT XXVI/2, No. 468.

[120] Translation followed that of Heimpel 2003: p. 379.

Ḫammurabi suggests that in order to resolve the dispute, Zimri-Lim has first to pull his troops out of the disputed region, and then a committee consisting of peer kings ("brothers") would be established to arbitrate the question of Hit. Ḫammurabi adds that he commits himself in advance to abide by the judgment of this committee.

The second case is a dispute between Rim-Sin king of Larsa and the king of most probably Ešnunna over free traffic on the waterways. According to a letter sent by Rim-Sin to his envoys at the court of Ešnunna (A.7535),[121] the traffic on the river was blocked by the king of Ešnunna due to his building of dams. When his request to open the watercourse was denied, Rim-Sin instructed his envoys to return home. The envoys then requested permission to leave and at the same time submitted a suggestion to resolve the dispute. There were two ways opened before their king to solve the dispute—arbitration by the Great King of Elam or judicial process through an ordeal by the Rivergod. Yet, despite the fact that their king would have surely won the case had he chosen trial by ordeal, he chose the more compromising way by appealing to the Elamite king.

As a matter of fact, we do not have so far any evidence of an actual implementation of the river ordeal to solve territorial disputes between independent states.[122] But there is now a document that attests to the possible implementation of such an ordeal for another sort of dispute between two independent polities. According to two duplicate letters found in Kültepe,[123] an Assyrian merchant was arrested as a hostage by the authorities of an unnamed Anatolian country. This was done to exert pressure on the Assyrian merchant colony in Kültepe to surrender another person suspected of spying and cooperating with the enemy. In their negotiation with the authorities of that country, the representatives of the Assyrian colony argued that the arrested merchant was innocent and ignored the charge that they knew anything about the other suspected person. Instead, they proposed that the arrested merchant should be allowed to either take an oath "by the dagger of (the god) Aššur" to prove his innocence, or to "go to the river", namely to go or to be thrown into the river in order to have the River-god judge whether he is guilty or not.

[121] Cited and discussed by Rowton 1967: p. 268f.; cf. S. Lafont 2000: p. 571f. with notes 25–26 for further literature.

[122] For this ordeal and its employment by the civil law in private litigations see Frymer-Kensky 1977; Durand, ARMT XXVI/1, pp. 509–539. See further the articles of van Soldt 2003 and van den Hout 2003.

[123] Kt n/k 504 and Kt 93/k 145; see Günbatti 2001; Larsen 2007.

6. Extradition and Asylum

A wide variety of refugees and runaways is attested in the available documents of the second millennium. In discussing the issue, we have to distinguish between the following categories of runaways: (1) runaway slaves; (2) captives of war escaping from their captors but unable to return to their homeland; (3) deserting soldiers who were afraid to return home; (4) dependent artisans escaping from their masters; (5) indebted peasants, who after losing all their property deserted their fields and joined bandit gangs; (6) free civilians who ran away from a blood avenger or for some other reasons; and (7) political refugees. To the above categories we have to add a somewhat different category of refugees, that of tribes, clans, communities or families, who for one reason or another were compelled to leave their homelands and cross the border to seek other pastures or agricultural land.

While their legal status and the prospect for survival differed in each case, they all shared a common fear lest they be extradited into the hands of those looking for them. This fear was founded on the fact that in this period many of the regions of the Near East were bound together by a network of treaties where the provisions for extradition of runaways often took an important place.[124] Most if not all of these runaways would have liked to find a new hospitable and safe place to settle down and earn a living, for roaming about alone in a foreign country was quite dangerous. First, there was the defenseless status of the alien and the fear lest he be abused by the local people.[125] Next, there was always the fear lest he be discovered by his pursuers. Finally, there was the fear he be delivered to his pursuers by the local authorities due to extradition agreements. A person fleeing from his city or country had therefore the choice of taking the risk of entering a foreign city and there hiring himself out as a soldier or a laborer, or living along the fringe of the populated regions by joining

[124] For a survey of provisions of extraditing runaways in treaties, see Snell 2001: pp. 86–98. For evidence from Mari on the extradition of fugitives, intimating the existence of extradition clauses in the treaties of the Old Babylonian period, see Sasson 2007. For Late Bronze Age examples, see in the next chapter.

[125] About the shaky status of an alien, the following Mesopotamian saying is very instructive: "A resident alien in another city is a slave": Lambert 1960: p. 259 (sub Sm 61: 16–17). For the status of the alien, see Pirenne 1958 and Cardascia 1958. It recalls the biblical warning not to oppress, deceive or deny legal rights to the alien (e.g., Ex. 22, 20; 23, 9; Deut. 24, 17; 27, 19), as well as the charges of hurting the alien voiced by the prophets (Jer. 7, 6; 22, 3; Zech. 7, 10; Mal. 3, 5; Ps. 94, 6).

the bands of homeless and becoming one of the highwaymen who raided the fields around the villages and cities in the vicinity.

Of these categories of runaways, political refugees, and those belonging to or working for the palace or the nobility, as well as captives of war, deserting soldiers, and dependent artisans, were of primary importance for the state. To these categories we have to also add the runaway slaves, who might have belonged to wealthy private persons but were not members of the nobility. On the other hand, the fate of indebted peasants and free civilians who left their homelands seems to have been of less concern to the state. In any case, they were not specified explicitly as a category of runaways to whom the provisions of extradition applied.

We have already noted some concern to the runaways issue in the treaty of the 23rd century concluded between Naram-Sin of Akkad and an Elamite king, and in the Old Babylonian treaty between Šadlaš and Nērebtum where both parties undertook not to enlist a runaway soldier of the other party (lines 47–50).[126] Although these treaties do not speak explicitly about extradition, the actual meaning is to be deduced. The above-mentioned three commercial treaties from Kültepe, concluded by the city of Aššur with rulers of some Anatolian cities, are more explicit in this regard. In those treaties, the stipulated extradition is concerned not only with murderers (Kt. n/k 794: 7–11; Kt. 00/k 6: 39–45; Kt. 00/k 10: iv, 19'–20'), but also with the extradition of Babylonian merchants—the commercial competitors of the Assyrian merchants who happened to come to these Anatolian cities—in order to be executed (Kt. n/k 794: 11–15). An extradition stipulation occurs also in a not yet published treaty from Tell Leilan, concluded between Till-Abnu, king of Apum, and Yamṣi-Ḫandu, king of Kaḫat (L87–1362); but in this case, it concerns runaway slaves.[127] These occurrences of stipulated extradition should be viewed as only a small sample of a much greater bulk of material pertaining to an issue which was one of the most common concerns of rulers throughout the history of the Ancient Near East, when failure to assent to demand of extradition was often regarded as *casus belli*.[128] And while the rich archives of Mari have contributed considerably to this issue,[129] they still leave us with questions regarding the different rules pertaining to the various types of runaways in this period.

---

[126] See above in this chapter, p. 69 with note 85.
[127] Reported by B. Lafont 2001a: p. 286 (sub T8).
[128] See the instances collected in Elgavish 2003: pp. 43–45.
[129] For which see Sasson 2007.

Asylum is an issue relevant to extradition. While one might have expected to find in the rich documentation of this period evidence of holy places as providing refuge for runaways, similar to the Biblical "cities of refuge" (Num. 35: 6–28; Deut. 19: 1–13; Joshua 20: 1–9), nothing of this kind has turned up until quite recently. However, the recently published Mari letter A.746, sent by the emissary Dâriš-libur to his king Zimri-Lim of Mari, does provide such evidence.[130] It deals with Zimri-Lim's request submitted to Yarim-Lim, king of Aleppo, to extradite four enemy rulers who after having been defeated managed to escape to the city of Emar, in the territory of Aleppo. In a response to that request, Yarim-Lim argued that "Zimri-Lim must have clearly forgotten . . . that in the territory of (the god) Addu fugitives are not to be handed into custody."

7. Diplomatic Law

Messengers and messages are attested already in the royal inscriptions of the Early Dynastic III period,[131] and the employment of diplomatic messengers in interstate relations is certainly much older. Yet, information regarding the rules and customs regulating the exchange of diplomats became available for the first time only from the Old Babylonian period. In recent years, the institution of diplomatic messengers and messages in the Ancient Near East was discussed by a number of scholars who treated its various aspects and brought to the fore the available rich information about this institution.[132] The main source for this information as pertains to the Old Babylonian period is the rich royal archives of Mari.[133] However, the greater part of this information pertains to the realms of international relations and state administration, and only a smaller portion relates to international law. It is this latter portion, which is mainly concerned with the powers and immunities of the diplomat as well as with his obligations, that will be reviewed here.

---

[130] Recently published as document No. 8 by Durand 2002.

[131] See above in Chapter One, note 61.

[132] For general discussions of the diplomatic institution in the Ancient Near East, see Meier 1988; Green 1989; Elgavish 1998 and 2000; Oller 1995; B. Lafont 2001b. For studies pertaining to this institution in the Old Babylonian period, see next note. For studies dealing with the Late Bronze period, see the next chapter, notes 2 and 298.

[133] For more recent discussions related to the period under consideration here, and upon whose works the following brief review is based, see B. Lafont 1992 and 2001a: pp. 294–314; Durand 1997.

A permanent diplomatic mission was unknown in the Ancient Near East. There is some evidence, however, that in this period, "many kings maintained a 'house' in foreign capitals that functioned as an economic and mercantile unit as well as a place in which to lodge messengers",[134] and the king of Mari even maintained a permanent personal postal service in Aleppo.[135] Instead of a permanent mission, once diplomatic relations were established, messengers were exchanged on regular basis to the extent that the regular exchange of messengers between kings became a sign of their cordial relations with each other, and the interruption of such exchange as indicating some tension or crisis in their relations.[136] Two main kinds of diplomatic delegations are attested in the Mari letters: delegations on transit, which only used Mari as a comfort station on their way to their destination without being officially received there, and delegations where Mari was their final destination. The composite of a diplomatic delegation varied according to circumstances. It could be composed of only one messenger traveling alone[137] or up to a very large delegation, which included interpreters,[138] secretaries and personal servants,[139] accompanied by a military escort with up to hundreds of soldiers.[140] The rank of the messengers varied from simple carriers of royal messages to high-ranking diplomats. Those latter came usually from the aristocracy and served as high-ranked royal officials or military officers, although none of them was a professional diplomat.

We do not have any document which specifies the set of rules that regulated the exchange of messengers. Yet, from the many letters that refer to the experiences of these messengers, and particularly their complaints of misconduct,[141] it is clear that these exchanges were conducted according to a quite developed set of rules. The treatment the diplomatic messengers were entitled to receive was according to their rank, although the extent those rules were observed was quite often depended on the nature of the relations between the kings involved.

---

[134] Villard 1995: p. 873. See B. Lafont 2001a: p. 294f. note 324 for details.

[135] A.2937, an unpublished document cited by B. Lafont 2001a: p. 294 note 324, which is due to appear in ARMT XXVI/3.

[136] See e.g. the above quoted letter of Anum-ḫirbi of Mama (above p. 54) quoting the request of Waršama, the ruler of Kaniš: "Let your messenger come to me and let my messenger come regularly to you" (lines 52–55).

[137] ARMT XIV, 117: 11 (=LAPO 16, 396).

[138] See e.g. ARMT XXVII, 116; see further Durand 1997: p. 592.

[139] See B. Lafont 1992: p. 169 note 12, and p. 183 note 94; Lafont 2001a: p. 295 note 329.

[140] ARMT I, 88 and 123; II, 5; XIV, 98; XXVI/1, 174 and 183.

[141] See e.g. ARMT II, 76; XIII, 32; XXVI/2, 323, 370, 384: 67'–71'.

Messengers in transit were requested to present to the authorities in the transit areas an official document issued by their king to the effect that they are diplomats going on his mission. The following letter, from the abovementioned archives of the Assyrian merchants at Kanish is an example of this kind of accreditation letter given to the emissary by his authorities:

> Thus the envoys of the City (of Aššur) and the Kanesh colony to all the colonies: our messengers Aššur-rabi and Ikuppiya have been sent to give instructions. Give them two escorts. (Each) colony must help them reach the (next) colony![142]

M.8990, from Mari, is another, actually unique type of this kind of document:[143]

> Yaspuqi-El, envoy of (the king) Ṣura-Ḫammû, (coming) from (the city of) Aḫunâ, (accompanied by) 100 soldiers (with) 1 *šagatum* as his guide, (coming) from Ašlakkâ, (going) to Mari.

We have here the name of the messenger, the identity of his king who sent him, the place from where he departed, his escort and his destination. The document was sealed by the king's seal to ensure its authenticity. That such a document was indeed indispensable we learn from ARMT XIV, 52, where the governor of Sagaratum reports to his king, Zimri-lim of Mari, that he denied free passage to an emissary from Ekallâtum going to Carchemish, since that person was not equipped with the proper document.[144]

Apart from such a diplomatic passport, the messengers should have been provided by a letter of accreditation intended for the ruler to whom the emissary was dispatched.[145] At least in certain cases, this letter might have been identical with the instructions given to the messenger by his king including the object of his mission.[146] Without such a document, messengers might have been suspected about their honesty and the real

[142] BIN 6: 120, for which see Larsen 1976: p. 248.

[143] Published by G. Bardet in ARMT XXIII, p. 20; cf. B. Lafont 1992: p. 172f.

[144] Related to these laissez-passer documents are letters of introduction, for which see the three examples from Tell Shemshara: Eidem and Læssøe 2001, Nos. 31–33 (SH.916, 907 and 895).

[145] For a reference to such a document, see ARMT XIV, 122 (=LAPO 16, 368).

[146] For such instructions given to messengers (*wûrtum*), see ARMT VI, 27 (= LAPO 16, 424), and B. Lafont 2001a: pp. 297 and 301.

intention of their mission, and were liable to be interrogated meticulously by the authorities of the receiving state.[147]

At the border of the destined state, the diplomatic messenger might have been denied entrance, even if provided with the proper document.[148] Even after entering the destined territory, messengers might have been denied access to the hosting king and were not permitted to present their credentials.[149] On the other hand, once entering the territory under the jurisdiction of the receiving king, it was the responsibility of that king to ensure the safety of the diplomatic delegation and to take care of hosting, accommodating, feeding, and even clothing its members. Having been admitted into the royal audience, after the ceremonial greetings and the delivering of the gifts he brought, the messenger broke the sealed envelope that contained the letter sent by his king,[150] and read it out in the front of the hosting king and in the presence of the audience. This, however, might have deterred the messenger from openly delivering his message, since in the regular royal audience, apart from the local high-ranked officials and notables, all the foreign delegations that happened to be present there took part. That could also have included delegations from adversary states of the sending state. In such an occasion, the messenger might have been invited to a secret council of the hosting king, to which only the closest allies and advisers were invited.[151] After he finished his mission and was about to leave the receiving country, the messenger had to await permission to leave (*wûrtum*).[152] On his departure, he regularly was provided with provisions for the way[153] and was accompanied by a messenger of the receiving king, who also served as a guide.

The idea of diplomatic immunity was at this age still quite undeveloped.[154] Indeed, there are some indications that royal messengers did enjoy some degree of immunity.[155] Thus we find that a severe crisis in the relations between Elam and Babylon did not deter the Elamite messen-

---

147 See Eidem and Læssøe 2001: No. 11 (SH.[illegible]).

148 See the letter A.2988+A.3008 = LAPO 16, 282. The messengers of the king of Ešnunna were stopped at the border and were denied entrance into the territory of Mari.

149 See ARMT XIV, 122 (=LAPO 16, 368); XXVI/2, 368 and 370.

150 See ARMT XXVI/2, 490.

151 See ARMT XXVI/2, 327 with note a; ARMT XXVI/2, 414 (for which see B. Lafont 1992: p. 176, note 57). See further ARMT XXVI/2, 307.

152 See e.g. ARMT XIII, 31; XVIII, 19 (=LAPO 16, 407 and 409).

153 See ARMT I, 17; XXI, 189.

154 See more recently Elgavish 2000.

155 B. Lafont 2001a: p. 296.

gers from traveling to Babylon with diplomatic messages,[156] and that foreign emissaries in transit who came from unallied countries and passed through Mari were nevertheless welcome there. Also, when it happened that a Babylonian delegation was suspected of harboring a fugitive slave, the authorities at Mari preferred recourse to divination rather than open a direct investigation and interrogation of its members.[157] However, by far the great bulk of negative evidence indicates that no messenger could take for granted that he was invulnerable. Thus we find that Ḫammurabi of Babylon arrested envoys of Ešnunna,[158] Larsa,[159] and Elam.[160] Ḫammurabi also intercepted a diplomatic delegation circulating between Qatna and Larsa,[161] and the king of Aleppo similarly intercepted Elamite messengers on their way to Qatna.[162] The worry lest their messengers would be intercepted by adversary kings motivated kings to either send their messages through messengers of allied states,[163] or in the disguise of merchants, or else under the protection of Bedouin groups[164]—the two category of people for whom the routes were opened even in times of war.[165] But dangers of attack waylaid messengers along the routes not only from adversary states, but also from brigands seeking spoil and ransom-money.[166] In order to evade these dangers, messengers of different countries used to travel together and on particularly important missions, to be accompanied by a military escort.

---

[156] See ARMT XXVI/2, Nos. 361 and 370, and the discussion of D. Charpin there on pp. 149–151.

[157] A. 1890, not yet published; briefly summarized by Charpin and Durand 1997: p. 381, note 100.

[158] ARMT XXVI/2, 370: 40'; 449: 36.

[159] ARMT XXVI/2, 372: 33.

[160] ARMT XXVI/2, 363: 26.

[161] ARMT XXVI/2, 383: rev. 17'.

[162] LAPO 16, 298 (A.266).

[163] ARMT XXVII, 71. Ḫammurabi of Kurda sent his messages through Babylonian messengers.

[164] ARMT XXVI/2, 526 (merchants); ARMT VI, 27 (=LAPO 16, 424; Bedouins).

[165] Charpin & Durand 1997: pp. 377–381.

[166] ARMT II, 123; XIV, 86.

CHAPTER FOUR

THE NEAR EAST IN THE LATE BRONZE AGE (1600–1200 BCE)

While the Old Babylonian Period documentation was dominated by a single culture, that of the Late Bronze Age was multi-cultural. This was reflected in the change of the period nomenclature—from one dominated by language to one dominated by archeological artifacts. The Akkadian language, which had become the language of diplomacy, was now required to serve as a bridge between many different languages and cultures, such as Hittite, Hurrian, Canaanite, and Egyptian, that were integrated into a network of diplomatic relations.[1]

The relevant documentation of this period is perhaps not as rich as that of the Old Babylonian period, but is compensated by the extremely valuable and important information we get on international relations and law[2] gleaned from many parity and subordination treaties,[3] edicts and verdicts,[4] as well as from rich diplomatic correspondence[5] and royal inscriptions.[6]

1. The Political Scene

Although the documented geographical scene expanded in this period, the political system in Mesopotamia, northern Syria and Anatolia remained in fact much similar to that of the previous Old Babylonian Period. This political system may be described as a multi-pole system, headed by some half-dozen

[1] There is no up-to-date detailed historical survey of the Ancient Near East of this period as it exists for the Old Babylonian Period. For a briefer survey, see Kuhrt 1995: Vol. 1, pp. 185–381. For a very detailed and up-to-date historical survey of Anatolia and the Hittites in this period, see Bryce 1998; Klengel 1999, and for Syria in this period—Klengel 1992: pp. 84–180. The history of Ugarit is treated in detail by Singer 1999. The relations of Egypt with the other regions of the Near East in this period are treated by Redford 1992: pp. 125–237. For the Hurrians, see Wilhelm 1989 and 1995, and for Assyria and its relations with its neighbors in this period, see Harrak 1987, and Mayer 1995: pp. 167–249.

[2] For the international relations of this period, see more recently Liverani 2001; Cohen and Westbrook (eds.) 2000, and Bryce 2003. The international law of the age is treated by Westbrook 2000 and 2003, as well as Beckman 2003.

[3] See below in §3.

[4] The more important were translated in Beckman 1999, Nos. 28–38B.

[5] The main collections of translations are: Moran 1992; Edel 1994; Hagenbuchner 1989: pp. 240–416. For the international archives of Ugarit, including diplomatic letters, treaties, edicts and verdicts, see Nougayrol 1956; Nougayrol et al. 1968: pp. 65–131; Bordreuil (ed.) 1991.

[6] For the main collections of royal inscriptions, see below notes 8, 9 and 10.

relatively powerful kings, each of whom governed a cluster of small satellite city-states ruled by petty kings or tribal chiefs. They were bound to their suzerain by a loyalty oath and in many cases by a written treaty, upon which the subordinate ruler took the oath of loyalty. Indeed, the number of powers in this period was somewhat reduced, but the real significant change in this system was the re-appearance of the empire. The main powers that now dominated the political scene were Egypt, Mittani, Ḫatti, Assyria and Babylonia. Egypt by this time took over Nubia in the south and expanded up to central Syria in the north. Mittani, a Hurrian kingdom, which was established around 1500 in the Upper Khabur region, had expanded eastward up to the Zagros mountains, and westward to northern Syria and the gateway to Anatolia where it confronted the Hittites. The Hittites, on their part, succeeded around 1350 to expand to northern and central Syria at the expense of Mittani and Egypt. In the east, the city of Ashur (Aššur) started from 1366 on to expand westward at the expense of Mittani, and eventually came to clash with the Hittites. To these main powers, we have to add Babylonia, although not really yet an empire, which had expanded over southern Mesopotamia.[7]

2. War

The royal inscriptions of the Assyrians[8] and the Hittites[9] are our main sources of information about the rules of war for this period.[10]

2.1. *Opening Hostilities*

2.1.1. *Declaration of War*

As was demonstrated in the previous chapters, a declaration of war sent in advance to an opponent is attested already in the Early Dynastic Period IIIb (25th–24th centuries), and echoes of this practice reach us from the

---

[7] For the various types of organization of these empires, see below in section 2.3.1.

[8] Grayson 1987a (=RIMA I).

[9] The main texts are: (1) The *Text of Anitta* (*CTH* 1) = Neu 1974; Hoffner 1997a; (2) The *Annals of Ḫattušili I* (*CTH* 4) = Houwink Ten Cate 1984; Beckman 2006; (3) The *Deeds of Šuppiluliuma* (*CTH* 40) = Güterbock 1956; Hoffner 1997b; (4) The *Annals of Muršili II* (*CTH* 61) of which two sets have survived: the *Ten Year Annals* and the *Comprehensive Annals*, for which see Goetze 1933; for a recent edition of the *Ten Year Annals* see Grélois 1988; cf. Beal 2000; (5) The *Apology of Ḫattušili III* (*CTH* 81) = Otten 1981; cf. van den Hout 1997.

[10] To these one may add the many descriptions of war campaigns in the Egyptian royal inscriptions of this period. For the 18th Dynasty, see Sethe 1914 (Urk. IV 1–313); Burkhardt et al. 1984 (Urk. IV 315–1225); Helck 1961 (Urk. IV 1227–2179). For the 19th Dynasty, see Kitchen 1993, 1996, 2000, and 2003. I, however, have to leave it to those who are more familiar with the Egyptian royal rhetoric and its pitfalls.

Old Babylonian Period as well.[11] More references we have from the Late Bronze Age. Summonses to battle sent in advance to an adversary are found in the Hittite historiographic document of the 14th century "*The Deeds of Šuppiluliuma*", composed by king Muršili II concerning the military campaigns of his father Šuppiluliuma I.[12] According to fragments 18–19,[13] Šuppiluliuma, while still acting under his father Tudḫaliya III, sent a demand to Anzapaḫḫaddu, the king of Arzawa, to return Hittite subjects. When the demand was ignored, Šuppiluliuma sent him a summons to battle: "[Come], let us fight!" (fragment 19: 14–15). Some time later, upon launching a campaign against Mittani, Šuppiluliuma, already acting as the king of Ḫatti, sent to the king of Mittani a similar summons to battle ("Come, let us fight"), a call that was ignored. Then, after entering the land of Mittani, Šuppiluliuma sent another call to that king, but, again, the latter preferred to ignore it and, shutting himself in his capital, he let Šuppiluliuma despoil the country (fragment 26).[14]

Further references for such a call to war preceding hostilities are found in the "*Annals*" of Muršili II. In his third regnal year, Muršili sent a message to Uḫḫaziti, the king of Arzawa, demanding the extradition of Hittite runaway subjects. When the latter rejected the demand and started mobilizing his army, Muršili sent him the following message:[15]

> Because I asked you to return my subjects who came to you and you did not give them back and you kept calling me a child and you kept belittling me, now, come, we will fight. Let the Storm-god, my lord, decide our lawsuit.

Then, in his seventh regnal year, Muršili sent a message to Anniya, king of Azzi-Hayaša, demanding him to extradite Hittite runaway subjects, and complaining about the latter's pillage raid on Hittite territory. When Anniya rejected this demand, Muršili responded by sending Anniya the following message:[16]

[11] See above in Chapter One, p. 18f. and Chapter Three, pp. 51–54.

[12] Güterbock 1956; Hoffner 1997b.

[13] Güterbock 1956: pp. 79–81.

[14] Güterbock 1956: p. 84f. The beginning of the episode is broken, but from what we are told in the prologue to the treaty drawn up by Šuppiluliuma to Šattiwaza of Mittani (*CTH* 51.I; Beckman 1999, No. 6a), some exchange of messages did precede these summons to battle (A obv. 1–16).

[15] The "*Ten Year Annals*", Bo II 43: obv. II 28–36; KBo 3.4: obv. ii, 9–14 (Goetze 1933: pp. 40/41, 46/47; Grélois 1988: pp. 77–79; Beal 2000: p. 85).

[16] The "*Comprehensive Annals*", KUB 14.17: rev. iii, 14–19 (Goetze 1933: p. 98/99).

> I came and encamped at the border of your land. I did not attack your land and I did not plunder it of civilian-captives, cattle and sheep. But you started hostilities [with My Majesty] and came and [attacked] Dankuwa [and empti]ed [it]. Let the gods take a stand on my side and judge the [legal case] on my side.

Still in the records of the same year, but previous to the Anniya affair, we find the following Muršili's description:[17]

> The next year (=Year 7) I went to Tipiya. While my father was in Mittani, Piḫḫuniya, man of Tipiya, marched and repeatedly attacked the Upper Land. He advanced as far as Zazziša and he looted the Upper Land and carried it (=the loot) down into the land of the Kaška. He took all the land of Ištitina and turned it into his pasture. When in Kaška there had never been a single ruler, suddenly this Piḫḫuniya ruled like a king. I, my Majesty, went toward him and sent him a messenger. I wrote to him: "Send out to me my subjects whom you took and led down into Kaška." Piḫḫuniya wrote back to me as follows: "I will not give anything back to you. And if you come to fight me, I will not take a stand to fight you anywhere in my own territory, I will come to your land and I will take a stand to fight you in the midst of your land." When Piḫḫuniya had written this back to me and did not give my subjects back to me, I went to fight him. I attacked his land.

One more reference to the Hittite practice of sending a declaration of war in advance is provided by the letter RS 34.165 found in Ugarit (Ras-Shamra, 12 km north of Latakia on the Syrian coast), which was sent to the king of Ugarit by an Assyrian king referring to the Hittite king Tudḫaliya IV.[18] After a much damaged opening (lines 1–11) we find in the first part of the letter (obv. 12–39) the following description:

> [12]And T[udḫaliya king of] Ḫa[tti] so he wrote [13]to m[e]: "Why [14]did you conquer and capture [... of?] my all[y]? [15]Come, let us fight! Is it not [16]so? (Now) I have set out against you for batt[le]!" [17]But I sent to him thus: "Why [18]are you coming against me? Have I set out against you?!" [19–20]And I, on that day, mustered my soldiers and my chariots. (But) I did not (managed yet) to reach the city of Taidu [21]and Tudḫaliya, king of Ḫatti, a second messenger of his [22–23]he sent to me holding two tablets of war and one tablet of peace. The two tablets of war [24]he presented me (first). (However,) when my soldiers [25]heard the hostile words [26]they were eager to march (to battle), and the messenger [27]of the king of Ḫatti saw (it). When three days [28]passed, the messenger of the king of Ḫatti presented to me the tablet of peace. [30]And in the

[17] The "*Ten Year Annals*", KBo 3.4, rev. iii, 67–86 (Goetze 1933: pp. 86–93; Grélois 1988: p. 85; Beal 2000: p. 87; Beal's translation is adapted).

[18] Lackenbacher 1991: pp. 90–100, No. 46; cf. Harrak 1987: pp. 140–142, 185–187. For the historical background, see also Singer 1985: pp. 100–123.

> tablet, so was written: [31]"(I swear by) the Storm-god and the Sun-god (who) may know whether I am hostile [32]to the king of Assyria, my brother, [and whether I am not] [33](rather) in peace (with him); whether the runaways [34]I would not return to him, and the soldiers of [........] [35]who fled from before the king of Assyria [36]and enter the land of Ḫatti, [37]whether to the king of Assyria I would not deliver! [........]." [38](Further on,) "Why brothers (like) us would be with one another [39]at war?!"

The rest of the obverse side of the letter is too damaged, while the reverse side is devoted to describe the moves that eventually brought about the war between Ḫatti and Assyria. The letter blames the Hittite king for it and justifies the Assyrian moves, which evidently ended in the defeat of the Hittites. The fact that the letter was addressed to the king of Ugarit, a subordinate of the Hittite king, renders it as an act of propaganda in an effort to loosen the allegiance ties of Ḫatti subordinate kings to their suzerain and to win them over to the Assyrians. In any case, it reflects the need of aggressive kings to take into account the negative effect that their moves in stirring up a war would bear upon allied countries. Turning to the content of the part of the letter quoted here, it depicts the Hittite king as intending to employ the declaration of war as only a diplomatic pressure exerted to achieve his goals, rather than to actually open a war. The fact that such a declaration needed two tablets indicates that it contained a detailed accusation raised against the Assyrian king as a justification for the declaration of war. The justification in this case, as it appears in lines 13–14, was an Assyrian military offensive against a Hittite subordinate country (*bēl māmītu* = "who had sworn allegiance").[19] An example of such a document is the Hittite so-called "*Indictment of Madduwatta*",[20] which is devoted to a detailed accusation against that ungrateful and treacherous subordinate ruler who violated his loyalty oath.

The Hittite records also disclose that the Hittites at least, if not also other peoples of the Ancient Near East, regarded a failure to declare war in advance as a "defilement", namely an offense against the norms of world order as determined by the gods,[21] an offense that was considered to arouse their rage. This comes out clearly in the Hittite autobiographic composition from the 13th century, the so-called "*Apology*" of the king Ḫattušili III, in a passage quoted in the previous chapter.[22]

---

19 Cf. *CAD* Vol. 10/1 (M/1), p. 192b, sub.mng. 1e.
20 *CTH* 147 = Beckman 1999, No. 27 (pp. 153–160).
21 See Moyer 1969: pp. 17–20, referring to Douglas 1966.
22 Chapter Three, p. 52f. and the text quoted.

The concept that a failure to declare war in advance is an offence against the gods is reflected also in an accusation made by the Hittite king Tudḫaliya (I/II or III) against the Hurrian king as appeared in the treaty drawn up by the former to Šunaššura king of Kizzuwatna.[23] After having accused the Hurrian king of denying the extradition of Hittite subordinates who started hostilities, we find as follows (i, 20–25):

> The Hurrian did not extradite my "slaves" to me, the Sun. His soldiers (and) his chariots he dispatched; in the Sun's absence they sacked the country Išuwa. All the captives, cattle (and) sheep, which they seized, they brought to the Hurri country. I, the Sun, stayed somewhere else to fight against some (other) enemy. The Hurrian transgressed the oaths.

Denying extradition of Hittite subordinates, and raiding Hittite territory, were two clear violations of the oaths in the treaty between the Hittite and the Hurrian kings, violations absolutely sufficient to justify the renunciation of the treaty with the Hurrians, the target of this accusation. If still the Hittite drafters emphatically inserted here a third offense of attacking from behind the back of the Hittite king, namely without declaring war in advance, it was no doubt in order to blacken the image of the Hurrian king and depict him as a sinner to the divine judges.[24]

Nevertheless, as far as we may deduce from the Hittite military records, it seems that the Hittites did not always feel it necessary to precede an attack by a formal declaration of war. First, there was no place for such a declaration when the Hittites launched an attack in reprisal for an enemy attack. Thus, we find that Šuppiluliuma I sent his army to raid Amka, an Egyptian territory, in reprisal for the Egyptian attack on Kinza, without preceding it by a formal declaration of war.[25] And when the Hurrians attacked the Hittite army in Murmuriga, Šuppiluliuma mobilized troops and chariots against them without first sending any demand or warning.[26]

---

[23] *CTH* 41.I = Beckman 1999, No. 2.

[24] This in order to cause the gods to spurn the sinner's appeal to them for aid against the Hittites. Such an expression of the gods' rage is found e.g. in a prayer to the god Šamaš (*CTH* 372) where we find a reference to "a person at whom the gods are angry and whom they reject" (i 46–47; Singer 2002: pp. 36ff.). For a detailed discussion of this Hittite accusation against the Hurrians, see Altman 2004a: pp. 406–411.

[25] "*The Deeds of Šuppiluliuma*", fragment 28: A iii 1ff. (Güterbock 1956: p. 94). The Egyptian attack on Kinza is recounted there on A ii 21ff.

[26] "*The Deeds of Šuppiluliuma*", fr. 28: A ii, 21ff. See also the case in fr. 14: 38' regarding the Arzawaean army, which seems to have invaded Hittite territory (cf. line 36'), and fr. 15: F iv 16'ff. regarding an Arzawaean attack on Tuwanuwa, a Hittite territory.

It also seems that the Hittites drew a distinction between organized states headed by kings and tribal communities, regarding the kind of enemies to whom it was required to send such a declaration before the onset of hostilities. Thus we find that Šuppiluliuma I, while having preceded his campaigns against Arzawa and Mittani by sending a formal declaration of war to their kings,[27] never mentioned doing it before launching an attack on troublesome tribal communities. Similarly, his son, Muršili II, sent both a demand for redress and a declaration of war to the king of Arzawa and the king of Azzi-Ḫayaša.[28] But none of his campaigns that were launched against the troublesome tribal communities of the Kaška in the north, or against the tribal peoples on the eastern border, are said to have been preceded by a formal declaration of war. It is quite symptomatic that the only reference at least to a message demanding redress sent by Muršili to the Kaška people was sent only when they were ruled by a king.[29]

Turning to the Assyrians, a call for an ordeal by battle is found in the Assyrian literary composition *"The Epic of Tukulti-Ninurta I"*, which was composed in honor of the reigning Assyrian king Tukulti-Ninurta I (1243–1207).[30] A similar call seems to occur also in another Assyrian epic honoring the Assyrian king Adad-nirari I (1305–1274), where in tablet V, obv. ii 8', we find what seems to be a letter of this king to the Babylonian king Nazi-Maruttaš calling for battle.[31] A further reference to such a call is found in a Babylonian chronicle devoted to the history of the wars of the Kassite kings of the 14th–13th centuries,[32] where we find in iii, 10–15 the following narrative:

> King Ḫurba-tela of Elam [appealed] to Kurigalzu (II, of Babylonia): "Come! Joint battle, you and me, at Dūr-Šulgi!" Kurigalzu, having heard and [...], marched on Elam to conquer it. King Ḫ[urba-tela] of Elam [joined] battle with him at Dūr-Šulgi. He beat a retreat before him, and Kurigalzu infl[icted] a defeat on him.

---

[27] *"The Deeds of Šuppiluliuma"*, fr. 19: 14–15 and fr. 26 respectively.

[28] King of Arzawa: *"Ten Year Annals"*, Year 3: Bo II 43, obv. ii 29–33; KBo 3.4, obv. ii 9–14 (Goetze 1933: pp. 40/41, 46/47; Grélois 1988: pp. 77–79; Beal 2000: p. 85). King of Azzi-Ḫayaša: *"Comprehensive Annals"*, Year 7, KUB 14.17: rev. iii 5–25 (Goetze 1933: pp. 88–101).

[29] See the reference in note 17 above and the text quoted.

[30] Edition and discussion: Machinist 1978. Recent translation: Foster 1993b: Vol. I, pp. 209–229. The call is mentioned in IIIA, 19'–20'.

[31] The epic survived in a much damaged condition. The reference is according to Machinist 1978: p. 273f. citing Weidner 1963.

[32] Grayson 1975: pp. 56–59, 170–177 (Chronicle 22 [P]); Glassner 2004: pp. 278–281 (Chronicle 45). Glassner's translation is adopted here.

While all these references do not prove that the Near Eastern people of this age always adhered to the customary rule that war should be preceded by a formal declaration addressed to the opponent, they do assert that this rule was widely acknowledged, even if not always practiced.

2.1.2. *The Indictment Ceremony*

A summons to war was conceived as a call for an ordeal by battle. This is clearly stated in the above-quoted call of Muršili II to Uḫḫaziti, the king of Arzawa, and to Anniya, the king of Azzi-Ḫayaša, as well as in that of Ḫattušili III to Urḫi-Teššub. Yet, in order that the gods would investigate the case and render their verdict on the battlefield, the parties, and particularly the wronged party, were requested to appeal formally to these divine judges, presenting them with a detailed indictment, and asking for authorization to wage war and for divine help. This request and practice was already demonstrated in the previous chapter for the Old Babylonian period. The Late Bronze Age provides further examples. Thus, for instance, we find the Assyrian king Adad-nirari I claiming that his attack against Šattuara, king of the land Ḫanigalbat, who had rebelled against him, was made "by the command of (the god) Aššur, my lord and ally, and (by the command) of the great gods who decide in my favour."[33] His successor Šalmaneser I (1273–1244) claims that before he launched an attack against the land Uruaṭri (later Urarṭu) he prayed to the god Aššur and the great gods; and that before turning against the rebellious Qutu, "I prayed to Aššur and the great gods, my lords, and they gave me a straight answer, a firm yes."[34] A more detailed description of such an appeal is given by the Hittite king Muršili II in the opening of his "*Annals*":

> When I, My Majesty, set on my father's throne, while I had not yet gone against any of the enemy foreign lands who were in a state of hostilities with me, I concerned myself with and preformed the regular festivals of the Sun-goddess of Arinna, my lady. I held up my hand to the Sun-goddess of Arinna, my lady, and said as follows: "O Sun-goddess of Arinna, my lady! The enemy foreign lands who have called me a child and belittled me, have begun seeking to take away the borders of the Sun-goddess of Arinna, my lady. Stand by me, O Sun-goddess of Arinna, my lady. Destroy those enemy foreign lands before me." The Sun-goddess of Arinna heard my words and stood by me.[35]

---

33 RIMA I, A.0.76.3 (p. 135f.): 7–9

34 RIMA I, A.0.77.1 (pp. 181ff.): 28–29, and 92–94, respectively.

35 The "*Ten Year Annals*", KBo 3.4, obv i, 19–27 (Goetze 1933: pp. 20–23); cf. Beal 2000: p. 84, whose translation is followed here.

The divine answer to the king's appeal was supposed to be given by the oracle before the battle.[36]

Naturally, any one of the parties involved in a conflict that wished to launch an attack was required to appeal for divine authorization and help. Yet, a more sophisticated regulation might have been stipulated in advance upon concluding a peace treaty. Such a regulation is found in a survived fragment of a treaty concluded in the 15th century between a Hittite king and an Anatolian ruler (*CTH* 28), where the following regulation is stipulated (lines 15'–18'):[37]

> Furthermore, when we had slaughtered a sheep (=upon concluding an alliance), we put under oath the following (regulation): "So long as we have not yet certified the verdict (of the gods) through an oracle, the Sun would not seize your land, and you would not seize the Sun's land."

A detailed description of the procedure that preceded the onset of war is given in the above-mentioned Assyrian literary composition "*The Epic of Tukulti-Ninurta I*".[38] The epic concentrates on the conflict that had developed into an open war between the Assyrian king and Kaštiliaš, the king of Babylonia, and which ended with an Assyrian victory. The epic reached us quite damaged, and the source and origin of the conflict are unknown to us. But it seems that the Babylonian king had launched a plundering raid on Assyrian territory, an act which constituted a violation of the treaty that had existed between these kings. In revenge, the Assyrians first arrested Babylonian traveling merchants on charges of spying, despite the fact that they were provided with official letters of accreditation. But when they were brought before the Assyrian king, he released them out of respect for international custom.[39] The Assyrian king turned then to the Sun god, the supreme divine judge, presenting him with the treacherous behavior of the Babylonian king, and asking him to punish Kaštiliaš by causing his defeat in battle and granting victory to the one who scrupulously observed the treaty (IIA, 12'–24'). This indictment was performed by raising "the tablet of oath (=treaty) (made) between us and read(ing it) out to the lord of heaven" (IIIA, 9').[40] Following this indictment ceremony,

---

36 For the methods of getting answers by the Hittites, see Beal 2002a. For Hittite inquiries about divine approval of a military campaigns, see Beal 2002b: pp. 32–35.

37 Otten 1967.

38 See note 30 above.

39 Machinist 1978: pp. 211–212, 214–215; Foster 1993b: p. 214f.

40 That in such a case the relevant documents should have been read aloud in the presence of (the images of) the gods, we learn also from the Hittite letter to the king of Assyria, KBo 18.24 (679/z): obv. i, 13–14 (Hagenbuchner 1989: II, p. 242).

Tukulti-Ninurta sent a letter to Kaštiliaš accusing him of treachery, and enumerating the long history of treacherous acts on the part of Babylonian kings toward Assyria (IIA, 25'ff.). After a much damaged section, we find the Assyrian king sending Kaštiliaš a second message, again accusing him of various offences against Assyria and summoning him to an ordeal by battle (IIIA, 1'–20').

Another detailed description of an indictment ceremony is found in the Hittite ritual text so-called, "*Ritual before Battle*".[41] The text, of which some excerpts follow, presents both the details of the ritual to be performed and the verbal address of the indictment against the Kaškean people to be presented to the divine judges:

> When they perform the ritual at the boundary of the enemy country.... [10]they speak as follows: "See! (the god) Zitḫariya is appealing to all the gods. The sanctuaries which had long been assigned to Zitḫariya's worship, the countries which have fallen into turmoil, ... [16] the Kaškeans have taken them. The Kaškeans have begun war. They boast of their power (and) strength. They have made light of you, O gods! See! Zitḫariya [20]is appealing to all the gods; he brings his complains before you. So pass judgment on his case, all ye gods! Let it be of great concern to the gods! In fact they (the sanctuaries) have been taken away by these people not from Zitḫariya alone, [25]they have been taken away from all you gods, all of you; ... Pass judgment on your own case in passing judgment on the case of Zitḫariya! [35]Blot out the Kaškean country, O gods! Let every single god take thought for his place of worship and win it back! ...."

In this first column, the Hittites took up the specific case of the god Zitḫariya, namely the loss of his sanctuaries to the Kaškeans, to appoint him the prosecutor in the divine court of justice, and to make his own case the concern of every single god. In the second column, of which a further excerpt follows, the enemy gods are summoned to the divine court of justice:

> [II, 1]And he (the priest) speaks as follows: "O gods of the Kaškean country! We have summoned you before this assembly. Come ye, eat (and) drink![42] Hear ye the accusation [5]which we bring against you! The gods of the Ḫatti land have done nothing against you, the gods of the Kaškean country. [10]They have not put you under constraint. But ye, the gods of the Kaškean country, began war. Ye drove the gods of the Ḫatti land out of their realm and took

41 *CTH* 422, for which see von Schuler 1965: pp. 168–173; Goetze 1969: p. 354f., whose translation is followed here.

42 Since old days, it was conceived that the assemblies of the gods, including assemblies that were called up for rendering a verdict, were accompanied by eating and drinking.

> over their realm for yourselves. [15]The Kaškean people also began war. From the Hittites ye took away their cities and ye drove them out of their field (and) fallow and out of their vineyards. The gods of the Ḫatti land and the (Hittite) people [20]call for bloody vengeance. . . . ."[43]

This latter part of the ritual introduces us to a new concept we have not yet encountered: the involvement of different pantheons in interstate conflicts. Indeed, we had already come across the problem when dealing with the Sargonic kings, who, following their campaigns beyond the borders of southern Mesopotamia, had to deal with foreign gods.[44] However, in documents of that earlier period no clear sign of tension between the involving pantheons could be discerned. The most we find is that some Sargonic kings claimed that their campaigns were fought "for the god Enlil" or "for the goddess Aštar", rendering these deities into imperialistic warriors, eager to enlarge their domains at the expense of foreign gods.[45] In the Ur III royal inscriptions, one finds the kings of Ur III presenting the gods as taking part in their battles,[46] and we occasionally find similar claims also in the inscriptions or year-names of some Old Babylonian rulers.[47] But all these cases do not amount yet to a clear confrontation of two different pantheons. The closest earlier example of a summons issued to a patron god of an opponent state, of which I am aware, is a prophetic vision sent to Zimri-Lim, king of Mari, in ARMT XXVI/1 196: lines 2'–14'. According to this letter, the god Tišpak, the titular god of Ešnunna, a state hostile to Mari, was summoned to appear before a divine tribunal where he was given an adverse judgment.[48] This would suggest that the divine world, as

---

[43] For a similar indictment against the Kaškeans, but without the ritual details, see the prayer of Arnuwanda and Ašmunikal to the Sun-goddess of Arinna about the ravages of the Kaška (*CTH* 375): Singer 2002: pp. 40–43.

[44] For details, see above Chapter Two, pp. 30–32.

[45] Op. cit. p. 28f. with notes 34–35.

[46] Op. cit. p. 41f. with note 93. Note there also the reference to the royal hymn "*Šulgi F*", where Nanna, the titular god of Ur, requests that "May he (= Šulgi) subjugate the foreign land for me!"

[47] Thus we find Nūr-Adad of Larsa to claim that he is the "subduer of the foreign lands for the god Utu" (RIME 4, E4.2.8.1: 11; E4.2.8.3: 20–21; E4.2.8.4: 17–18), and Kudur-mabuk is presented as he "who by the decree of the gods Nanna and Utu seized Kazallu, tore down its walls, (and) made it submit" (RIME 4, E4.2.13.3: 16–19). In the year-name 31a of Ḫammurabi of Babylon we find the assertion that the gods An and Enlil marched in front of his army; in his year-name 32a he presents himself as he who "gains victory for the god Marduk", and in year-name 35a he ascribes the destruction of the city walls of Mari and Malgium to orders given by the gods An and Enlil; for a more recent on-line edition and translation of Mesopotamian year-names prepared by M. Sigrist and P. Damerow, see http://cdli.ucla.edu/dl/yearnames/yn_index.htm.

[48] For a more recent discussion of this letter, see Sasson 1995..

envisioned by the people of that age was far from a peaceful world, so that rivalry might have existed among the gods, the more so among different pantheons. Another manifestation of this rivalry is the belief that peace could only be reached between two adversary countries if peace was first reached between their patron gods. Thus we find Tušratta, king of Mittani, in one of his letters to Amenhotep III, king of Egypt, expressing his wish that "may the gods grant it, and may (the god) Teššub, my lord, and (the Egyptian god) Aman make flourish forever, just as it is now, this mutual love of ours" (EA 19: 14–16).[49] And following the conclusion of the peace treaty between Ḫattušili III, king of Ḫatti, and Ramesses II, king of Egypt, we find Ramesses declaring in his letter to Kupanta-Kurunta, king of Mira-Kuwaliya as follows:

> The good relationship which I, Great King, King of Egypt, established with the Great King, [the King of Ḫatti], my brother, consists of good brotherhood and good peace. The Sun-god (of Egypt) and [the Storm-god (of Ḫatti) gave it] forever.[50]

Similar expressions appear in the Akkadian version of this treaty.[51]

These reflections of rivalry relationships between different pantheons, which may have amounted to open enmity, raise a question. Insofar as the parties involved in a conflict acknowledged the same pantheon, there should have been no problem. There should also have been no problem upon concluding a treaty between two parties who venerate different pantheons since both would have invoked the main gods of both pantheons. But what would have been the case when oaths had been violated and both parties were required to bring their case before a divine tribunal? Obviously, gods of the two pantheons involved were supposed to participate in it. But who was then supposed to preside over that tribunal which would investigate and punish the transgressor, and how was a verdict reached? Who was supposed to preside over the divine assembly before whom the Kaškean gods were summoned to appear? The answer seems to be simple: no one! In such a scene of a divine international tribunal, where any religious image was simply a reflection of the human world, and in a mortal international scene dominated by multi-powers, there

---

49 Translation follows Moran 1992: p. 43.

50 *CTH* 166: obv. 10–12 = Beckman 1999, p. 130 No. 22D.

51 *CTH* 91: A obv. 9–13 = Beckman 1999, No. 15). For a quotation, see below in section 3.2.3. See also the Egyptian version, §2. For both versions, see the more recent edition of Edel 1997: pp. 18–21.

was no room for a dominant figure to preside over such a multi-pantheon tribunal. That human world also lacked any kind of international organization, such as today's UN, that might have served as a model for a divine international tribunal. Unfortunately, the above-quoted "*Ritual before Battle*" is too vague in this regard, and it is not entirely clear whether beside the gods of Ḫatti and the gods of the Kaškeans other neutral gods were considered to have participated in that assembly.

Yet, the situation was not much better when the two opponent parties revered the same pantheon. That is because the ancients modeled their divine judges on their human judges, with all their strengths and weaknesses. The gods were not perceived as omniscient. There is ample evidence, at least in the second millennium, that the ability of the gods to know what was going on in the world without embarking on an inquiry of their own was believed to be limited, and that it was necessary to inform them of events on earth. Hence, much the same as in the case of a mortal human trial, the outcome of a divine trial, either by a multi-pantheon or by a mono-pantheon court, could not be foreseen with certainty. It depended upon the quality of the legal arguments presented by each side with the advocates and influential intercessors representing the litigants, as well as the enticements and bribes offered to the judges by both sides. In order to succeed in a divine court, it was therefore advisable to try to convince the gods of the rectitude of the appellant and the guilt of the other party. At the same time, however, it was also advisable to try to win them over through sacrifices or promises of various favors.[52]

2.2. *During the War*

Fundamentally, there was a distinction in treatment between an enemy country and a rebellious country. Although in many, if not most cases,

---

[52] The existence of such concepts among the Hittites is indicated in the first place by the "*Evocatio Ritual*", for which see e.g. *CTH* 423: ii 20–36 (ed.: Haas and Wilhelm 1974: p. 234ff.): "And she (the Old Woman) says as follows: 'Behold, I have placed for you, gods of the enemy city, a *gulšan* beer jug; on the left I placed for you covered tables. I spread out for your trails with white cloth, red cloth, blue cloth; let these clothes be your trails! Set out on these and turn to the king in favour! Turn away finally from your own lands!' As soon as the Old Woman has finished saying these words, she sacrifices one sheep to the gods of the enemy city and one sheep to the goddesses of the enemy city." (translation adapted from Singer 1994: p. 83f.). For a Hittite attempt to bribe the gods of the enemy with promises that would be fulfilled after the battle, see KBo 33.216: obv.[?] 5′–9′ (Otten 1962: p. 76; De Roos 1989), where we read: "If you, (the gods) Ninurta, Kumarbi (and) [...] will give to me (and) I will def[eat] the king of Aššur [...] I will erect 3 stelae [and to each] godhead I will give 1 ox and 8 sheep [(and) festivals] I will establish and [.......]." For other Hittite military rituals preformed to ensure success in battle, see Beal 1995.

the cause behind the war was a violation of some treaty, still the treatment of a rebellious country seems to have been more harsh and at times even ruthless; the more so in case of a stubborn rebellious country. But there seems to be still some differences among the various peoples of the Ancient Near East in this regard.

About the behavior of the Assyrians we learn from their royal inscriptions, starting with the inscriptions of Adad-nirari I, which describe his dealings with the Hurrian country of Ḫanigalbat (=Mittani):

> 4–14When Šattuara, king of the land Ḫanigalbat, became hostile[53] against me, and committed hostilities; by the command of (the god) Aššur, my lord and ally, and (by the command) of the great gods who decide in my favour, I seized him and brought him to my city Aššur. I made him take an oath and then allowed him to return to his land. Annually, as long as (he) lived, I regularly received his tribute within my city, Aššur.
> 15–51After his death, Uasašatta, his son, revolted, rebelled against me, and committed hostilities. He went to the land of Ḫatti for aid. The Hittites took his bribes but did not render him assistance. With the strong weapons of the god Aššur, my lord; with support of the gods Anu, Enlil, and Ea, Sîn, Šamaš, Adad, Ištar, and Nergal, most powerful among the gods, the awesome gods, my lords; I captured by conquest the city Taidu, his great royal city, the cities Amasaku, Kaḫat, Šuru, Nabula, Ḫurra, Suduḫu, and Waššukanu. I took and brought to my city, Aššur, the possessions of those cities, the accumulated (wealth) of his (Uasašatta's) fathers, (and) the treasure of the palace. I conquered, burnt, (and) destroyed the city Irridu and sowed salty plants over it. The great gods gave me to rule from the city Taidu to the city Irridu, the city Eluḫat and Mount Kašiieri in its entirety, the fortress of the city Sudu, the fortress of the city Ḫarrānu, to the bank of the Euphrates. As for the remainder of his (Uasašatta's) people, I imposed upon (them) corvée (lit. "hoe, spade, and basket"). But as for him, I took out from the city Irridu his 'wife of the palace', his sons, his daughters, and his people. Bound I brought them and his possessions to my city, Aššur. I conquered, burnt, and destroyed the city Irridu and the cities within the district of the city Irridu and sowed salty plants over them.[54]

As we progress with the Assyrian royal inscriptions of Adad-nirari I's successors, the treatment of the conquered communities become more severe. Now we find, for the first time in Assyrian inscriptions, references

[53] The verb here is *ikkirūma* from *nakāru* = "to become hostile" but also "to rebel". Grayson translated here "rebelled", but since we do not have any information that Ḫanigalbat had already before become subordinated to Assyria, I prefer to translate here "became hostile".

[54] RIMA I, A.0.76.3 (p. 135f.): 4–51.

to mass punishment. Thus, we read in the inscriptions of Šalmaneser I (1273–1244) the following accounts:[55]

> [27–46]...the land Uruaṭri rebelled against me. I prayed to the god Aššur and the great gods, my lords. I mustered my troops (and) marched up to the mass of their mighty mountains. I conquered......—eight lands and their fighting forces; fifty-one of their cities I destroyed, burnt, (and) carried off their people and property. I subdued all of the land Uruaṭri in three days at the feet of Aššur, my lord. I took a selection of their young men (and) I chose them to enter my service. I imposed upon them (the conquered regions) heavy tribute of the mountains forever.
>
> [47–53]The city Arinu, the holy city founded in bedrock, which had previously rebelled (and) disregarded Aššur: with the support of Aššur and the great gods, my lords, I captured (and) destroyed that city and sowed salty plants over it. I gathered (some of) its earth and made a heap of it at the gate of my city, Aššur, for posterity.
>
> [56–87]When by the command of the great gods (and) with the exalted strength of Aššur, my lord, I marched to the land Ḫanigalbat,...Šattuara (II), king of the land Ḫanigalbat, with the aid of the armies of the Hittites and the Aḫlamu, captured the passes and watering-places (in) my (path)....I struck, and brought about their defeat. I slaughtered countless numbers of their extensive army....I butchered their hordes (but) 14,400 of them (who remained) alive I blinded (and) carried off. I conquered nine of his fortified cult centers (as well as) the city from which he ruled and I turned 180 of his cities into ruin hills. I slaughtered like sheep the armies of the Hittites and Aḫlamu, his allies. At that time I captured their cities...I became ruler over these lands and set fire to the remainder of their cities.

The same behavior continued with Tukulti-Ninurta I (1243–1207). While we find him to be more forgiving of those who opposed Assyria for the first time, stubborn rebellious countries were treated severely:[56]

> [iii, 2–7]The hordes of princes of Abulê, king of the land of the Uqumenu, I captured (and) brought them bound to my city, Aššur. I made them swear by the great gods of heaven (and) underworld, I imposed upon them the [exacting] yoke of my lordship, (and then) I released them (to return) to their lands. [...] rebellious [cities] I subdued at my feet and imposed (upon them) corvée. Annually I receive with ceremony their valuable tribute in my city, Aššur.
>
> [iii, 30–iv, 23]All the land of Šubaru, the entirety of Mount Kašiiari as far as the land Alzu, which previously, during the reign of Shalmaneser (I), king of the universe, my father, had rebelled and withheld tribute, had united itself under one command. I prayed to the god Aššur and the great gods, my lords,

55 RIMA I, A.0.77.1 (pp. 181ff.).
56 RIMA I, A.0.78.1 (pp. 231ff.).

> (and) marched up to Mount Kašiiari. (As) with a bridle I controlled the land of the Šubaru, the land Alzu, and their allied kings. I conquered the great cult center of the land Purulimzu. I burnt them (the inhabitants) alive (and) the remnants of [their] army I took as captives.... 180 of their fortified cities I destroyed, ravaged, burnt, (and) turn into ruin hills. I added the regions of the lands Alzu, Amadanu, Niḫanu, Alaia, Tepurzu, and Purulimzu to my land. I took from them hostages, subdued (them) at my feet, and imposed (upon them) corvée.

Turning to the Hittites, we also find them taking harsh measures against rebellious communities. But not carrying out the same atrocities as those described by Tukulti-Ninurta I, or at least they would not have admitted them publicly.[57] As far as we can glean from the available sources, the Hittites did not make any distinction in treatment of a rival country headed by a king differently from a tribal, semi-nomad group headed by an acknowledged chief or a gang of brigands. One cannot find any significant difference in the way the Hittites treated the troublesome tribal communities of the Kaška in the north or the tribal peoples on the eastern border, as compared to their treatment of enemy states such as Arzawa. The regular treatment of the tribal enemy communities, as mentioned in the "*Deeds of Šuppiluliuma*" and in Muršili II's "*Annals*", was burning down the towns and, on occasion (evidently, when the local population did not flee), taking into captivity the non-combatant population (NAM.RA) together with their cattle and sheep. As for the enemy troops, we hear that the Hittite king "smote" or "slew" them and that "the enemy troops died in multitude." Occasionally, those who survived were taken as captives (LÚ.MEŠ ŠU.DAB). Very rarely do we find that Šuppiluliuma I "slew the whole tribe",[58] which might have also included the non-combatant population. Yet, burning down towns, killing the enemy (troops), and taking away combatants and non-combatants as captives to Ḫattuša occurred also with regard to the countries of Arzawa and Mittani.[59]

---

57 See below in section 2.3.2 regarding war captives by the Hittites, where evidence is cited suggesting that the Hittites, at least in certain occasions, blinded war captives.

58 "*Deeds of Šuppiluliuma*", fr. 15: F iv, 9' (Güterbock 1956: p. 75).

59 "*Ten Year Annals*", Year 3, KBo 16.1: ii 56'–58'; KBo 3.4 + KUB 23.125: ii 41–45 (Grélois 1988: pp. 59/78 and 61/80); see also "*Deeds of Šuppiluliuma*", fr. 35: 30'–32' (restored; Güterbock 1956: p. 111) for burning down Ḫarrān and the land around Waššukanna in the territory of Mittani. Note, however, the different treatment and the different expressions employed in Muršili II's "*Ten Year Annals*" when referring to the conquest of Arzawa in Year 4 and to the conquest of two fortified cities of Azzi-Ḫayaša in Year 10.

2.3. *After the War*

2.3.1. *Organizing the Conquered Territories*

There was more than one type of organization for the conquered territories. The Egyptian empire in Nubia during this period was based on full annexation. The local dynasties were replaced by an Egyptian regime backed by a network of colonies, strongholds, and garrisons, and a policy of acculturation of the Nubian elite.[60] The type of government and economy established by the Egyptians in Nubia were largely a copy of that of Egypt. Most, if not all, of the Nubians must eventually have found themselves working as peasant farmers on land that was owned by the crown, local princes, government administrators, and by the temples that were built throughout the region. Certain temples in Egypt were also endowed with land and with the right to exploit or tax certain resources in Nubia.[61] The Egyptian empire in Asia, on the other hand, while annexing the territories that it conquered, left the local Canaanite dynasties on their thrones with their administrations, but controlled them through resident and traveling commissioners. The actual status of the Canaanite subordinate kings was no different from that of the Egyptian mayors in Egypt,[62] and contrary to the Hittite system, and most likely also to the Mittanian and Assyrian systems, their position and status were not guaranteed by a written treaty.

The Assyrian empire (designated as the Middle Assyrian empire during this period),[63] contrarily, was based on the suzerain-subordinate ("vassal") system. The defeated kings were either left on their thrones or were replaced by other members of their dynasty. Their loyalty was secured by a loyalty oath most probably backed by a written subordination treaty, and their main obligation was the payment of yearly homage and tribute.[64] Since, however, no Middle Assyrian subordination treaty has turned up so far, we do not know the details of this system. Annexation, in any event, was reserved for cases of rebellious countries as was demonstrated by the policy conducted by Adad-nirari I in dealing with Ḫanigalbat,

---

[60] See Trigger 1976; Adams 1977; Smith 1995.

[61] Trigger, op. cit., p. 129.

[62] For a more recent discussion, see Redford 1990. For the Ramesside period, see also Higginbotham 2000.

[63] For the growth and the organization of the Middle Assyrian empire in northwestern Mesopotamia, see Machinist 1982; Harrak 1987: pp. 129–131, 190–205, 267–277; Liverani 1988; Cancik-Kirschbaum 1996.

[64] See the inscription of Adad-nirari I quoted above in section 2.2 (RIMA 1, A.0.76.3: 4–14).

displayed above in his quoted royal inscription. In his first campaign to Ḫanigalbat, Adad-nirari only reduced it to a subordinate country, leaving its king on the throne after had sworn an oath of allegiance; his main obligations were to pay a yearly homage and tribute. It was only after Uasašatta rebelled that Adad-nirari annexed part of Ḫanigalbat, deported its royal family to Aššur, built a palace for the Assyrian administration in the capital Taidu, and seems to have ruled Ḫanigalbat as a province. Later on, following an attempt by Šattuara II with Hittite help to overthrow the Assyrian rule there, Šalmaneser I, whose royal inscription is quoted above, launched another campaign into Ḫanigalbat. Doing this, he not only extended his dominion over Ḫanigalbat but also applied there a drastic administrative policy, never attested elsewhere before, as may be inferred from his abundant archives found in the city of Aššur and in north Syrian sites.[65] A series of administrative centers, some of them are attested as palaces, were implanted in the occupied land like islands in a sea of native Hurrians. Following the extensive destruction of local settlements, their people were displaced within Ḫanigalbat, together with their domestic animals, to work the extensive agricultural lands that surrounded the Assyrian administrative centers. There is no indication that the Hurrians, namely the local subordinated population, were involved in private businesses or public administration. On the contrary, the known archives belong only to homogeneous new Assyrian settlers, who had the monopoly of agricultural production. They imposed their legal system, controlled the water resources, and administered the Hurrian temples. The settlers were organized in a hierarchy of functions and were centered in regional administrative palaces. Each palace had a high degree of economic, administrative, military and legal authority. They were in constant contact with the metropolis Aššur and with the king through a network of messengers. Yet, there is no sign that this Assyrian colonization was accompanied by an attempt at acculturation. This picture leads to the conclusion that Ḫanigalbat was ruled through an Assyrian network of colonies that monopolized human and territorial resources for the benefit of the central power in Aššur.[66]

The Hittite system of subordinate countries, while also largely based on the suzerain-subordinate system, seems to be more elaborate.[67] These

[65] The following summary is taken from Harrak 1987: pp. 190–205, 279–282.

[66] Harrak 1987: p. 204. See also Liverani 1988, especially p. 90.

[67] The following summary is based on my paper Altman 2003a, where more detailed discussion with due references may be found.

countries may be sorted into two basic categories: conquered countries and self-subjugated countries. In case of a country conquered in the course of war, the conqueror acquired rights *in rem* on that country, which means full control of the conquered territory and a free hand in dealing with it. The conquered country became the property of the conqueror's country under the full authority of its king. Cities that rejected an offer of surrender were subjected to burning and destruction, their population was exiled and its possessions—confiscated. The Hittite king could treat the conquered territory and its royal family as he wished. He could remove the family from the throne, and then either annex the country, turning it into a province ruled by a Hittite official as part of the Hittite homeland.[68] He could also grant it to a member of his own royal family as an appanage land, or to any other person whom he might install as subordinate king. Alternatively, he could split it into separate units or detach parts and transfer them to the jurisdiction of other allied or subordinated kings. In all these cases, the granted country (save the one gifted to his allies) remained the property of the conqueror's country. What the suzerain granted was rather the right to use it, namely the right to enjoy, hold, occupy, and profit from the fruits of that political entity. The rights the grantor had over the grantee were rights *in personam*, based on the subordination treaty drawn up for the latter, which detailed his obligations to his Hittite suzerain (for these treaties see below in §3.3). One of the most important obligations, beside the obligation to pay annual homage and tribute, was to provide military forces upon demand of the Hittite king, when there was an attack on Hittite territory, or when the Hittite king set out on an offensive campaign. The provinces, on the other hand, namely the annexed territories, were requested to provide regular contingents.[69] In some more favored cases, the Hittite king also undertook some obligations in behalf of his subordinate king, such as to protect the latter's throne and country from any internal or external enemy and to ensure that throne for the subordinate's offspring.[70]

The second, more favored category of Hittite subordinate countries were those that were self-subjugated. Such a country was one whose king, on his own initiative, appealed to the Hittite king to accept him

[68] The Hittites annexed only those territories that either bordered their homeland or were close to it with no significant political interspace.

[69] See Beal 1992: pp. 71–104.

[70] See, e.g., *CTH* 42 (Ḫuqqana): A i 33–34, 36–38; *CTH* 75 (Talmi-Šarrumma): A rev. 4–5, 7, 13–16.

into political subordination ("vassalage"), usually in return for military assistance and protection.[71] The rights the suzerain acquired in this case should have been only rights *in personam*. That is, the suzerain's legal relations with the self-subjugated king were contractual relations, as between a creditor and debtor. The suzerain had the right to impose certain obligations on the subordinate,[72] including the payment of an annual tribute, and the right to limit the latter's ability to act freely in foreign affairs. But the suzerain had no claim on the territory of the subordinate king nor any direct authority over his people. The terms of subordination imposed on a self-subjugated king very likely followed accepted rules which the suzerain was quite restricted to change. Moreover, on his part the suzerain also had some obligations to his subordinate king. He had to protect the latter and his country, and usually also to secure its throne for the latter's offspring; in certain cases—for the latter's explicitly designated heir. In case the subordinate king passed away, the suzerain was entitled—if he had not otherwise promised—to intervene in the hereditary succession by either approving or denying the heir apparent. But he could not remove the local dynasty from the throne, nor was he allowed to change the borders of the subjugated country at will. In case the line of the subordinate king was exhausted, the subordinate country would not have been annexed by Ḫatti, but its throne would very likely have been granted to some local person. The obligations of the subordinate king, as well as the suzerain's undertakings, were backed by a ceremonial oath taken by both before the images of the gods.[73] The military protection and help the subordinate king received from his overlord were regarded as a consideration for his subjugation, and once he had accepted this "payment" for his submission, he was not allowed to retract. This was all the more true after he had sworn an oath that put the transaction under divine sanction.

The Hittites seem to have also differentiated within the group of self-subjugated countries between countries that had been fully sovereign before subjugation to the Hittites and those that had previously been subject to another overlord. The treaties drawn up for the former might have

---

71 Countries in point are Ugarit (*CTH* 46), Amurru (*CTH* 49, 62, 92), and Mittani (*CTH* 51, 52).

72 Noteworthy among these are the obligations to send troops and chariots on request of the Hittite king; to protect the Hittite king and his legitimate heir from any enemy, and to make once a year a visit to the Hittite king to pay him homage.

73 See my paper Altman 2003b.

granted some special privileges which did not appear in Hittite ordinary subordination treaties.[74]

There are some further characteristics of Hittite imperialism which may be mentioned.[75] In contrast to Egyptian and Assyrian policy, we do not find the Hittites establishing colonies in occupied territories. There are indeed some references to garrisoning soldiers in conquered territories, and also some references to building forts for those garrisons.[76] But building or rebuilding cities, to be populated by Hittite civilian settlers, is attested so far only in regard to Hittite border zones, as in the cases of Tiliura and Tarḫuntašša. Also, as far as I am aware, there is so far no clear evidence of Hittite policy of forced or deliberate acculturation in occupied territories,[77] although there are some indications that to some extent an unforced acculturation of the elite class in the subordinated countries did indeed take place.[78]

2.3.2. *The Fate of the Captives of War*

As we have seen above in Chapter Two, exiling a defeated population, either in its entirety or only selected parts, was an old practice in the Ancient Near East. Captives were taken on raids—mainly to sell them into slavery or for ransom—or following a conquest of a foreign territory. Deportation of defeated communities to be settled in the victor's country is attested in Egypt and Mesopotamia already in the third millennium.[79] Egyptian royal inscriptions from the New Kingdom (ca. 1560–1070) record the deportation of great numbers of people in the course of military campaigns.[80] Some were settled in strongholds, forming some kind of military colonies; others were settled in villages around certain temples, forming

---

[74] An example in point is the subordination treaty drawn up by Šuppiluliuma I to Šattiwaza of Mittani, *CTH* 51 (=Beckman 1999, No. 6a).

[75] The following characteristics were previously treated by me in Altman 2008a.

[76] Beal 1992: pp. 231–237.

[77] In fact, the *"Instructions to the BĒL MADGALTI"*, iii 9–16 (von Schuler 1957: p. 47) provides a positive indication that the Hittites *did not* try to impose their culture on the annexed territories, at least not in matters of law, for this high official is instructed that upon judging cases in his jurisdiction he should honor the local customs.

[78] See Singer 1992.

[79] For Mesopotamia see the references in Chapter Two, p. 43. For captives employed in the Egyptian military forces see Fisher 1961: pp. 44–80. Foreign captives and their flocks may have been used by the Egyptians for internal colonization: see Eyre 1987a: p. 37.

[80] Helck 1971: pp. 342–347.

distinct ethnic communities, in order to build and staff temples; still others were granted by the Pharaohs to their warriors or to temples as slaves.[81]

Turning to the Hittites,[82] war captives were usually brought to the capital Hattuša, but occasionally the destination given is to the king's personal estate. Occasionally we also read that the king allowed his troops to take them as semi-free servants, and some captives might have been donated to the temple estates of Hittite deities.[83] According to Law 40 of the Hittite Laws,[84] the Hittite king assigned fields to war captives for cultivation, and they assumed obligations in connection with that land-holding. According to the "*Instructions to the BĒL MADGALTI*", the provincial governor was instructed to take care of these captives to settle them, and provide them with fields, seeds, cattle, sheep, wool for making clothes, and firewood.[85] Further information about the fate of war captives taken by the Hittites is provided by documents discovered in the excavation at Maşat-Höyük (old Tapika, a Hittite frontier town).[86] One of the administrative documents found there, HKM 102,[87] records a list of those captured in battle who were listed to be ransomed by their people, in which after most of the names a ransom price was set. Several of those named persons were designated as "blind". Although no details were given regarding the circumstances how those persons lost their sight, their large proportion in the list suggests that they were blinded by the Hittites. According to one of the letters found there,[88] at least some of the blind persons were employed in a mill house. Regarding the social status of the Hittite war captives, they generally enjoyed a higher social position than ordinary slaves.[89]

Mass deportation by the Assyrians started with Adad-nirari I (1305–1274). The Assyrians used those deportees as a useful workforce. The deportees, including men and women of different skills as well as children of all ages,

---

81 Bakir 1952: pp. 31, 109–117; Eyre 1987b: pp. 184–190, 209f.

82 The following information is taken from Hoffner 2002.

83 Ḫattušili I relates in his "*Annals*" that he donated the slaves and maid servants that he took as captives from Ḫaḫḫa to the temple of the Sun-goddess of Arinna: KBo 10.1: rev. 11–14; KBo 10.2: rev. 15–20 = Houwink Ten Cate 1984. Administrative texts recording temples inventories mention non-combatant captives as belonging to the temple labor force: Hoffner 2002: p. 65 with note 22. For the term NAM.RA denoting exiled civil population see Alp 1950–51.

84 Hoffner 1997c.

85 (A) KUB 13.2: iii 36–41; (B) KUB 31.84: iii 60–71 = von Schuler 1957: pp. 48–50.

86 Hoffner 2002: pp. 65–70.

87 For which see del Monte 1995: pp. 103–111.

88 Alp 1991: No. 58.

89 Hoffner 2002: p. 62 with note 3 for references.

constituted a heterogeneous group. They were provided with rations of food, wool and very likely oil. The amount received varied according to the sex, age, and occupation of the deportees, as well as the number and age of the children dependent on their mothers. They were allocated, according to their sex, age and skills, construction projects, farming of large agricultural estates, and very likely traditional workshops of handicrafts, such as weaving, where women and young boys were generally employed.[90]

2.3.3. *The Attitude to Temples and Gods' Images of the Enemy*
In contrast to the "*Annals*" of Ḫattušili I, discussed in the previous chapter, the Hittite documents of the Middle and New Kingdom do not refer to taking the gods of the defeated enemies into captivity, leaving one to wonder about the reason. Instead, we do find isolated, emphatic references about a respectful attitude shown by Hittite kings to certain enemy's temples that were spared and left untouched out of respect for their divine owners. Thus we are told by Muršili II about the behavior of his father Šuppiluliuma I when he conquered the upper citadel of Carchemish as follows:

> since [my father (Šuppiluliuma)] feared the gods,... he let no one in[to the presence(?) of (the deities) [Kubaba(?)] and Lamma, and he did not intrude into any [of the temples]. (Rather,) he bowed (to them) and gave [.......]. But from the lower town he removed the inh[abitants], silver, gold, and bronze utensils and carried them to Ḫatti.[91]

Muršili II also tells us that when he destroyed the land of Ḫurna and the city of Ḫurna,

> because there was a temple of the Storm-god of Ḫurna behind the city of Ḫurna, I spared it and they did not plunder it. The servants of the god who were at the back of it, I left unmolested, and they are still dwell there. But (the cities of) Kapperi, Karaššuwa and Ḫurna I made tributaries.[92]

Assyrian royal inscriptions of this period also make no reference to the practice of removing the images of the enemy's gods. Such references first appear in the royal inscriptions of Tiglath-pileser I (1114–1076), to be discussed in the next chapter. What we do have about the Assyrian attitude to the enemy's temples in this period is a reference made in a much

[90] Saporetti 1970; Freydank 1975 and 1980; Garelli, Charpin and Durand 1982.
[91] "*The Deeds of Šuppiluliuma*", fragment 28: A iii 32–41 (Güterbock 1956: p. 95; Hoffner 1997b: p. 190).
[92] "*Comprehensive Annals*", Year 25$^{?}$, KUB 19.37: rev. iii, 42–47 (Goetze 1933: p. 176/177).

later Babylonian chronicle referring to the treatment of Tukulti-Ninurta I (1243–1207) of Esagil, the main temple of Babylon, and Marduk, its god:

> Tukulti-Ninurta (I) returned to Babylon... He battered down Babylon's wall, cru[shed] the Babylonians. Among the booty, he carried away the riches of the Esagila and Babylon. He took the great lord Marduk [out of] his [dwel] ling-place and made him set out for Assyria.[93]

In this case, Marduk's image was removed to the city of Aššur where he was no doubt welcomed as an honorable guest and was provided for.[94]

3. Treaties

A major contribution to the study of international law of the Late Bronze Age in the Near East is provided by the many treaties surviving from this period, the great majority of which are subordination treaties (conventionally called "vassal treaties").[95] In almost all of these treaties, the Hittites are a party to them, either on a parity standing or as those who dictated their terms.[96] The others, non-Hittite treaties, are four parity treaties from northern Syria: two from Alalaḫ of the 15th century, and two from Ugarit.[97] Apart from the distinction between parity treaties and subordination

---

93 "*Chronicle of the Kassite Kings*" (= "Chronicle P"): iv 3–6 (Glassner 2004: No. 45, pp. 278–281).

94 Cf. van Driel 1969: p. 54; Machinist 1978: p. 525. This event is the topic of a pseudonymous Babylonian literary composition so-called "*Marduk Prophecy*", where Marduk relates of his sojourns in Ḫatti (after have been taken by the Hittites in 1594), in Assyria (having been taken by Tukulti-Ninurta I) and in Elam. According to the text, Marduk blessed Assyria during his residence there. For the text, see Foster 1993b: Vol. I, pp. 304–307.

95 For avoiding the conventional use of the term "vassal" in the context of the political life of the Ancient Near East, see above in the previous chapter, note 56.

96 For a convenient list of the Hittite treaties, see Beckman 1999: pp. 6–8, who enumerates 37 treaties, of which the better preserved 22 documents are translated in that book. For an up-to-date list of all the documents that are regarded as Hittite treaties, see <http://www.hethport.uni-wuerzburg.de/SVH>. Many of these are, however, mere fragments or too broken, and the designation of some of them as treaties is doubtful. The basic edition of the Hittite treaties written in Akkadian is Weidner 1923, and of those written in the Hittite language is Friedrich 1926 and 1930. The basic study of the Hittite treaties is still Korošec 1931. A more recent study which deals also with non-Hittite treaties is that of McCarthy 1978, which includes a detailed list of previous studies. Of the long list of the more recent studies, note particularly Zaccagnini 1990. See also Beckman 2003: pp. 759–764 ('3. Treaties'). For a more recent detailed bibliography, see Beckman 1999: pp. 197–211, to which one may add Altman 2004a. Quoted passages from the Hittite treaties which are included in Beckman's book (1999) are his translations with, occasionally, only minor changes and clarification additions made within brackets.

97 See note 147 below, Nos. 7–10.

treaties, the available treaties may be further sorted into regular comprehensive treaties with an overall regulation of the mutual relations between the two parties, and limited treaties or protocols devoted to a limited number of issues.

3.1. *Parity and Subordination Treaties: General Features*

3.1.1. *Some Common Formalities*

Almost all the available treaties of this period are written on clay tablets. Only one subordination treaty written on a bronze tablet has been discovered so far.[98] Another treaty, the parity treaty concluded by the Hittite king Ḫattušili III and the Egyptian king Ramesses II,[99] according to a note preserved in its Egyptian versions, was originally written on a silver tablet. Its two versions, however, survived only as copies: the version sent by Ramesses II to his Hittite partner was written in Akkadian and preserved in two copies made on clay that were found in the Hittite archives in the Hittite capital Ḫattuša (Boğazköy today), while the (Akkadian) version, sent by Ḫattušili III to Egypt was translated into Egyptian and copied onto the walls of two Egyptian temples. According to a note preserved in the Ulmi-Teššub treaty,[100] this treaty was also originally inscribed on a metallic (iron) tablet. Nevertheless, these few instances are not sufficient to clarify whether it was mandatory for the final draft of a treaty to be engraved on a metal tablet.[101] The fact that some treaties written on clay were found bearing the official royal seal,[102] indicating thereby they were the final draft, suggests otherwise.

The language usually employed was Akkadian, the diplomatic language of this period; although treaties drawn up by the Hittites to Anatolian rulers and preserved in the Hittite archives were found written only in the Hittite language, suggesting that they were originally written in that language. Yet, copies of treaties written in Hittite but composed originally

[98] The treaty drawn up by Tudḫaliya IV, king of Ḫatti, to Kurunta, his cousin, king of Tarḫuntašša: Otten 1988 (StBoT Beiheft 1); Beckman 1999, No. 18C.

[99] Edel 1997; Beckman 1999, No. 15.

[100] *CTH* 106: rev. 22; Beckman 1999, No. 18B, p. 113.

[101] *Pace* Beckman 2003: p. 761, sub 3.4.

[102] These include the parity treaty between Taḫurwaili of Ḫatti and Eḫeya of Kizzuwatna (KBo 28.107–109+), for which see Otten 1971; two subordination limited treaties (or protocols) drawn up by the Hittite king Šuppiluliuma I to Niqmaddu II of Ugarit and found in Ugarit, RS 17.227 and RS 17.340+17.369A (*PRU* IV, pp. 40, 48, and 52); a parity treaty concluded between Aziru of Amurru and Niqmaddu II—RS 19.68 (*PRU* IV, p. 284); parity treaties between the cities of Carchemish and Ugarit, RS 17.230, RS 17.146, RS 17.115 and RS 18.19 (*PRU* IV, pp. 153–160 respectively); and two parity treaties found in Alalaḫ, AT 2 and 3.

in Akkadian were also found in the Hittite archives in addition to their originals.[103] These copies might have been made for the needs of the Hittite chancellery. Also copies in the Ugaritic language and written in the Ugaritic alphabet, made for the local chancellery of a treaty composed by the Hittites in Akkadian, were found in the Ugarit archives beside its original Akkadian version.[104] Finally, the abovementioned copies of the Ḫattušili III—Ramesses II treaty found in Egypt on the walls of two Egyptian temples present an Egyptian translation written in Egyptian hieroglyphs of a version originally composed in Akkadian.

Regarding sealing, the common practice is also not entirely clear. On the one hand, there is the fact that, except for one treaty having a seal,[105] all the treaties found in the Hittite capital Ḫattuša (Boğazköy) lacked seals. Yet, while for almost all there is no indication in their text that they had ever been sealed, still three of them do have such an indication.[106] In addition, all the Hittite treaties that were found outside of the Hittite homeland,[107] as well as the non-Hittite treaties found in Alalaḫ and Ugarit, are sealed.[108] There is also the fact that the parity treaty between Taḫurwaili of Ḫatti and Eḫeya of Kizzuwatna does have a seal,[109] and that Hittite edicts and verdicts also have seals.[110] Finally, one may note that in his letter to Niqmaddu II, king of Ugarit, the Hittite king Šuppiluliuma I promised Niqmaddu to grant him "a sealed tablet of treaty."[111] These facts lead to the assumption that treaty-documents of this age, if not mere first drafts or copies made for the needs of the chancellery, should have been sealed. Subordination treaties, edicts and verdicts, however, were sealed only by the suzerain, at least the copy handed over to the subordinate

---

103 *CTH* 21 with Išputaḫšu of Kizzuwatna; *CTH* 41 and 131 with Šunaššura of Kizzuwatna; *CTH* 49 with Aziru of Amurru; *CTH* 51 and 52 with Šattiwaza of Mittani; *CTH* 62 with Duppi-Teššub of Amurru.

104 Akkadian: RS 17.227 (with many duplicates, three of which are sealed; *PRU* IV, pp. 40–44); Ugaritic: RS 11.772+ (*PRU* IV, pp. 44–46).

105 The treaty between Taḫurwaili and Eḫeya, referred above in note 102.

106 The Šunaššura treaty (*CTH* 41.I; Beckman 1999, No. 2): i 1; the Talmi-Šarrumma treaty (*CTH* 75; Beckman 1999, No. 14): A obv. 5, and the Kurunta treaty (StBoT Beiheft 1; Beckman 1999, No. 18C): iv 44–45.

107 These include the two limited treaties or protocols drawn up to Niqmaddu II of Ugarit RS 17.227 and RS 17.340+17.369A, and the Hittite-Egyptian treaty, for which see note 114 below.

108 For which see above note 102.

109 See note 105 above.

110 E.g., RS 17.237 and RS 17.62 (*PRU* IV, pp. 63–67); RS 17.335+ (*PRU* IV, pp. 71–75); RS 17.382+ (*PRU* IV, 80–83); RS 17.130, RS 17.137, RS 17.229, RS 17.238 and RS 17.28 (*PRU* IV, pp. 103–110); RS 17.133, RS 17.352, RS 17.35, RS 17.362 (*PRU* IV, pp. 118f., 121–124).

111 RS 17.132: lines 51–52 (*PRU* IV, pp. 35–37; Beckman 1999, No. 19: end of §5).

party.[112] In the case of parity treaties, these might have been sealed by the two partners on the same copy,[113] or, as in the case of the Hittite-Egyptian treaty, each of the parties sealed the copy he handed over to his partner.[114] Where the treaty was inscribed on a metal tablet, the seal was imprinted on a bulla attached by a cord through a hole in the metal tablet.[115]

The main copies of the treaty, save for those made for the needs of the chancellery, were kept in the main temples of the two partners, placing them in front of the divinities' images. Thus, for instance, we have the following statement made at the end of the Kurunta treaty (§28):[116]

> This document is made in seven copies and is sealed with the seal of the Sun-goddesses of Arinna and the seal of the Storm-god of Ḫatti.[117] One tablet is deposited in the presence of the Sun-goddess of Arinna, one tablet in the presence of the Storm-god of Ḫatti, one tablet in the presence of Lelwani, one tablet in the presence of Ḫebat of Kizzuwatna, one tablet in the presence of the Storm-god of Lightning, and one tablet in the presence of Zitḫariya. And Kurunta, king of the land of Tarḫuntašša, has one tablet in his residence.

This convention to place copies of the treaty in the main state temples has a bearing on the question whether it was mandatory, at least in this period, for treaties to be concluded in writing. This convention, and the fact that in case of a treaty breach the wronged party had to read the violated

---

112 Note the following clarification made at the end of the so-called "*Arbitration of Syrian Disputes by Muršili II of Ḫatti*" (*CTH* 63: A iv 2–13; Beckman 1999, No. 30): "The fact that this tablet of legal disputes has not now been sealed is because the king of the land of Carchemish, Tudḫaliya, and Ḫalpaḫi were not in the presence of My Majesty. For this reason this tablet has not been sealed. When the king of the land of Carchemish, Tudḫaliya, Ḫalpaḫi, and Tuppi-Teššup come into the presence of My Majesty, they will come as a group before My Majesty, so that I, My Majesty, can question them concerning the disputes. And whoever makes some arguments, I, My Majesty, will listen to it. Then at that time they will seal this tablet of legal disputes." (Beckman's translation).

113 A good example is the treaty between Niqmepa of Alalaḫ and IR.^{d}IM of Tunip, AT 2.

114 This conclusion is based on the version preserved on the walls of the Egyptian temples, at the end of which there is a description of only two seals, one belonging to Ḫattušili, the other to the Hittite queen Puduḫepa (Edel 1997: p. 82/83, §30). Note that also in exemplar A, of the version sent by the Egyptian king to Ḫatti and preserved there in two copies (*CTH* 91), there are on its reverse side, lines 10'–11', damaged references to two seal imprints (Edel, pp. 12, 78 and 80: §30; cf. Beckman 1999: p. 100). Of these seals, one for sure belonged to Ramesses, while the other might have belonged very likely to his chief queen Nefertari.

115 As may be inferred from the find of the Kurunta bronze tablet treaty (StBoT Beiheft 1; Beckman 1999, No. 18C).

116 Ibid. Beckman's translation is adopted.

117 For these and other similar 'divine seals' mentioned in the texts see Watanabe 1989; I owe this reference to Prof. Itamar Singer, Tel-Aviv University.

treaty to the gods upon appealing to them,[118] suggest that at least in case of treaties concluded between more advanced and established states it was indeed mandatory in this period to conclude treaties in writing.

3.1.2. *Structure*

The most conspicuous and meaningful feature that distinguishes the treaties of this period from those from Mari and Tell Leilan of the 18th century, is the shift of the list of gods by whom the oath was taken from the opening of the treaty toward its end. The Old Babylonian treaties from Mari and Tell Leilan, by placing at their very opening the adjuration formula combined with a list of the gods by whom the oath should be taken, appear as oath documents, which accord their designation as "tablets of oath" (*ṭuppi nīš ilim* = "tablet of [an oath by] the life of the god"). The oath thus appears as the most crucial act in creating a contractual commitment by the parties taking the oath. The Late Bronze treaties, in contrast, put the list of the gods at the end of the treaty, just before the curses and the blessings section, and actually omitted any adjuration formula. This is not to say that the parties were not sworn in; the oath they took on the treaty is mentioned in various ways in the stipulatory section.[119] Moreover, the gods invoked in this list were explicitly summoned "to the assembly for this oath. They shall stand, observe, and listen. And they shall be witnesses."[120] Furthermore, the curses warn that the one who violates the oath would be punished by "the gods of the oath."[121] But the crucial act which established the contractual relations between the parties was their agreement to enter these legal relations as stipulated in the document. The oath taken was only intended to put these relations under divine sanction, which would then turn the curse and the blessings into being potentially operative. Accordingly, the treaties of the Late Bronze Age are designated as *ṭuppi rikši* "tablet of treaty ("bond")", *išḫiul* in Hittite.[122]

---

118 See in section 2.1.2 above.

119 Thus, e.g., in the Niqmepa treaty (*CTH* 66; Beckman 1999, No. 9) Niqmepa is warned: "if you do not fight [wholeheartedly], you will transgress the oath" (end of §2); and *passim* in the subordination treaties. For references to the oath in parity treaties, see e.g. AT 2: 74–75; AT 3: 40–42; *CTH* 25: 10; RS 19.68 (*PRU* IV, p. 284f.): 4, 11, 42, 44, 46.

120 The Manapa-Tarhunta treaty (*CTH* 69; Beckman 1999, No. 12): §13, A iii 48'–51'.

121 Thus, e.g., the curse of the Niqmepa treaty (*CTH* 66; Beckman 1999, No. 9: §20) warned that "if Niqmepa does not observe these words [of] the treaty and of the oath, then these oath [gods] shall destroy Niqmepa together with…, his wives, his sons, his grandsons, his [household], his city, his land, and his possessions."

122 For the terms that were employed for designating "treaty" in this period see more recently Zaccagnini 1990: pp. 51–67.

The reasons behind this change should be sought very likely in the means used by the ancient peoples to remove the dangers inherent in a breach of oath, means such as incantations,[123] or appeasement of the gods through sacrifices.[124] These means should have resulted in at least some disregard for oaths,[125] and this seems to be true also with regard to the attitude of the people of this period to the curses, which also seem to be regarded as something that could be avoided.[126] The curses as well as the blessings in these treaties were evidently regarded more as prayers and petitions to the gods, who would punish the transgressor and favor the observer of the treaty.[127] However, the very fact that curses and blessings were attached to the treaties, oaths were taken at the concluding of the treaties, and gods were invoked as witnesses, indicate that these were still regarded as necessary means to render the treaty an effective instrument. It seems therefore that while these means could not enssure the observance of the treaty by the subordinated party, they were still deemed necessary to enable the wronged suzerain to appeal to the divine judges to punish the offender.[128] This change in structure and its conceptual significance is particularly conspicuous in the Hittite subordination treaties where the so-called "historical prologue" replaced the adjuration formula

---

[123] For such incantations see tablets III and IV of the "*Šurpu*" series (Reiner 1958: pp. 19ff.).

[124] Cf. Muršili's "*Second Plague Prayer*", §8: Goetze 1929: pp. 204ff. For relevant Hittite material note further *CHD* 3/1, p. 63, *sub* c.: KUB 30.45: ii 15, "tablets of rituals to help various offenders, including one who has sworn falsely."

[125] The extent to which the oaths to a treaty could be disregarded may be learned from a letter of Šamši-Adad I, IM 62089 (Eidem and Læssøe 2001: No. 1), where Šamši-Adad I complains about the misbehavior of a subordinate ruler by the name Jašub-Addu: "previously he followed the ruler of Šimurrum. He left the ruler of Šimurrum and followed the ruler of the Tirukkeans. He left the ruler of the Tirukkeans and followed Ja'ilānum. He left Ja'ilānum and followed me. He left me and now follows the ruler of Kakmun. And to all these kings he has sworn an oath! Within just three years he made alliances with these kings and broke them!" (lines 6–17).

[126] This is implied in the expressions *arrat la pašāri* = "a curse that cannot be dispelled", and *arrat la napšuri* = "irreversible curse" (e.g. *BBSt.* No. 5: iii 33; No. 7: ii 15; No. 8: iii 25; cf. *CAD* A/II, pp. 235, *sub.* 1a1'–2'). These expressions indicate that regular curses could be revoked by the one who was cursed. This is also implied by the existence of counter-incantations designed to revoke curses: see e.g. "*Šurpu*", Tablets IV–VI (Reiner 1958: pp. 25–35).

[127] Note that the curses and blessings in Hittite state treaties are formulated as cohortative (*lu*-) or precative (*li*-): e.g. *CTH* 51.I: A rev. 58ff.; *CTH* 52.I: rev. 25ff.; *CTH* 49.I: A rev. 12′–20′.

[128] The ambivalent attitude of the ancients toward their gods in such matters can perhaps be compared to our attitude to the United Nations. Despite its shortcomings, each side in an international conflict wants its point of view to be heard in that forum; at least in order to ensure that the U.N. does not side with and help the other party to the conflict.

and the list of the divinities at the opening of the treaty, reflecting thereby the recourse to divine judgment (see below §3.3.1).

3.1.3. *Entry into Force*

We probably have to distinguish in this matter between parity treaties and subordination treaties. In the case of parity treaties, if not otherwise explicitly stipulated, the treaty seems to have come into force the moment both parties took the oath.[129] In the case of subordination treaties, we very likely have to distinguish between the moment when the general obligation of loyalty of the subordinate party toward his overlord was created, and the moment when the detailed terms of the treaty came into force. The general obligation of the subordinate party was created the moment he agreed to enter under the suzerainty of the overlord and when the latter accepted him as a subordinate. All the more so when the would-be suzerain had provided the would-be subordinate with military aid and the latter accepted it. The detailed terms of the treaty, on the other hand, would have become in force only when both parties (or in certain cases, only the subordinate) took an oath by the gods on these terms.

In certain cases, however, we find an explicit clause regarding the entry of the treaty into force. In the parity treaty concluded between Idrimi and Pilliya (AT 3) the following provision was given:

> In whatever day Baratarna (= Idrimi's overlord) swears the oath by the gods with Idrimi—from that day (on) it is dictated to return fugitive.

In the subordination treaty of Manapa-Tarḫunta of the Land of Šeḫa River (*CTH* 69 = Beckman 1999, No. 12), Muršili II dictated the following provision under what condition the treaty would enter into force (§4: A i 58–59): "If you carry out these matters (= to hand over all the civilian captives) [then] I will take [you] as a subordinate."

---

[129] See e.g. in the treaty concluded between Aziru of Amurru and Niqmaddu II of Ugarit, RS 19.68 (*PRU* IV, p. 284f.): 5–12: "The claims Aziru has against Ugarit… in the day the oath is established, they are cancelled." In view of the fact that each of the parties took the oath in his respective residence, the coordination of the exact time when both parties would take it could not be ascertained. But contrary to the case with the unilateral treaties of the Old Babylonian period, where the inability to ascertain the timing of the swearing of the two partners might have created a problem, with bilateral treaties such a coordination was not so significant, since the performing of one's obligations was conditioned by the performance of the other's obligations.

It may be noted that no date, detailing the day, month and year when the treaty was concluded, is to be found in the available treaties of this period.

3.1.4. *Provisos, Escape Clauses, and Concern about Wrong Interpretation*[130]
In certain cases, the drafters of a treaty found it necessary to insert an escape clause on behalf of either one or both parties in order to avoid conflicting commitments. Such a clause appears in the treaty concluded between Niqmepa of Alalaḫ and IR-IM of Tunip (AT 2: 73–75):

> [The king] of the Hurrian people is my (over)lord! If <the words of the treaty (or: any provision of the treaty)> would conflict with (the interests) of the king of the Hurrian people, I would not break (my former) oath to the Hurrian king, my (over)lord, (and) these (specific?) terms (of the treaty) would be exempted from the (present) oath.[131]

In this case, one of the two parties (or both of them)[132] was worried lest a situation would arise, in which his commitments according to the present treaty would conflict with his former commitments given under oath to his overlord, the Hurrian king.

Another escape clause, applying to both parties, is given in the parity sections of the Šunaššura treaty (*CTH* 41.I: ii, 42–48 and 52–58 = Beckman 1999, No. 2: §§28 and 31).[133] Lines 42–48 (and the corresponding lines 52–58 with only the names of the kings respectively changing places) read as follows:

> If some country starts war against the Sun (=the Hittite king), (and) Šunaššura is bound to this coun[try] by his oath (literally: this country is to Šunaššura under his oath), (and if) the Sun requests auxiliary troops, Šunaššura (nevertheless) will send auxiliary troops.[134]

---

130 This section is based in part on my article Altman 2005a.

131 For the various translations offered to this stylistically poorly worded clause, as well as the arguments in favor of my own translation as is given here, see Altman 2005a: p. 440f.

132 While Alalaḫ is known to have been subordinated to the Hurrian king at that time, it is not known whether it was also the case with Tunip. Yet, the first person singular wording of the paragraph in question, as throughout the entire document, without identifying the speaker, allows ascribing this declaration to either of the two parties.

133 For the observation that this treaty contains both a parity and a subordination treaty, see below in section 3.1.5.

134 My translation; for arguments in favor of this translation, as well as for some further examples, see Altman 2005a: pp. 435–439.

> (Yet,) if Šunaššura provides the troops (and) says: "Against the enemy lead them out!" he (the Sun) may lead them out. If he (Šunaššura) does not say this, they will remain in his (the Sun's) country to guard (it).

In this case, both parties reserved the possibility to avoid taking an active part in the military campaign of the other party.

The Šunaššura treaty provides us yet with a further example of the Hittite drafters' concern lest there would be created a situation that their partner would be unable to stand by his promises due to a conflict of his commitments. Behind this concern was the fact that the land of Kizzuwatna, located in the Cilician plain, previous to the conclusion of the present treaty with the Hittites was subordinated under oath to the Hurrian king from whom it had defected to the Hittites. In the prologue to the treaty with Šunaššura its king, the Hittite drafters took pains to make clear that Šunaššura severed all his connections with the Hurrian king and that the land of Kizzuwatna has no commitments any more to the latter. Among the various statements given there to this effect, we find the following statements (i, 30–32): "Now the (people of the) land of Kizzuwatna... from the Hurrian (king) they separated and shifted (allegiance) to the Sun." Then, in lines i 34–36: "The land of Kizzuwatna rejoices very much over its liberation. Now the land of Ḫatti and the land of Kizzuwatna are free from their oaths (to the Hurrian king)." In these statements, the Hittite drafters asserted two claims: Kizzuwatna is no longer bound by oath of allegiance to the Hurrians, and Kizzuwatna is satisfied with this new situation. But the drafters were not content with this and inserted in iii 48–49 the assertion that "in the future, the land of Kizzuwatna never will turn (back) to the land of the Ḫurri!" Finally, in iv 25–31 they added the following assertion:

> Furthermore: We will certainly erase the tablet of the oath which had been made previously (= the treaty concluded with the Hurrian king). We will indeed discard the word of the ruler of Ḫurri. Moreover, Šunaššura (the king of Kizzuwatna) is no longer [the subject] of the ruler of Ḫurri. We will make another tablet (of oath between us). In addition, Šunaššura must not send his messenger to the ruler of Ḫurri, and he must not allow the messenger of the land of Ḫurri into his land.

It may be noted that all these assertions were given in a legal document over which Šunaššura, the king of Kizzuwatna, took an oath, thereby expressing his consent to these assertions. The only plausible explanation that suggests itself to these assertions is that they were all intended to deprive Šunaššura from claiming in the future that he was still bound by an oath to the Hurrians and was therefore denied the ability to take any military or politically action against the Hurrian king. In other words, Šunaššura's consent to these assertions deprived him of the possibility of claiming "frustration" due to a conflict of commitments.

Another kind of reservation is found in the subordination treaty drawn up by Muršili II to Kupanta-Kurunta of Mira-Kuwaliya (*CTH* 68: C i 33'–38'; A i 27 = Beckman 1999, No. 11: §§9–10):

> C i 33'You shall not found a single city in the direction of the Astarpa River, or in that of the Siyanta River. If you do found even a single city, you will have transgressed the oath, and I will come as an enemy and attack it.... C i 38'(Yet,) a single sacred city belonging to Mašḫuiluwa (=Kupanta-Kurunta's adopter father) himself is situated on the Siyanta River; A i 27it shall be exempted from the oath.

Finally, in the subordination treaty Muršili II drew up for Niqmepa of Ugarit we find the following proviso (*CTH* 66 = Beckman 1999, No. 9: §1):

> Now you, Niqmepa, come before the King! But if it is ever impossible for you to come—perhaps some matter will arise before you—it shall be exempted from the oath.

On the other hand, confined however only to the subordination treaties, we find that the Hittite drafters made every effort to deprive the subordinate party of any possible loophole to evade the fulfillment of his obligations by allegations based on wrong interpretation of the provisions. Time and again we find the warning that "if you would do [so and so] you will transgress the oath." Thus, for instance, in the Targašnalli treaty (*CTH* 67 = Beckman 1999, No. 10): §4, obv. 24'–27', Targašnalli is warned to

> have regard for the garrison troops which I, my Majesty, have left behind for you as you have regard for your[self], your household, and your servants. Sustain them and treat them well. You shall not mistreat [them in any way]. If you do mistreat them in any way, you will thereby have transgressed the oath.

Another clarification that recurs in the Hittite subordination treaties reads as follows:

> Alternatively, if he (the subordinate king) commits some misdeed, thinking as follows: "Although I am under oath and subject to the treaty, either let the enemy defeat him, or let him defeat the enemy. I don't want to know anything about it," and if he should write to that enemy, saying: "The troops of Ḫatti are now coming to attack. Be on guard!"—he will transgress the oath.[135]

[135] The Tette treaty, *CTH* 53; Beckman 1999, No. 7: §4, A ii 25–32.

3.1.5. *Amendment and Modification of Treaties*

The fact that the treaties were inscribed on clay tablets means that once having been dried they could no longer be changed, and treaties inscribed on metal tablets had the same effect. For this reason, the curses at the end of the treaties regularly warned the parties against violating the words of the treaty rather than changing its wording.[136] In case the tablet happened to be damaged or stolen, an authentic duplicate might be prepared.[137] In case there was a need to make amendments, either a new treaty was drawn up detailing explicitly the amendments,[138] or a kind of protocol or edict was issued.[139] In case there was a need to change the terms of the treaty for the worse, an entirely new treaty was needed, a treaty that totally ignored the older one.[140]

Another way the Hittite drafters of treaties chose to cope with the need for later changes is presented by the treaty of Šunaššura of Kizzuwatna (*CTH* 41.I = Beckman 1999, No. 2). As was observed by V. Korošec (1982), this treaty underwent a later revision that changed the nature of the treaty from that of an almost parity treaty to that of an ordinary vassal treaty, reflecting a reduction of Kizzuwatna's status. This was done by adding lines i 38–48,[141] and iii 37–iv 39, which are indicative of a subordination treaty, while retaining the older, parity part, i 1–4, 49–iii 36 and iv 40–66. This inevitably created some contradictory provisions.[142]

3.1.6. *Termination of the Treaty*

Three situations might have terminated the treaty: (1) violation by one of the parties; (2) one of the parties passed away; (3) one of the parties was removed from power and was no longer able to carry out his obligations.

---

136 Only very rarely do we find warning against "altering" the words of the treaty tablet, as is the case with RS 17.340+ (Beckman 1999, No. 4), which might be understood as referring to changes in the wording.

137 Such was the case with the Talmi-Šarrumma treaty (*CTH* 75; Beckman 1999, No. 14), originally drawn up by Muršilli II. After it had been stolen, it was replaced by a new copy made and sealed by Muwattalli II, Muršili's son and successor, who also preceded it with a note to this effect.

138 Such is the case of the treaty that was drawn up by Tudḫaliya IV for Kurunta (Beckman 1999, No. 18C).

139 As is the case with the edict issued by Ḫattušili III to Kurunta: *CTH* 97; Beckman 1999, No. 18A. See also *CTH* 106 (Beckman 1999, No. 18B) drawn up to Ulmi-Teššub (=Kurunta?); note there particularly §5.

140 Such is the case of the Šaušgamuwa treaty (*CTH* 105; Beckman 1999, No. 17). For discussion, see Altman 2004a: pp. 439–460.

141 To my mind, also lines i, 5–37.

142 Best apparent in the military provisions: compare the provision in §57 (A iv 19–24) with those in §§28–34 (A ii 42–69).

(1) *Violation of treaty*: The people of the Ancient Near East very likely did not distinguish between "condition" and "warranty", namely between a major term that goes to the root of a contract or treaty, whose breach entitles the wronged party to treat the contract as discharged, and a secondary term of minor importance whose breach entitles that party only to damages. Any breach of whatever term might have entitled the wronged party to see himself as discharged of his undertakings in that treaty and justified his taking actions to punish the violator.[143] This concept is clearly presented in the prologue of the Šunaššura treaty, *CTH* 41.I: i, 25, 32–36 (Beckman 1999, No. 2):

> [25]The Hurrian transgressed the oaths.... The Hurrian sinned against [33]the Ḫatti country, but against the country Kizzuwatna he sinned greatly.... [35]Now the Ḫatti country and the country Kizzuwatna [36]are free from their oaths (to the Hurrian king).

It may be noted that the oaths of the wronged party are not considered void; the claim here is rather that the wronged party is only freed of his undertakings.[144]

(2) *One of the parties passed away*. More usually, such an event should not have affected the validity of the treaty, since the deceased's legal successor would normally have inherited his commitments; but a follow-up treaty was then expected to be concluded. It is only when it was an ad hoc treaty, concluded personally between two rulers, without any declared

---

143 Indeed, in the Hittite treaties we find quite often a warning that such and such an act would constitute a breach of the oath. See e.g. *CTH* 49.II: ii 12'–39', 40'–46'; iii 12'–16', 29'–34'; iv 6'–11'; *CTH* 53: A ii 16–32; 40–47; iii 41–52; *CTH* 62.II: B ii 4'–9'; A ii 3'–12', 22'–24', 38'–45'; iii 7–11, 18–22; *CTH* 67: obv. 5'–9', 22'–23', 27'; rev. 21–24, 25–32, 35–42, 43–49, 51–54. However, as this small sample demonstrates, such a warning may appear in almost every paragraph or stipulated case. On the other hand, in certain treaties, such as those of Šattiwaza or Kurunta, there is no such a warning. It seems, therefore, that these warnings were intended rather to emphasize the provisions that the drafters deemed them as vulnerable to wrong interpretation by the subordinate. These warnings reflect, thus, the drafters' concern to forestall in advance any possible opening left to the subordinate party to repudiate his obligations on the pretext that a certain situation is not under oath. Cf. further such remarks as "this too shall be placed under oath" as appears in e.g. *CTH* 67: rev. 32 (Beckman 1999, No. 10: §11), or, occasionally, "it shall be exempted from the oath" (ibid., 35–36). We very rarely find that the treaty also stipulates a certain behavior of *Hittite* people, that is on the part of the suzerain, a transgression against the oaths (taken by the suzerain); cf. e.g. *CTH* 62.II: A ii 30'–37' (Beckman 1999, No. 8: §10). Here also we have to understand it as emphasizing the fact that *also* such a behavior would constitute a breach of the treaty.

144 Cf. the statement in the Ḫuqqana treaty (*CTH* 42; Beckman 1999, No. 3), §36: "But if you in any way do evil, then, I, My Majesty, will treat you badly. I, my Majesty, shall be free from this oath before the gods."

intention to be continued into the next generation,[145] that the treaty ceased to be in force.

(3) *One of the parties was removed from power* and was no longer able to uphold his obligations. In such a case, if the removed party were not replaced by his legal successor who took over his commitments, the treaty would have been considered to expire. In case both parties were interested in continuing the terms of the treaty, they would have had to conclude a new treaty. In the case of a subordination treaty, when the suzerain was removed the situation might have been a bit more complicated. Since the subordinated party was bound personally to the removed suzerain, he had the right to see himself as absolved of his obligations. As long, however, as the new regime would have honored the previous suzerain's undertakings on behalf of the subordinate party, there might have been no justification for the latter to repudiate the treaty. The more so in case he was explicitly sworn in to pledge loyalty also to "the land of Ḫatti." Yet, on the other hand, Hittite subordination treaties regularly obligated the subordinate king to protect the suzerain and his legitimate heirs from any usurper, and to fight such a usurper. Thus, a usurpation event necessarily would have brought the subordinated king into a situation of conflicting commitments, which would compel him to claim frustration of treaty.[146]

In case of a treaty between two cities, the treaty was considered to be continuously in force, unless one of the cities ceased to exist, and as long as each of them kept to the terms of the treaty.

3.2. *Parity Treaties*

3.2.1. *Structure*

To date we have at least ten parity treaties from this period,[147] but in only five have all their main parts survived, and of these treaties, only one

[145] For such an expressed declaration ("for ever"), see in the Hittite-Egyptian treaty (*CTH* 91; Beckman 1999, No. 15): §§3–5 (*passim*). Another kind of expression to this effect is by emphasizing that the terms are valid also for the next generation, as is e.g. the case with the Ḫuqqana treaty, *CTH* 42 (Beckman 1999, No. 3): A i, 33–34, 36–37 ("Later, I will protect your sons, and my son will protect your sons").

[146] We do have actually such a case pertaining to the relations of the Hittite king Šuppiluliuma I, who was an usurper, with Niqmaddu II of Ugarit; for discussion see Altman 2004a: p. 247f. For case where the subordinated king was sworn to loyalty to the land of Ḫatti, see below §3.3.2 with note 208.

[147] The list of the Hittite parity treaties includes the following treaties: (1) between Telipinu of Ḫatti and Išputaḫšu of Kizzuwatna (16th century; *CTH* 21; del Monte 1981: p. 210); (2) between Zidanta of Ḫatti and Pilliya of Kizzuwatna (15th century; *CTH* 25; Otten

may be regarded as an ordinary comprehensive treaty.[148] The following structure suggested here should, therefore, be taken with due reservation. The basic structure of these parity treaties seems to be as follows: (1) Preamble, which presents the parties of the treaty;[149] (2) stipulatory section; (3) curses on the party who would fail to adhere to his obligations.[150] In case there was a need to add the time when the agreement would enter into force, or to insert an escape clause, it was placed before the curses section. The parity treaty concluded between Idrimi of Alalaḫ and Pilliya of Kizzuwatna (AT 3) may illustrate this structure:[151]

> Tablet of agreement. When Pilliya and Idrimi took an oath by the gods and made this binding agreement between themselves (as follows):
>
> They will always return their respective fugitives; (i.e.) if Idrimi seizes a fugitive of Pilliya, he will return him to Pilliya, and if Pilliya seizes a fugitive of Idrimi, he will return him to Idrimi. Anyone who seizes a fugitive, and returns him to his master, (the owner) will pay as prize of capture 500 (shekels of) copper if it is a man, one thousand as prize of capture if it is a woman. However, if a fugitive from Pilliya enters the land of Idrimi and nobody seizes him, but his own master seizes him, he need not pay a prize

1951; (3) between a Hittite king and Padditiššu of Kizzuwatna (15th century; *CTH* 26; Beckman 1999, No. 1); (4) between Taḫurwaili of Ḫatti and Eḫeya of Kizzuwatna (15th century; Otten 1971: pp. 66–68); (5) Three succeeding versions of a treaty between Tudḫaliya I/II (or III) of Ḫatti with Šunaššura of Kizzuwatna: [I] *CTH* 131; Beckman 1999: p. 26 [§§11–14]; [II] *CTH* 41.II; Beckman 1999: p. 25f.: §§1–10; [III] *CTH* 41.I: i 49—iii 36 (Beckman 1999: No. 2; cf. Korošec 1982); (6) between Ḫattušili III of Ḫatti and Ramesses II of Egypt (13th century; preserved in two versions: in Akkadian, found in Ḫattuša, the Hittite capital, and in Egyptian, found in Egypt inscribed on the walls of the temple of Amon at Karnak and of the Ramesseum; for both versions see Edel 1997). In addition, there are two treaties found in Alalaḫ (of the 15th century) and two treaties found in Ugarit: (7–8) between Niqmepa of Alalaḫ and IR.^{d}IM of Tunip, and between Idrimi of Alalaḫ and Pilliya of Kizzuwatna (AT 2–3; recent translation: Hess 2000a); (9) between Niqmaddu II of Ugarit and Aziru of Amurru (14th century; RS 19.68 = *PRU* IV, p. 284f.), and (10) a limited parity treaty between the cities of Carchemish and Ugarit drawn up by Ini-Teššub, king of Carchemish (northern Syria, 13th century; RS 17.146 [and 18.115] = *PRU* IV, pp. 154–160; see also RS 17.230 and 18.19 = *PRU* IV, pp. 153f., 169). Due to the fact that many treaties were preserved in very bad condition, we cannot be sure about the exact number of the parity treaties, but the following two very fragmentary treaties may very likely be added to this list: *CTH* 134—between a king of Ḫatti and a king of Egypt (see most recently Singer 2004: pp. 591–607), and *CTH* 28—between a Hittite king and Ḫuḫazalma of an unknown polity (Otten 1967).

148 These are treaties Nos. 6–10 of the list in the previous note, with treaty No. 6 as the exceptional.

149 Survived in treaties Nos. 2, 5 (version III), 6, 7–10.

150 Survived in treaties Nos. 6 (Egyptian version, which includes also a blessing formula), 7–10.

151 Following the translation of Reiner 1969: p. 532, while restoring lines rev. 30–35 erroneously omitted there. The division into separated sections is mine in order to make it more conspicuous.

> of capture to anyone. And if a fugitive from Idrimi enters the land of Pilliya and nobody seizes him, but his own master seizes him, he need not pay a prize of capture to anyone. In whatever city (it is suspected that) they conceal a fugitive, the mayor and five elders will make a declaration under oath.
>
> From the very day on which Barattarna[152] has sworn (this) oath by the gods together with Idrimi, from that day on it is decreed that fugitives have to be returned.
>
> Whoever transgresses this agreement, ^{d}IM, Šamaš and Išḫara, and all the (other) gods will destroy him.

What is not so typical in this treaty is the fact that its sections, as well as its various clauses, are not separated from each other by a horizontal ruling, as is more common both in parity and subordination treaties in this period.

The Hittite-Egyptian treaty presents yet three additional sections: (1) following the preamble and before the stipulatory section there is a short reference to the past relations between the two countries, followed by declarations of the parties indicating their intention to create "great peace and great brotherhood between them forever"; (2) a list of the divine witnesses, followed by (3) a blessing formula in addition to the curse.[153] Regarding the latter two sections, we cannot be sure whether the other five Hittite parity treaties also contained a list of divine witnesses and a blessings section, since the closing section (or sections) of these treaties are lost. Yet, since the other four treaties from northern Syria *certainly* did not have these two sections, we cannot deny the possibility that we have here two distinct traditions: Syrian, which did not include a list of divine witnesses[154] and a blessing section, and Hittite, which did include these sections. However, it seems more likely that the differences stem from the fact that all the other four "Syrian" treaties are limited treaties or protocols, while the Hittite-Egyptian treaty presents a structure of a much expanded peace treaty with an overall regulation of the mutual relations between

---

152 The king of Mittani, the overlord of Idrimi.

153 The two latter sections were preserved only in the Egyptian version. The section of the curses and blessings, which in treaties Nos. 7–10 (without blessings) closes the treaty, is followed in the Egyptian version by two more paragraphs concerning extradition of runaways, which clearly belong to the previous stipulatory section. This seems to be a failure of the Egyptian scribes who translated the original Akkadian text sent by the Hittite king into Egyptian and copied it onto the walls of the temples; see Spalinger 1981: p. 348f.

154 Note, however, that also these treaties, in their curse section, do refer to a limited number of divinities as those who would implement the curse upon the party who violates the agreement.

the two parties. The fact that some Hittite subordination limited treaties also lacked divine witnesses and a blessing section support the latter suggestion.[155] Regarding the reference to the past relations and the declarations of the parties, as far as we may infer from the parity sections of the Šunaššura treaty (*CTH* 41.I: i, 1–4, 49—iii, 36),[156] the expanded peace treaty might not always have included them. Accordingly, the regular structure for an ordinary, comprehensive peace treaty would be as follows: (1) Preamble; [(2) an optional section: statement about the intentions of the parties in concluding the treaty, with or without a possible reference to their previous relations;] (3) stipulations; (4) a list of the divine witnesses; (5) a curse and blessing section.

3.2.2. *The Parties to the Treaty*

Parity treaties were concluded in the first place between two kings. Comprehensive peace treaties are expected to have been concluded between two fully sovereign rulers. More limited treaties, regulating the political and commercial relations between two neighboring states, and concerning particularly frequent problems like runaway slaves and trespasses, could have been concluded also between rulers one of whom or both were not fully sovereign. Namely, it might have been concluded between two rulers subordinated to the same overlord;[157] between a sovereign ruler and a ruler subordinated to a third party;[158] or between two rulers subordinated to different overlords.[159]

Apart from parity treaties concluded between rulers, we also have a treaty (or treaties) concluded between two cities, Carchemish and Ugarit, which were subordinated to the same overlord, the Hittite king.[160] The copies of this treaty that survived concerned the commercial relations of these cities, and provided for the case of merchants of one of the cities who would be killed in the territory of the other city.

---

155 See RS 17.340 and RS 17.227 (Beckman 1999, Nos. 4 and 28A). Both these documents do not have a blessing section and the list of divine witnesses is combined with the curse.

156 See the last paragraph of section 3.1.5 above.

157 This may be the case with AT 2 (see note 132 above with the accompanied text).

158 This most probably is the case of AT 3 quoted above, where only Idrimi seems to have been subordinated at that time to the Mittanian king (note that only Idrimi is required that his suzerain Barattarna would also take the oath).

159 The last two cases, however, were possible only when their respective suzerains, or the two fully sovereign kings, were in friendly relations, based on a peace treaty, with each other.

160 RS 17.230, 17.146, 18.115, and RS 18.19 (*PRU* IV, pp. 153–160).

This treaty between the cities of Ugarit and Carchemish raises yet a question about the nature of the institution designated "the City". While the treaty was concluded by Ini-Teššub, the king of Carchemish, it is presented as the treaty between the cities Carchemish and Ugarit.[161] It seems to indicate that Ini-Teššub, who was also the Hittite viceroy whose jurisdiction covered all the territories under Hittite suzerainty in Syria including the two city-states involved, acted here as an arbitrator in his capacity of Hittite viceroy, while the two cities were represented by their elites.[162]

3.2.3. *Characteristics of Parity Treaties*

The wording of the above quoted parity treaty between Idrimi of Alalaḫ and Pilliya of Kizzuwatna (AT 3) may be taken as typical to the parity treaties of this period: impersonal and objective, a bilateral document that contains the reciprocal obligations of both parties.[163] This is true not only of the limited treaties or protocols, but also of the comprehensive treaty of Šunaššura as may be inferred from its parity sections (*CTH* 41.I: i, 1–4, 49–iii, 36). In this regard, these treaties continue the tradition presented by the Old Babylonian bilateral treaty between Šadlaš and Nērebtum, and differ from that of the parity unilateral Old Babylonian treaties discovered in Mari and Tell Leilan—treaties discussed in the previous chapter.

Two treaties, however, do not entirely accord with this format: the treaty between Niqmepa of Alalaḫ and IR.ᵈIM of Tunip (AT 2), and that between Ḫattušili III and Ramesses II. AT 2 opens with a preamble introducing the two parties of the treaty much the same as the other parity treaties of this period, and has the seals of *both* parties. Yet, it differs from

161 While the preamble of RS 17.230 presents the agreement as having been concluded between "Initeššub, king of Carchemish, and the people of the land of Ugarit", the preamble of RS 17.146 presents the treaty as an agreement between "the land of Carchemish and the land of Ugarit." Note that while the Ugaritic king is not mentioned as a party, the treaty does refer to merchants "of the king of Ugarit" (RS 17.146: 4–5), indicating that at the time the treaty was concluded there existed a king over Ugarit.

162 In Ugarit, this elite was composed of a college of 'elders' or 'fathers' which legally represented the community, particularly in case of crimes committed in their territory by someone unknown; see Vita 1999: p. 483f. (sub 3.8.2), with the references to previous literature cited there. In the Amarna letters we find the 'City' to represent and handle the affairs of the cities of Tunip (EA 59), Irqata (EA 100) and Byblos (EA 139–140) on the Lebanese coast, when their king died or was absent. In EA 149: 57–60 the "people of Arwad" are said to have entered into agreement under oath with the ruler of Sidon and Aziru of Amurru in order to cooperate in fighting against Tyre.

163 At times, however, the scribe may have changed from a third person to first and second person as it seems to be the case with the much damaged treaty between Zidanta and Pilliya (*CTH* 25).

the other parity treaties of the period by it being formulated unilaterally in the first person, although employing such designations as "I"—"you", "my land"—"your land", which may fit each of the parties without a need to repeat each provision twice. This deviation is particularly conspicuous when comparing it to AT 3, the bit earlier treaty from Alalaḫ. AT 2 differentiates from AT 3 also in its designation as a "tablet of the (oath by the) life of the gods" (*ṭuppu ša nīš ilāni*), continuing thereby the Old Babylonian tradition, whereas AT 3 is called *ṭuppi rikši* "tablet of treaty ('bond')". These divergences seem to reflect the fact that the format that (a bit later?) took hold by the Hittites and sometime later in Syria was not yet firmly established in 15th century Syria, and that AT 2 seems to reflect rather a transitory stage.

Another kind of deviation from the more common format of the available parity treaties of this period is presented by the opening section of the two versions of the treaty between Ḫattušili III and Ramesses II. While the various clauses of the stipulatory section are formulated reciprocally in the third person, yet following the preamble and preceding the stipulatory section there is a unilateral declaration in the first person singular, which is addressed to the partner. This presents the document as the unilateral undertaking of the party who drew up the version. Following is a quotation of the opening of the Ramesses' copy (written in Akkadian) which was sent to Ḫattušili:[164]

> A obv. 1–3 The treaty which Ramesses Meriamun, Great King, King of Egypt, Hero, concluded on a tablet of silver with Ḫattušili, Great King, King of Ḫatti, his brother, in order to establish great peace and great brotherhood between them forever.
> 3–7 Thus says Ramesses Meriamun, Great King, King of Egypt, Hero of All Lands; son of Minmuarea (=Seti I), Great King, King of Egypt, Hero; grandson of Minpaḫtarea (=Ramesses I), Great King, King of Egypt, Hero; to Ḫattušili, Great King, King of Ḫatti, Hero; son of Muršili, Great King, King of Ḫatti, Hero; grandson of Šuppiluliuma, Great King, King of Ḫatti, Hero:
> 7–13 Behold, I have now established good brotherhood and good peace between us forever, in order likewise to establish good peace and good brotherhood

[164] Beckman 1999, No. 15: §§1–5, whose translation was adopted here with small changes (the division into separated paragraphs is Beckman's; see his introduction there on p. 96). The Akkadian version survived in some fragments constituting two exemplars (A and B; for the score, see Edel 1997: pp. 5–12), a fact which helps in restoring the damaged lines. For the parallel Hittite document (written originally in Akkadian but found translated and copied in Egyptian hieroglyphs) see besides Edel 1997, also Kitchen 1996: pp. 79–85. In the present quotation, I omitted the brackets indicating restoration in order to facilitate reading. Note that the parallel version introduces the parties in reverse order.

in the relations of Egypt with Ḫatti forever. Behold, as far as the relations of the Great King, King of Egypt, and the Great King, King of Ḫatti, are concerned, from of old and forever by means of a treaty the god has not allowed the making of war between them. Behold, Ramesses Meriamun, Great King, King of Egypt, is doing this in order to bring about the relationship which the Sun-god and the Storm-god established for Egypt with Ḫatti in accordance with their relationship from the beginning of time, so that for eternity he might not permit the making of war between them.
13–18And Ramesses Meriamun, Great King, King of Egypt, has indeed created <it> (the relationship) on this day by means of a treaty upon a tablet of silver, with Ḫattušili, Great King, King of Ḫatti, his brother, in order to establish good peace and good brotherhood between them forever. He is my brother, and I am his brother. He is at peace with me, and I am at peace with him forever. And we will create our brotherhood and our peace, and they will be better than the former brotherhood and peace of Egypt with Ḫatti.
19–21Behold, Ramesses, Great King, King of Egypt, is in good peace and good brotherhood with Ḫattušili, Great Prince of Ḫatti, Behold, The sons of Ramesses Meriamun, <Great King>, King of Egypt, are at peace and brothers with the sons of Ḫattušili, Great King, King of Ḫatti, forever. And they will remain as in our relationship of brotherhood and of peace, so that Egypt will be at peace with Ḫatti and they will be brothers like us forever. (*Here start the bilateral provisions of the treaty*)

A similar unilateral statement, made by Ḫattušili, appears in his version sent to Egypt. It would seem that this strange combination of bilateral reciprocal formulation of the terms of the treaty with unilateral statements was adopted in order to reinforce the liability of the parties.

Another statement included in the above quoted declaration of Ramesses, which was intended to reinforce the treaty, referred to the past relations of the two countries. In the Ramesses copy sent to Ḫatti, this reference is quite brief (A obv. 9–11): "Behold, … from of old and forever by means of a treaty the god has not allowed the making of war between them". In A obv. 17–18, there is one more short reference to the past: "Behold, we will create our brotherhood and our peace, and (they will be) better than the former brotherhood and peace of Egypt with Ḫatti." The copy sent by Ḫattušili to Egypt has yet a longer, more specific reference (§2):[165]

[165] The following translation follows mainly that of Kitchen, taking into account, however, also Edel's translation (pp. 21, 23). Line numbering follows that of Edel. Note that the designations "King" and "Prince" follow Edel's rendering of the Egyptian titles *p3-ḥq3-ʿ3 n Kmt* for the Egyptian ruler and *p3-wr-ʿ3 n Ḫt* for the Hittite. Kitchen preferred to employ the title "Great Ruler" for both kings, but a more accurate rendering would be "the Great Ruler of Egypt" and "the Great Chieftain of Ḫatti" respectively (so e.g. Schmidt 1973:

> Formerly, since eternity, ... God did not permit hostilities to arise between them through a treaty. But, in the time of Mu(wa)talli, the Great Prince of Ḫatti, my brother, he fought with Usimare Setepenre, the Great King of Egypt. But now, as from today,—see: Ḫattušili, the Great Prince of Ḫatti, [makes] a treaty to (re)establish the relationship which Re made and which Seth made—with the land of Egypt and the land of Ḫatti—to prevent hostilities ever arising between them again.

And then, after a few more sentences, we find once again a reference to the past (§5: 24–29):

> As for the standing treaty which has been current ("here") in the time of Šuppiluliu(ma), the Great Prince of Ḫatti, and likewise the standing treaty which existed in the time of Mu(wa)ttalli, the Great Prince of Ḫatti, my father (*sic*),—I hold firm to it. See, Ramesses Meriamun, the Great King of Egypt, also holds firm to the [treaty/peace] which he has made together with us, beginning from today. We (both) hold firm to it, (and) we shall remain within this regular relationship.

The common, main message of these references to the past is that the present treaty is but a follow-up treaty—a continuation of the long-term contractual relations between Egypt and Ḫatti—and that this treaty is intended to strengthen the ties between the two countries. This assertion was quite obviously designed to grant the treaty greater binding power, the more so as it was displayed as a fulfillment of the will of the supreme gods.[166]

The Hittite-Egyptian treaty, being the only parity treaty of which the versions held by its two partners survived, provides some further important information. First, each of the two partners drew up his own version, sealed it, took an oath over it, and sent it to his partner to be placed in the partner's main temple in front of the image of his main god. This is echoed in Ramesses II's letter Kupanta-Kurunta of Mira-Kuwaliya:[167]

---

pp. 113ff.). The discrimination between these titles is the product of the Egyptian scribes who translated the Akkadian text into Egyptian and copied it onto the walls of the temples, reflecting thereby their ideological conceptions of the superiority of the Pharaoh. Such discrimination for sure did not appear in the original version.

[166] It may be noted that while the Ramesses' version, in accordance with this intention, entirely disregarded the belligerent relations that existed between the two countries for about three generations, Ḫattušili's version chose to bring it up. This was done no doubt out of Hittite internal politics, in order to besmirch the name of Muwattalli, Ḫattušili's deceased brother, in the eyes of the gods and the Egyptians, and hence—indirectly—also to besmirch the name of Muwattalli's son and legitimate heir Urḫi-Teššub, whom Ḫattušili had removed from the throne, but who still posed a threat to Ḫattušili at that time.

[167] *CTH* 166: rev. 14'–16'. Edel 1994: I, pp. 74–77, No. 28; Beckman 1999, No. 22D.

> The written version of the oath which [I made] for the Great King, the King of Ḫatti, my brother, has been set at the feet of [the Storm-god] and before the Great Gods. They are witnesses [to the words of the oath].

This fact is also echoed in two of Ramesses II's letters to Ḫattušili III, KUB 3.51 and KBo 28.1,[168] where the exchange of copies is discussed. That would mean that each of these copies was placed not in the main temple (or temples) of the party who drew it up, but rather in that of the other party. And yet, as may be inferred from Ḫattušili's copy, whose list of divine witnesses together with the curses and blessings sections were preserved, the main gods of *both* parties together with their respective pantheons are invoked as witnesses to the undertakings of the respective partners.[169] These *two* pantheons are also invoked to punish the violator, and to bless the one who shall keep the terms of the treaty. Accordingly, we have to understand that in case one of the parties would disregard his undertakings, the wronged party would have to appeal to his own gods, reading aloud to them the violated terms of the version handed to him by the violator on concluding the treaty, and to ask them to intervene on his behalf by calling up the other party's gods to join in punishing the violator.

Next, these two versions of the Hittite-Egyptian treaty enlighten us about the reciprocal formulation of the stipulatory section. Disregarding the deviations of the hieroglyphic version that resulted from the need of the Egyptian scribes to serve internal propaganda[170] or from their failure to read correctly the original version sent by Ḫattušili,[171] still the provisions that survived are not entirely identical in the two versions and not all the provisions are reciprocal. Both versions stipulate that upon the death of the Hittite partner, should the Hittites commit an offense against his legitimate heir, Ramesses would send troops to help him regain the throne (Beckman's §11, Edel's §10). Nothing, however, is said about Ḫattušili's obligation to guarantee the legitimate royal succession in Egypt.[172] In addition, regarding the obligation of both partners to help each other in case of an

---

[168] Edel 1994, Nos. 2 and 4.

[169] "As for these terms . . . a thousand gods, of gods male and female belonging to the land of Ḫatti, together with a thousand gods, of gods male and female belonging to the land of Egypt they are with me as witnesses who have heard these terms" (Kitchen's translation).

[170] This includes the description that preceded the preamble, describing how the Hittite emissaries arrived to beg peace, and the title "Great Prince" employed to designate Ḫattušili (see note 165 above).

[171] See note 153 above.

[172] Cf. Edel 1997: pp. 38–41, 85.

enemy attack on either of them (Beckman's §§7–10, Edel's §§6–9), while the version sent by Ḫattušili included an escape clause, which allowed the partner not to personally take part in fighting this enemy, the version sent by Ramesses did not have this escape clause. These two deviations suggest that the two versions exchanged between the two partners did not need to be necessarily fully identical nor fully reciprocal.

Another important piece of information regarding this exchange of versions emerges from the Egyptian royal correspondence that followed the conclusion of the treaty. In KBo 28.1: obv. 5'–12', a letter mentioned above, Ramesses informs Ḫattušili that he had disseminated the treaty throughout Egypt so that all Egypt, dignitaries as well as ordinary people would hear about the agreement and its details, and he urges Ḫattušili to do the same as soon as he gets the Egyptian version of the treaty. This is the first time, and so far also the only case, where we hear about this practice.[173] In Egypt it was reflected by the fact that copies of the treaty were inscribed on the walls of two very important temples, the temple of Amon at Karnak and the Ramesseum. But we have to wait until the 8th century BCE to find a similar reflection in three stelae from Sefire in north Syria, presenting the treaty concluded between Bar-Ga'yah, king of KTK, and Mati'el, king of Arpad.[174] The same is known to have been later practiced in ancient Greece, where in Athens and most of the other Greek city-states it was common to erect permanent records, including marble steles, of treaty documents.[175]

We are less informed regarding the swearing-in procedures, but we may presume that it was not much different from those of the Old Babylonian period. Namely, each party took the oath in front of the images of his own gods as well as of the images or emblems of the partner's gods[176]

---

[173] Yet, in the subordination treaties we do find a reflection of this requirement of publicizing in the demand that the treaty should be read periodically in the presence of the subordinate king and his court; see the quotation in note 198 below.

[174] Fitzmyer 1995; see below in the next chapter.

[175] See Phillipson 1911: p. 398; Adcock and Mosely 1975: p. 177f., and more recently Bederman 2001: p. 171f. This practice is known also from ancient Rome; note e.g. the treaty concluded in 497 BCE between Rome and all the Latin states, known by the name "*foedus Cassianum*", which, according to Cicero (*pro Balbo* 53; cf. Livy 2.33.9), was inscribed on a bronze pillar and was set up in the Forum.

[176] This is suggested by the list of divine witnesses and the formulae of curses and blessings preserved in the Hieroglyphic version of the Hittite-Egyptian treaty, which refer to the pantheons of *both* parties; see the quotation in note 169 above.

brought by the latter's emissaries.[177] Those emissaries also supervised or even administered the swearing-in of their host.[178]

3.2.4. *The Issues Dealt with in the Available Parity Treaties*

The most common issue treated in the available parity treaties is the extradition of runaways, whether runaways in general or more specifically political refugees[179] and slaves.[180] Some treaties also deal with the return of other categories of people crossing the border, whether forcibly such as kidnapped,[181] or voluntarily such as families or whole communities looking for subsistence across the border.[182] Second in frequentness is the issue of defensive alliance.[183] In certain cases, the parties reserved their rights to restrict the deployment of their supporting troops only as garrison troops in the ally country when its army goes off to battle an enemy country.[184] In no case, however, do we have a non-ad hoc offensive alliance. Related to the security issues are provisions dealing with the obligation to provide the allied party with political and military intelligence, particularly any information about rebellious conspiracies.[185] Other issues deal with the honorable treatment of the ally's royal messengers;[186] thefts and murders,[187] ceasing hostilities and promises not to wage war against each other,[188] returning settlements taken in the course of war and promises to refrain from fortifying certain settlements,[189] renouncement of all claims,[190] and

---

177 This is suggested by EA 164, a letter sent by Aziru, ruler of Amurru, to Tutu, a high Egyptian official. In response to the latter's demand of him to report to the Egyptian royal court, Aziru put the following request (lines 28–34): "My lord, I am afraid of the king, my lord, and of Tutu. Here are (the images of) my gods and my messenger. Tutu and the magnates of the king, my lord, I would put under oath, and then I will make the journey."

178 The fragment of the 15th century parity treaty between a Hittite king and a ruler by the name Ḫuḫazalma of an unknown polity (*CTH* 28; edited by Otten 1967) preserved a reference (line 15') to a certain ceremony on concluding a treaty, in the course of which a lamb was slaughtered.

179 Runaways in general: treaties numerated as Nos. 5 [I–II], 6 and 7 in the list in note 147 above; political refugees: treaties Nos. 1, 3, 4 and 6.

180 Treaties Nos. 7 and 8.

181 Treaty No. 7.

182 Treaties Nos. 1, 3, 4 and 7.

183 Treaties Nos. 1, 4, 5 [I and III], 6 and 9.

184 Treaties Nos. 1, 4 and 5 [I and III]; see the quotation from the Šunaššura treaty in section 3.1.4 above.

185 Treaties Nos. 3, 4 and 5 [I and III].

186 Treaties Nos. 3, 4 and 5 [III].

187 Treaties Nos. 3 and 7.

188 Treaties Nos. 5 [III] and 6.

189 Treaty No. 2.

190 Treaty No. 9.

finally the obligation to help the legitimate heir of the signatory partner to gain the throne when his father died.[191]

3.3. *Subordination Treaties*

Subordination treaties are treaties dictated and drawn up by a suzerain for an inferior party, stipulating the latter's obligations, and frequently including also some obligations of the suzerain. The fact that such a treaty is a unilateral dictation of the suzerain was made expressly clear in the Alakšandu treaty (*CTH* 76: A iii 73–77 = Beckman 1999, No. 13: §16):

> Furthermore, this tablet which I have made for you, Alakšandu, shall be read out before you three times yearly, and you, Alakšandu, shall know it. These words are by no means reciprocal. They issue from Ḫatti.

To date we have at least 19 subordination treaties and supplements drawn up by Hittite kings, which are either comprehensive or limited subordination treaties (or protocols).[192] In addition, there are many more documents, which are too fragmentary to ascertain whether they are parity or subordination treaties,[193] or whether they are treaties or mere edicts,[194] or whose designation as treaties rather than loyalty oaths may be questioned.[195]

---

[191] Treaties Nos. 5 [III] and 6.

[192] These are the treaties of (1) Šunaššura of Kizzuwatna (*CTH* 41.I; Beckman 1999, No. 2); (2) Ḫukkana of Ḫayaša (*CTH* 42; Beckman 1999, No. 3); (3–4) the limited treaty and protocol of Niqmaddu II of Ugarit (RS 17.227 and RS 17.340+; Beckman 1999, No. 28A and 4 respectively); (5) Aziru of Amurru (*CTH* 49; Beckman 1999, No. 5); (6–7) Šattiwaza of Mittani (*CTH* 51 & 52; Beckman 1999, No. 6A & 6B); (8) Tette of Nuḫašše (*CTH* 53; Beckman 1999, No. 7); (9) Duppi-Teššub of Amurru (*CTH* 62; Beckman 1999, No. 8); (10) Niqmepa of Ugarit (*CTH* 66; Beckman 1999, No. 9); (11) Targašnalli of Ḫapalla (*CTH* 67; Beckman 1999, No. 10); (12) Kupanta-Kurunta of Mira-Kuwaliya (*CTH* 68; Beckman 1999, No. 11); (13) Manapa-Tarḫunta of the Šeha-River Land (*CTH* 69; Beckman 1999, No. 12); (14) Alakšandu of Wiluša (*CTH* 76; Beckman 1999, No. 13); (15) Talmi-Šarrumma of Aleppo (*CTH* 75; Beckman 1999, No. 14); (16) Bentešina of Amurru (*CTH* 92; Beckman 1999, No. 16); (17) Šaušgamuwa of Amurru (*CTH* 105; Beckman 1999, No. 17); (18) Ulmi-Teššub of Tarḫuntašša (*CTH* 106; Beckman 1999, No. 18B); (19) Kurunta of Tarḫuntašša (StBoT Beiheft 1; Beckman 1999, No. 18C). Note that the so-called "Šattiwaza—Šuppiluliuma treaty" (*CTH* 52; Beckman 1999, No. 6B; enumerated above as number 7) is actually not a treaty but a kind of supplement attached to the Šattiwaza treaty (number 6 above) presenting Šattiwaza's declaration. For another possible example of such a supplement see note 211 below.

[193] E.g., the treaty concluded with Ḫuḫazalma (*CTH* 28), and the treaty concluded with Lab'u of Tunip (*CTH* 135).

[194] E.g., the document issued by Šuppiluliuma I to Šarri-kušuḫ (*CTH* 50).

[195] To these belong the documents drawn up by Arnuwanda I to the men of Išmerika (*CTH* 133; Beckman 1999, No. 1A), and to the Kaška people (*CTH* 138–140; von Schuler 1965: pp. 109–140).

3.3.1. *Structure*

On the basis of the above mentioned 19 documents, the conventional structure of the Hittite subordination treaties is as follows: (1) An introduction presenting the suzerain as the one who dictated the document;[196] (2) a historical prologue reviewing the historical and legal background of the present treaty;[197] (3) a stipulatory section; (4) a "tablet clause", fixing the place where the tablet of the treaty is kept,[198] and (occasionally) stipulating that it should be read periodically in the presence of the subordinate king and his court;[199] (5) a list of the gods invoked to witness the conclusion of the treaty and to sanction the treaty;[200] (6) curses and blessings invoked upon the subordinate king depending whether the terms of the treaty are violated or observed.

The two components that differentiate the Hittite subordinate treaties from the parity treaties of this period are the so-called "tablet clause", and the so-called "historical prologue". However, the "tablet clause" is attested only in four documents belonging to three treaties and the requirement

196 Exceptions are the Šattiwaza treaty (*CTH* 51; Beckman 1999, No. 6A), which omits the conventional introduction, and the Šunaššura treaty (*CTH* 41.I; Beckman 1999, No. 2) whose introduction is a remnant of an earlier parity version (see the last paragraph of section 3.1.5 above).

197 An exception is the Aziru treaty (*CTH* 49; Beckman 1999, No. 5), where the prologue is set after specifying the general loyalty obligation of Aziru, and the yearly tribute he has to pay.

198 A good example of this clause is found in the Šattiwaza treaty (*CTH* 51.I; A rev. 35–37; Beckman 1999, No. 6A: §13): "A duplicate of this tablet is deposited before the Sun-goddess of Arinna, since the Sun-goddess of Arinna governs kingship and queenship. And in the land of Mittani a duplicate is deposited before the Storm-god, lord of the *kurinnu* of Kahat. It shall be read repeatedly, for ever and ever, before the king of the land of Mittani and before the Hurrians."

199 The reference to the place where the copies of the treaty are kept appears in the Šattiwaza treaty (*CTH* 51.I; Beckman 1999, No. 6A): A rev. 35–37; the Šattiwaza's Declaration (*CTH* 52.I; Beckman 1999, No. 6B): rev. 8–10, and the Ulmi-Teššub treaty (*CTH* 106; Beckman 1999, No. 18B): obv. 38'. In the Kurunta treaty (StBoT Beiheft 1; Beckman 1999, No. 18C) it appears at the end of the treaty. The requirement that the document should be publicly read appears only in four documents: the Šattiwaza treaty (*CTH* 51.I; Beckman 1999, No. 6A): A rev. 36–37; the Šattiwaza Declaration (*CTH* 52.I; Beckman 1999, No. 6B): rev. 7–8; the Kupanta-Kurunta treaty (*CTH* 68; Beckman 1999, No. 11): §28, I iv 1'; and the Alakšandu treaty (*CTH* 76; Beckman 1999, No. 13): A iii, 73–75. While many treaties are too fragmentary to determine whether originally they included such a requirement, the treaties of Aziru, Duppi-Teššub, Manapa-Tarḫunta and Kurunta definitely did not include it. The criteria for including or omitting these requirements in a subordination treaty cannot at present be determined.

200 An exceptional case is presented by the Ḫuqqana treaty (*CTH* 42; Beckman 1999, No. 3), where this list, followed by the curses and blessings section, divides the stipulatory section into two.

that the document should be publicly read appears only in three documents, belonging to two treaties.[201] On the contrary, the so-called "historical prologue" seems to be an indispensable component in the Hittite subordination treaties. In a recent study devoted to this component and its function in the Hittite treaties, it was concluded that this section is characteristic of the so-called Hittite "vassal treaties" and related legal documents drawn up by a suzerain for his subordinate kings or communities. Its function was to present an argument or a set of arguments with a legal message, justifying the imposition of obligations on the subordinate party, and depriving that party of the ability to contest the validity or legality of the treaty. Such a prologue was likely to appear not only in subordination treaties but also in any Hittite state document imposing on a subordinate party certain obligations or restrictions, which involved infringement of some enshrined or traditional rights of that party.[202] Thus, we find it also in edicts issued to subordinate rulers[203] as well as to local communities within the kingdom.[204]

Except for the "historical prologue" and the "tablet clause", which are characteristic of subordination treaties, the structure is the same as that of the parity treaties of this period.

3.3.2. *The Parties to the Treaty*

Subordination treaties were concluded in the first place between the suzerain and his subordinate king. In cases where the subordinated country did not have a local king, the would-be suzerain might have elevated a local personage to kingship, but upon concluding the treaty, the local populace were also made party to the side of that personage.[205] This is true also in cases where there was some doubt as to whether the personage

[201] See note 199 above.

[202] See Altman 2004a: pp. 473–481. For a detailed summary see Altman 2004b.

[203] A good example is the edict issued by Muršili II to Abiradda of Barga (*CTH* 63; Beckman 1999, No. 30): §§2–5 (A i 3–ii 5).

[204] The edict issued by Ḫattušili III to the city of Tiliura (*CTH* 89; von Schuler 1965: pp. 145–148).

[205] Such is the case of the treaty drawn up by Šuppiluliuma I to Ḫuqqana of Ḫayaša: *CTH* 42; Beckman 1999, No. 3. While the first three columns present the agreement with Ḫuqqana, column iv, which was attached to the treaty as an appendix, presents an earlier accord with the (notable) people of Ḫayaša: see Beckman 1999: p. 27. Further examples of treaties concluded with elders of Anatolian communities are *CTH* 146, which included a treaty with a group of elders (Beckman 1999, No. 27a), and *CTH* 27, which seems to be a treaty drawn up by an unknowen Hittite king with a *ḫabiru* gang (Otten 1957; Carruba 1969: pp. 237f.).

imposed on the subordinate land would be accepted and acknowledged by the local populace.[206] The subordinated party was sworn in to pledge loyalty to the signatory suzerain, his sons and grandsons, rarely also to the queen.[207] Only most rarely do we find that the subordinate king was sworn in by "an oath to the king of Ḫatti and the land of Ḫatti, and to my sons and grandsons."[208] This rarity reflects the fact that the Hittite kings were much concerned lest the subordinate king would transfer his loyalty to a usurper belonging to another branch of the Hittite royal family or to some other Hittite personage, no less than they were concerned lest he would transfer it to a foreigner overlord.[209]

3.3.3. *Main Characteristics of Subordination Treaties*

Contrary to the parity treaties, subordination treaties were drafted in only one version, by the suzerain, as a dictated agreement, and a copy of it sealed by the suzerain was handed to the subordinate party.[210] In certain cases, a supplementary document was added, phrased as a declaration made in the first person by the subordinate party, confirming the assertions made by the suzerain in the prologue of the main text and adding details which strengthen the subordinate's commitment to his overlord.[211]

206 This was the case of the treaty drawn up by Šuppiluliuma I to Šattiwaza of Mittani (*CTH* 51+52; Beckman 1999, No. 6A–B), where we find that the treaty should be read repeatedly "before the king of the land of Mittani and before the Hurrians" (*CTH* 51.I: §13, A rev. 36–37; *CTH* 52.I: §8, rev. 7–8), and that the curses and blessings refer to "you, Šattiwaza, and you Hurrians" (*CTH* 51.I: §§15–16; *CTH* 52.I: §§ 9–10). Moreover, *CTH* 52.I, §11, presents the oath that Šattiwaza and the Hurrians took together. For another treaty whose curse explicitly addresses apart from the subordinate king also his people see the Manapa-Tarḫunta treaty (*CTH* 69; Beckman 1999, No. 12): §20.

207 The Bentešina treaty (*CTH* 92; Beckman 1999, No. 16): §9, obv. 39, and the Ulmi-Teššub treaty (*CTH* 106; Beckman 1999, No. 18B): §9, rev. 5; §10, rev. 8. Both treaties were drawn up by Ḫattušili III.

208 Duppi-Teššub treaty (*CTH* 62.II; Beckman 1999, No. 8): §5, A i 21'–22', 27'–28'. See there also §8, A ii 14' (restored). Indeed, here and there we find that a specific treaty is "of Ḫatti". Thus we find in the Alakšandu treaty (*CTH* 76; Beckman 1999, No. 13): §16, A iii 76–77, that the treaty "issues from Ḫatti." In Šuppiluliuma I's letter to Niqmaddu II of Ugarit (RS 17.132 = *PRU* IV), lines 19–21, Niqmaddu is requested to observe "the treaty and the peace of Ḫatti."

209 Cf. the Ḫuqqana treaty (*CTH* 42; Beckman 1999, No. 3): §§2 and 11, and the Šaušgamuwa treaty (*CTH* 105; Beckman 1999, No. 17): §§6 and 9.

210 Two examples of such a sealed copy handed to the subordinate are the limited treaties or protocols RS 17.227 and RS 17.340, for which see Schaeffer 1956: pp. 1–6, figs. 2–6.

211 The only certain example available is the wrongly so-called Šattiwaza—Šuppiluliuma treaty (*CTH* 52; Beckman 1999: No. 6B), which is actually a supplementary document attached to the subordination treaty drawn up by Šuppiluliuma I to Šattiwaza of Mittani (*CTH* 51; Beckman 1999, No. 6A); for discussion, see my paper Altman 2005b, and for more expanded Altman 2004a: pp. 296–323. Another possible example is in all probability *CTH* 96

The Hittite subordination treaties stipulated highly defined, clearly expressed terms imposed upon the subordinate party. These were worded more usually in the second person but at times in the third person. The most common and important demands were the military obligation, providing political and military intelligence, rendering yearly tribute, and paying yearly homage. On the other hand, the Hittite suzerain also made some explicit promises to the subordinate party, the more important of which were the promises to protect the subordinate king and his land from any enemy from within or without and to safeguard the throne of the subordinate king for his offspring. It was only in the case of a rebellious country that such promises were omitted.[212] Regarding the yearly tribute, the amount and the content were explicitly defined, either in the treaty itself[213] or in a supplemental document,[214] so that even if it constituted a heavy burden, at least it was a fixed amount and the subordinate king could be assured that no further demand in that regard would be made. Moreover, when later circumstances called for a reduction in the amount of the tribute or other obligations, a due adjustment was made.[215]

Regarding the subordinate's foreign relations, the key formula was "you shall be at peace with my friend and hostile to my enemy", followed by an updated list of those countries that are friends of the Hittite king and those that are enemies.[216] This meant that the subordinate king was allowed to conclude parity treaties, including commercial relations, not only with other countries subordinated to the Hittites but also with countries outside Hittite suzerainty, on the condition that they or their suzerain

---

(ed. Beckman 1989/90: 291), a fragmentary document worded as a declaration made by Kurunta of Tarḫuntašša, which might have been attached to *CTH* 106 (Beckman 1999: No. 18B), the treaty Ḫattušili III drew up for him (under the name Ulmi-Teššub).

[212] This is the case of the treaties of Kupanta-Kurunta (*CTH* 68; Beckman 1999, No. 11), Manapa-Tarḫunta (*CTH* 69; Beckman 1999, No. 12), and Šaušgamuwa (*CTH* 105; Beckman 1999, No. 17).

[213] So in the treaties of Aziru (*CTH* 49.II; Beckman 1999, No. 5): §1; Tette (*CTH* 53; Beckman 1999: No. 7): §3, and Duppi-Tešub (*CTH* 62.II; Beckman 1999, No. 8): §5.

[214] Examples: RS 17.227 (and duplicates) and RS 11.732 (*PRU* IV, pp. 40–43, 47–48; Beckman 1999: No. 28A and B).

[215] Thus, following the detachment of the small kingdom of Siyannu from the authority of the king of Ugarit, Muršili II reduced the amount of tribute imposed on the king of Ugarit: RS 17.382+380 (*PRU* IV, pp. 80–83; Beckman 1999, No. 31B). For another case see *CTH* 97 and 106 (Beckman 1999, No. 18A and 18B: §6).

[216] For the formula, see e.g., the Niqmepa treaty (*CTH* 66; Beckman 1999, No. 9): §2, lines 13f. For a good example of an updated list, see the Šaušgamuwa treaty (*CTH* 105; Beckman 1999, No. 17): §§11–12, where the name of Aḫḫiyawa was erased by the scribe after it had been written on the tablet (cf. Beckman 1999: p. 124 note 23).

maintain friendly relations with the Hittite king.[217] The same regulation was evidently true also in the Mittanian system of subordinate countries, as may be inferred from the parity treaty concluded between Pilliya of Kizzuwatna and Idrimi of Alalaḫ, who was subordinated to Baratarna, the king of Mittani (AT 3). In this specific case, and very likely also in other similar cases, the overlord of the subordinate party were requested to take an oath on the treaty beside his subordinate (see above section 3.2.1 for full quotation).

More often, both the suzerain and the subordinate king took the oath. It was only when the suzerain did not make any promise that he would not take the oath.[218] In either case, whether only by the subordinate or by both, the oath was taken by the gods of both parties, and copies of the agreement were placed in the main temples of both parties.[219]

Finally, regarding the "historical prologue",[220] its basic arguments in justifying the imposition of obligations on the subordinate party are found in the prologues of what may be called "Constitutive (Subordination) Treaties". Namely, treaties that impose a subordinate status on an inferior party not previously subordinated to the Hittites, and establish his relations with his suzerain. In the case of subjugation by force, the prologue presents the justification of the war that forced the defeated party into subordination.[221] In the case of self-subjugation, the prologue includes a description of the circumstances that caused the inferior party to submit to the Hittite suzerain, and the consideration he received for his submission.[222]

---

217 See in the Šaušgamuwa treaty (previous note), §13, where, following the deterioration of relations between Ḫatti and Assyria, Šaušgamuwa was banned from letting Assyrian merchants enter his country.

218 See Altman 2003b.

219 I am aware of only one document, the Šattiwaza declaration (*CTH* 52; Beckman 1999, No. 6B), that according to what may be inferred from the damaged first lines of §8 was placed only in the main temple of the subordinate party; for the assumed reason, see the references in note 211 above.

220 The views expressed in this regard in this and in the following paragraphs are based on Altman 2004a.

221 See the Manapa-Tarḫunta treaty (*CTH* 69; Beckman 1999, No. 12): §§1–3.

222 The available examples are a limited treaty (or protocol) issued to Niqmaddu II of Ugarit (RS 17.340+; Beckman 1999, No. 4); the Šattiwaza treaty and its supplementary document (*CTH* 51+52; Beckman 1999, No. 6A–B); and the Tette treaty (*CTH* 53; Beckman 1999, No. 7). To these one may add the Kupanta-Kurunta treaty (*CTH* 68; Beckman 1999, No. 11). This latter treaty, while belonging to the category of "Modificative Treaties", refers to the case of Mašḫuiluwa of Mira who found shelter in the Hittite court, which provided the Hittites with the legal basis to claim suzerainty over that country.

3.3.4. *Follow-Up and Modification Treaties*

"Follow-Up (Subordination) Treaties" are treaties designed to reinforce and continue the contractual relations that had been established in a previous generation through "Constitutive Treaties".[223] Accordingly, their prologues either explicitly (in most cases) or implicitly refer to the former relations, with much emphasis being put on demonstrating this continuation. The terms of these treaties either follow the terms of the original treaty without any modification or at most include some improvements. Where there was such an improvement, or when any other special favor was conferred on the subordinate party, the drafters did not fail to present it emphatically, since such an act only added to the subordinate's commitment to his overlord.[224]

Where neither modification nor improvement was intended, we would have expected that no new treaty would be drawn up, but, as may be inferred from the few available cases, this is not always so. In two or three cases, follow-up treaties were drawn up on the occasion when both parties, the suzerain and the subordinate king, succeeded their fathers.[225] In another instance, a follow-up treaty was drawn up on the occasion when a new subordinated king succeeded his father.[226] In two other cases, no new treaty was drawn up when a new Hittite king replaced his father,[227] but in

---

[223] The available documents that may be ascribed to this category are: (1) Treaty drawn up by Tudḫaliya II (or III) for Šunaššura of Kizzuwatna (*CTH* 41.I; Beckman 1999, No. 2); (2) edict issued by Šuppiluliuma I to Niqmaddu of Ugarit (*CTH* 47; Beckman 1999, No. 28A); (3) treaty drawn up by Muršili II for Duppi-Teššub of Amurru (*CTH* 62; Beckman 1999, No. 8); (4) treaty drawn up by Muwattalli II (originally: Muršili II) for Talmi-Šarrumma of Aleppo (*CTH* 75; Beckman 1999, No. 14); (5) treaty drawn up by Muwattalli II for Alakšandu of Wiluša (*CTH* 76; Beckman 1999, No. 13); (6) treaty drawn up by Ḫattušili III for Bentešina of Amurru (*CTH* 92; Beckman 1999, No. 16); (7) treaty drawn up by Tudḫaliya IV for Kurunta of Tarḫuntašša (StBoT Beiheft 1; Beckman 1999, No. 18C).

[224] See e.g. the treaties of Duppi-Teššub (Hittite version, *CTH* 62.II; Beckman 1999, No. 8): §4, A i, 11'–18', and of Bentešina (*CTH* 92; Beckman 1999, No. 16): obv. 13–33.

[225] The treaties of Talmi-Šarrumma (*CTH* 75; Beckman 1999, No. 14), and Bentešina (*CTH* 92; Beckman 1999, No. 16). The third case is alluded to in the Hittite version of the Duppi-Teššub treaty (*CTH* 62.II; Beckman 1999, No. 14), where, according to what may be inferred from copy C, lines 15–17, it seems that Muršili II drew up a follow-up treaty for Ari-Teššub, the father of Duppi-Teššub.

[226] The treaty of Duppi-Teššub.

[227] One case concerns Talmi-Šarrumma of Aleppo in the new reign of Muwattalli II (*CTH* 75; Beckman 1999, No. 14). The latter only made a new *copy* of the one that was drawn up for Talmi-Šarrumma by Muršili II and was "stolen" (A obv. 3–8), but there is no reference that any new treaty had ever been drawn up by Muwattalli II for Talmi-Šarrumma. The second case concerns Bentešina of Amurru. As is evident from his presence at the ceremony of the conclusion of the treaty drawn up for Kurunta by Tudḫaliya (StBoT Beiheft 1: §28, iv, 36; Beckman 1999, No. 18C), Bentešina still reigned over Amurru

another case, two successive Hittite kings drew up a treaty for the same subordinated king.[228] It seems, thus, that a follow-up treaty was required whenever the subordinate signatory passed away and was replaced by his legitimate heir, but it was not mandatory when only the suzerain signatory died and was legitimately succeeded by his son.

The reason for this difference seems to be due to the fact that Hittite subordination treaties explicitly stipulated the commitment of the subordinate party not only to the signatory suzerain but also to his son and grandson that would ultimately and legitimately succeed him. On the other hand, these treaties quite usually obligated only the subordinate signatory party but not his next generations. Indeed, occasionally we do find an expressed wish that the good relations be continued also between the next generations of the signatories.[229] In two cases there is even an explicit request that the terms of the treaty be observed not only by the subordinate signatory but also by his heirs down to the second and third generation, and that he and his heirs would maintain their loyalty to the signatory suzerain and his heirs.[230] But there are as many treaties that request only the loyalty of the subordinate signatory, not even hinting at his offspring being subordinated to this obligation.[231] Moreover, where the curses and blessings sections were preserved to the extent that enables any conclusion, we find them to refer only to the case where only the subordinate signatory himself would or would not observe his undertakings.[232] This, in turn, suggests that, notwithstanding the implicit or explicit understanding

when Tudḫaliya ascended the throne. Yet there is no evidence that Tudḫaliya ever drew up a new treaty for him.

228 This is the case of Kurunta of Tarḫuntašša, in whose treaty, drawn up by Tudḫaliya IV, there is an explicit reference to the treaty previously drawn up for him by Ḫattušili III.

229 See the Kupanta-Kurunta treaty (*CTH* 68; Beckman 1999, No. 11): §13 and the Talmi-Šarrumma treaty (*CTH* 75; Beckman 1999, No. 14): §13.

230 See the treaties of Alakšandu (*CTH* 76; Beckman 1999, No. 13): §6, B ii 11–19, and Kurunta (StBoT Beiheft 1; Beckman 1999, No. 18C): §21, iii 21–31.

231 These are the treaties of Šunaššura (*CTH* 41.I: §12, A i 55–59); Ḫuqqana (*CTH* 42: §§2–5, A i 6–34; note that in §6, A i 35–40 it is the Hittite king who promises that he *and his son* will benevolently protect Ḫuqqana and his sons); Duppi-Teššub (*CTH* 62.II: §5, A i 19'–28'); and Niqmepa (*CTH* 66: 4–9). Other treaties, like those of Aziru, Šattiwaza, Tette, Targašnalli, Manapa-Tarḫunta, Bentešina, Šaušgamuwa, and Ulmi-Teššub, are too damaged so that we cannot determine whether they include such a request.

232 Available examples are the treaties of Ḫuqqana (*CTH* 42: §§10–11, A ii 2–13); Aziru (*CTH* 49.I: §§17–18, A rev. 12'–20'; restored); Šattiwaza (*CTH* 51.I: §§15–16, A rev. 58–75, and *CTH* 52.I: §§9–11, rev. 25–39, 40–62); Tette (*CTH* 53: §17, A iv 46'–57'); Duppi-Teššub (*CTH* 62.II: §§21–22, A iv 21–32); Niqmepa (*CTH* 66: §§20–21); Targašnalli (*CTH* 67: §15, left edge 3'–4'; restored); Manapa-Tarḫunta (*CTH* 69: §§20–21, A iv 29'–46'), and Alakšandu (*CTH* 76: §21, A iv 31–46).

that each party inherited the commitments of his forefathers, this understanding was not considered to have sufficient obligatory force and a new personal commitment and oath were required. The few available examples of follow-up treaties, however, do not allow us to determine whether this request was merely desirable or rather indispensable.

Regarding the justification of the continuation of the political subservience of the subordinate country in the second or later generation, while the prologues of these treaties claim that the present subordination is but a continuation of former relations, they hardly refer to the circumstances that led to the original subjugation and are not concerned with its justification. In all the available cases, the prologues stress instead the loyal behavior of the vassal king after becoming subordinated to Ḫatti.[233] This behavior discloses his implied consent to the continuation of his subordination to the Hittite suzerain, and constitutes an argument of a "lack of protest". In three cases (*CTH* 62, 76, and 92), the text adds a claim to an uninterrupted continuation of that subjugation over a long period of time, coupled with a reference to the way by which this subjugation was originally achieved. Where these three latter claims appear together—that is, a lack of protest over a long and uninterrupted period of subjugation coupled with a reference to the original circumstances that led to the subjugation—they amount to what may be regarded a claim for the right of possession.

In case of a rebellion of the subordinate country, a new treaty was drawn up as a replacement of the previous subordination treaty, worsening the former terms of the subjugation. Where the former treaty contained promises of the suzerain in favor of the subordinate party these promises were entirely ignored in the new treaty.[234]

4. Dynastic Marriage Alliances

Although dynastic marriages were quite a common institution in the Ancient Near East, no written formal agreement of such arrangement has reached us so far, nor do we know what rights the father of the bride

[233] Except for the Talmi-Šarrumma treaty (*CTH* 75; Beckman 1999, No. 14), where the section dealing with Talmi-Šarrumma's father has not been preserved. But one may rightly assume that this lost section also contained a reference to the loyalty of the latter.

[234] Examples in point are the treaties of Kupanta-Kurunta (*CTH* 68; Beckman 1999, No. 11) and Šaušgamuwa (*CTH* 105; Beckman 1999, No. 17).

acquired on giving his daughter in marriage to a foreign king. Nevertheless, we are fortunate to have at least some of the royal correspondence exchanged between royal courts in the Late Bronze Age pertaining to dynastic marriage,[235] from which we learn about some conventional rules. Thus, we learn that in case of a proposal of a marriage alliance between two royal houses, the parents of the bride would have stipulated their assent to the proposal on the condition that their daughter would became the main wife of their future son-in-law.[236] This, in turn, implies that in case she would give birth to a son, he would become the legitimate heir of his father. In order to ensure this condition was fulfilled and their daughter was treated properly and with due respect, her parents would stipulate that she be allowed to meet with and speak to their messengers.[237] Such an alliance might have contributed to closer relationships between the two royal courts to the degree that the two countries were regarded as "one".[238]

235 EA 1–5, 11, 14, 19–22, 24–25, 29, 31–32; Edel 1994: I, Nos. 34–68, 103–110.

236 In EA 20: 8–9, 15–16, Tušratta, the king of Mittani, expresses his expectation that his daughter will become the "Mistress of Egypt". According to KBo 28.21+22: obv. 38'–41', and KBo 28.23: obv. 37–41 (Edel 1994: I, Nos. 42 and 43; for the latter see also Beckman 1999, No. 22F), Puduḫepa, the Hittite queen, stipulated that her daughter will be made the chief queen of Egypt, a request that was accepted by Ramesses II. For such a demand, see also KBo 1.23 (Edel 1994: I, No. 68, for which see his discussion in Vol. II, p. 256). See further KBo 7.11:obv. 11'–15' (Edel 1994: I, No. 37 [p. 94/5]; II, p. 153f.) where Ramesses quotes from two letters sent to him by the kings of Babylonia and Ḫanigalbat (Mittani) requesting that their daughters in the Egyptian harem be made the chief queen instead of the Hittite princess, requests denied by him.

237 See EA 1: 10–61 for a quoted complaint of the Babylonian king to the king of Egypt for having forbidden his messenger to see and talk with his daughter in Egypt, and Amenhotep III's response. For stipulating in advance this issue, see the letter KUB 26.89: 5'–8' (Edel 1994: I, No. 104), from Ramesses II to Puduḫepa, and KUB 21.38 (Edel 1994: I, No. 105; Beckman 1999, No. 22E), from Puduḫepa to Ramesses.

238 Thus we find Tušratta, king of Mittani, expressing his expectation that when his daughter will be brought to Egypt to become its "mistress", "on that day shall Ḫanigalbat (=Mittani) and Egypt be [one]" (EA 20: 16–17; for the restoration, see Moran 1992: p. 49, note 3). Two generations later we find the Hittite Queen Puduḫepa, in her letter to Ramesses II, KUB 21.38: rev. 13–14 (Edel 1994: I, No. 105; Beckman 1999, No. 22E), expressing her belief that "now I know that the land of Egypt and the land of Ḫatti will become one country." Similar expression appears in a letter written by Ramesses II to Puduḫepa, KUB 3.63 (Edel 1994: I, No. 51), obv. 17–20: "The Sun-god and the Storm-god, and the gods of the land of Egypt and the land of Ḫatti caused it that the two great lands will become for ever one land." Note, however, that the same expression and wish—"our two great lands will become one land"—also appears in the Egyptian-Hittite correspondence in connection with the conclusion of the peace treaty with no reference to any marital alliance: KBo 8.14: 6 = Edel 1994: I, No. 5.

These arrangements, on the other hand, might have opened the door for the father of the bride to intervene legally in the affairs of his son-in-law's country. Such a case is actually known from two later Mesopotamian chronicles.[239] According to these sources, the Assyrian king Aššur-uballiṭ I (1363–1328) gave his daughter in marriage to a Babylonian king, who was later succeeded by his son born to that Assyrian-born queen. However, following an uprising in Babylonia, this reigning son was murdered and was replaced by a usurper. Aššur-uballiṭ marched then into Babylonia, defeated and slew the usurper, and set the son of his murdered grandson on the throne.[240]

A legitimate case of intervention with regard to throne succession in an allied country, however, might have resulted not only from dynastic marriage but also from a parity treaty which stipulated that in case one of the signatories passed away, his surviving partner should help the deceased's legitimate successor to gain the throne.[241] A case in point, which brought about deterioration of relations between Ḫatti and Babylonia, is described in a letter sent by the Hittite king Ḫattušili III to Kadašman-Enlil II of Babylon (obv. 7–17):[242]

> When your father and I established friendly relations and became affectionate brothers, we did not become brothers for a single day. Did we not establish brotherhood and friendly relations in perpetuity? We [then] set down [an agreement] with one another as follows: "We are mortal. The survivor shall protect the children of the one who goes first to his fate." Then when your father went to his fate while the gods prepared [longevity for me], I wept for him like a brother. [After] I had fulfilled [my mourning responsibilities] for your father, I dried my tears and [immediately] dispatched a messenger, writing to the noblemen of Babylonia as follows: "If you do not protect the progeny of my brother in regard to rule, I will become hostile to

239 The Assyrian "*Synchronistic Chronicle*", a concise history of the relations between Assyria and Babylonia through the 15th–8th centuries, and the Babylonian "*Chronicle of the Kassite Kings*" (known also by the name "*Chronicle P*"), a history of the wars of the Kassite rulers of Babylonia in the 14th–13th centuries. For both chronicles, see Glassner 2004: pp. 176–183, and 278–281.

240 "*Synchronistic Chronicle*": A i, 8'–17'; "*Chronicle of the Kassite Kings*": i, 5'–14'; (Glassner 2004; pp. 178/9 and 278/9 respectively).

241 For an example in point, see the Hittite-Egyptian treaty: Edel 1997: pp. 38–41 (§10); Beckman 1999, No. 15 (§11). The Akkadian version, sent by Ramesses to Ḫattušili, has the following provision: "And the son of Ḫattušili, King of Ḫatti, shall be made King of Ḫatti in place of Ḫattušili, his father, after the many years of Ḫattušili, [King] of Ḫatti. And if [the people] of Ḫatti commit an offense against him, then [Ramesses], beloved of Amon, must send [infantry] and chariotry to his aid and take revenge for him" (Beckman's translation adapted).

242 *CTH* 172 = Beckman 1999: No. 23 (p. 139, §4), whose translation is adopted.

> you. I will come and conquer Babylonia. But if an enemy somehow arises against you, or some matter becomes troublesome for you, write to me so that I can come to your aid."

As it turned out, this declaration of intention was never put to the test, but there is no wonder that it caused a deterioration of diplomatic relations between the two countries following an angry response by Itti-Marduk-balāṭu, the Babylonian vizier: "You do not write to us like a brother. You pressure us as if we were your subjects."

5. Managing Conflicts and State Responsibility

When conflicts, such as concerning borders or problems related to dynastic marriage, arose between two rulers subordinated to the same suzerain, it was up to the suzerain to act as arbitrator to solve it or to hand down his verdict. A case in point is the verdict given by the Hittite king Muršili II in the dispute between the king of Ugarit and the citizen of the neighboring land of Mukiš[243] over their common border (RS 17.237: obv. 1–16; rev. 2'–8'):[244]

> [1][Thus says the S]un Muršili, the Great King, K[ing of Ḫatti,] [2]the son of Šuppiluliuma, the Great King, the Valiant:
>
> ---
>
> [3][Regarding] the settlements of the borders of Mukiš, [4][which] Šuppiluliuma to Niqmaddu, [5][the kin]g of Ugarit, in a tablet of binding [6]has sealed them, and (about which) now Niqmepa, [7]the son of Niqmaddu, approached the Great King (saying) thus: [8]"Regarding these settlements, the citizen of Mukiš, [9]took me, Niqmepa, to court." [10]And Muršili, the Great King, [11]investigated this case, [12]and these settlements, which of old [13][t]o Ugarit are they, [14]now Muršili, the Great King, [15][to] Niqmepa, king of Ugarit, [16][thus?] he gave them? [17]....... field...... [18]...........
> [Rev...]............... [2'][Now.... Muršili, the Great King,] [3'][to Niqmepa,] the king of U[g]ar[it and] to his sons (and) [his grandsons] thus he gave them. [4'][Forever,] later on, the citizen of Mukiš, [5'][regarding] these [settlements] shall not claim [6'][in cou]rt against Niqmepa and against his sons [7'](and) [his grand]sons. Forever! [8'][Wh]oever protest, this tablet will answer him! (*Here follow curses on whoever would alter the wording of this tablet*)

---

243 No local king is known to have ruled over Mukiš in that period; the City of Mukiš should have evidently been administered by the local elite.

244 *PRU* IV, 63–65. Duplicates or parallels: RS 17.62, 17.339 A, and 17.366 (*PRU* IV, 65–70).

According to this document, Muršili handed down his verdict, not on the mere ground that his father Šuppiluliuma I had ratified these settlements as belonging to Ugarit, but rather based on an investigation he himself had conducted, which found that the settlements in question had "of old" (*ša laberti*) been in Ugarit's possession. The document, however, does not explicate how long before Ugarit had held them. A similar case is recorded in another document found in Ugarit, RS 17.123 (*PRU* IV, p. 230), which is a verdict of a Hittite king whose name is not mentioned, regarding a dispute between Ugarit and Siyannu over some territory.[245] In this case also, the verdict was given in favor of the one who held it "of old" (*ša ultu dārīti*).[246]

While the above two cases pertained to the realm of public international law, also cases of private litigations, involving litigants of different states subordinated to the same suzerain, might have been brought before the suzerain himself if one of the litigants was a subordinate king. Thus we find in AT 13 a case brought up before Šauštatar, king of Mittani/Ḫanigalbat, by a Mittanian private person residing in Alalaḫ against Niqmepa, king of Alalaḫ, arguing that because of his Mittanian citizenship (*ḫanigalbatūtū* = Ḫanigalbat-ship) he is not liable for some compulsory services required by the Alalaḫ authorities.[247] More often, however, private litigations involving citizens of different states seem to have been brought before some high official acting on behalf of the suzerain.[248]

Apart from managing such disputes that broke out, the suzerain might have taken care to minimize ahead the possibility of conflicts between his subordinated kings by obligating them to maintain peaceful and friendship relations. Several instances of such steps taken by Hittite kings are

---

[245] See also RS 17.368 (*PRU* IV, 77f.) and RS 16.170 (*PRU* IV, 78).

[246] Other instances of territorial and other disputes brought before the suzerain are: Niqmepa, the king of Alalaḫ, brought a case against Šunaššura, the king of Kizzuwatna, before Šaušštatar, king of Mittani, in regard to dispute over the city of Alawari (AT 14); Ḫattušili III, king of Ḫatti, gave an award in the dispute between Niqmepa, king of Ugarit, and the merchants of Ura (RS 17.130 = *PRU* IV, pp. 103–105); the royal divorce of Ammištamru II, king of Ugarit, and the daughter of Bentešina, king of Amurru, was arranged by Tudḫaliya IV, king of Ḫatti (RS 17.159 = *PRU* IV, p. 126f.), while the secondary issues relating to this divorce were discussed before Ini-Teššub, king of Carchemish, in his capacity as the viceroy of the Hittite suzerain over Syria (RS 17.396 = *PRU* IV, p. 127f.).

[247] In this instance, Niqmepa won the case, but the document does not provide any reasoning for this ruling.

[248] For such litigations within Hittite jurisdiction, see the cases brought before Ini-Teššub, king of Carchemish, the Hittite viceroy over Syria, e.g. RS 17.108, 17.110, 17.128, 17.226, 17.355 (*PRU* IV, pp. 165, 178, 179, 208, 209, respectively), or the case brought before Armaziti, son of the Hittite king, RS 17.314 (*PRU* IV, p. 189).

known. Thus we find in the treaty drawn up by Šuppiluliuma I to Šattiwaza of Mittani the following provision:[249]

> You (Šattiwaza) shall not again act independently, nor transgress your treaty, nor shall you seek further territories for yourselves. Prince Piyaššili (king of Carchemish) and Prince Šattiwaza—their territories [will be . . .] for one another. If a city of Prince Piyaššili writes secretly to Šattiwaza, then Šattiwaza must reveal its secret communication. He must seize its messenger and send him to Piyaššili, his brother(-in-law). Nor will Šattiwaza write in a furtive(?) manner to a city of Piyaššili. Piyaššily and Šattiwaza are bound to one another in brotherhood.
>
> If Šattiwaza summons Piyaššili to the city of Irrite or to Taite for consultation(?), Šattiwaza shall not plan any evil against Piyaššili, his brother, and he may not cause another man to undertake evil against Piyaššili. And the cities which Šattiwaza has given up to Piyaššili shall not plan any evil matter or maliciousness against Piyaššili. If Piyaššili summons Šattiwaza to Carchemish for consultation(?), Piyaššili shall not plan any evil matter or maliciousness against Šattiwaza. Whatever cities of Šattiwaza are situated on the banks of the Euphrates shall be retained, but he shall not seize another city on the bank of the Euphrates.

Similar provisions we find in the treaties drawn up by Muršili II to Targašnalli of Ḫapalla, to Kupanta-Kurunta of Mira-Kuwaliya, and to Manapa-Tarḫunta of the Land of the Šeḫa River,[250] as well as in the edict he issued to Abiradda of Berga,[251] and in the treaty Muwattalli II drew up for Alakšandu of Wiluša.[252]

Such a policy might have resulted in a network of treaties concluded between the various subordinated kings belonging to the same suzerain. Although we do not have so far a clear example of such a treaty,[253] we do have at least an example of a limited agreement pertaining to commercial life concluded between two city-states under Hittite suzerainty. The agreement, discovered in Ugarit and of which we have four parallel but not

---

[249] *CTH* 51.I; Beckman 1999, No. 6A: §11–12: A rev. 23–34. Beckman's translation adapted.

[250] *CTH* 67 (Beckman 1999, No. 10): §§8–10; *CTH* 68 (Beckman 1999, No. 11): §25, and *CTH* 69 (Beckman 1999, No. 12): §§7–12, respectively.

[251] *CTH* 63A (Beckman 1999, No. 30): §§7–9.

[252] *CTH* 76 (Beckman 1999, No. 13): §14, A iii 31–44.

[253] There are, however, two uncertain candidates for such a treaty, one pertaining to the Hittite suzerainty, the other to the Mittanian. One is the treaty between Aziru of Amurru with Niqmaddu II of Ugarit (RS 19.68 = *PRU* IV pp. 284–286), but it is uncertain whether it was concluded before or after both became subordinated to the Hittites. The other one is the treaty concluded between Niqmepa of Alalaḫ and IR.IM of Tunip (AT 2), for which see note 132 above.

identical documents,[254] was concluded between the city-states of Ugarit and Carchemish in the presence of Ini-Teššub, the king of Carchemish,[255] acting very likely in his capacity as the Hittite viceroy over the Hittite territories in northern Syria. Both cities were represented very likely by their elites.[256] RS 17.230 reads as follows:

> [1]Ini-Teššub, king of the land of Carchemish, [2]with the people of the land of Ugarit, [3]concluded this treaty. [4]If a man of Carchemish [5–6]is killed in the land of Ugarit, [7–8]If they (the people of Ugarit) catch the one who killed him, [9–12]he will pay three times the (value of the dead) person, as well as three times the (value of) his goods that were disappeared. [13–14]But if they do not find the one who killed him, they will pay three times (his value) as blood money recompense. [15–19]And for his goods that have disappeared, for all that disappeared they will pay (only) their capital value. [rev. 20–23]And if a man of the land of Ugarit is killed in the land of Carchemish, the recompense is the same.

The document is sealed in the center of its obverse with the seal of Ini-Teššub. Documents RS 17.146 and 18.115 are far more detailed, and explicitly provided for the case of merchants of the one city killed in the territory of the other.

Matters were more complicated when they concerned litigations, royal or private, against foreign individuals of countries not subordinated to the same suzerain. Two such cases are referred to and discussed, among other matters, in the above mentioned letter sent by the Hittite king Ḫattušili III to the Babylonian king Kadašman-Enlil II.[257] In the first case (rev. 14–25), the Babylonian king complained that some of his merchants were killed in the lands of Amurru and Ugarit, and in a third land whose name is damaged. These lands were subordinated to Ḫatti, and therefore within Hittite jurisdiction. In responding to this, Ḫattušili instructs the Babylonian king about the ordinary procedures as they are conducted in Ḫatti:

> If the (Hittite) King hears about it, [they pursue] that matter. They apprehend the murderer [and deliver him] to the relatives of the dead man, [but they allow] the murderer [to live. The place] in which the murder occurred is purified. If his relatives will not accept [the compensatory silver], they may make the murderer [their slave]. If a man who has committed an

---

254 RS 17.230, 17.146, 18.115, and the very broken fragment RS 18.19 (*PRU* IV, pp. 153–160).

255 See note 161 above.

256 For "The City" as a partner in treaties, see above in section 3.2.2 with note 162.

257 *CTH* 172: rev. 14–25, 26–33 = Beckman 1999, No. 23: §§10–11; Beckman's translation is adapted.

> offense against the King [escapes] to another land, killing him is not permitted. Ask, my brother, and they will tell you. [...] thus. Would those who do not kill a malefactor kill a merchant? [But in regard to] the Subarians, how should I know if they are killing people? Now [send] me the relatives of the dead merchants so that I can investigate their lawsuit.

Responding to the second allegation, the Hittite king wrote as follows (rev. 26–33):

> Concerning Bentešina (king of Amurru) of whom my brother wrote to me: "He continually curses my land"—when I asked Bentešina, he replied to me as follows: "The Babylonians owe me three talents of silver." Right now, a servant of Bentešina is on his way to you so that my brother can decide his lawsuit. And concerning the curses against the land of my brother, Bentešina swore an oath to my gods in the presence of Adad-šar-ilani, your messenger. If my brother does not believe this, let his servant who heard Bentešina when he continually cursed the land of my brother come here and oppose him in court. And I will put pressure on Bentešina. Bentešina is my subject (=subordinate king). If he has cursed my brother, has he not cursed me too?

The next two paragraphs (§§12–13: rev. 34–48) deal with a Babylonian complaint that a Babylonian physician, namely a highly valued expert, who had been sent to Ḫatti, died after he had been detained there in an infringement of the custom.[258] The Akkadian term employed to designate this infringement of the custom is *ul parṣu* "not (according to) custom." While the semantic range of the term *parṣu* is quite wide,[259] and is attested already in the third millennium, in the Late Bronze Age it was introduced into the realm of international relations and law to designate an accepted custom or rule that should not be transgressed.[260] The Hittite equivalent term to *ul parṣu* is *natta āra* "not correct", "not right", "not ethical".[261]

Returning to the above mentioned complaint of the Babylonian king, similar complaints regarding detention of physicians or offenses committed against foreign merchants and even diplomatic messengers, whether

---

258 See in §13 (rev. 44): "Detaining [a physician] is not right!"

259 According to the *CAD*, Vol. 12 (P), pp. 195ff., it has the following meanings: rite, ritual; temple office, prebend, income from a prebend; divine authority, power, office; symbol, insignia; authoritative decision, command, decree; custom, practice.

260 For recent discussion, see Artzi 2005: pp. 474–479.

261 For a recent study devoted to this Hittite term, see Cohen 2002; for its connection with the Akkadian *parṣu*, see there pp. 27–33, and for its employment in treaties and diplomatic correspondence, see pp. 97–130.

or not employing the above terms, are also found in other diplomatic letters exchanged between the royal courts of this age.[262] In one of these letters, the Amarna letter EA 8 sent by the Babylonian king Burra-Buriyaš to the Egyptian king, the Babylonian king complained about offenses committed against his merchants while they were in Canaan on their way to Egypt. There we find the following comment of the Babylonian king (lines 25–33):

> [25]Canaan is your country, and [its] kings [are your subordinates]. [26]In your country I was robbed. Interrogate [them and] [27]repay the money that they took away. [28]And the people who [killed] my servants—[29]put them to death and avenge their blood. [30]And if you would not kill these people, [31]they will return and, be it a caravan belonging to me [32]or your messengers, they will kill, and [33]messengers between us will be cut off.

This complaint, the same as the above quoted two passages from Ḫattušili III's letter to Kadašman-Enlil II, reflects the concept that the suzerain is responsible for all the offenses committed in the territories of his subordinated kings against people of an allied king.

The concept that a sovereign ruler is responsible for hostile actions carried out by people of his land also in other territory is echoed in EA 38, a letter sent by the king of Alašiya (= Cyprus, or part of it) to the king of Egypt, his 'brother'. The king of Alašiya rejects there the addressee's accusation that people of Alašiya took part in piratical raids carried out by men of Lukki on Egyptian territory.

An interesting case with a similar accusation, but where there was some uncertainty as to whose jurisdiction was the city from which the raids were carried out, is brought up in the letter KBo 1.14[263] sent by a Hittite king, evidently Ḫattušili III, to an Assyrian king. In the obverse, lines 6–18 we read:

> [6][...the city of] Turira keeps raiding my land. [7][From there—the land of Car]chemish, from here the land of... [8][they are raiding]. The king of the land Ḫanigalbat keeps writing to me [9][thus]: "[The city of Tu]rira is mine! from there I keep writing (to you)." [10](But) Turira is (either) mine or yours (=of the Assyrian king); [11]the affair of Turira is not the concern of the king of Ḫanigalbat. [12]Don't you know that when (the people of) Turira keep raiding the land [13]they take the booty into the city Turira?! [14](And that) my subjects who ran away, into Turira they go (for hiding)! [15]If Turira is yours, smash (it, but as to) my subjects who are staying in the city, [16]do not approach their

262 E.g., EA 7: 73–82; 8: 8–42; 35: 30–34.

263 Goetze 1940: pp. 26–31; Harrak 1987: pp. 68–75.

> property! If Turira is not yours, [17]write to me and I will smash it; (as to) your soldiers who are staying in the city I will not approach their possessions.

Turira, located in north Mesopotamia, not far from Carchemish, belonged to the land of Ḫanigalbat (previously Mittani), which three generations before came under Hittite suzerainty, but more recently was conquered by the Assyrians who stationed soldiers in Turira. The Hittite king actually ironically accused the Assyrian king for ignoring his responsibility to prevent the raids ("Don't you know...?"), as well as allowing runaway Hittites having refuge in Turira. The Hittite king also entirely dismissed the responsibility of the king of Ḫanigalbat in this affair and put it on his suzerain, while making it clear that in case the Assyrian king fails to solve the problem, he, the Hittite, would assume responsibility and attack Turira.

A more explicit complaint against an ally for having provided protection to someone who was continuously raiding the territory of the complainer is found in the so-called '*Tawagalawa letter*' (*CTH* 181), sent very likely by the Hittite king Ḫattušili III to a king of Aḫḫiyawa (Achaians of the Greeks). It concerns the hostilities carried out by a certain Piyamaradu, formerly a Hittite subject of high rank, who had become a freebooter and was carrying out raids on Hittite territory. There, in lines iii, 52–iv, 6, we find the following complaint:[264]

> Further, ... (Piyamaradu) is saying this: "I will go over into the land of Māsa (or) the land of Karkiya, but the civilian captives, my wife, children and the household I will leave here." So what does this mean? During the time when he leaves behind his wife, children and household in my brother's (= the king of Aḫḫiyawa's) land, your land is affording him protection. But he is continually raiding my land! And whenever I have prevented him in that, he comes back into your territory. Are you now, my brother, favourably disposed *to this conduct*?
>
> (If not,) now, my brother, write him at least this one thing: "If not, then either, arise and go forth into the land of Ḫatti, (since) your lord (=the Hittite king) has settle his account with you, (or) if not, (then) come into the land of Aḫḫiyawa, and in whatever place I settle you, you must remain there.... Arise ... and settle down in another place! So long you are at enmity with the king of Ḫatti, be at enmity from (some) other country! Don't be at enmity from my country! If your heart is in the land of Karkiya (or) the land of Maša, then go there!"

264 Edition: Sommer 1932: pp. 1–194. Translation adapted from Hoffner 2009: p. 310. For the background, see there pp. 296–301, as well as Bryce 1998: pp. 320–324.

6. Refugees and Extradition

The information we have about the issue of extradition from the Old Babylonian period is much expanded in the Late Bronze,[265] including many more examples of treaties including extradition provisions.

An example of a parity treaty devoted entirely to the extradition of fugitive slaves is the one concluded between Idrimi of Alalaḫ and Pilliya of Kizzuwatna (AT 3), quoted above in §3.2.1 of this chapter. More elaborated provisions related to fugitive slaves are found in the parity treaty of the next generation from Alalaḫ, between Niqmepa of Alalaḫ and IR.dIM of Tunip:[266]

> [22]If a fugitive slave, male or female, flees from my country to yours, [23]you must size him and return him. If anyone else seizes him [24]and delivers him to you, you [shall keep him] in your prison, [25]and when his owner arrives, you shall hand him over. [26]If the slave is not residing (there), you shall provide (the owner) an escort, and in whatever town he is residing [27]he (the owner) may seize him. (In any town where) he is not (found) residing, the mayor and five elders [28]shall be sworn in (by the owner): "If my slave stays among you, you must notify me." [29]If they do not agree to swear, but return the slave, [they go free]. [30]If they take the oath, and later he discovers his slave [among them], [31]they are thieves and their hands shall be cut off, [32](and) they will pay 6,000 (shekels of) copper to the palace.

This treaty also provides provisions regarding the emigration of individuals, voluntarily or forcibly, to the partner's country (lines 17–21):

> [17]If anyone of my country [enters your country], [18]if you hear of it you must [... and] inform me. [19]If he resides in your country, you must seize him and deliver him (to me).

> [20]If there are captives from my country who are sold in your country, [21]you must seize him together with the one who sells it, and deliver them to me.

In contrast to the cases of runaway slaves and of kidnapped, which do not required any further clarification, and in contrast to the case of people who emigrate in search of sustenance dealt with in lines 54–58 of the same treaty (see below), the reason behind the emigration of the individual referred to in lines 17–19 is not specified. Yet, in view of the fact

---

265 For more recent discussions, see Liverani 2001: pp. 66–70; Snell 2001: pp. 86–98; Altman 2002; Elgavish 2003.

266 AT 2: 22–32; for more recent translations, see Reiner 1969: p. 531f.; Dietrich and Loretz 1997; Hess 2000a: pp. 330–31.

that he was not granted with the right of sojourn, contrarily to the case of families seeking sustenance, we may understand the case as referring to one who have committed some crime.[267]

The parity treaty of the 15th century between a Hittite king whose name was not preserved and Paddatiššu of Kizzuwatna introduces yet a further question in this regard: what would be the rule in case the emigrante denies any involvement in crime?[268]

> If a subject of Paddatiššu plots against his lord and then enters Ḫatti, [and] Paddatiššu sends after the fugitive, saying as follows: "He revolted against me. I will have him returned!"—[If] the charge is true, the fugitives must be returned. But if the fugitive denies it, claiming: "I [myself] am not in revolt against him"—his word is false. Whatever trustworthy men of the land Kizzuwatna [the Great King (=the Hittite king)] may ask for an oath will swear an oath about this, and the fugitive must be returned.

The emigration of families, communities, clans and tribes to another country also might have caused much concern to their homeland. For in contrast to the situation in many developed industrial countries nowadays, where the continuous influx of foreign workers exerts an ever growing pressure upon the local resources, it seems that in many countries in the Ancient Near East, if not in all, there was a chronic shortage of manpower. In such a case, kings welcomed new immigrants who either voluntarily or through coercion entered their countries.[269] At the same time, these kings were reluctant to let their own population emigrate to other countries.[270]

---

[267] Erica Reiner (1969: p. 531) seems to reach a similar conclusion, since she restored (as a possible restoration) in line 17: "If someone from my land [*plots against me*]."

[268] *CTH* 26: §§1–2 (Edition: Mayer 1953: pp. 112–119. Recent translation: Beckman 1999, No. 1). These two paragraphs present a parallel stipulation in which only the names of the respective kings and their countries change places. §2, which is much better preserved, is quoted here (Beckman's translation).

[269] This is demonstrated in the first place by the wide employment of the practice of deportation of defeated communities to be settled in the victor's country, for which see above in this chapter under §2.3.2. The positive attitude—at least of the Hittites—toward new immigrants is best reflected in many Hittite subordination treaties which contain a stipulation to the effect that in case a community sets out and enters the land of the subordinate king, he must turn them over to the king of Ḫatti: *CTH* 49.I: F 1'–3'; 49.II: iv 1'–5' (Aziru); *CTH* 53: A iii 41–52 (Tette); *CTH* 62.II: A iii 12–22 (Duppi-Teššub); *CTH* 66: 61–69 (Niqmepa). The Hittite positive attitude toward a deported population is best reflected in the "*Instruction to the BĒL MADGALTI*": (A) KUB 13.2: iii 36–41; (B) KUB 31.84: iii 60–71 = von Schuler 1957: pp. 48–50. This governor (of the frontier district?) was instructed to take care of the deportees, to settle them, and to provide them with fields, seeds, cattle, sheep, etc.

[270] As far as it concerned Hittite policy, it may be seen in the provisions made in many Hittite subordination treaties stipulating that any fugitive coming from Ḫatti—be it either a Hittite citizen or a deportee who was brought to Ḫatti but managed to run away—who

Referring to the case of the emigration of tribes, clans, communities or families to another country in search of sustenance, the treaty concluded between Niqmepa, king of Alalaḫ and IR-ᵈIM, king of Tunip (AT No. 2), has the following provision (lines 54–58):[271]

> [If families] enter into your land to find subsistence,[272] (be aware) lest you should not guard them much the same as your land;[273] (be aware) lest, much the same as your land, you should not trust them. Whenever they want to [retur]n to my land you must gather them and return them to [my land], and one single family in your land you may not detain!

In spite of the somewhat fragmentary condition of this paragraph, its message is fairly clear: If a number of families emigrate on their own free will from their homeland to another country, their host cannot evade his responsibility to protect them, and must accept them with friendship. Above all, whenever they want to return to their homeland, the host cannot detain them and is required to enable them to return. The right of these families to free movement and protection was thus acknowledged here much the same as in the case of foreign merchants. An acknowledgement, in the realm of interstate relations, of the norm according to which a free person seeking refuge and sustenance was not subject to enslavement against his will, is already attested in the Old Babylonian treaty between the city-states of Šadlaš and Nērebtum of the 19th century.[274] In that treaty, and more explicitly in the treaty between Alalaḫ and Tunip, a clear distinction is drawn between the law of a runaway slave and the law

---

entered the subordinate country, should be extradited to the Hittite king. In some cases, the Hittites had granted the other party with the same right (Šunaššura—*CTH* 41.I: A ii, 11'–iii, 13), or at least promised him to return needed craftsmen who would run away from him (Targašnalli—*CTH* 67: obv. 39'–40'; Kupanta-Kurunta—*CTH* 68: E iv, 32'–41'; Alakšandu—*CTH* 76: A iii, 65–67). In the case of Ugarit, it was granted that the Hittites would return Ugaritic fugitives (RS 17.234 = *PRU* IV, p. 107f.), or that Niqmaddu would be entitled to keep any fugitive who would come to him from the neighboring countries (RS 17.369A = *PRU* IV, p. 52). In other cases, the Hittites stressed their rule that it is not permitted for the king of Ḫatti to return a fugitive who came to him: *CTH* 49.II: iv, 12"-14" (Aziru; restored); *CTH* 51.I: A rev. 9–19 (Šattiwaza); *CTH* 66: 73–78 (Niqmepa); *CTH* 67: obv. 36'–38' (Targašnalli); *CTH* 68: E iv, 41'–45' (Kupanta-Kurunta); *CTH* 76: A iii, 62–64 (Alakšandu). It may be noted, however, that the stated Hittite rule, that no foreign fugitive who fled to Ḫatti is to be returned, not necessarily and not in every case was derived from, or was a symptom of, a shortage of manpower. In many cases, it might have derived from political considerations.

271 The following discussion is based on my article, Altman 2002.

272 For *butalluṭu* see *CAD* Vol. 2 (B), p. 62b (mng. 11: "to be provided with food"); *AHw* p. 99b sub *balāṭu(m)* II Dt. ("Unterhalt, Versorgung empfangen").

273 I take *šumma la* as a strong asseveration.

274 Discussed in Chapter Three, pp. 67–69. For this norm in the realm of the Old Babylonian civil law, see Altman 2002: pp. 324–329.

of free families who seek temporary refuge in another country. Whereas in lines 22–23 of the Alalaḫ treaty quoted above, the parties agree to extradite fugitive slaves, this obligation is not at all stipulated regarding free families in lines 54–58. The only obligation of the host is to see to the well-being of these families, and to allow them to return to their homeland whenever they so desire. Admittedly, the very fact that the right of those families to return at will to their homeland had to be explicitly stipulated in a treaty may indicate that it had not yet become widely acknowledged, or that it was quite often ignored. Nevertheless, it does show that this norm was at least known in this part of the 'Fertile Crescent' already in the 15th century.

Another 15th century treaty referring to the law of families or communities crossing the border in order to find sustenance is the treaty drawn up by the Hittite king Tudḫaliya I/II to Šunaššura of Kizzuwatna, in whose prologue this issue occupied an important place.[275] Before discussing the relevant passage, some preceding clarification regarding this prologue is, however, needed. The matter that much concerned the Hittite drafters of the prologue was the fact that the land of Kizzuwatna, located in the Cilician plain, was previously subordinated under oath to the Hurrian king from whom it had defected to the Hittites. The Hittites, on their part, were bound to the Hurrians by a peace treaty, which meant that by taking control of Kizzuwatna as a vassal country they violated that treaty. This, in turn, rendered their new treaty with Šunaššura vulnerable to a claim on the part of Šunaššura that this treaty was illegal for it involved an offense against a third party.[276] The Hittite drafters of the present treaty with Šunaššura were faced thus with the need to render the defection of Kizzuwatna from the Hurrians as legitimate. To this end they built a sophisticated set of arguments, which apart from providing us the opportunity to get some insight into the drafters' legal conceptions, provide us with a rare example of how new norms of international laws might have been created. In the following, I will concentrate only on the arguments related to the issue of communities crossing the border in order to find sustenance.[277]

[275] *CTH* 41.I; recent translation Beckman 1999, No. 2.

[276] For the acknowledgment by the Hittites of the idea of illegality of treaty that involved an offense against a third party, see the discussion in Altman 2004a: pp. 191–198.

[277] For a detailed discussion of this prologue see Altman 2004a, Ch. XIII, and there, pp. 417–426 for discussing the issue of communities crossing the border.

In order to justify the defect of Kizzuwatna from the Hurrians, the Hittite drafters brought up an old episode of confrontation between the Hurrians and the Hittites about the control over the land of Išuwa (A i, 8–20, 25–32):[278]

> [8]When [...] the (people of) the land of Išuwa, "slaves" of the Sun, [9][star]ted hostility against the Sun, (I,) the Sun, went to fight with them. [10]I overpowered the land of Išuwa, but [the people of Išuwa] [11]fled before the Sun (and) descended to the Hurri land. I, the Sun, sent word [12]to the Hurrian (king): "Extradite my 'slaves'!" But the Hurrian sent word back [13]to the Sun as follows: "No!"
>
> ---
>
> [14]"Those communities had previously, in the days of my grandfather, come to the Hurri land, [15](and) had settled there, and, indeed, [16]they later went to the Ḫatti land as refugees. [17](But) now, certainly, the cattle [18]have chosen their stable; they definitely [19]have come to my land."
>
> ---
>
> [20]The Hurrian (king) did not extradite my 'slaves' to me, the Sun....
>
> ---
>
> [25–26]The Hurrian transgressed the oaths. (I,) the Sun, sent word to the Hurrian as follows: "If some land [27]would secede from you (and) to the land of Ḫatti [28]shift (its allegiance), how would such a case be (considered)?" The Hurrian [29]sent word to me, the Sun, as follows: "Exactly the same!"
>
> ---
>
> [30]Now the (people of the) country Kizzuwatna are Hittite cattle, [31](and) chose their stable. From the Hurrian [32]they separated (and) shifted (allegiance) to the Sun....

The precedent of the Išuwa affair, as posed here, is given in four paragraphs, each devoted to a different subject. Lines 14–19 present the Hurrian arguments, which were introduced here in order to constitute a precedent for the case of Kizzuwatna. According to the Hurrian arguments, the people of Išuwa were originally free people who chose to settle on Hurrian territory. Admittedly, they later entered Hittite territory, but they did so as "refugees" (LÚ.MEŠ *munnabtūti*) who had the right to return to their homeland, and their host was forbidden to enslave them; this, in accordance with the law of stray oxen who return to their stalls of their own accord.[279] Lines 8–13 present the historical background from the viewpoint of the Hittites. The Hittites, for their part, did not deny the

278 Translation follows Goetze 1940: pp. 36–39, with minor changes.

279 The main idea of the "stray oxen" model was expressed by the words "the cattle have chosen (literary: 'recognized') their stable" (lines 18–19, 31; cf. Isaiah 1: 3: "The ox knoweth his owner, and the ass his master's crib"). This was based on the ability of cattle to return

Hurrian claim that the people of Išuwa came to Ḫatti as "refugees", nor did they deny that refugees have the right to return to their homeland at will. What the Hittites did deny was that this right might be applied to the *people of Išuwa*. The Hittite argument is that although these people had entered Ḫatti as "refugees", because of their hostile acts against their Hittite host they had forfeited their right to this status, together with the right to return to their homeland. Their hostility brought about a Hittite military operation against them, with the result that their settlements were conquered and they were reduced to the status of "slaves", the property of the Hittite king. Their flight to the Hurrians was, therefore, a flight of "slaves", and the Hurrian king was obligated to return them by virtue of his treaty with Ḫatti. His failure to do so (line 20) constituted a violation of the Hittite-Hurrian treaty. Lines 20–24 present then the transgressions of the Hurrians against Ḫatti, which provide a pretext for the Hittite king to see himself discharged of his obligations toward the Hurrian king (lines 32–33; 35–37). Finally, lines 25–29 present what may be regarded as the most problematic argument: the claim that the Hurrian king had acknowledged in the past, in connection with the Išuwa episode, the principle that any vassal country (or rather any former *Hittite* vassal country) has the right to return to its former overlord.[280] By his words "exactly so!" the Hurrian king acknowledged the status of "refugees", which he had demanded for the people of Išuwa, as applicable to whatever (Hittite) vassal country defected to him. Thus, since Kizzuwatna previously belonged to Ḫatti (lines 5–6), its return to the Hittites only accorded with the principle acknowledged by the Hurrian king, and should not be considered as an offense against the Hurrians.[281]

The treaty from Alalaḫ (AT 2), and less patently the Šunaššura treaty, apart from pointing out the "right of return", implies that free refugees

---

by themselves to their stable, which, in turn, may have been used whenever the identity of the true owner of stray cattle was subject to dispute. Cf. Goetze 1940: p. 37, note 148.

[280] It should be noted that this by no means should be interpreted as asserting the privilege of self-determination. Such a right was unknown in the Ancient Near East, and acknowledgment of the right of a subordinate country to change its suzerain at will, would have put an end to the entire political system of subordinate countries, and would have rendered the loyalty oath worthless. One may, however, still understand it not as a sweeping right but rather as a special rule agreed by the Hurrians entitling the formerly Hittite subordinate countries, that are now or would be under Hurrian suzerainty, to return to Ḫatti.

[281] While I tried to summarize and simplified the main argumentation, it should be noted that this argumentation is much more complicated and involved many questions that could not be presented here. For a detailed discussion, see Altman 2004a: Ch. XIII.

who emigrate voluntarily also had the "right of sojourn". That is, that they are entitled to stay as long as they wish in their place of refuge and that it was up to them to decide when to return home.

A clear distinction in this regard between captives and free people who emigrate voluntarily seems to appear also in the above-mentioned "*Tawagalawa letter*" (*CTH* 181), sent very likely by the Hittite king Ḫattušili III to a king of Aḫḫiyawa. In a quite broken passage which concerns the status of a group of 7000 civilian deportees who seem to have been taken by force from a Hittite territory (iii, 7–17) the Hittite king suggested the following procedure to clarify their status:[282]

> My man will come. You, my brother, must put the leaders on trial?.... Let my (own) man also be present. And if... says: "*I crossed over*? as a fugitive", let him stay there. But if he says: "He forced me," then let him come back to me.

Notwithstanding the much-damaged condition of these lines, their message is still quite clear: while captives should be returned, those who of their free will crossed the border to another country may stay there.

This latter right, however, was not always accepted, and sovereign kings were apt to deny their citizens the right of travel to another country, particularly when it concerned entire communities. This may be inferred from the stipulations concerning transhumant population in the above-mentioned parity treaty concluded between Paddatiššu of Kizzuwatna, and a Hittite king. In lines 17'–20' of what has survived of this treaty we find the following:[283]

> [If the population of a settlement] of the Great King (=the Hittite king), including its women, its goods, and its large and small cattle, sets out and enters the land of Kizzuwatna, [Paddatiššu] must seize them and return them to the Great King. And if the population of a settlement of Paddatiššu, [including] its [women], its goods, and its large and small cattle, sets out and enters Ḫatti, [the Great King] must seize them and return them to Paddatiššu.

A similar provision appeared in all probability also in two other treaties concluded between Ḫatti and Kizzuwatna,[284] and much later in the treaty

[282] Hoffner 2009: p. 309 (§9).

[283] *CTH* 26 (Beckman 1999, No. 1).

[284] In the treaty concluded between Telipinu and Išputaḫšu of Kizzuwatna (KUB 31.82: 7'–8'), and in the treaty concluded between the Hittite king Taḫurwaili and Eḫeya of Kizzuwatna (170/u+: 5'–7'); for both see del Monte 1981: p. 211. The pertaining clause of both treaties has survived in very fragmentary condition.

between Ḫattušili III and Ramesses II.[285] It seems that in the case where an entire community crossed the border into another country, other considerations were brought into account, causing its king to deny it the right of traveling abroad. The reason behind such a denial was no doubt the reluctance of kings to lose a source of income taxes, at that time usually in the form of agricultural products, and a source of manpower for the army and for public works. But of no less importance was also the fact that, when it came to a population living in border districts, leaving their home and moving into an adjacent country made those districts vulnerable to incursions by hostile foreign forces.

It is because of these considerations that I would doubt whether the "right of return", acknowledged in the prologue of the Šunaššura treaty and in the treaty between Niqmepa of Alalaḫ and IR-^{d}IM of Tunip, was widely accepted as a right of the refugees themselves rather than that of their former king, who had great interest to have them return to his country.

Yet, not only in the case of communities but also in a case of individual refugees, if they were not subject to extradition agreements, could there have appeared a prohibition to admit them into the service of the host king? We have already noted a provision to this effect that appeared already in the treaty of the 23rd century concluded between Naram-Sin of Akkad and an Elamite king, and in the 19th century treaty between the city-states of Šadlaš and Nerebtum, discussed in the previous chapter,[286] where in lines 47–50 there is the provision that "A soldier of Sumunumḫim, Ammi-dušur shall not enlist; a soldier of Ammi-dušur, Sumunumḫim shall not enlist." A similar prohibition is found in the treaty concluded between Ḫattušili III and Ramesses II.[287] After stipulating the requirement to extradite noblemen who fled to the country of the other party, or communities who crossed the border into the other's country, the text goes on and stipulates that—

> *Akkadian Version* (*CTH* 91: obv. 46–48; cf. 52–53)
>
> [If] one man come <or> if two [men, who are not known (= not noblemen) come to Ramesses mai-Amon] in order to enter [his] service, then R[amsses

[285] Edel 1997: pp. 42–49 (§§11 and 13) for the relevant clauses. Cf. Kitchen 1996: p. 82f. (§§7–8) for the hieroglyphic version, and Beckman 1999: p. 98f. (§§ 12 and 14) for the Akkadian version.

[286] See above in Chapter Three, p. 69 with note 85.

[287] Edel 1997: pp. 42–49, §§12 and 14.

> mai-Amon shall seize them and deliver them in the hand of Ḫa]ttušili, King of Ḫatti.
>
> *Egyptian Version* (§12; cf. §14)
>
> If [one] man or two men, who are not known fl[ee from the land of Egypt] and come to the land of Ḫatti to become servants of the other (king), then they shall not be allowed to remain in the land of Ḫatti, they shall be brought (back) to Ramesses meri-Amon the Great King of Egypt.

The prohibition to allow such people to enter the service of an allied king no doubt was made in order to discourage defections of needed manpower to another country.

In the last mentioned treaty there is the following liberal far-reaching provision which prohibited the parties to severely punish the runaway who was handed over to them:[288]

> If a man flees from the land of Egypt—be it one, two or three—and they come to the Great Ruler of Ḫatti, the Great Ruler of Ḫatti shall seize them and have them brought back to Usimare Setepenre (=Ramesses II), the Great King of Egypt. But as for (any)one who shall be (so) brought to him, to Ramesses II Meriamon, the Great Ruler of Egypt, let not his offence be taken into account; let not his house, his wives (or) his children be destroyed; [let] him [not be killed], let not his eyes, ears, mouth or feet be harmed; and, on the whole, let no crime be held against him. Likewise, if (any)one flees from the Ḫatti-land... (*and so forth the reverse case*).

Some idea about how the extradition was carried out is provided by the following letter of the king of Beirut sent to the king of Ugarit:[289]

> Thus says the King of Beirut; to the King of Ugarit, my good brother, speak (as follows): May you be well! May the gods protect you! My brother, there is a citizen of Ašqalon in my city, in the territory of my port-commissioner; and he used to steal from the house estate of my port-commissioner and then he fled to Ugarit, and (subsequently) departed to Alašiya. But now he came back to your land! Now, my (accredited) official I am sending to you. And you, my brother, arrest that man and deliver in the hands of my official! Do not hold (him) back!

When the self-surrender of a high dignity person was on the agenda, the latter might have stipulated his assent by being accompanied by a high official. We read about such a case in the so-called "*Tawagalawa letter*"

---

[288] Edel 1997: pp. 54–61, §§17–18; Kitchen 1996: p. 85 (§9); Beckman 1999, No. 15: §§18–19. The stipulation of the hieroglyphic version, which was better preserved, is followed.

[289] First published by Arnaund and Salvini 2000. The revised translation adapted here follows that of P. Artzi and J. Klein in Artzi, Klein and Elgavish 2003: p. 24f.

(*CTH* 181), mentioned already above,[290] which was sent by a Hittite king (most likely Ḫattušili III) to a king of Aḫḫiyawa. According to the letter, when the Hittite king set out on his campaign to the Lukka lands harassed by Piyamaradu, he summoned the latter to surrender to him. About Piyamaradu's reaction we read in col. i, 6–15:[291]

> When I (=the Hittite king) reached the town Šallapa, he (Piyamaradu) sent a man to meet me (saying): "Take me as (your) vassal. Send the crown prince to me, that he may escort me to Your Majesty." So I sent to him the crown prince, (saying): "Go, stand him alongside yourself on the chariot and escort him here." But he (Piyamaradu) snubbed the crown prince, and said "no". Yet is not the crown prince the equivalent of the king? (The crown prince) held him by the hand, but he said "no" to him and demeaned him in the presence of the lands. And (as if that were not enough,) he said this in addition: "Give me kingship here on the spot. If you don't I will not come (to Ḫatti)."

Piyamaradu, fearing for his life, refused to surrender and, managing to escape, he found refuge in Aḫḫiyawan territory. The entire episode is retold in i, 66–ii, 8 with additional details. The crown prince was instructed as follows (ii, 5–8):

> "Go, assure him with an oath, take his hand (as a gesture of protection) and conduct him to me." And concerning the supposed plot to kill him because of which he was afraid, is murder a thing permitted in the land of Ḫatti? It most certainly is not!

Having failed to convince Piyamardu to surrender, the Hittite king still did not give up and extended a far-reaching offer to him (ii, 58–77):[292]

> I have just sent out Dabala-Tarḫunta, the charioteer. And (this) Dabala-Tarḫunta is not some men of low rank; from (my) youth as charioteer he has been mounting the chariot beside me. He used to mount the chariot alongside your brother Tawagalawa too. Have I not offered safe conduct to Piyamaradu? Now safe conduct (works) this way in Ḫatti: If they send… to someone, they may not harm him. But with regard to the safe conduct I transported this (message): "Come, make your case before me! Then I will put you on the road. And I will write to my brother (the king of Aḫḫiyawa), how I will put you on the road. If you are satisfied, let it be (so). But if you are not satisfied, then my man will escort you back into the land of

290 See note 264 and the accompanied text.

291 Following the translation of Hoffner 2009: p. 302 and the interpretation of Singer 1983: p. 211. See also Bryce 1998: pp. 320–324. According to the colophon at the end of the letter, what we have actually is only the third tablet of a much longer letter.

292 Translation follows Hoffner 2009: p. 302. Clarifications in brackets are mine.

> Aḫḫiyawa in the same manner as he came (here with you). Otherwise, let this charioteer remain in his (Piyamaradu's) place (=as hostage) while he (Piyamaradu) comes and while he comes back there." Who is this charioteer? Because he has (a wife) of the Queen's family—in the land of Ḫatti the family of the Queen is highly respected—is he not much more to me than just an in-law? But he shall remain in his (Piyamaradu's) while place while he comes (and) returns.

Finally, there is also a case of extracting and smuggling out a rebellious ruler wanted by his suzerain. The case is narrated in the Hittite text KUB 19.15+KBo 50.24, recently reconstructed and published by J.L. Miller.[293] In this text, the Hittite king Muršili II recounts the flight of his subordinate Tette, the rebellious ruler of Nuḫašše, to Egypt. Its obverse i, 5'–28' reads as follows:

> Then [...]became hostile$^{(pl.)}$ towards me, and Titti, [my servant] wrote [to] the ['ma]n'$^{?}$ of Egypt (saying): "[Send] troops and chariots, [and]...*shall*...me forth, and [I] will arise [and] come to the land of Egypt." Then the troops and chariots of the land of Eg[ypt] came, and Titti arose and went to the land of [Eg]ypt. When however, I wrote to 'Arma'a[294] (saying): "Since Tetti was m[y] servant, why then did you send your troops and chariots and [bring] him a[way]? Give my [serv]ant back to me!" ['Arma'a] did not give [him ba]ck [to me], nor did he [even wr]ite back to me. Then it came about that Zirtaya, [his] servant, wrote to me (saying): "Sen[d] troops and chariots and I will arise, and [come] to Ḫattuša." So I sent troops and chariots, and they brought Zirt[aya, his servant], to Ḫattuša. Then 'Arma'a w[rote] to me (saying): "Since [Z]irtaya is my servant, [giv]e hi[m back to me]!" But I wrote back to him (saying): "An[d you]? Wh[y] did you [not g]ive Tetti back to me?" Then 'Arma'a remain totally quiet [and] said [nothing] at all! [So] we were [not] on good terms with one another. We were [not] at all on [goo]d$^{?}$ terms.

These two cases ended with only a deterioration of the diplomatic relations between Ḫatti and Egypt. In other cases, when the wronged party considered his military forces as sufficient to punish the one who violated an extradition agreement, a refusal to comply with such an agreement would have constituted a *casus belli*.[295] In any case, the wronged king was entitled to have considered the treaty he had with the one who violated

---

[293] Miller 2007: p. 252f. The quoted lines were already previously treated by Stefanini 1962: pp. 11–19.

[294] Identified by Miller (pp. 253–256) with Haremhab in his role as viceroy and commander of Egypt's Asian territories.

[295] See the cases referred to above in notes 13, 15, 16 and 17 and the accompanied texts.

it as void, and himself as discharged of his obligations according to this treaty.[296]

7. Diplomatic Law

Much information about the regulations that controlled diplomatic relations in this period is provided by the relatively rich correspondence exchanged between the royal courts at this time.[297] This correspondence, added to the diplomatic letters of the previous period, has enriched our knowledge of how diplomatic relations were conducted in the Ancient Near East,[298] although many questions still remained open.

Diplomatic missions in this period consisted in most cases of only one senior messenger, who might have been assisted by a junior staff, and sometimes accompanied by an interpreter,[299] or by a scribe.[300] The senior messengers tended to be of aristocratic background, and although not professional diplomats, at least some of them are known to have served their country as diplomats for many years.[301] Moreover, some of them acquired a good reputation and were preferred and welcomed in foreign royal courts.[302] The messengers were provided with appropriate documents requesting that courtesies be extended to them. There were two categories of these documents: passports, which were to be presented to the rulers in the transit areas, and letters of accreditation that were intended for the ruler to whom the emissary was dispatched.[303] A good example of a passport from this period is EA 30, issued most likely by the king of Mittani:

---

296 As may be inferred from the prologue of the Šunaššura treaty discussed above in p. 157.

297 The main collections of translations are: Moran 1992; Edel 1994; Hagenbuchner 1989: pp. 240–416, and Hoffner 2009. For the international archives of Ugarit, including diplomatic letters, treaties, edicts and verdicts, see Nougayrol 1956; Nougayrol et al. 1968: pp. 65–131; Bordreuil (ed.) 1991.

298 In addition to the studies cited in Chapter Three, notes 132–133, see the following studies which concentrated on the Late Bronze Age documents: Cohen 1996a and 1996b; Cohen and Westbrook 2000; Westbrook 2000a and 2000b; Liverani 2001; B. Lafont 2001b; Bryce 2003.

299 See the Amarna letters EA 11: 5–6 and 21: 24–26.

300 EA 24: iv, 37.

301 For two such persons see Kitchen 1999: p. 138.

302 EA 11: 13–15; 21: 24–32; 24: ii, 57–58, 86; iv, 21–29, 53–56.

303 For which see D. Elgavish in Artzi, Klein and Elgavish 2003: pp. 30–34.

> To the kings of Canaan, subordinates of my brother (the king of Egypt), thus the (Mittanian) king: Now, I have sent Akiya, my messenger, to hasten to the king of Egypt, my brother. No one may hold him back. Bring him safely into Egypt and entrust (him) in the hand of the (border) fortress commander of Egypt. Let [him] go on hurriedly. And (regarding) his presents, he is to owe nothing.[304]

As for the letter of accreditation, there were two types of credentials: a separate document entirely devoted to the presentation of the emissary, and a combined letter devoted to some matter of concern, and an introduction of the agent sent to deal with that matter.[305]

The messenger also carried a tablet with a written message enclosed in a sealed envelope, ensuring thereby its authenticity. Upon arrival at his destination, the messenger was supposed to read out the letter to the addressee, and to be able to discuss and negotiate with him the issues on the agenda. The hosting king would expect the messenger to be honest, but there was always the concern that he might misrepresent the exact message of his king, or, when reporting to his king, the correct response of the host.[306] The customary rule that emissaries would be accompanied on their way back to their homeland by emissaries of the hosting king provided the latter with the possibility to verify the message received from the foreign emissaries by interrogating his own emissaries, and to verify that his own response would be delivered correctly.

The exchange of messengers was conducted according to a quite developed set of rules that regulated the proper attitude to foreign emissaries, including issues pertaining to hosting, accommodating and feeding the diplomatic delegation. However, the extent those rules were observed was

---

[304] In translating the problematic last sentence I followed Moran 1992: p. 100 with note 5. Oppenheim (1967: p. 134) suggested a different translation: "And nobody should for any reason lay hand on him."

[305] Ibid., p. 31f. For an example of a combined letter, see the letter of the king of Beirut quoted above on p. 160.

[306] Thus we find in the Šunaššura treaty (*CTH* 41 I: A iv 32–39; Beckman 1999, No. 2: §59) the following provision: "Furthermore: In regard to a tablet which I, My Majesty, send you, … and the words <of> the messenger, which he speaks orally in response to you—if the words of the messenger are in agreement with the words of the tablet, trust that messenger …, But if the words of the speech of the messenger are not in agreement with the words of the tablet, you … shall certainly not trust the messenger and shall certainly not take to heart the evil content of that report of his" (Beckman's translation). An interesting case of disagreement among the Hittite envoys sent by Ḫattušili III to Ramesses II, concerning the exact instructions the Hittite king gave them orally, is reported in two letters sent by Ramesses II to the Hittite king and separately to Puduḫepa, the Hittite queen: Edel 1994: I, Nos. 42–43 (pp. 100–109).

quite often depended on the nature of the relations between the kings involved.

The idea of diplomatic immunity, on the other hand, was at this age still quite undeveloped.[307] Senior messengers might have been detained by the recipient king even for several years,[308] while their current communication with their king was carried out by junior members of the delegation. Nevertheless we find in the diplomatic correspondence of the period such complaints as "to treat a messenger badly is against the acceptable custom" (KBo 7.11: obv. 6'), or "to kill a messenger is against the accepted custom" (KUB 3.61: rev. 2), or "to put fetters on the hands and feet of messengers is against the accepted custom", and "to detain messengers in their place (of service) is against the accepted custom" (KUB 3.81: 6' and 14').[309] One may see in these and similar complaints the embryonic germs of what have later grown as the doctrine of diplomatic immunity.

307 See more recently Elgavish 2000.

308 E.g., EA 3: 14; 7: 49–52; 28: 113; 36: 18; 38: 23–24.

309 Edel 1994: I, Nos. 37, 39 and 40 respectively. These quoted complaints were voiced by the Hittite king Ḫattušili III when he found that his messenger by the name of Zawa was arrested in Egypt by Ramesses II as a result of this messenger's misbehavior. For the background and the restorations of the relevant damaged lines, see Edel 1994: Vol. II (Kommentar), pp. 151–153, 157–159. For another instance of messengers who were arrested following some misbehavior, see EA 29: 173–179.

CHAPTER FIVE

THE NEAR EAST 1200–330 BCE

1. The Political Scene

The 12th century BCE, dubbed "the crisis years" and seen in terms of political and cultural history, may be considered as the major watershed in the history of the Ancient Near East.[1] The Hittite kingdom, having been attacked by the so-called "Sea-Peoples", entirely disappeared, taking with it its subordinated kingdoms such as Amurru, Ugarit, Alašiya (Cyprus) and others in northern Syria and Anatolia. The Egyptian Asian Empire also collapsed, and the Canaanite cities along the Mediterranean coast suffered various degrees of destruction. At the same time, the Israelites invaded Canaan, and new kingdoms were established by the Ammonites, Moabites, and Edomites in Transjordan. The Philistines occupied Philistia, the territory that was later named after them. The Arameans expanded from the Syro-Arabian desert westward into southern Syria, and northward into Upper Mesopotamia where they established new petty kingdoms. In south-central Anatolia, Cilicia, and northern Syria, new so-called "Neo-Hittite" states that seem to have been of a mixed ethnic origin were established. After the mid-eleventh century, Assyria and Babylonia began to undergo territorial retrocession under the pressure of invading Aramean tribes, which sometime later established many settlements in Babylonia. Finally, about the same time as the Aramean influx, Chaldian groups whose exact ethnic origin is not clear penetrated into Babylonia. In the wake of these events, the sources for the transitional period of the 12th–10th centuries became extremely scanty and the Near East entered a "Dark Age".[2]

When in the latter part of the tenth century the curtain started to rise again above the political stage of the Near East, we encounter the beginning of a process which transformed this stage from one dominated by

[1] See the various articles in Ward and Joukowsky 1992.

[2] For the transitional period of the 12th–10th centuries in the Levant see the articles in Gitin et al. 1998, and Oren 2000.

multi-powers to one dominated by only one single power.[3] It started with the Assyrian king Aššur-Dan II (934–912), who in reaction to the pressure exerted by the Aramean tribes, set out on a series of campaigns in an effort to recover the territories held by the Assyrians in Upper Mesopotamia under the Middle Assyrian Empire; an endeavor crowned with success by 745. At that time, the political scene of the Near East was still very much similar to that of the Late Bronze Age, dominated by some great powers and many smaller kingdoms and petty principalities. By 745, however, the scene dramatically changed when the Assyrian king Tiglath-pileser III (744–727) set out on a new series of campaigns that expanded Assyrian sovereignty far beyond the Euphrates, Assyria's traditional western frontier. Most of Syria and Lebanon were conquered then and annexed.[4] At the peak of Assyrian power in the late eighth and seventh centuries, the Neo-Assyrian Empire stretched from Anatolia to Egypt and from Cyprus to Iran. Following a massive deportation policy, Assyria became a multiracial and multi-ethnic state.[5]

With Aššurbanipal (668–627), the last great Assyrian king, Assyria seems to have reached its peak. But already during his reign it started to deteriorate and by 605 its empire was divided between Media and Babylonia. We know next to nothing about the Median Empire (615–550),[6] and as far as it concerns issues of international law, the information we have about the Neo-Babylonian Empire is also very meager. Indeed, with the establishment of the Neo-Babylonian kingdom (605–539)[7] there starts a rich flow of documentary sources, consisting of tens of thousands of texts. However, they all came from temple and private archives, and save for a few texts, we have no state archives from this period. And while we do have a large number of Neo-Babylonian royal inscriptions,[8] they mostly deal with building works in Babylonia and only few deal with

---

[3] For the most detailed review of the political changes and developments during the period from the tenth through the sixth centuries, namely from the rise of the Neo-Assyrian empire up to the end of the Neo-Babylonian empire (539), see *CAH*[2] Vol. III/1, Chs. 6–13, and Vol. III/2. A shorter, but still a detailed review is that of Kuhrt 1995, Vol. II.

[4] For the achievement of Tiglath-pileser III as the one who founded the Assyrian empire, see Garelli 1991.

[5] Postgate 1989.

[6] For what is known about the Medes, see Diakonoff 1985. For more recent discussion about the history and nature of this empire, see the collection of papers edited by Lanfranchi et al. 2003, particularly the articles of M. Liverani (pp. 1–12), M. Jursa (169–179), and R. Rollinger (289–319).

[7] For its political history, see *CAH*[2] Vol. III/2, Ch. 27, and Kuhrt 1995: II, pp. 589–622.

[8] Langdon 1912; Berger 1973.

foreign affairs. The Median and the Babylonian kingdoms were replaced by the Achaemenid empire whose formation started around 550 with the conquests by Cyrus II (the Great; 559–530) and Cambyses II (530–522). It lasted until it was conquered by Alexander (the Great) between 334 and 323. However, despite its relatively long duration and the largest territory of any Ancient Near Eastern empire—stretching from the Hellespont to north India, including Egypt most of this period and extending into central Asia—we hardly have any substantial information regarding international law.[9] One possible explanation for this is the fact that it had no rival that could challenge its power.

So, for the time being, the main contribution we have to the issue of international law during that period comes from Assyrian sources. This contribution is supplemented to a certain extent by the Bible. Yet, biblical law was limited to certain aspects of the rules of war and the prerogatives of the king, while some other related matters can only be deduced from incidents recorded in the historical or prophetic writings.[10]

2. War

The royal inscriptions of the Assyrians[11] and to some extent the Bible are our main sources of information about the rules of war from this period.

2.1. *Opening War*

2.1.1. *Declaration of War*

As in the case of the previous periods so also for the first millennium, available references to a declaration of war preceding the launch of a military attack are very rare, to say nothing of real messages of such a declaration actually sent to an adversary king. What we do have are only few references to such a declaration in royal inscriptions or other documents, or in the Bible. One such reference is found in Sargon II's "*Letter to the Gods*", which is addressed to the god Aššur, to the gods of destiny who abide in

---

[9] For a review of the available sources, see Kuhrt 1995: II, pp. 647–652, and pp. 652–701 for the history and organization of this empire. More detailed discussions are found in *CAH*² Vol. IV, pp. 1–286; Gershevitch 1985; Cook 1983; Dandamaev 1989; Dandamaev and Lukonin 1989; Briant 2002.

[10] For the contribution of the Bible to the issues under discussion, see Rosenne 1993.

[11] For these, see *ARAB* I (§§216ff.) and II; RIMA 2–3; Bauer 1933; Borger *Ash.* and *BIWA*; Frame 1995: pp. 133–34, 143–154, 160, 163–268; Fuchs 1994 and 1998; Lie 1929; Luckenbill 1924; Piepkorn 1933; Tadmor 1994; Streck 1916.

the city of Aššur, and to the city of Aššur and its people at the end of his eighth campaign (714).[12] In line 111 we read that Urša, the king of Urarṭu, after having drawn up his battle line, sent a messenger to Sargon telling him "about (his) preparations for the approaching battle."[13]

A detail description of an exchange of messages prior to launching a retaliation campaign is found in Esarḫaddon's so-called *"Letter to the God Aššur"*, in which the Assyrian king provides the god with a detailed account about his campaign against the land of Šubria on the shores of Lake Van.[14] The account starts with the enumeration of the repeated Assyrian demands sent by Esarḫaddon to the ruler of Šubria to surrender Assyrian subjects who had fled to Šubria in seeking refuge, and ends with an Assyrian refusal to accept the latter's messages of repentance for having repeatedly refused to comply. In this case, it may be noted, the final Assyrian refusal did not include a reference to an explicit declaration of war, very likely because Šubria was regarded then as a client state bound to the Assyrian king by a subordination treaty,[15] and the text already provided the needed justification for a retaliatory act. We may assume that while such a justification was mandatory in any case, a formal declaration of war was needed only between independent rulers.

In the *"Annals"* of Aššurbanipal there is a reference to a written declaration of war sent by him to Indabibi, king of Elam, by the hand of the latter's messenger.[16] It was sent in the wake of Indabibi's refusal to surrender

---

[12] Thureau-Dangin 1912. English translation: *ARAB* II, pp. 73–99. For this genre of texts see Borger 1957–1971: p. 575f.; Pongratz-Leisten 1999: pp. 210–227. For discussion, see Oppenheim 1960.

[13] According to the interpretation of Oppenheim (1960: p. 139), this bit of ethnographic information—"a chivalrous custom indicates a ceremonial and formalized attitude toward warfare that was quite alien to Assyrian military practices in which the tactics of the raider were clearly preferred"—was intended "as a foil for the subsequent long winded self-presentation of Sargon. The writer may have wanted to contrast the naïve pride, if not arrogance, of the Urarṭean king with the elaborate and wordy piety of Sargon." Still we may regard it as authentic information, as Oppenheim himself seems to have regarded it.

[14] Borger, Ash.: pp. 102–109 (§68): Gbr. I–Gbr. II, i, 35. For a discussion of this letter, see Oppenheim 1979: pp. 125ff., and more recently Leichty 1991. For the historical background, see A.K. Grayson, in *CAH*² III/2, p. 129f.

[15] The small land of Šubria, having been located between the kingdoms of Assyria and Urarṭu, fulfilled the role of a buffer state between the two rival kingdoms. But in the wake of the decline of Urarṭu in the latter half of the reign of the Assyrian king Sargon II, Šubria was forced to yield to Assyrian pressure. For a recent review of the relations between Šubria and Assyria, see Parker 2001: pp. 230–246.

[16] *ARAB* II, §878; Bauer 1933, Vol. II, p. 17: ix, 73–82. For reading his name as Indabibi, rather than Indabigash, see Brinkman 1984: p. 101, note 506. Note that in a previous letter sent to Indabibi (*ABL* 1151), Aššurbanipal addressed him as his "brother" (Waterman

Assyrian subjects, a fact suggesting that this declaration was preceded by an Assyrian demand to return those subjects:

> Since you did not send to me those people, (I) declare (as follows): I shall come and your cities I shall destroy, (and) [the people] of the cities of Susa, Madaktu (and) Ḫidalu I shall take as captives. From your throne I shall remove you, and another (person) I [shall install] on your throne. [The fa]-te which I made befall Teumman I shall make happen to you.

That Aššurbanipal indeed considered sending a declaration of war in advance of starting hostilities as obligatory, and what is of no lesser importance that such a declaration should be based on a justifiable case, are reflected by his indignation over a surprise attack by Urtaku, the Elamite king:[17]

> On my sixth campaign I marched against Urtaku, king of Elam, who was not mindful of the favors of the father that begat me, and did not maintain friendly relations. When hard times arose in Elam and there was a famine, I sent him grain to keep his people alive, grasped his hand. Those of his people who had fled before the hard times and settled in Assyria until rain fell in his land and there was a harvest—those people, who had kept themselves alive in my land, I sent back to him. The Elamite, an attack by whom I had never considered with my heart, of whose enmity I had not even thought,... Urtaku, with whom I was not at enmity, mustered his army, rushed the war into the land of Karduniash.

One more reference to a declaration of war is included in a Late Babylonian document, now in the British Museum, BM 55467, which seems to be a unique document.[18] It is a copy made in the Achaemenid or Seleucid period of a Babylonian document, probably dating to the first part of Nabopolassar's reign (626–605).[19] It opens by enumerating Assyrian crimes made against Babylon by Sennacherib (704–681). These crimes provided the justification for the author's declaration of his intention to avenge Babylon (rev. 3) and destroy Nineveh (rev. 4–8). According to the modern editor of the text, the elaborate literary style and language of the text, however, leads one to consider it as part of a ceremony performed

1931: Vol. II, p. 301f.), a fact attesting the independence and legally equal standing of this Elamite king.

[17] Streck 1916, Vol. II, p. 104/105: iv, 15–32; Piepkorn 1933, pp. 56–59: Edition B, iv, 18–34, whose translation is adapted here.

[18] Gerardi 1986. The name of the author of the text was not preserved, nor the name of the addressee.

[19] Ibid. p. 31 with note 10, and p. 37f.

in Babylon before the army was dispatched, and as a propaganda device to secure the support of allies and other Babylonian cities in Babylon's struggle with Assyria.[20] Whether or not that was indeed the purpose of the text, it nevertheless does reflect, if not necessarily the need for sending a declaration of war to the adversary, at least the need for having a justified case for launching an attack.

An example of sending an adversary king a summons to battle, which is a kind of declaration of war, is found in the Bible, in II Kings, 14:8–11 (II Chronicles 25:18–21):

> Then Amaziah sent envoys to King Jehoash son of Jehoahaz son of Jehu of Israel, with this message: "Come, let us confront each other." King Jehoash of Israel sent back this message to King Amaziah of Judah: "... Because you have defeated Edom, you have become arrogant. Stay home and enjoy your glory, rather than provoke disaster and fall, dragging Judah down with you." But Amaziah paid no heed; so King Jehoash of Israel advanced, and he and King Amaziah of Judah confronted each other at Beth-Shemesh in Judah.

It was suggested that the biblical legal duty to make a call for peace before launching an attack on a foreign city (Deuteronomy 20:10) is "an early instance of a legal duty of making a declaration of war."[21] As a matter of fact, such a practice, which was actually a call to submit, is known to have been followed also by the Assyrians (see e.g. II Kings 18:1–37) and by other nations (e.g. Judges 11:4–28; I Samuel 11:1–2). But it was motivated by the drive to save time, resources and lives of the attackers rather than from humane feelings. The biblical precept in Deuteronomy 20:10 takes this practice one step further by rendering it as a legal obligatory duty, which should be regarded as a forerunner of the modern laws of human rights.[22]

2.1.2. *Appeal to the Gods and the Justification for the War*

Just as for the Old Babylonian period and the Late Bronze Age, also for the period under discussion here, before setting out on a military campaign kings were required to get divine authorization. Thus, e.g., we read in one of Tiglath-pileser I's royal inscriptions (1114–1076) as follows:

[20] Ibid. p. 33f.

[21] Rosenne 1993: p. 535, note 53.

[22] Since the Bible distinguishes between a compulsory war, which is a religious duty (*mitzvah*), and an optional war (*reshut*), there is a question whether this precept applied only to the optional war or to both. For contradictory opinions, see Rosenne, op. cit. p. 535f. with note 53.

> At that time, with the exalted might of the god Aššur, my lord, with the firm approval of the god Šamaš, the warrior, with the support of the great gods with which I have ruled properly in the four quarters and have no rival in battle nor equal in conflict, at the command of the god Aššur, (my) lord, I marched to the lands Nairi whose distant kings, on the shore of the Upper Sea in the west, had not known submission.[23]

We have a prayer addressed to the god to grant permission and extend help in the above-mentioned Sargon II's "*Letter to the Gods*".[24] In this letter, which provides a detailed account of his achievements in his eighth campaign, we find among other things a description of his treatment of Ursâ, the king of Urarṭu, preceded by quite a lengthy accusation against that ruler (lines 92–95):

> Ursâ, the Urarṭian, who does not respect (*lit.* guard) the word of (the gods) Aššur and Marduk, who does not fear the curse of the lord of lords,—a mountaineer, of murderous seed, who was without judgment, whose speech was evil, whose lips kept bawling indecencies, who had no respect for the honored name of (the god) Šamaš, supreme judge of the gods, and who was forever, without let-up, overstepping his bounds: after (all) his earlier sins, he committed the grievous offense of destroying this land and overwhelming its people.

Then, after detailing his accusation against Ursâ, we have in lines 123–126 the following account:

> Because I had never yet come near Ursâ, the Urarṭian, and the border of his wide land, nor poured out the blood of his warriors on the (battle-)field, I lifted my hands, praying that I might bring about his defeat in battle, turn his insolent words against himself, and make him bear his sin. The god Aššur, my lord, heard my words righteous (indignation), they pleased him and he inclined to hear my just prayer. He granted me my request. He sent at my side his terrible weapons, which in their going forth... despoil the rebellious.

More direct examples of appeals to the gods to obtain permission to launch an attack are found in the corpus of queries addressed by Assyrian kings to Šamaš, the Sungod.[25] Thus, among the queries addressed by Esarḫaddon (680–669), we find the following query:[26]

---

23 RIMA 2, p. 20f. (A.0.87.1): iv 43–51.

24 Thureau-Dangin 1912; for the English translation of the following quotations, see *ARAB* II, pp. 79 (first part of §152) and 81 (end of §153, beginning of §154).

25 Starr 1990. The queries are addressed to the god Šamaš as the patron of divination ("lord of the [oracular] verdict"; ibid. p. lxx, note 61).

26 Ibid. No. 28 (p. 32): 1–8.

> Šamaš, great god, give me a firm positive answer to what I am asking you! … (Should) Esarḫaddon, king of Assyria, who is now intent on sending men, horses and troops, as he wishes, to (the city and territory of) Siriš, (and) whom your great divinity knows, in accordance with the command of your great divinity, Šamaš, great lord, (and) your favorable decisions, should the subject of this query, Esarḫaddon, king of Assyria, strive and plan? Should he send men, horses and troops, as he wishes, to Siriš? Is it pleasing to your great divinity?

A similar appeal is found among the queries addressed by Assurbanipal, king of Assyria (668–627):[27]

> Šamaš, great lord, give me a (firm) positive answer to what I am asking you! Should Nabû-šarru-uṣur, chief eunuch, and the men, horses, and army [of] Assurbanipal, king of Assyria, which are at [his disposal, go to recover the fort]resses of Assyria which the Manneans conq[uered? If he go]es, [will he], be it through friendliness and peaceful nego[tiations, or by waging war, or by [whatever tr]icks, [recover] these fortresses? … Is it decreed and confirmed in a favorable case, by the command [of your great divinity, Šamaš, great lord]?[28]

As a reflection of such appeals to the gods and their response, we find in the Neo-Assyrian royal inscriptions, almost routinely, the statements that the campaign was carried out under the command of the god. Thus, e.g., Tiglath-pileser I claims that:

> i, 46The god Aššur (and) the great gods … 48–49commanded me to extend the border of their land. Their mighty weapons, 50–51deluge in battle, they placed in my hands. 51–54I gained control over lands, mountains, towns, and princes who were hostile to the god Aššur and I subdued their districts. … 59–61I added territory to Assyria (and) people to its population. I extended the border of my land and ruled over all their lands.[29]

While we hardly find justification of the campaigns in the Neo-Assyrian queries to the gods,[30] we do find it *post factum* in the royal inscriptions and in such documents as the "*Letters to the Gods*". According to B. Oded

---

27 Ibid. No. 267 (p. 244f.): obverse, 1–9; restoration of the damaged lines is based on the reverse, 7–11, which repeat the question, and on other similar queries.

28 For further similar queries addressed to the god asking his approval to set out on a campaign, see Starr, op. cit. Nos. 7, 8, 30, 31, 34, 60, 62, 63, 78–82, 84, 94, 96, 101, 105, 108, 110, 270–272.

29 RIMA 2, p. 13 (A.0.87.1): i 46–61.

30 In few of the queries mentioned above in note 28 there is, however, a very brief note to the fact that the planned campaign is intended to recover an Assyrian fortress or territory captured by the enemy, or as a response to his aggressive movements: see Nos. 30, 31, 78, 267.

who studied in depth these justifications,[31] the Assyrian royal inscriptions present the following twelve different pretexts in order to provide a legitimate *casus belli*: The outset of the campaign was (1) "by the command of the god"; (2) to punish evildoers; (3) a response to hostilities; (4) to protect a protégé and aid allies; (5) against usurpers; (6) to punish violators of an oath of loyalty; (7) to quell rebellion; (8) to enforce order and peace; (9) to punish those who sin against the gods; (10) to avenge and exact retribution for killing an ally or loyal dependent of Assyria, or as a punishment for treasonable behavior, disloyalty and ingratitude; (11) to demonstrate force and glory; (12) as an achievement of the Assyrian king's mission to unify the world under his dominion. Thus, according to Oded, "by stating the grounds for war with marked religious overtones the Assyrians demonstrate that they possessed the notion of *causa iusta* and that they were sensitive to the religious and moral aspect of warfare."[32]

Yet, we do not find here any appeal to a divine judgment, as we have encountered in the Middle Assyrian epic of Tukulti-Ninurta I.[33] This, and the fact that most of the available queries addressed to the god Šamaš lack any of the above claims, make one suspect whether we have here a real motivation to justify the war. In fact, many of the above pretexts can be taken as a mere political propaganda aimed at the gods—to whom these inscriptions were addressed in the first place—presenting their human agent as a capable war-leader, who on the one hand effectively protects their domain, and on the other hand expands it.[34] These inscriptions portray the Assyrian king as an ideal king, as he wishes to appear in the eyes of gods and men,[35] and the reasons presented for launching a campaign were aimed at serving this image. They by no means can be taken to reflect a common notion of *causa iusta* shared by all the peoples of the Near East in that period. They rather reflect an attitude typical for a state, which claimed world domination[36] with hardly any sensitivity to the common concepts of international law, nor to the enshrined rights of other peoples.

The claim that the war was made "by the command of the god", which render the war a "divine war" (conventionally called "holy war"), was not limited, however, to the Assyrians. While the many expressions of "divine

---

[31] Oded 1992.
[32] Ibid. p. 178f.
[33] Above, p. 96.
[34] Cf. Oded 1992: pp. 181–190 and the literature cited there.
[35] Ibid. pp. 181–184.
[36] For this claim, see ibid. pp. 163–176.

war" in the Old Testament are better known,[37] it may in fact be found all over the Near East during this period. Thus, e.g., we find in Judges 4: 6–7 the following message of the prophetess Deborah:

> She summoned Barak son of Abinoam of Kedesh in Naphtali, and said to him, "The Lord, the God of Israel, has commanded: Go, march up to Mount Tabor, and take with you ten thousand men of Naphtali and Zebulun, And I will draw Sisera, Jabin's army commander, with his chariots and his troops, toward you up to the Wadi Kishon; and I will deliver him into your hands."

A similar claim is found in the inscription of Mesha, king of Moab (lines 14–16):[38]

> And Kemosh said to me: "Go, take Nebo from Israel!" And I went in the night, and I fought against it from the break of dawn until noon, and I took it, and I killed [its] whole population.

It may be noted that earlier in this inscription, lines 4–13, the text gives an historical background to the war of Mesha against Israel who for many years oppressed Moab. Yet, also in this case, we do not necessarily have to take these lines as a justification for Mesha's actions; they were rather meant to glorify his achievements. Nor should the reference to Kemosh's order (line 14) be taken as a justification or pretext for conquering Nebo. Had it been intended to serve as a justification, we would have expected it to be placed earlier in the text, in order also to justify his earlier military acts. It seems that as far as it concerned political propaganda, addressed either to the gods or to the people, what was important to be presented during this period was not a justification of military acts but rather the close relations between the king and the gods, as well as showing the king as the one who fulfills their command. It may be noted that we also do not find in the Bible any justification for conquering Canaan, save for the claim that God had promised this land to the Children of Israel. And also in this case, this claim does not seem to serve any kind of justification but rather to show that God realized his old promise.

Indeed, this does not mean that the need to justify military acts was entirely ignored during this period; we occasionally do find here and there such justifications. But I cannot avoid the feeling that we encounter in this period some regression from the idea of a world controlled by divine justice through divine judgment.

---

37 See e.g., von Rad 1958; Miller 1973; Lind 1980; Kang 1989.

38 K.A.D. Smelik's translation in Hallo and Jounger 2000: p. 137f.

2.2. *During the War*

The cruelty with which the Assyrians treated at least some of their enemies is well known. One of the most horrible descriptions is found in the inscriptions of Aššurnaṣirpal II (883–859):[39]

> I crossed over to Mount Kašiiari (and) approached the city Kinabu, the fortified city of Ḫulāiia. With the mass of my troops (and) my fierce battle I besieged (and) conquered the city. I felled with the sword 800 of their combat troops, I burnt 3,000 captives from them. I did not leave one of them alive as a hostage.... I made a pile of their corpses. I burnt their adolescent boys (and) girls. I flayed Ḫulāiia their city ruler (and) draped his skin over the wall of the city Damdammusa. I razed, destroyed (and) burnt the city. (Col. i, 106–110).
>
> I approached the city Tēla ... I besieged (and) conquered the city. I felled 3,000 of their fighting men with the sword.... I burnt many captive from them. I captured many troops alive: from some I cut off their arms (and) hands; from others I cut off their noses, ears, (and) extremities. I gouged out the eyes of many troops. I made one file of the living (and) one of heads. I hung their heads on trees around the city. I burnt their adolescent boys (and) girls. I razed, destroyed, burnt, (and) consumed the city. (i, 113–ii, 1).
>
> (I) approached the city Ammali ... In a clash of arms I besieged the city (and) conquered (it). I felled with the sword 800 of their combat troops. With their corpses I filled the streets of their city (and) with their blood I dyed their houses red. (ii, 54–56).

And so on. Yet it was argued that

> The alleged cruelty of Assyrians is a modern myth exaggerated beyond all proportion. It is true that Assyrians, like their contemporaries and successors, did commit terrible atrocities in war and that they did cause civilian populations considerable suffering both during and after war. However, such atrocities were not inflicted summarily but as just punishments for perjury prescribed in the curse sections of broken treaties.[40]

Similar assertions regarding this behavior, which was designated as "calculated frightfulness",[41] were voiced by various scholars.[42] It was argued that such horrible measures were applied only in cases where the enemy resisted peaceful overtures or when one or more groups of cities were singled out for a major onslaught. This practice proved to be extremely effective, since once the surrounding peoples heard of these acts they sur-

---

[39] RIMA 2, p. 201 (A.0.101.1).

[40] Parpola 2003: p. 1060f.

[41] Olmstead 1923: p. 81.

[42] See e.g., Olmstead, op. cit. pp. vii–viii; W. von Soden 1963: pp. 131–2.

rendered to the Assyrian army without further resistance. Thus, in practice only certain pockets of resistance were subjected to this treatment.[43]

However, even if we were to agree with that opinion, and would have agreed as well that also other contemporary peoples might have committed terrible atrocities in war,[44] still, it is remarkable that we do not find them boasting of, nor even admitting it in their royal inscriptions. Moreover, it may be noted that the passages quoted above were taken from an inscription engraved on huge stone reliefs, which lined the walls and floors of the Ninurta temple at Calah,[45] to which no ordinary Assyrian citizen, let alone foreigner had access. The detailing of the atrocities perpetrated during battle was, therefore, not addressed to diplomatic emissaries of neighboring independent countries, or to the subjugated people under Assyrian rule, but primarily to the Assyrian gods; in this specific case, to god Ninurta, to whom the inscription is explicitly addressed (i, 1–9). Thus, in contrast to the horrible things done on battlefields, the above detailing of atrocities could not have been intended to serve a "calculated frightfulness". In this case, the boasting of the king of such actions was rather aimed to gain him prestige in the eyes of the gods. This boasting is what makes the Assyrians appear so cruel to modern man. On the other hand, the fact that we do not find such a boasting by other contemporary nations[46] suggests that, while atrocities might have been done everywhere in the Ancient Near East, they were condemned and denounced.

Turning to the Israelite treatment of defeated populations in the Bible, according to Deuteronomy 20:10–18 there is a distinction between a 'compulsory war' defined as a religious duty that was launched according to the command of God against the seven nations who occupied the land of Canaan, and an 'optional war', launched against peoples outside of the Land of Canaan. In a compulsory war, the command was to kill the entire population (vers. 16–18); while in an optional war, the precept is to spare the women and children (14). Other related biblical rules concern marriage with a female captive of war (ibid. 21:10–14) and the prohibition against destruction of fruit trees (20:19).[47]

---

43 A.K. Grayson in *CAH*² III/2, p. 221.

44 See e.g. Judges 1,7; II Samuel 8,2; I Kings 11:15–16.

45 A.K. Grayson in RIMA 2, p. 191.

46 By "contemporaries" I mean also those of the second millennium.

47 For more recent discussion with references to previous literature, see Wright 2008.

Regarding the fate of the defeated soldiers killed in battle, while the practice to grant them a burial is known from earlier periods,[48] it is not attested after the Old Babylonian period. However, some biblical references suggest that the practice was still known at least by the Israelites.[49] According to Joshua 10:26–27, after the kings of Jerusalem, Hebron, Jarmuth, Lachish, and Eglon were killed and hanged on trees, at the end of the day Joshua commanded that they be taken down and be buried in a cave (cf. Deuteronomy 21:22–23). According to I Kings 11:15, Joab went up to Edom "to bury the slain". In Ezekiel 39:11–13, Ezekiel prophesies against Gog that Israel would bury him and his entire multitude. Finally, in Psalms 79:2–3 the author complains bitterly against the enemies for having given the dead bodies of the people of Israel to the fowls of heaven and to the beasts of the earth, with none to bury them.

2.3. *After the War*

2.3.1. *The Neo-Assyrian Treatment of Subjugated Countries*[50]

The Assyrians employed two forms of control over lands they subjugated: (1) a client-states ("vassal") system[51] according to which the native dynasties were left on their thrones after having taken an oath over a subordination treaty that was drawn up by the Assyrian king; (2) a provincial system whereby the subjugated territory was annexed and turned into a province, governed by Assyrian officials.[52] In general, it seems that the Assyrians preferred the client system as long as the subordinated country remained loyal, and only when and where that system failed was annexation adopted.[53] While one might interpret such a policy as adherence to some international law, it would seem rather to have been derived from an economic consideration. The client system would avoid large military and administrative expenditures with regard to the maintenance of a province; particularly if the territory concerned was located far from the Assyrian homeland.

---

[48] See in Chapter One, p. 19; Chapter Two, p. 33 with notes 56 and 57; Chapter Three, p. 64 with note 66.

[49] I owe the following references to Spigel 1990: p. 254f.

[50] For a recent review, see Grayson 1995.

[51] I hereby follow Postgate 1992: p. 252, in replacing the conventional ill term 'vassal' by 'client'.

[52] For these two systems, see Pečírková 1977 and 1987; Eph'al 1979; SAA 5: pp. xxi–xxx; Yamada 2000: pp. 300–308. For mixed, transitional cases attested mainly in the ninth century, see Postgate 1992: p. 256f.

[53] Cf. Grayson 1995: p. 964.

2.3.1.1. *Client States*

Our information regarding the client system is unfortunately quite limited. This is due to the fact that only two or three severely damaged Neo-Assyrian client treaties with large lacunae are available.[54] But it is also due to the fact that Assyrian royal inscriptions when referring to reducing a subjugated country to client status, except for the tribute obligation, do not detail all its obligations. The subordinate king was bound to his suzerain through a subordination treaty reinforced by oaths and curses. The main obligations imposed on the client king, as far as we can infer from the available documentation, may be summarized as follows: (1) to protect the life of the Assyrian king, his sons and his magnates;[55] (2) to go forth with his army to accompany the Assyrian king whenever the latter goes to war;[56] (3) to report annually to the Assyrian king in order to pay him homage and to bring his annual tribute (*madattu*) and gift (*nāmurtu*; Babylonian *tāmartu*);[57] this latter obligation could, however, be fulfilled

---

[54] For the Neo-Assyrian treaties, see SAA 2; for discussion, see below section 3: "Treaties".

[55] See the treaty drawn up by Aššur-nerary V for Mati'-ilu, king of Arpad (SAA 2, No. 2: reverse, v 1–7: "If our death is not your death, if our life is not your life, if you do not seek (to protect) the life of Aššur-nerari, his sons and his magnates as your own life and the life of your sons and officials, then may (the god) Aššur, father of the gods, who grants kingship, turn your land into a battlefield, your people to devastation, your cities into mounds, and your house into ruins."

[56] Op. cit. reverse iv, 1–3: "[If the Assyrian army] goes to war at the orders of Aššur-nerari, king of Assyria, and Mati'-ilu, together with his magnates, his forces and his char[iotry] does not go forth (on the campaign) in full loyalty, may (the god) Sin... (here follows a long set of curses)". Aššurnaṣirpal II, on his Mediterranean campaign, mobilized troops from the subordinated territories of Bit-Bahian, Bit-Adini, Carchemish and the Patinu (RIMA 2, p. 216f. [A.0.101.1]: iii 56–77). When Šalmaneser III set out on his campaign against Que in his 20th regnal year, he mustered "all the kings of Ḫatti" (RIMA 3, p. 55 [A.0.102.10]: iv 22b–24a). Sargon II, in his Cyprus Stele, ii 9–12, declares as follows: "I imposed upon them (the land of Ḫamath) tax and tribute, corvée work and the obligation to join expeditions as the kings my forefathers had imposed on Irḫulena (the king) of Ḫamath"; for the reading, see more recently Yamada 2000: p. 182 with note 367. References to calls for military service addressed to client states are found in some of the letters belonging to the correspondence of Sargon II: SAA 5: Nos. 97, 139, 199, and 200. Finally, Aššurbanipal, on his first campaign against Egypt, mustered "22 kings of the seacoast" (Rassam Cylinder: i 68–74 = Streck 1916: II, p. 8/9 = *ARAB* II, p. 293, §771; cf. Cylinder C: i 23–51 = Streck 1916: II, pp. 138/9–140/41 = *ARAB* ii, p. 340f., §876).

[57] See e.g. in Sennacherib's final edition of his *Annals*, Col. ii, line 67 (Luckenbill 1924: p. 31): "I imposed upon him the payment of tribute (in the form of) present to my majesty". Failure to pay the yearly tribute was regarded as a rebellion. Thus we find in Aššurbanipal's inscriptions the following complaint regarding the conduct of Yauta' the Arabian: "(he) violated his oath to me, drew off the yoke of my dominion. He restrained his feet from asking my health and kept back from bringing me his gift. The people of Arabia he incited to revolt with him" (Piepkorn 1933, p. 82: 1–4). For a detailed study of the *madattu* and

through messengers.[58] The client king was also required to send regular reports about political and military matters in his region.[59] In order to maintain a closer eye on the subordinate king, the Assyrians might have appointed an Assyrian official (*qēpu*), accompanied by a small military garrison, at the client court. In the treaty that Esarḫaddon drew up for Baal, king of Tyre, the latter was instructed, among other things, not to accept nor listen to whatever messenger who would come to him, without the Assyrian royal deputy present, nor to open a letter sent to him by the Assyrian king without the presence of that deputy.[60] In some cases, the Assyrians to some extent also tried to control the foreign trade of the subordinated countries by forbidding the subordinate kings to export certain goods to a particular destination, and by levying taxes.[61] On the other hand, in case the client king was proved loyal, the Assyrian king might have granted him some privileges. This was done by Esarḫaddon in his treaty drawn up to Baal of Tyre. In that treaty the latter was granted free access for Tyre's ships and merchants to an array of ports of trade and all the cities within Assyrian territory along the seacoast, and in the mountains. It also guaranteed against harmful behavior, for which they would, however, continue to pay tolls as in the past (rev. iii, 18–30).

2.3.1.2. *Annexed Territories and Deportation of Population*

When the client system failed and the subordinate king revolted,[62] his territory was annexed to "the Land of Aššur"[63] and reorganized into a province; the local dynasty was removed and replaced by an Assyrian governor, and the social elite and large sections of the local population

---

nāmurtu, see Postgate 1974: pp. 111–130, 146–162. For further basic studies, see Martin 1939; Jankowska 1969; and more recently Bar 1996.

58 Cf. Postgate 1974: pp. 123–126.

59 This is exemplified by several letters sent by the client kings to the Assyrian king. See e.g., SAA 1: Nos. 30, 31, 42, 104; SAA 5: Nos. 35, 44, 45, 110.

60 SAA 2, No. 5: Reverse iii, 11–14.

61 See the letter of Qurdi-Aššur-lamur, ND 2715: Saggs 2001: pp. 155–158. The letter, dated to the reign of Tiglath-pileser III, refers to the fact that he imposed a tax on the lumber brought down from the Lebanon range by the people of Tyre, by then a subordinate state (lines 10–11); that he appointed tax inspectors over the custom houses of the entire Lebanon range, who also kept watch on the harbor 11–14a); and that he forbade the Sidonians to export timber to Egypt and the Philistine cities (24–27).

62 Although, actually, in many cases only after repeated rebellions.

63 For this phrase denoting Assyria proper, including the newly annexed territories but not the client states, see Postgate 1992: p. 251f.

were deported and replaced by a foreign population deported from other regions of the empire.[64]

Deportation of defeated communities, either in their entirety or selected groups to be settled in the victor's country, was an old practice in the Ancient Near East from the third millennium onwards.[65] However, the systematic implementation of mass deportation as an imperial policy is attested only by the Assyrians, starting with Tiglath-pileser III (744–727). This coincides with the great upsurge of Assyrian expansionist policy in his reign. From the reign of Aššur-dan II (934–912) up to the end of the Assyrian empire (612) 157 cases of deportation are known, of which 124 cases occurred during the period of 117 years, from the reign of Tiglath-pileser III up to that of Aššurbanipal (668–627). In 43 cases, the deportees were enumerated and came to a total of 1,210,928 persons, while in nine other instances their total given was 107,705+X.[66] Generally speaking, deportation was employed as a punishment for a rebellious territory and accompanied its annexation, but in fact it was much more than just a punishment. It was intended to weaken recalcitrant countries and sources of potential threat. By deporting the leading citizens and high-ranking civil and military officials, as well as skilled workers, the Assyrians reduced the likelihood of a fresh uprising against them as well as the possibility of a national revival. At the same time, the transportation of the population from settlements in strategic areas meant that these places could be populated by Assyrian soldiers and citizens, in order to set up Assyrian strongholds and to establish provincial centers, logistic bases and colonies.[67]

The conquest of a rebellious country was liable to bring about widespread devastation with much of the economic base of the region and its infrastructure destroyed, while the massive deportation of the local population would have left the country depopulated. If the Assyrian intention was not to retain that ruined region as a buffer state or region (see below), it necessitated taking measures to restore it. The incorporation of such an annexed territory into the Assyrian provincial system was made through the establishment of a fortified administrative center and a network of strongholds. Once forts or garrison towns established the military

---

[64] The following information is taken from Oded 1979.
[65] See above Chapter Two, p. 43; Chapter Three, p. 63 with note 52; Chapter Four, p. 106.
[66] Oded 1979: pp. 10–11.
[67] Ibid., pp. 43–45.

stability of the area, the process of the consolidation of the region through agricultural colonization started. This included the establishment of new rural villages settled by Assyrian citizens and people deported from various parts of the empire to be employed in agricultural production.[68] Some Assyrian letters from the reign of Sargon II (721–705) indicate that the forts might have had surrounding arable land with fields allocated to the fort personnel.[69]

However once annexed, its people, whether the original local population or the new incoming deportees, became, at least theoretically, Assyrian citizens with full civil rights and subject to the same obligations imposed on all the Assyrian people.[70] Yet, many essential questions directly relating to the social and legal status of the deportees and their descendants cannot be unequivocally answered.[71] It seems in fact

> that the socio-economic and legal status of the deportees was not uniform and their conditions were not identical. There were masters and dependents, full freemen and chattel slaves, soldiers and civilians, labouring freemen and labouring dependent persons, townsmen and villagers, free peasants and dependent farmers, free land holders, tenants and *glebae adscripti*. The rights and duties of the individual deportee were determined by a wide range of circumstances. The position of any particular deportee also depended on his occupation, on the employer, on the function he was singled out to perform, on his personal ability, and on the specific conditions prevailing in the place where he lived.[72]

Following the annexation, an Assyrian cult was introduced, and the people of the newly created province were required to acknowledge the majesty of Assyria's great gods, and expected to bear the tax burdens for the upkeep of their temples (see below). This might have been followed by some kind of acculturation, as may be inferred from Sargon's cylinder inscription inscribed in commemoration of the founding of his new capital at Dûr-Šarrukin:[73]

---

68 Parker 2001: p. 82f. For Assyrian citadels, fortresses and colonies in subjugated territories, see further Tadmor 1975: pp. 36–40; Oded 1979: p. 44f.; Parker 1997.

69 SAA 5: Nos. 15 and 109.

70 Oded 1979: pp. 81–86. There is no evidence that citizens of newly acquired territories were subject to any form of racial, social, or religious discrimination vis-à-vis ethnic Assyrians; cf. Parpola 2003: p. 1061.

71 Oded 1979: p. 75, and see the detailed discussion on pp. 75–115.

72 Oded 1979: p. 115.

73 Fuchs 1994: pp. 43–44/296: 72–74 (= *ARAB* II, §122 whose English translation is adopted here).

> People of the four regions of the world, of foreign tongue and divergent speech, dwellers of mountain and lowland... I carried off at Aššur, my lord's command, by the might of my scepter. I united them ("made them of one mouth") and settled them therein. Assyrians, fully competent to teach them how to fear god and the king, I dispatched to them as scribes and superintendents.[74]

Yet the introduction of the Assyrian cults did not preclude the continued practice of the local, native cults, and they seem to have remained unaffected. No similar imposition of Assyrian cults is attested with regard to the client states.[75]

The obligations imposed on the newly created province were the same as those imposed all over Assyria, save the cities of Aššur, Harran, and some old Babylonian cities which were granted exemptions (see below). These obligations were of two kinds: obligation to pay agriculture taxes and the duty of personal service. The agriculture taxes included in the first place corn-tax (*nusāḫē* and *šibšu/tibnu;* mainly barley and its straw), which might have included fruits of some kind, the produce of orchards;[76] and taxation of sheep, goats and oxen (*iškāru*).[77] The latter might have included the taxing of animal products such as wool and hides. The provinces, through their governors, were also obligated to supply regular offerings (*ginû*) to the temple of the god Aššur, the national god, at the city of Aššur. These offerings consisted of sheep, corn, and emmer. This duty was shared among the provincial governors who took it in turns.[78] Next were the taxes imposed on commercial activities. These were imposed on quays, on the commercial houses where trade was conducted, on ferries or crossings, on town gates, and perhaps also on water-borne traffic, and very likely were aimed only at merchants and those involved with trade.[79] The other obligations consisted of service duties, first of which was the military service. Apart from a general levy of the population, called up exceptionally for the duration of a major campaign, there were men who were given a plot of land in return for performing state service for limited periods of time during the year (*ilku*). They were allowed, however, to fulfill their obligations by fitting out others to undertake their military

[74] Cf. the account in II Kings, 17:24–28.
[75] Cogan 1974: pp. 51–55, 112; idem 1993.
[76] Postgate 1974: pp. 174–189, 206–7.
[77] Ibid., pp. 94–104, 207–8.
[78] Ibid., pp. 213–215.
[79] Ibid., pp. 131–4, 212–3.

service instead of serving in person.[80] These people, called "king's men" (*ṣāb šarri*), could be recruited from distant parts of the empire. Different regions might supply different branches of the army, which meant that they might have been required to leave their homes and serve wherever the king assigned them.[81] Apart from these 'king's men' recruited for military service, other people were levied under the same *ilku* system by the same process as the soldiers for royal corvée work (*dullu ša šarri*).[82]

2.3.1.3. *Buffer States and Zones*

Apart from the above two kinds of sovereignty over subjugated countries, in certain cases the Assyrians chose not to impose any type of imperial rule. This policy was adopted whenever the cost of maintaining imperial control was seen as far outweighing the benefits. In such a case, the neutrality of these buffer states or zones was seen as valuable due to their geographic location between areas of Assyrian territorial control and hostile states. There were two kinds of buffer areas: states and zones. The buffer state retained its autonomy, which was tolerated and even encouraged by its neighbors as long as it maintained its neutrality. The buffer zone had no viable political structure, nor was it controlled by any outside political force. It was regarded by its rival neighbors to be largely empty space, or no-man's land, and since it physically separated the rival states, it provided a degree of security for them.[83]

A policy attested during the reigns of Tiglath-Pileser III (744–727) and Sargon II (721–705) concerning regions bordering deserts was to integrate nomads groups into the Assyrian control system. This was made in order to secure these nomads' loyalty, as well as to establish a barrier against the incursion of other nomads from the desert into the settled areas. According to this policy, leaders of Arabian groups were entrusted with the task of supervising the traffic through border areas.[84]

2.3.1.4. *Cities with Civic Privileges*

A limited number of cities within the Assyrian empire were granted special charters, which included some civic rights and privileges that were put down in writing and were reported as having been inscribed on ste

[80] Ibid., pp. 63–93, 218–226.

[81] Ibid., p. 224f.

[82] Ibid., pp. 226–229. Unfortunately, nothing is known of how the obligation to perform *ilku* service was assessed, who precisely was liable, and the length of time served; cf. Postgate 2000: p. 106.

[83] Parker 2001: pp. 94–97, 155–157, 251–253.

[84] See for details Eph'al 1982: pp. 93–100.

lae[85] set up very likely in public areas. Apart from the city of Aššur, the old religious capital of Assyria,[86] and later Ḫarran in Upper Mesopotamia,[87] some old Babylonian cities also enjoyed such a status; among them the cities of Sippar, Nippur, Babylon and Borsipa are particularly mentioned.[88] This privileged status, known by the name *kidinnūtu*,[89] granted the people of these cities freedom from corvée work, military service, and a tax exemption. A Babylonian literary political pamphlet, set under the guise of an omen text and known by the name of "*Fürstenspiegel*" or "*Advice to a Prince*",[90] enumerates the privileges of the inhabitants of Nippur, Babylon, and Sippar, and provides detailed information concerning this institution. It reveals that the privileges might have also included matters of litigation, and forbade the Assyrian king to impose fines or imprisonment on the citizens of the privileged cities or to treat them unjustly. These privileges seem, however, to have applied only to native-born citizens. We learn this from a letter (*ABL* 878) in which some citizens of the city of Babylon seem to have requested the Assyrian king to extend these privileges also to their non native-born women. In order to support their claim they argue that "whoever enters inside it (=Babylon), his privileged status is secured" and that "not even a dog that enters inside it is killed!"[91]

2.3.1.5. *The Assyrian Attitude to Temples and Gods' Images of the Conquered Territories*

Removal of the gods' images of a defeated enemy started to be mentioned in the Assyrian royal inscriptions with Tiglath-pileser I (1114–1076). These inscriptions often report the fact that the gods of the enemy were taken

---

[85] See in the document called "*Advice to a Prince*" (below note 90), line 51, which warns the (Assyrian) king lest he would "alter their inscribed (treaty) stele".

[86] See particularly the document called "*Aššur Charter*": Saggs 1975.

[87] *ARAB* II, §§ 54, 78, 92, 102, 104, 107 (Fuchs 1994: pp. 343 [2.4: 10–12], 307 [2.2: 5], 303 [2.1: 10], 362 [2.5.5: 10–11], 300 [1.3: 6–8], 296 [1.2.1: 13–15] respectively), and 182.

[88] See the inscriptions mentioned in the previous note, which also mentioned that Sargon granted "freedom" to the cities of Dēr, Ur, Uruk, Eridu, Larsa, Kullaba, Kissik, and Nēmed-Laguda.

[89] Originally an old Elamite term meaning to be under divine protection (*kidinnu*), symbolized by a sacred ensign, which was perhaps displayed on the city gate. See the discussion of Leemans 1946. At least some of these Babylonian cities had for a very long period already enjoyed such privileged status, which the Assyrian kings Sargon II and Esarḫaddon only renewed.

[90] Lambert 1960: pp. 110–115.

[91] SAA 18: No. 158. For discussion of the status of these cities see Oppenheim 1977: pp. 120–125; Reviv 1988, and more recently Kuhrt 1995: Vol. II, pp. 612–617.

together with the booty to Assyria without detailing their status there.[92] In certain cases, however, we find a more detailed account that reports hostile treatment of these deported cult images ranging from mere humiliation, by being donated to the main Assyrian gods as slaves, up to total eradication. Thus we read in the inscriptions of Tiglath-pileser I that "I gave to the god Adad, who loves me, 60 copper kettles together with their gods",[93] and that—

> At that time I donated the 25 gods of those lands, my own booty which I had taken, to be door-keepers of the temple of the goddess Ninlil, beloved chief spouse of the god Aššur, my lord, (the temple of) the gods Anu (and) Adad, (the temple of) the Assyrian Ištar, the temples of my city, Aššur, and the goddesses of my land.[94]

Similar statements are found in the inscriptions of Aššur-dān II (934–912) and Adad-nārārī II (911–891).[95] About more harsh treatment, we read in Sennacherib's inscriptions recounting his management of the rebellious city of Babylon: "The gods dwelling therein,—the hands of my people took them, and they smashed them. Their property and goods they seized."[96] Aššurbanipal's account of his campaign against Elam gives the following details:[97]

> [vi, 27–47]The *zikkurat* (temple tower) of Susa... I destroyed. Šušinak, their god of revelation, who dwells in seclusion, the work of whose divinity no one has (ever) seen, the gods Šumudu, Lagamaru, Partikira... (*19 Elamite gods are enumerated*)...—these gods and goddess, together with their paraphernalia, their property, their vessels, as well as their priests and attendants(?), I carried off to Assyria.... [vi, 62–69]The sanctuaries of Elam (*in the environs of Susa*) I desecrated. Its gods (and) goddesses I counted as powerless ghosts (*zaqīqi*). Their secret groves, into which no stranger (ever) penetrates, whose borders he never (over)steps,—into these my soldiers entered, saw their mysteries, and set them on fire.

These hostile actions reflect a concept—first clearly attested in the Late Bronze Age[98]—according to which the divine world was split by contend-

---

92 Actually, not in every victorious encounter do we find a note about deporting the enemy's gods; it rather seems that this act was carried out selectively.

93 RIMA 2, p. 16 [A.0.87.1]: ii, 61–62.

94 RIMA 2, p. 20 [A.0.87.1]: iv 32–39.

95 "I gave their gods as gifts to Aššur, my lord." RIMA 2, p. 134 (A.0.98.1): 58; p. 144 (A.0.99.1): 16–17, respectively.

96 Luckenbill 1924: p. 83, line 48.

97 Streck 1916, II, pp. 52–55 = *ARAB* II, §810.

98 See Chapter Four, pp. 98–100

ing divine groups, with human wars reflecting the conflicts between the national gods of the contending states. In case of victory on the battlefield, the victor would have claimed that his national gods are more powerful.[99] And by rendering the gods of the defeated enemy into subordinates or even powerless ghosts he would have realized his gods' claim to universal rule. However, references to such extreme treatment of the enemy's cultic statues are very rare and it seems to be very extraordinary behavior.[100]

2.3.2. *The Neo-Babylonian Treatment of Subjugated Countries*

There is hardly any substantial information about the organization of the Neo-Babylonian Empire. While there is evidence that the Babylonians maintained both the client and provincial systems, we lack sufficient information as to whether these systems were adopted as they were from the Assyrians, or whether these systems were entirely reorganized.[101]

The Neo-Babylonian Empire did not adopt the Assyrian practice of cross-deportation. The evidence indicates clearly that the Babylonians deported populations only in one direction—into the Babylonian heartland, and settled them in discrete enclaves, named after the ethnicon or place of origin of the settled exiles. There is no evidence that the Babylonians ever replaced the deportees of one territory by deportees from another region.[102] Regarding the fate of the deportees,[103] some of them were enslaved, particularly qualified craftsmen, and were distributed among palace, temple, and private households.[104] The majority, however, were settled on state land which they farmed independently, paying state taxes and carrying out services that often included military service.[105]

It was noted above that under the Assyrian regime some old Babylonian cities enjoyed special privileges. A characteristic feature of these cities was self-rule by free and legally equal members of society united

[99] See the second address of the Rab-shakeh to the people of Jerusalem, II Kings 18: 33–35, which echoes this concept.

[100] Cf. Oppenheim 1979: pp. 131–134, who, on discussing Esarḫaddon's letter to the god Aššur, pointed out the reflections of what seem to be "a spirit of dissent and criticism" expressed by the citizens of the city of Aššur of at least some of the ways in which the Assyrian imperialistic aspirations were implemented. For a different interpretation of this letter and its motive see Eph'al 2005.

[101] See more recently Vanderhooft 1999: pp. 89–114.

[102] Vanderhooft 1999: p. 110f.

[103] The following information is based on Dandamaev 1991: pp. 252–275.

[104] For enslaved prisoners of war in temple households, see Dandamaev 1984: p. 472, and p. 107 for private households.

[105] Dandamaev 1991: p. 269.

in a popular assembly around the principal temple of the city. However, the status of the citizens of these cities was inheritable and passed on from father to sons, and was applied to freemen who lived in the city and owned land in the city or in the rural district over which the power of the people's assembly extended. These qualifications deprived the deportees of the rights of citizenship, and they enjoyed no civic rights. Yet, in cases where they were settled in distinct regions, they could create their own organization of local self-government under the guidance of their own elders.[106]

2.3.3. *The Achaemenian Empire Treatment of Subjugated Countries*

According to Herodotus (Book III, 89ff.), our only good source on the Achaemenid provincial organization, Darius divided the realm into twenty provinces, or satrapies, each with a governor (satrap), and each with a fixed annual tax or tribute. Yet not all peoples who owed allegiance to the king were included within a satrapy. Thus, the Ethiopians and the Arabs were apparently not included as taxpayers within a province, but both provided military units to Xerxes' army. In 480, both were included in the Old Persian list of peoples within the empire, and both contributed 'gifts' (δῶρα) at regular intervals. The Arabs' "gifts" were said to have been 1,000 talents of frankincense a year.[107] Beside these, there were also client but nominally independent states, such as Cilicia, which apparently did not owe anything financially or militarily to the empire.[108] All the other peoples of the empire apparently contributed troops to the army with each contingent being armed and equipped in its native fashion.[109]

Each satrapy had subdivisions, which could have been governed by locals in contrast to the satraps who were drawn exclusively from the highest levels of the Persian aristocracy. Some satrapies, which included a multiplicity of different political entities, were usually governed along traditional lines by their own authorities.[110]

---

[106] Ibid. pp. [illegible].

[107] For the status and payments of the Arabs in the Achaemenid period see Eph'al 1982: pp. 206–210.

[108] Young 1988: p. 87f.: for the imperial organization, see there pp. 79–111.

[109] Young 1988: p. 92.

[110] Kuhrt 1995: II, p. 696f. Thus, e.g., was the case with the subdivisions of the satrapy "Beyond the River": Yehud with its main city Jerusalem was administered by Jews and retained its sacred laws and its priests; Samaria was governed by the local family of Sanballat; the Phoenician cities continued to be ruled by their traditional dynasts; and Ammon was probably ruled by a local governor (Kuhrt, op. cit. p. 697; for this satrapy see further Eph'al 1988).

The Achaemenid rule was characterized by its leniency and tolerance. Persian systems of social organization, customs or religious beliefs were not imposed on the conquered peoples. Local forms of government, economic organization, political structure and law were left undisturbed, as long as they did not conflict with imperial needs.[111] This policy, established in the reign of Cyrus, seems to have continued, with the possible exception of Cambyses' behavior in Egypt,[112] unchanged under Darius, and there is nothing to suggest that it did not remain characteristic of the Achaemenids to the end of their dynasty.[113] Also the policy toward local religions was benign. We know that the Achaemenids contributed to local cults in Egypt and Babylonia, and also granted some privileges to the temples in Jerusalem and Magnesia-on-the-Maeander.[114] But they were careful to punish rebellious people by destroying their shrines.[115] From the Achaemenid period we have a number of examples of deportation, but generally it was a punishment inflicted on communities that had revolted, and was not systematically applied as an instrument of imperial policy as with the Assyrians.[116]

3. Treaties

In sharp contrast to the great number of treaties available from the Late Bronze Age, we have actually only four or five treaties from the first millennium, all in quite fragmentary condition.[117] Of these, one is a parity treaty from the ninth century;[118] two or three are Neo-Assyrian subordination ("vassal") treaties of the eighth and seventh centuries;[119] and one

---

[111] See Young 1988: pp. 42f. and 103f.

[112] See the discussion of his reign by Young 1988: pp. 47–52.

[113] Young 1988: p. 103.

[114] Kuhrt 1995: II, p. 699.

[115] Herodotus 6.19; 8.53.

[116] Cook 1985: p. 285f.

[117] For all the available treaties of this period, save that of the Sefire stelae (for which see below), see SAA 2. All the quoted texts of these treaties follow Parpola and Watanabe's translation. The number of the available treaties, and consequently the following discussion, differ, however, from those of Parpola and Watanabe in SAA 2: pp. xv-xliii, and those of Parpola 2003: pp. 1054–1059.

[118] Between the Babylonian king Marduk-zakir-šumi and the Assyrian king Šamši-Adad V (SAA 2: No 1).

[119] These are the treaty drawn up by Aššur-nerary V for Mati'ilu of Arpad, and the treaty drawn up by Esarḫaddon for Baal of Tyre (SAA 2: Nos. 2, and 5, respectively). To these we have very likely to add the so-called Aššurbanipal's "treaty" with the Qedar tribe (SAA 2: No. 10, pp. xxxiii, 64–65), for which see below.

treaty from northern Syria of the eighth century written in Aramaic whose nature, whether parity or subordination, is not entirely clear.[120] While this small corpus may be expanded with some additional documents,[121] their fragmentary condition nullifies any attempt to define them conclusively as treaties, let alone to infer from them any substantial information pertaining to the treaties of this period.

To the documents disqualified as treaties we have also to ascribe Esarḫaddon's so-called "vassal treaties" concluded with Median chieftains.[122] Although these latter documents were and still are too often regarded as treaties, yet already since their publication in 1958 many scholars have argued that they present nothing more than a loyalty oath imposed by Esarḫaddon on various sections of the Assyrian population.[123] For that matter, one may note that these documents entirely lack the most important components essential to a vassal treaty—a demand for full commitment and loyalty to the *current* suzerain, namely Esarḫaddon. Also, there is no set of provisions regulating the proper behavior toward *this* suzerain, such as a demand for periodic visits to pay him homage; a demand for yearly tribute, and a demand for military help in case of war against a foreign enemy. Indeed, it was suggested that these documents "could also secondarily be put to use as treaties concluded with vassals", and "it seems quite possible that these texts really were meant to function as 'vassal-treaties', instruments relegating the oath-taking rulers to a status of permanent vassalage."[124] Yet, even were we to accept that suggestion, and considering the close affinity they exhibit with the available Neo-Assyrian subordination treaties, it is still questionable how far we may rely on these loyalty oaths in reconstructing the structure and characteristic features of the regular Neo-Assyrian subordination treaties.[125]

---

120 The treaty was concluded between Bar-Ga'yah, king of KTK (a country which has not been identified so far), and Mati'el, king of Arpad (Tell Rif'at to the north of Aleppo). For a more recent edition and discussion with references to previous literature, see Fitzmyer 1995, and Fitzmyer 2000 for translation only.

121 SAA 2: Nos. 11–13, which may be vassal treaties. On the other hand, Nos. 3, 4, 6, 7, 8, and 9, are in all probability loyalty oaths.

122 Wiseman 1958a; SAA 2: No. 6.

123 First to express hesitation to regard it as a "vassal treaty" was Labat 1960: p. 294. More assertive critics were those of Gelb 1962: p. 161; Watanabe 1987: p. 4, and more recently with more detailed arguments Liverani 1995. For the status of Media at that time and its relevance to questions of these "vassal treaties", see recently Lanfranchi 1998.

124 Parpola, in SAA 2: pp. xxx–xxxi.

125 It may be noted, however, that the term *adê* (Aramaic עדי), employed for designating "treaty" in this period, was used as well to designate a "loyalty oath" sworn by the citizens to their king. For this term and its meaning, see more recently Tadmor 1982: pp.

Thus, in view of the very small number of treaties available from this period, and particularly in view of their fragmentary condition, the conclusions we may draw from this corpus are very limited and provisional.

The earliest of these treaties is the much damaged treaty of the Babylonian king Marduk-zakir-šumi with the Assyrian king Šamši-Adad V. While there are some clear indications that Babylonia was the stronger party in the treaty,[126] nothing of what has survived necessarily suggests that it is a subordination treaty. It seems rather to be a parity treaty which allows some advantages to the Babylonian party. There are also some indications that it was composed in Babylonia: the text is written in the Neo-Babylonian dialect and inscribed in a Neo-Babylonian script;[127] the curses formulae invoked first (if not only) the principal Babylonian gods; and most of the survived curses are very similar to the epilogue to the Old Babylonian laws of Ḫammurabi.[128] If it was indeed written in Babylonia, it very likely followed a Middle/Neo-Babylonian treaty-making tradition, of which unfortunately we know next to nothing. And since the opening and closing sections are missing, we can hardly define any significant features of this treaty. All that can be said is that the treaty seems to be worded bilaterally, citing the obligations of both parties in the same document. The changeover from the stipulatory sections to the curses section is not interrupted by a list of divine witnesses as in the case of the Hittite-Egyptian treaty. And the curses section is not accompanied by some ritual acts, nor are the curses interwoven with the individual stipulations, as is the case with the Neo-Assyrian subordination treaty drawn up by Aššur-nerari V for Mati'-ilu of Arpad (see below).

One feature deserves, however, special attention: this piece of treaty is written on a small black stone fragment that was found in the library of Aššurbanipal, and is so far the only known Mesopotamian treaty written on stone.[129] It was suggested that this may be the Babylonian exemplar of the treaty sent officially to Assyria, paralleling presumably an Assyrian exemplar sent to Babylon.[130] Yet, taking into account that the version sent to Assyria would have most probably been written on clay, it is quite likely

142–143; Grayson 1987b: pp. 128–9; Parpola 1987b: pp. 180–183; Brinkman 1990: pp. 95–105; Fitzmyer 1995: 57–59.

126 Cf. Brinkman 1968: p. 204f.

127 Cf. Brinkman 1990: p. 107.

128 Cf. Brinkman 1990: p. 97. For the curses of the Old Babylonian laws of Ḫammurabi see more recently Roth 1995: pp. 136–140.

129 Ibid.

130 Noth 1961: p. 143, note 73.

that the present fragment belonged to a copy that was originally kept in Babylon and was taken from there as booty by some later Assyrian king. At any rate, the fact that it was written on stone indicates that it was intended to be better preserved, or more likely, to be publicly viewed. If so, it may be taken as following a practice first attested in 13th century Egypt, where the treaty concluded between Ḫattušili III and Ramesses II was copied on the walls of the Amun temple at Karnak and the Ramesseum, and as a forerunner of the Sefire stelae (see below).[131]

Moving on to the Neo-Assyrian subordination ("vassal") treaties, one may immediately note a sharp deviation from the form and structure of the Hittite "vassal treaties". This is apparent already in the preamble. Whereas the common preamble of the Hittite subordination treaties presents the document as the treaty dictated by the Hittite king, who is presented alone,[132] the Neo-Assyrian preamble presents the document as the *adê* (= "treaty") concluded by the two identified parties.[133] All the preambles of the available Neo-Assyrian subordination treaties suffered much damage, but still that of the treaty drawn up for Baal of Tyre may serve as an illustration of these preambles:

> [The treat]y (*adê*) of Esarḫad[don, king] of Assyria, son of [Sennacherib, likewise king of Assyria, with Baa]l, king of Tyre, with [...], with a]ll [Tyrians], young and old [...]

While the preambles of the available Neo-Assyrian subordination treaties seem to present the same tradition, it does not seem to be the case with their other sections. Starting with the treaty drawn up by the Assyrian king Aššur-nerari V (754–745) with Mati'ilu, the king of Arpad (northern Syria),[134] whose opening sections were entirely lost, the first extant section of the treaty (i, 1'-9') calls for a curse upon Mati'ilu, his family and his people, should he violate the treaty, and is followed in the next section by a long elaborate ritual (i, 10'-35') of which its first part (lines 10'-20') is quoted here:

---

[131] On looking for a still earlier forerunner, one may go back to the "*Stele of the Vultures*" of the 24th century, discussed above in Chapter One, p. ...., but the long gap in time renders this suggestion very problematic.

[132] For the Hittite subordination treaties see previous chapter.

[133] Survived in the treaty of Esarḫaddon with Baal of Tyre (SAA 2: No. 5; restoration follows that of No. 6), and it can be restored in the treaty(?) drawn up to the Qedar tribe (Parpola and Watanabe: No. 10). Cf. also SAA 2: No. 11, as well as the preamble of the loyalty oaths in SAA 2: Nos. 6 and 8.

[134] SAA 2: No. 2, pp. xxvii–xxviii, xliii–xliv, xlvi, 8–13.

> 10'This spring lamb has not been brought out of its fold for sacrifice, nor for a banquet, nor for a purchase, nor for (divination concerning) a sick man, nor to be slaughtered for [...]: it has been brought to conclude the treaty of Aššur-nerari, king of Assyria with Mati'-ilu. If Mati'-ilu [sins] against th[is] sworn treaty, then, just as this spring lamb has been brought from its fold and will not return to its fold and [not behold] its fold again, (in like manner) may, alas, Mati'-ilu, together with his sons, daughters, [magnates] and the people of his land [be ousted] from his country, not return to his country, and not [behold] his country again.

Such a combination of cursing and rituals is found also in another treaty of which the same Mati'-ilu was a party. In stele I of the Aramaic treaty from Sefire, to be discussed below, we find it preceding the stipulatory sections. A combination of cursing and rituals is found already in some Hittite loyalty oaths like the "*First and Second Soldiers Oaths*",[135] but not in Hittite treaties, and its appearance in the treaties of Mati'ilu seems to be either a new development or of an older tradition unattested so far.

As for its following stipulatory sections, the preserved stipulations warn Mati'-ilu lest he should conceal or protect any chariot-fighter or cavalryman (iii, 19'ff.); lest he will not go forth with his army when the Assyrian army goes to war at the order of the Assyrian king (iv, 1ff.); or "if our death is not your death, if our life is not your life, if you do not seek (to protect) the life of Aššur-nerari, his sons and his magnates as your own life and the life of your sons and officials" (v, 1–4). And more generally, "if Mati'-ilu sins against this treaty" (v, 8–9). While these demands generally resemble Hittite stipulations, the structure of these stipulatory sections differ greatly from that of the Hittites, for each of the stipulations is followed by an elaborate curse. Moreover, while we find this style later in Esarḫaddon's so-called "vassal-treaties" with the Median chieftains, it does not appear in Esarḫaddon's "vassal treaty" drawn up to Baal of Tyre, nor in the Qedar tribe treaty, and it also does not occur in the Aramaic treaty from Sefire of which the same Mati'-ilu was a party. This feature, then, seems to represent a treaty-making tradition of which we do not have any information to date.

Finally, there is the adjuration section that should be regarded. In the treaty drawn up by Aššur-nerari V for Mati'ilu, this section was put at the end of the document (vi, 6ff.), resembling thereby the Hittite practice of putting the lists of the gods toward the end of the treaties. Yet it does not follow the style of these Hittite lists, but rather that of the adjuration

135 *CTH* 427. Edition: Oettinger 1976.

section of the Old Babylonian treaties of the 18th century from Mari and Tell Leilan:

> [6]You are sworn by Aššur, king of heaven and earth! [7]Ditto by Anu and Antu! Ditto by Illil and Mullissu! [8]Ditto by Ea and Damkina! Ditto by Sin and Nikkal! [9]Ditto by Šamaš and Nur! Ditto by Adad and Šala! [10]Ditto by Marduk and Zarpanitu! Dittu by Nabû and Tašmetu! [11]Ditto by Ninurta and Gula! Ditto by Uraš and Ninegal! [12]Ditto by Zababa and Babu! Ditto by Nergal and Laṣ! [13]Ditto by Madanu and Ningirsu! [14]Ditto by Ḫumḫummu and Išum! [15]Ditto by Girra and Nusku! Ditto by Ištar, Lady of Nineveh! [16]Ditto by Ištar, Lady of Arbela! [17]Ditto by Adad of Kurbail! [18]Ditto by Hadad of Aleppo! [19]Ditto by Palil, who marches in front! [20]Ditto by the heroic Pleiades! [21]Ditto by Dagan and [M]usuruna! [22]Ditto by M[elqarth and Esh]mun! [23]Ditto by Kub[aba and Kar]huha! [24]Ditto of Hadad, [...] and Ramman [25]of [Damascus]! [26][Ditto by]...[......]! (*Break*)

It may be noted that the list, which starts with the main Assyrian and Babylonian gods, also includes North Syrian and Hittite gods (lines 18 and 23), as well as Canaanite gods (lines 21, 22, 24–25).

Turning to the treaty drawn up by Esarḫaddon (680–669) to Baal of Tyre,[136] the sections that immediately follow the preamble did not survive. We cannot be sure therefore whether the treaty did or did not include a historical prologue, or whether an adjuration section followed the preamble, as in the treaty of the Qedar tribe (see below), or was put at the end of column III or the beginning of column IV. These badly damaged sections were followed by some stipulatory sections, whose style generally resembles that of the Hittite subordination treaties, and differs greatly from that of the Mati'ilu treaty.[137] The treaty is closed by quite a long section of curses (iv, 1'–19'), which invokes beside the great gods of heaven and earth, the gods of Assyria, the gods of Akkad (=Babylonia), and the gods of Eber-nari ("Across-the-River" = northern Syria), also some Syrian and Canaanite gods.

The last Neo-Assyrian document to be treated here is what was regarded as a "vassal treaty" drawn up by Aššurbanipal (668–627) to the Qedar tribe.[138] Following the much damaged preamble (i, 1'–2'), there is what seems to be a brief adjuration section (obv. 3'), followed by what seems to be a "historical prologue" (obv. 4'–11'), which presents the justification

136 SAA 2: No. 5, pp. xixx, xliv (Diagr. 1, no. 5), xlvii, 24–27.
137 For the content of these stipulations see above on page {157}.
138 SAA 2: No. 10, pp. xxii–xxiii, xxxiii, 64–65.

for the Assyrian demands, and ends with a curse section whose beginning only has been preserved:[139]

> 3'[(*Swear* by the gods) Aššur], Mullissu and Š[*erua*]:
>
> ---
>
> 4'[*Considering* th]at Yauta' (the rebellious king of the Qedar) the malef[actor] handed all [Arab]s over to destruction [through] the iron sword, and put you to the sword, 8'[and that Aššur]banipal, king of Assyria, your lord, put oil on you and turned his friendly face towards you, 12'you shall not strive for peace with Yauta', 14'you shall not [... with] your brothers, [your] unc[les...
>
> (*at least 6 lines of the beginning of the reverse are broken away*)
>
> rev. 1'You shall [........]; [you sh[all keep] his feet [off...] and shall not send [...] after him by the hand of anyone, (but), considering the *terrible* things which he did, you shall make every effort to kill him.
>
> ---
>
> 8'[May (the gods) Aššur, Mu]llišu, Sin, Šamaš, [Bel, Na]bû, Ištar [of Nineveh, Iš]tar of Arbela], Nergal [....... (*Rest destroyed*)

The document seems to be very limited in its demands, by only requesting that the Qedar tribe "shall not strive for peace with Yauta'", and "shall make every effort to kill him" (obv. 12'–13'; rev. 5'–7'). Since these two demands open and close the stipulatory section of the document, it would seem that they were the only concern of the document. This, and the fact that no demand is made here to maintain loyalty to the Assyrian king, render this document rather as a protocol either preceding or supplementing an existing subordination treaty. In either case, it should be regarded as a limited agreement that could not take the place of a regular subordination treaty. The section that immediately follows the preamble (obv. 3') seems to be a shortened form of adjuration,[140] and this would clearly set its structure apart from that of the Hittite subordination treaties and would make it similar to that of the Old Babylonian treaties from Mari and Tell Leilan.[141] The next section, however, displays a clear historical prologue, which is similar to that of the Hittite subordination treaties and is found already in the 17th century treaty from Alalaḫ,[142] but does not occur in the older Old Babylonian treaties. These two sections, taken together with the preamble, render this treaty with the Qedar tribe

---

139 A comparison with the curse section of the Baal treaty suggests that the curse section of the Qedar treaty should have been quite condensed.

140 Cf. SAA 2: p. xxxvii.

141 Discussed above in Chapter Three, pp. 69–73.

142 Discussed above in Chapter Three, pp. 73–75.

of a hybrid tradition, and anyway there is a question how far its structure was typical of a regular Neo-Assyrian subordination treaty.

Lastly, we have to consider the eighth century treaty concluded between Bar-Ga'yah, king of KTK, and Mati'el, king of Arpad, which was found inscribed on three stelae at Sefire in northern Syria. It seems that these three stelae present copies of two or three (subsequent?) versions of one treaty. But despite the many studies devoted to these stelae, the question whether this treaty was parity or a subordination treaty still remains open. Considering the fact that I have only recently studied this treaty in detail,[143] I will confine myself to only a few notes presenting the conclusions reached in that study.

Some facts seem to favor the conclusion that it is a subordination treaty. The provisions are formulated unilaterally, specifying only Mati'el's obligations, while no collateral version presenting Bar-Ga'yah's obligations is known. There is also no evidence so far that the Old Babylonian practice of formulating parity treaties in two separate collateral unilateral documents was also practiced in the first millennium. On the other hand, none of the contents of the Sefire provisions necessarily implied the subordination of Mati''el, and what is more, there are some exclusive characteristic features of a parity treaty. These are: (1) the restriction of the military obligation to defense only;[144] (2) the declaration made in Stele I C 1, "Thus have we spoken [and thus have we wr]itten", which discloses that the agreement was reached mutually, with no one dictating it; and, perhaps, (3) the absence of a "historical prologue".[145] These, and the fact that at least in the Old Babylonian period there existed a different practice of formulating parity treaties, do suggest that we may have here a parity treaty.

There is, however, a further aspect to be considered. If this treaty were indeed a parity treaty composed in two parallel unilateral versions, each

---

143 Altman 2008b.

144 Compare the Assyrian subordination treaty drawn up by Aššur-nerary V to Mati'ilu of Arpad (SAA 2: No. 2); rev. iv, 1–7 (quoted above in note 56), which obligates Mati'ilu to go forth with his magnates, forces and chariots to accompany the Assyrian king whenever he goes to war.

145 The fact that the Qedar treaty, although very likely not an ordinary vassal treaty but rather a protocol preceding or supplementing an existing subordination treaty, has what seems to be a "historical prologue" (obv. 4'–11'), would suggest that Neo-Assyrian vassal treaties might have included a "historical prologue", implying a continuation of the Hittite treaty-making tradition. If this conclusion is valid, then the absence of this component in the Sefire inscriptions, a component characteristic only of a subordination treaty (Altman 2004a: pp. 473–481), would suggest their parity nature.

presenting the obligations undertaken by one of the parties, we would have expected that the authorities of Arpad would have rather publicized the obligations undertaken by the king of KTK or else those of both parties.[146] The fact that they publicized only their own obligations may hint at the conclusion that this fact was imposed on them by KTK, which means that this is in fact a subordination treaty, according to which Arpad was subordinated to KTK. This consideration, however, is far from conclusive, and the question of the true nature of the Sefire documents should be considered as still open.

The typical features of the Sefire treaty have close similarities to the Neo-Assyrian treaties on the one hand, and some similarities to the Hittite "vassal treaties" on the other. But the treaty has some unique features as well that do not accord with either of these two traditions. The preamble, preserved only on Stele I, has the peculiar feature of being repeated twice, once on face A (1–6) and again on face B (1–6), so that it is not clear whether we have to take Face A as the beginning of the inscription or rather Face B.[147] The preamble's specification of the contracting parties is also unique. It reads as follows (Face A: 1–6):[148]

> [1]The treaty of Bar-Ga'yah, king of KTK, with Mati'el, the son of 'Attarsamak, the king [of Arpad; and the trea]ty [2]of the sons of Bar-Ga'yah with the sons of Mati'el; and the treaty of the grandsons of Bar-Ga'[yah and] his [offspring] [3]with the offspring of Mati'el, the son of 'Attarsamak, the king [of Arpad; and the treaty of KTK with [the treaty of] [4]Arpad; and the treaty of the lords of KTK with the treaty of the lords of Arpad; and the treaty of *Ḥa*[*bur*]*u* [5]with all Aram and with Miṣr and with his sons who will come after [him], and [with the kings of] [6]all Upper-Aram and Lower-Aram and with all who enter the royal palace.

Such a comprehensive list of the contracting partners of both parties is so far unique in the treaties of the Ancient Near East. It more closely resembles the opening of loyalty oaths, although in the latter only the subordinated party might be so detailed.[149] Moreover, the preamble on Face

---

146 Note the revised reading and translation of Stele I, Face A, lines 6–7 by Fitzmyer (1995: p. 43, and 2000: p. 213): "the st[ele with t]his [inscription] they have set up (as) this treaty". Accordingly, the stele was set up by *both* partners.

147 See more recently van Rooy 1989.

148 Fitzmyer 2000's translation is adopted; restoration of the damaged lines is based on the almost identical preamble preserved on Face B.

149 Cf. e.g. the preamble of "*Esarḫaddon's Succession Treaty*", in fact a loyalty oath: SAA 2: No. 6.

B adds in lines 4–6 the following statement: "and the treaty of the gods of KTK with the treaty of the g[ods of Arpad]. This is the treaty of gods, which gods have concluded." Namely, the gods of both parties are direct contracting partners in this treaty. It may be noted that in the Hittite-Egyptian treaty of the 13th century, the closest example we have to such a presentation, the Egyptian Sun-god and the Hittite Storm-god are only mentioned as having collaborated in bringing about that treaty, but not as the real parties to it. The wording, "the treaty of [party one] with the treaty of [party two]" (Face A, 3–4; Face B, 4–6), is also very peculiar suggesting that the treaty might have been composed in two parallel unilateral versions, each presenting the obligations undertaken by one of the parties, and that a similar stele with a collateral version presenting Bar-Ga'yah's obligations was erected in his territory.[150] Another unique feature, as far as I am aware, is the concluding declaration formula in Stele I C 1, "thus have we spoken [and thus have we wr]itten", disclosing that the agreement was reached mutually.

Finally, also remarkable is the practice to make the treaties public by copying them on stelae. This practice, which is known to have been later practiced in ancient Greece and Rome, where it was a consistent practice to erect permanent records including marble stelae of treaty documents,[151] has, however, Ancient Near Eastern forerunners. We have already mentioned above (on page 191) the ninth century treaty between the Babylonian king Marduk-zakir-šumi and the Assyrian king Šamši-Adad V that seems to reflect this practice. We also mentioned there the still earlier example from 13th century Egypt, where the Hittite version of the Hittite-Egyptian treaty was translated into Egyptian and was copied onto the walls of two important Egyptian temples, that of Amun at Karnak and the Ramesseum. Moreover, in one of the letters Ramesses II sent to Ḫattušili III, the Egyptian king informs Ḫattušili that he had disseminated the treaty throughout Egypt so that all Egypt, dignitaries as well as ordinary people, would hear about the agreement and its details, and he urges Ḫattušili to do the same as soon as he will get the Egyptian version of the treaty (KBo 28.1: obv. 5'–12').[152] A similar request we find in Sefire Stele I, Face B, lines 8–10: "Let not one of the words of thi[s] inscription be silent, [9][but let

[150] See Fitzmyer's comment on Face A, line 3 on page 64.
[151] See Chapter Four, p. 132, note 175.
[152] Edel 1994: I, No. 4.

them be heard from]*'Arqu* to Ya'd[i and] BZ, from Lebanon to Yabrud, from Damascu]s to *'Aru* and…"

A related example of this practice is mentioned in the abovementioned political-literary Babylonian document of the seventh century, the Babylonian *"Fürstenspiegel"* or *"Advice to a Prince"*, which concerns the civil privileges that were granted by the Assyrian king to certain Babylonian cities.[153] Line 51 of that document warns the (Assyrian) king lest he would "declare their treaties (namely the granted charters of privileges) void, or alter their inscribed (treaty) stele". Finally, this practice is hinted at also in the Old Testament.[154]

4. Rules pertaining to Maritime Traffic

References to cases pertaining to maritime traffic that may be used as sources for possible international law are very rare. For the period under consideration here, one such case is the following stipulation included in the above-mentioned treaty that Esarḫaddon drew up to Baal, the client king of Tyre (rev. iii, 15'–17'):[155]

> If there is a ship of Baal or the people of Tyre that is shipwrecked off the land of the Philistines or within Assyrian territory, everything that is on the ship belongs to Esarḫaddon, king of Assyria; however, one must not do any harm to any person on board the ship but one must return them all to their country.

A case in point of a shipwreck we have in a letter found in the archives of Ugarit sent by the king of Tyre to the king of Ugarit, "his brother" (namely, a peer bound to him through a parity treaty), RS 18.031:[156]

> To the king of Ugarit, my brother, speak: Message of the king of Tyre your brother.
>
> ---
>
> May you be well. May the gods guard and preserve you. Here with me it goes well. Is everything going well with you there? Answer me, please.
>
> ---

153 Lambert 1960: pp. 110–115.

154 Deuteronomy 27: 2–8. Note also the connection between standing stones and covenant in Genesis 31: 48, 52; Exodus 24: 4; Joshua 24: 26–27.

155 SAA 2: No. 5.

156 Recent edition: M. Dietrich et al. 1995: p. 178f., No. 2.38 (transliteration only). For the recent English translation adopted here, see Hoftijzer and van Soldt 1998: p. 334. The letter is to be dated generally to the 14th–13th centuries.

> As to a ship of yours that you sent to Egypt, that (ship) is in Tyre. Serious damage happened to it in a torrential rainstorm. They were found, and the *rb tmtt*[157] took all their grain from them. But I took all their grain (and) the crew, all that belonged to them, from the *rb tmtt*, and I gave it back to them. And another ship of yours is unloaded in Acco. Let my brother not be troubled about anything.

It was suggested that "the text makes it probable that there was a kind of international entente whereby ships of various nations and their cargoes were respected in time of peace."[158] Whether or not such an entente was shared also by other city-ports at that time is uncertain, but the letter does reflect relations based on a parity treaty that should have existed between Tyre and Ugarit. This is indicated by the use of the epithet "my/your brother", a convention that was conditioned on the mutual consent of the two parties to a treaty to upgrade their contractual relations to those of "brotherhood".[159] In view of the conditions of navigation in that period, one basic need of a port-city was to secure a friendly anchorage for its own vessels in case of an approaching storm. Another need was to secure the vessels against piracy while passing an unfriendly strip of coast. It was therefore in the interest of a port-city to come to terms with as many rulers of coastal areas along which its vessels were sailing. Unfortunately, while we do have references to such agreements,[160] no actual document of such an agreement has been recovered so far. Yet the above quoted letter surely reflects such a case.

Where such an agreement did not exist, or was ignored, there remains the sanction of possible retaliation by the wronged state. We are told of such a case in the Egyptian story called "*The Report of Wenamun*".[161] The papyrus that holds this story was written around the third decade of the eleventh century, directly after the events which are related in the story. Whether or not it reflects an actual mission, "it depicts a true historical

---

[157] Probably a high Tyrian official in charge of salvage operations; see Hoftijzer and van Soldt, op. cit. p. 334, note 2.

[158] Hoftijzer and van Soldt, loc. cit. note 1; the suggestion is ascribed to J.M. Sasson.

[159] See the letter KUB 23. 102 (Hagenbuchner 1989: Vol. II, pp. 260–264), sent by a Hittite king to an Assyrian king, where the writer declined the addressee's request to upgrade their relationships to those of "brotherhood".

[160] See e.g. the following Amarna letters (translation: Moran 1992), EA 83: 25–26 (a pact between the rulers of Sidon and Amurru); EA 89: 17–19 (a marriage alliance between the rulers of Tyre and Byblos); EA 136: 24–32 (a pact between the rulers of Byblos and Beirut).

[161] Wente 1972; Goedicke 1976; Lichtheim 1976: pp. 224–230. The following quotations follow Lichtheim's translation.

situation and a precise moment."[162] The story relates the bad experience an Egyptian envoy by the name Wenamun suffered on his way to procure pine trees from Byblos in Phoenicia. Toward the end of the story (2,74–83), we are told that Wenamun left Byblos on board a Byblian ship loaded with pine lumber on its way to Egypt. However, so the story relates,

> The wind drove me to the land of Alasiya (Alashia; Cyprus). Then the town's people came out against me to kill me. But I forced my way through them to where Hatiba, the princess of the town was. I met her coming from one of her houses to enter another. I saluted her and said to the people who stood around her: "Is there not one among you who understand Egyptian?" And one among them said: "I understand it." I said to him: "Tell my lady that I have heard it said as far away as Thebes, the place where Amun is: 'If wrong is done in every town, in the land of Alasiya right is done.' Now is wrong done here too every day?" She said: "What is it you have said?" I said to her: "If the sea rages and the wind drives me to the land where you are, will you let me be received so as to kill me, though I am the envoy of Amun? Look, as for me, they would search for me till the end of time. As for this crew of the prince of Byblos, whom they seek to kill, will not their lord find ten crews of yours and kill them also?" She had the people summoned and they were reprimanded.

Unfortunately, the remainder of the report is lost, but it suffices to show that even where a formal agreement did not exist, the mutual commercial interest of city-ports sharing the same sea route should have brought them to respect some unwritten entente concerning shipwrecks.

The extant part of this Egyptian story has two other episodes, which pertain to international rules related to port-cities and maritime traffic. The first one concerns the question of the limits of the responsibility of a city-port for crimes committed within its jurisdiction against a foreign vessel. It occurred when the ship on which Wenamun was sailing from Egypt to Byblos, moored at the city-port of Dor, a city of the Tjeker people (1, 10–21):

> Then a man of my ship fled after stealing one vessel of gold worth 5 *deben,* four jars of silver worth 20 *deben,* and a bag with 11 *deben* of silver; [total of what he stole]: gold 5 *deben,* silver 31 *deben.*
>
> That morning, when I had risen, I went to where the prince (of the city) was and said to him: "I have been robbed in your harbor. Now you

[162] Lichtheim 1976: p. 224. See also Wente 1972: p. 142, who notes that "the very format of the papyrus on which the report is written put it into the category of official documents."

> are the prince of this land, you are the one who controls it. Search for my money!"... He said to me: "are you serious? Are you joking? Indeed I do not understand the demand you make to me. If it had been a thief belonging to my land who had gone down to your ship and stolen your money, I would replace it from my store-house, until your thief, whatever his name, had been found. But the thief who robbed you, he is yours, he belongs to your ship. Spend a few days herewith me; I will search for him."

The thief was not found, and after nine days Wenamun left for Byblos. At this point in the story there are eight damaged lines, but from what has survived the following events may be reclaimed: After passing Tyre, Wenamun managed to seize 30 *deben* of silver from a ship he encountered which belonged to the Tjeker. He told the owners that he would keep the money until his money was found. The second episode, actually the next phase of the same episode, occurs when after a long and frustrated sojourn in Byblos Wenamun finally was about to leave with a cargo of timber (2, 62–74). Eleven ships belonging to the Tjeker people had come in demanding that the prince of Byblos arrest him for the money he took. The prince, however, declined their demand, answering: "I cannot arrest the envoy of Amun in my country. Let me send him off, and you go after him to arrest him." It is uncertain, however, whether it was a refusal to extradite an official Egyptian messenger, as the author of the text presents it, or that it stemmed from the fact that the crime was committed outside Byblos jurisdiction. In any case, it seems certain that the prince of Byblos wanted to avoid a confrontation with either Egypt or the Tjeker people, which would have harmed his relations with both.

5. Arbitration and Mediation

As was stated earlier in Chapter Three, the recourse to arbitration or mediation of some third party in disputes between states not dependent on him was hardly known in the Ancient Near East. What we do have in the Ancient Near East is the intervention and arbitration of a suzerain king in interstate disputes between two countries subordinated to him. Nevertheless, for the period under discussion one case of mediation is known.[163] It is related by Herodotus (Book 1, 74), describing the end of a five-year war between the Medes and the Lydians following an eclipse

[163] The episode is brought up by S. Lafont 2000: p. 577f.

of the sun, which according to modern calculation should be ascribed to the year 585:

> On one occasion they had an unexpected battle in the dark, an event which occurred after five years of indecisive warfare: the two armies had already engaged and the fight was in progress, when day was suddenly turned into night.... Both Lydians and Medes broke off the engagement when they saw this darkening of the day: they were more anxious than they had been to conclude peace, and a reconciliation was brought about by Syennesis, a Cilician, and Labynetus of Babylon, who were the men responsible both for the pact to keep the peace and for the exchange of marriages between the two kingdoms. They persuaded Alyattes to give his daughter Aryenis to Astyages, son of Cyaxares—knowing that treaties seldom remain intact without powerful sanctions. These nations have the same form of oath as the Greeks, but for additional confirmation they make a shallow cut in their arms and lick each other's blood.[164]

6. Extradition and Asylum

Generally speaking, in this period, the same as in the previous ones, the right of a state to claim extradition of its runaways depended on and was regulated through treaties concluded with the state that provided them refuge. A refusal to comply with such a request was regarded as a violation of that treaty and a *casus belli*.[165] Due to the meager number of treaties uncovered from this period and their poor condition, only three treaties, in which some stipulations regarding runaways were preserved, are available. In the parity treaty of Šamši-Adad V of Assyria with Marduk-zakir-šumi of Babylon,[166] there is in line 13, in much damaged context, a reference to fugitives. In the subordination treaty the Assyrian king Aššur-nerari V drew up for Mati'-ilu of Arpad, also within a damaged context, Mati'-ilu is forbidden to "conceal (or) protect (any) chariot-[figh]ter or cavalryman [...], nor send him to another country."[167] Finally, in the Aramaic treaty concluded between Bar-Ga'yah, king of KTK, and Mati'el, king of Arpad, in Stele III, there are two articles referring to fugitives:[168]

164 Herodotus, *The Histories*, translated by Aubrey de Selincourt (Penguin Books, Harmondsworth, 1954), p. 42. The eclipse of the sun was dated by astronomers to the 28 of May 585 BCE. For the ritual of licking the blood compare the ritual attested in Mari documents referred to in Chapter Three, p. 70.

165 See the instances collected in Elgavish 2003: pp. 43–45.

166 SAA 2: No. 1.

167 SAA 2: No. 2, obverse iii, 21–23.

168 Translation follows Fitzmyer 2000.

> Now if a fugitive flees from me, one of my officials, or one of my brothers, or one of my courtiers, or one of the people who are under my control, and they go to Aleppo, you must not gi[ve th]em food or say to them, "Stay quietly in your place", and you must not incite them against me. You must placate(?) them and return them to me. And if they [do] not [dwell] in your land, placate(?) (them) there, until I come and placate(?) them. But if you incite them against me and give them food and say to them, "Stay where [yo]u are and do not (re)turn to his region," you shall have been unfaithful to this treaty (lines 4b–7).
>
> And as for [k]ings [of my vicin]ity, if a fugitive of mine flees to one of them, and a fugitive of theirs flees and comes to me, if he has restored mine, I will return [his; and] you yourself shall [no]t (try to) hinder me. And if (you do) not (do) so, you shall have been unfaithful to this treaty (lines 19b–21).

What makes the first quoted article particularly interesting is the fact that it refers to Aleppo—at that time a city belonging to the country of Arpad—as the place the fugitive had chosen for asylum rather than Arpad, the capital. There, presumably in the temple precinct of Adad/Addu, the storm-god of Aleppo/Ḫalab, he might have expected to be provided with food, drink and shelter and be safe from extradition. It may be noted that the king of Arpad was not required to extradite the fugitive physically, but to keep him there if persuasion was not effective.[169] This reflects an old tradition of Aleppo or its Adad's temple as an asylum, which goes back at least to the 18th century, when Yarim-Lim, king of Aleppo declined a request to extradite four rulers who after having been defeated managed to escape to his territory. In his response to that request, he argued that "in the territory of (god) Addu fugitives are not be handed into custody."[170]

In Esarḫaddon's "*Letter to the God Aššur*" mentioned above we find an interesting piece of information about extradition.[171] The letter (or letters) is preserved in two cuneiform texts, K.7599 and K.2852+K.9662, which may be parts of two different letters dealing with the same affair.[172] They are concerned with Esarḫaddon's campaign against the land of Šubria in 673, a country situated between the Assyrian and the Urarṭian empires, which up to that time had enjoyed an independent status, and served as a kind of buffer state. As such, it was used by Assyrians and Urartian deserters, political fugitives, and criminals as an asylum, from where the Assyrian

169 Greenfield 1991.

170 See above in Chapter Three, p. 83, note 130.

171 See above note 14 and the accompanied text.

172 See Leichty 1991: p. 52.

and the Urarṭian authorities found it difficult to get them back.[173] The fragment K.7599[174] opens with the rationale of the campaign: the king of Šubria rejected Esarḫaddon's demand to extradite Assyrian political refugees who fled into Šubria. What makes this much damaged fragment so interesting is what has been preserved in line 7. According to this line, Esarḫaddon seems to have offered to provide these refugees with written amnesty and safe-conduct.[175] In the second tablet, K.2852+K.9662 (Gbr. II), col. i, line 1, we have the king of Šubria's confession that by rejecting Esarḫaddon's demand he transgressed the oath of the great gods, disclosing thereby that that demand was based on a treaty that he or his predecessors had concluded either with Esarḫaddon or one of his forefathers. In iii, 23–24 we are told what happened to the Assyrian fugitives who were the primary objective of the campaign against Šubria: Esarḫaddon spared their lives but cut off their hands, noses, eyes, and ears. Then, in the following lines, 28–34, Esarḫaddon tells us about another interesting case of extradition. Sometime before the above affair of the Assyrian refugees had broken out, there occurred a similar case with Urarṭian refugees who took refuge in Šubria, the extradition of whom Ursa, the king of Urarṭu, demanded from the king of Šubria but was similarly rejected. Then, after Esarḫaddon captured Šuberia, so we are told, he sought out and identified those Urarṭian refugees and returned them to Urarṭu "in order to keep the treaty" he had with the king of Urarṭu. What is of interest here is the fact that Esarḫaddon, having become the new ruler of Šubria, acknowledged thereby that that old treaty still applies to that newly acquired territory, and that the stipulation regarding extradition, which that treaty should have had, is valid with regard to those Urarṭian refugees who took refuge in Šubria before he took it under his control.[176]

---

173 See further SAA 5: p. xxiv, and the letters Nos. 32, 34, 35, 52, 54.

174 Borger, Ash.: p. 102, § 68: Gbr. I.

175 Oppenheim 1979: pp. 125ff., and more recently E. Leichty 1991. Such an offer recalls the incident of Piyamaradu and the far-reaching offer made to him by the Hittite king as described in the Hittite "*Tawagalawa letter*", dealt with in the previous chapter (p. 161f.). The above offer of Esarḫaddon also recalls the stipulation in the treaty between Ḫattušili III and Ramesses II, which prohibited the parties to severely punish the runaway who was handed over to them (see above Chapter Four, p. 160).

176 This does not exclude that Esarḫaddon had in fact other political considerations behind his decision to observe that treaty and to extradite those refugees to the king of Urarṭu; cf. the reason suggested by Leichty 1991: p. 55.

7. Diplomatic Law[177]

As was already stated above in Chapter Three, there is no clear evidence that permanent embassies were ever known in the Ancient Near East. Nevertheless, a passage in a letter from the Assyrian crown prince Sennacherib, *ABL* 196, concerning tribute brought from the subjugated country of Kumuḫa (Commagene), should be noted. It narrates that

> the emissaries of Commagene have come, bringing tribute and with it seven teams of mules. The tribute and the mules are entrusted in the Commagenean embassy, and the emissaries too are there, eating their own bread (8–14).[178]

The designation we have for the institution translated here "embassy" is É ᵐKUR-*ku-mu-ḫa-a-a* literally "house of the Kumuḫeans". Unfortunately, we have no further information about this or similar house, nor about its nature.

Whether or not this "house of the Kumuḫeans" indicates some kind of a permanent embassy, official diplomatic emissaries were not allowed to leave their host at will, and there are ample references to the fact that they might have been detained for many years. As far as it pertains to the period under discussion, this fact is echoed in the above-mentioned Egyptian tale "*The Report of Wenamun*" of the eleventh century.[179] There, in the course of a verbal duel between the Egyptian messenger Wenamun and the prince of Byblos, we find the latter referring to the fate of some Egyptian envoys who were detained by him for seventeen years until their death (2.51–52). A case of detention and maltreatment of an Assyrian envoy sent to the Aramaic tribe of Bit-Dakkuri is reported by the Assyrian governor of Nippur in the letter *ABL* 238 to the Assyrian king Aššurbanipal. According to this report, the messenger not only was maltreated but also was arrested.[180] In another letter, *ABL* 1260, sent by Aššurbanipal himself, he complains that despite the kindness he showed to the land of Elam, the messengers he sent to extend greetings were seized by the Elamites.[181] On the other hand, Aššurbanipal himself declared that two princes sent to him by Teumman, king of Elam, "with insults", were detained by him because of

---

177 For recent literature on diplomatic messengers and messages in the Ancient Near East, see Chapter Three, notes 132–133, and Chapter Four, notes 297–298.

178 SAA 1: No. 33.

179 See above note 161.

180 SAA 18: No. 192.

181 Waterman 1931: II, p. 376/7.

his great anger against their lord.[182] A more serious treatment is found in the letter *ABL* 1186,[183] where Aššurbanipal instructed the addressees how to handle the messengers of his rebellious brother Šamaš-šum-ukin: "you shall certainly kill the one to be killed and seize the one to be seized."

Maltreatment of foreign messengers by their host is reported also in the Bible. According to II Samuel 10:2–4, the king of Ammon injured the messengers of David sent to him with a message of condolence; he clipped off one side of their beards and cut away half of their garments at the buttocks, and sent them off. This act was taken by David as a justified *casus belli.*

A case told by Herodotus (Book 7, 133–138), although cannot be verified, at least discloses how people of his time considered maltreatment of foreign messengers. According to Herodotus, The Spartans killed Persian messengers sent to them by Darius I. Sometime later, the Spartans started to experience a failure to obtain favorable signs from their sacrifices, which they believed to be a divine punishment for their misdeed. In order to appease the gods, they sent to Xerxes, who succeeded Darius, two Spartan citizens who volunteered to sacrifice their lives in atonement for killing Darius' messengers. Xerxes, however, refused to kill them and sent them back to Sparta, saying that he would not behave like the Spartans who by their misdeed had broken the law which all the world holds sacred.

No less serious were the dangers *en route.* Mitta, king of Muški captured a delegation sent by Urik, king of Que, on its way to Urarṭu, Assyria's arch-enemy, and handed them over to Sargon II, king of Assyria, this in order to find favor with Sargon so that he would agree to establish diplomatic relations with Muški.[184] The insecurity of the journey of the diplomatic emissaries, either *en route* or at the destination court, is reflected in the corpus of queries addressed by Assyrian kings to Šamaš, the Sun-god.[185] Thus we find in No. 24 of this corpus the king Asarḫaddon asking the god whether the messenger he is planning to send to the king of Ḫubuškia will be attacked, seized and killed on his way by the Urarṭians, the Cimmerians, the Manneans, the Scytians, or by any other enemy. In No. 57, Asarḫaddon is asking whether he may send a messenger to the city lord

182 Weidner 1932–33: p. 180: 37–40.
183 Waterman 1931: II, pp. 320–23.
184 SAA 1: No. 1.
185 Starr 1990.

of Karkašši, and whether, if sent, this messenger will be seized and killed by that city lord.

To a certain extent an early kind of a diplomatic passport with which the messengers were provided, requesting that courtesies be extended to them,[186] might have reduced the difficulties the messengers could have encountered on their mission. For the period under consideration here, there are two references available to such documents as well as an actual document. The first reference is found in the above-mentioned tale "*The Report of Wenamun*".[187] In the very beginning of the tale we are told that the messenger Wenamun, having arrived from upper Egypt, presented his documents to the authorities in Tanis (located in the northeast portion of the Delta), who, after having read them, assured him that they will act according to what these documents request (1, 3–6). However, upon arrival at Byblos, his destination, when he was requested by the prince of Byblos to present his credentials, he realized that he had left them with the authorities in Tanis (1, 51–57):

> He said to me: "If you are right, where is the dispatch of Amun that was in your hand? Where is the letter of the High Priest of Amun that was in your hand?" I said to him: "I gave them to Smendes and Tentamun (the authorities in Tanis)." Then he became very angry and said to me: "Now then, dispatches, letters you have none. Where is the ship of pinewood that Smendes gave you? Where is its Syrian crew? Did he not entrust you to this foreign ship's captain in order to have him kill you and have them throw you into the sea? From whom would one then seek the god?[188] And you, from whom would one seek you?"

Besides depicting here the perils a messenger without relevant documents might have encountered on his way, it may be noted that the story clearly differentiates between two kinds of documents: one equivalent to a diplomatic passport, the other to credentials.

Another reference to these two kinds of documents is given in the Bible, in Nehemiah 2: 7–9, referring to those given to Nehemiah by the Persian king, Artaxerxes I:

> Then I said to the king, "If it please the king, let me have letters to the governors of the province of Beyond the River, directing them to grant me passage until I reach Judah; likewise a letter to Asaph, the keeper of the King's Park,

[186] For early examples see Chapter Three, p. 85; Chapter Four, p. 163.
[187] See above note 161; the translation of M. Lichtheim is adopted in the following quotation.
[188] Referring to the small icon of the god Amun which Wenamun had with him.

> directing him to give me timber for roofing the gatehouses of the temple fortress and the city walls and for the house I shall occupy." The king gave me these, thanks to my God's benevolent care for me. When I came to the governors of the province Beyond the River I gave them the king's letters. The king also sent army officers and cavalry with me.

In this case, Nehemiah was privileged to be provided not only by the proper documents but also with an armed escort, indicating that a diplomatic passport and credentials were not sufficient to provide full security to the messengers.

One actual example of such a "passport" survived from the Achaemenid period. It is a document written in Aramaic issued by Arsames, satrap of Egypt, to his estate manager and companions for a journey from northern Babylonia to Egypt. It addresses the regional superintendents along the route, ordering them to supply the satrap's party with precisely stipulated quantities of food for themselves and their horses, and to debit the amounts expended to Ersames' "account".[189]

---

189 Driver 1965: No. VI (pp. 27–28); cf. Kuhrt 2001: p. 116.

CONCLUDING REMARKS

The following remarks sum-up and highlight what the writer believes to have been accepted norms of behavior in the practice of interstate relations and law in the Ancient Near East, in particular those pertaining to human rights. They also provide some further observations that were not discussed in the previous chapters.[1]

Starting with some more general remarks, we note that nowhere in the available records from the periods under consideration here do we find a process of creating and establishing new accepted norms of interstate behavior.[2] It would seem then, that the attested concepts and norms were created and accepted long before they appeared in writing. This seems to be true whether they were first attested in Early Dynastic records, or quite later in those of the Old Babylonian period or even later. These norms seem to have emerged out of the need for ensuring the co-existence of various communities, and some of them might have predated the emergence of the earliest city-states. So far, there is nothing to support an assumption that these earliest norms were created, imposed and enforced by one powerful community or state on other communities. Yet, they were ascribed—very likely already in quite an early time—to the gods who were believed to constantly supervise their observance as part of the divine world order, a fact which imparted sanctity to these norms.

The basic image of the divine world, as it appears in the literary works of the historic era, reflects a kind of tribal society with a weak political organization and no monarchical institute. Such a society, however, no longer existed in the region where and when these literary works were written. It means that this image should have been created before the more advanced institutions, first and foremost kingship, came into being, namely before the foundation of the Sumerian dynasties at the beginning of the Early Dynastic period *ca.* 2900. Yet, this image failed to evolve and

---

[1] References will be confined here only for issues that were not discussed in the previous chapters.

[2] This is true also with regard to the prologue of the Šunaššura treaty (dealt with in Chapter Four), where the Hittite drafters attempted to expand the scope of the rights of a subservient state to self-determination. This attempt seems rather as intended to serve the specific needs of that treaty, while the very idea of self-determination of a state should have been rejected by all the powers of the age, including the Hittites.

lagged behind in following the changes that occurred over time in human political and social institutions. For once this image was put into writing, already in the third millennium, in the form of myths, epics and hymns, it became sanctified and fossilized making it resistant to change.

What did change over time was in the first place the image of the supreme god of the national pantheon, who came to be regarded as a powerful ruler at the expanse of the "democratic" assemblies of the lesser gods.[3] Another important change occurred toward the last third of the third millennium with the emergence of the idea that the divine world is also regulated by the same rules of justice as the human world, and that divine decisions are reached by divine trial. On the other hand, we find expressions that rendered the national gods as imbued with imperialistic aspirations. This image of the divine world became even more complicated when it started to involve different and even adversary pantheons.

Turning to the norms, the employment of a specific term to designate an infringement of the custom in the realm of interstate relations and law—the Akkadian term *ul parṣu* in the sense of "not (according to) custom", and its Hittite equivalent *natta āra* "not correct", "not right", "not ethical"—is first attested in the Late Bronze Age. Yet, the very idea that certain offenses against human beings should be regarded as sinful is attested already in the Early Dynastic period and no doubt prevailed a long time before.

Regarding norms of war, two preliminary actions seems to have been widely regarded as obligatory before opening hostilities: an appeal to the gods for divine authorization, and sending the enemy a formal declaration of war. The need for divine authorization stemmed from the basic concept that the borders of states were regarded as the creation of the gods, hence sacrosanct, and should not be violated. Consequently, wars required a sufficiently justified *casus belli*. While this need seems to have existed already in the Early Dynastic III period, it became even more expressive with the emergence of the idea that divine decisions are only reached by divine trial. These decisions were conceived to be regularly handed down on the battlefield, with the battle being regarded as an ordeal. Thus, before launching a military campaign, rulers were obligated to appeal first

[3] See Jacobsen 1976: pp. 75–91.

to their national god and then, through him, to the divine court, present their justified case, and ask for a divine decision in their favor.[4]

The need to send a formal declaration of war is also very old, although—so it seems—not always observed. It is already attested in the Early Dynastic period IIIb and continued to be attested down to the late seventh century. Regularly, such a declaration was sent by a messenger in the form of a written tablet that included a detailed accusation against the addressee, and might have also included a demand for redress in the form of an ultimatum. It is not certain, however, whether it was mandatory that such a declaration be put in writing. It is also not certain whether the requirement to send such a declaration in advance distinguished between various kinds of adversaries—whether it was a country headed by a king, a tribal semi-nomad group headed by an acknowledged chief, or a gang of brigands. While it seems that the Hittites used to send it only to countries headed by a king, we are not informed to what extent such a distinction was widely accepted by other peoples of the Ancient Near East.

The causes for launching military campaigns varied greatly, ranging from a mere plundering raid to a full-scale campaign with the intention of defeating and conquering an enemy country. In addition, there was not any homogeneity in the attitude to war, not through the long history of the Ancient Near East, or in any specific point of time throughout its long period. At one end, there were the semi-nomadic tribal groups for whom war was a way of life and a source for pride and wealth; at the other end were the settled city-states and territorial states, whose ideal was a peaceful life and economic prosperity, and not easily drawn into a war.

These differences in motivation and attitude necessarily had their impact on the behavior of armies during the course of the war. Open field battles were relatively rare in the Ancient Near East; more often, rulers, upon considering the enemy forces to overmatch their own forces, would have preferred to shut themselves within their fortified cities, taking into account the fact that siege operations normally could not last more than a few months. That is because, at least in the third and second millennium,

[4] Yet, at least in the seventh century, at the height of the Assyrian Empire if not already before, it seems that an Assyrian appeal to the gods before launching a military campaign was confined to pure divination seeking whether the campaign would succeed, without any attempt to justify it, no reference to divine trial, nor any appeal for authorization. It seems, that at that time, the Assyrians were sure that all their military acts matched the desire and goals of their supreme god to the extent that no justification or authorization was needed.

most states had, if at all, only a very limited standing army, and had to rely on a mobilized army that was composed of farmers who could be drafted only during the dormant agricultural season.

This limitation necessarily brought about different fate for many conquered cities. Those that readily accepted an offer to surrender were treated more mercifully. At most, their fortifications were demolished, their royal family might have been exiled and its domain confiscated. A new subordinated local ruler might have been installed then, and the burden of yearly taxes and military obligations were imposed on them; but the local population, however, was spared. Contrarily, cities that stubbornly rejected an offer of surrender, and particularly in cases of rebellion or violation of subordination treaty, suffered much harsher treatment. They were thoroughly plundered, and might have been burned to the ground and their people enslaved; in extreme cases, all males were executed. Alternatively, the entire community was exiled to another locality where it was mixed with other communities. The temples of the defeated enemy were plundered along with the statues of their gods and carried away. However, with rare exceptions where harsh treatment was employed as an instrument of terror, even in cases where cities stubbornly rejected an offer of surrender, the victorious army usually avoided atrocities including execution of the local population. This behavior may be interpreted as reflecting economic calculations and tactical and strategic considerations, rather than humane compassion. Yet, some recorded instances where the enemy was accused of crimes committed against a conquered population[5] suggest that avoidance of atrocities might have been influenced by a widely accepted acknowledgment that crimes against humanity are forbidden and are sins that are liable to be punished by the gods.

Upon conquering a territory, the conqueror faced two options. One was to turn it into a client territory, which meant allowing it an internal autonomy under a local ruler, and permitting it to keep an army. The other option was annexation, which meant putting it under the control of an official and taking over the burden of guarding its borders, as well as securing the loyalty of its population. This latter option had the advantage of exhausting the local resources, but also the disadvantage of draining the conqueror's manpower. The states of the Ancient Near East, including

[5] See e.g. the accusation against Gutium in Utu-ḫegal's inscription, above in p. 39 and the accusation against Urša the king of Urarṭu by Sargon II in his "*Letter to the Gods*", above in p. 172.

the Neo-Assyrian Empire, seem to have preferred the client system, and employed annexation only when the former option failed.

Deportation of a great section of the defeated population was widely employed by Ancient Near Eastern conquerors in order to strengthen their hold of newly conquered territories. Yet the exact fate that awaited those deportees varied according to the question whether the conqueror country suffered from a shortage of manpower or rather from a hunger for cultivated land, namely land which enjoyed sufficient rains or irrigation. A regime in want of land (or water), like the city-states of southern Mesopotamia, and the city-state of Aššur in the Old Babylonian period, would want to reserve any newly acquired land for its own citizens rather than granting it to captives. In that case, a deported enslaved population could provide that regime with a source of cheap labor for mining, roads and buildings construction, as well as working on the large estates of its elite. Contrarily, for a regime in want of manpower, like the Hittites and other empires during the Late Bronze Age, importing deportees and providing them with land and other means for subsistence was the most logical way to increase its agricultural products as well as its source of manpower for the army and for public works. At the same time, such a policy would have strengthened that regime's border districts that were vulnerable to incursions by hostile forces. In such a case, some of the war captives, particularly the women and children who were captured and carried away by the nobles and the warriors, might have been enslaved to be employed in private households and in the precincts of the palace and temples. Yet, the great majority was deported and settled in areas and border districts lacking settlers and were provided with land and the means for subsistence.

Contrary to what is known from Classical Greece, there is no evidence from the Ancient Near East for arranging a truce to bury the dead, nor a rule for returning the bodies of the enemy dead to their families. There are, nevertheless, some indications, attested as early as the Early Dynastic III period, that corpses of the defeated soldiers might have been granted a burial by the victorious army, but reference to such a norm disappeared during or after the Old Babylonian period.

Regarding treaties, there were two kinds: commercial and political. Of the former we have only a very few examples, too few to draw any meaningful conclusions. The political treaties are divided into two main categories: parity and subordination (conventionally called "vassal" or "client") treaties. Parity treaties may be further divided into two sub-groups: ad-hoc and limited treaties, and comprehensive treaties. With the exception of ad-hoc treaties, all the political treaties—contrary to treaties of Classical Greece—were not limited in time but were intended to be in force forever. Nevertheless, in order to strengthen the commitment of the parties, whenever a legitimate successor to one of the parties ascended the throne, a new draft of the treaty might have been drawn. On the other hand, when one of the signatories died without a legitimate successor, or was removed from the throne, the contractual connections between the two political entities would have been terminated.

At least from the Late Bronze Age on, if not already earlier, treaties seem to have been sealed by the parties, either by both parties in case of a parity treaty or only by the suzerain in subordination treaties. On the other hand, save for one Old Babylonian treaty, treaties did not have any date of when they were concluded. Their conclusion was made in the presence of the gods (statues or symbols) of both parties, in front of which and by whom the parties took an oath to observe the treaties, and the copies of which were deposited in the main temples of the parties. Another feature which is first attested in the 13th century, and of which we have so far only a few examples, is the practice to advertise in public the content of treaties, a practice well known later from ancient Greece and Rome.

While the structure of the political treaties underwent changes in time, it seems that in the 15th–13th centuries the various treaty-making traditions reached their climax and converged. Yet, no definite statement may be made to this effect because of the meager amount and poor condition of the examples we have from the first millennium. Anyhow, the Late Bronze Age introduced two significant changes, whose forerunners seem to appear already in the Old Babylonian period. One change is particularly noticeable in parity treaties: the parties exchanged similar versions, each of which contained the obligations of both parties, so that if one party violated the treaty, his violation also nullified the obligations of the wronged party. This change replaced the previous system attested in the Old Babylonian period according to which each of the parties drafted the obligations of the other party, who took an oath on that version containing only his obligations.

The second change pertained only to the subordination treaties and is known so far from only Hittite documents and edicts. Immediately following the preamble that introduced the suzerain as the one who dictated the treaty, there is a section—ranging in length from one sentence to several paragraphs—that is called by modern scholars "historical prologue" or similar designations. Its function was to present arguments justifying the imposition of obligations on the inferior party, with the intention to deprive that party of the ability to contest the validity or legality of the treaty. As a matter of fact, this section was likely to appear in any state document imposing on a subordinate party obligations or restrictions, which involved infringement of some enshrined or traditional rights of that party.

Unfortunately, because of the poor condition of the few available later treaties of the first millennium, it is not clear whether these two changes survived in that later period.

The available "historical prologue" sections in the Hittite documents, due to their above-defined function, are, in fact, potentially rich sources of international law conceptions that until most recently have unfortunately been ignored by scholars. They are particular valuable for their contribution to our knowledge of such issues as claiming lost territories, justifying launching a military campaign, subjugating and occupying foreign territories, and those pertaining to the validity and legality of the treaty. Following are some observations made on the basis of these sections.

Starting with issues pertaining to the binding force of subordination treaties, the arguments raised by the drafters in order to guarantee the suzerain's interests disclose their concern lest the subordinate party would raise a claim of duress, namely that he was forced by the suzerain into these contractual commitments, a claim which would render the treaty voidable. To this effect, they emphasized the fact that it was rather the would-be subordinate party, by his own initiative, that appealed to the would-be suzerain for protection and help in exchange for political subordination.[6] Another observable concern was lest the inferior party would claim that the very conclusion of the treaty, or else the acts that preceded and brought about this conclusion, involved an offense on the part of the suzerain against a third party, which claim would render the treaty illegal and hence unenforceable.[7] A further concern is lest the inferior party would claim "frustration", declaring that his promises given to another suzerain are still valid and therefore he is precluded from fulfilling his later-made promises to his new suzerain.[8]

Regarding issues of occupying conquered territory, we find that at least the Hittite lawyers acknowledged a claim for the "right of possession" in the realm of interstate law. This right was already acknowledged in the

[6] For discussion, see Altman 2004a: pp. 216–229.
[7] For discussion, see Altman 2004a: pp. 191–198.
[8] For discussion, see Altman 2005a.

Old Babylonian civil law, and it seems to have been adapted into interstate law in the 14th–13th centuries. From the few treaties that imply to this right, as well as from the biblical episode of Jephthah (Judges 11:12–27), it appears that this claim had to consist of three components: uninterrupted possession (or suzerainty) of the territory in question for at least two generations; lack of protest on the part of the subordinate king or people, and an assertion of lawful acquisition.[9]

Related to this "right of possession" is the rule of what one may call in modern terms "limitation of action". That is, a statutory limitation of time, beyond which an action is no longer valid or enforceable. According to this rule, holding back a claim to some position or territory beyond a certain statutory length of time, while throughout this time this position or territory was occupied by another, would have deprived a person of the right to claim it later. There are indeed some hints that the Hittite lawyers acknowledged such a rule,[10] but its details are still unknown to us.

Another circumstance under which a ruler may forfeit his claim to lost territory is also suggested by the episode of Jephthah in Judges 11:12–27. According to this narrative, in the event that a territory lost by one state to another was recovered by a third party, the first owner lost his claim to this territory. Some episodes preserved in Hittite documents suggest that this rule was acknowledged also by the Hittites and their neighbors.[11] But it is still not clear whether under such circumstances the first owner had entirely forfeited his title over his lost territory, or whether he was simply precluded from raising his claim as long as that territory was held by that third party.

---

[9] For discussion, see Altman 2001 and Altman 2004a: pp. 364–370, 375–378, 386–387, 392–394, 396. In the few documents pertinent to this right there is no clear evidence that the Hittites considered this right to have positive, acquisitive value, namely as acquiring title, making the usucapient owner. But it is still possible that they regarded it as of a negative, extinctive value, extinguishing the title of any other person.

[10] See discussion in Altman 2004a: Chapter XII, p. 353f., regarding the significance of the assertion of Kurunta's loyalty in the Kurunta treaty; and in Chapter XIV, pp. 444f. and 454, regarding the assertion of Aziru's loyalty in the Šaušgamuwa treaty. This issue has a bearing on such questions as after what period of time of acquiescence a subordinate ruler is no longer entitled to raise protest against the very legal basis of his subordination; or for what period of time a suzerain still has the right to claim back a country that had defected from him.

[11] This rule is suggested by the case of Aštata, lost to Šattiwaza of Mittani and recovered by Piyaššili of Ḫatti, as presented in the Šattiwaza treaty (*CTH* 51.I [Beckman 1999, no. 6a]: A rev. 18–21). Another case suggesting this rule is the case of Iyaruwatta in *CTH* 63a (Beckman 1999, No. 30), discussed in Altman 2004a: Chapter V, section A 3. This latter case, however, is more complicated due to the revolt of Barga under EN-urta against the Hittites.

The Ancient Near Eastern subordination treaties, as a rule, obligated the subordinated party to provide on request military help headed by the subordinate king himself or his son whenever the suzerain launched a campaign. The available parity treaties, contrarily, are only defense treaties that restricted the demand for military help to only cases when the other party's country, his throne, or the right succession of his legitimate heir, are under attack or in danger.

The most frequent found provisions in both parity and subordination treaties, and a matter that was liable to create much tension in interstate relations up to opening war, pertain to the extradition of runaway people, and particularly political refugees. Demands for extradition were usually based on and regulated through these treaties, and a denial of such a demand was regarded as a violation of the treaty and a *casus belli*. Yet, in the documents pertaining to this issue we find—albeit very few—references to some significant restrictions put on such a demand. One so-far unique restriction is found in the treaty concluded between Ḫattušili III of Ḫatti and Ramesses II of Egypt (early 13th century), which included a far-reaching liberal provision that prohibited the parties to severely punish the runaway who was handed back to them.[12] Two sources refer to a certain city as a religious asylum, from which no runaway is to be extradited.[13] Finally, there are indications that already in the Old Babylonian period, and more attested in the 15th century, it became acknowledged, at least in certain parts of the "Fertile Crescent", that free persons who leave their homeland and crossed the border of another country seeking sustenance were not regarded as extraditable refugees whose homeland may request their extradition. On the other hand, they were not subject to enslavement by their host country against their will, and they retain the right of return to their homeland.[14]

Frequent causes for tension in interstate relations in the Ancient Near East were plundering raids from a neighboring country. In case that country was subordinated to a third party, that party was held responsible for those hostile acts. The acknowledgement of this responsibility of the suzerain is attested already in the Old Babylonian period. In case both countries were subordinated to the same suzerain, any kind of dispute, either between the two subordinate rulers, or between their citizens,

---

[12] See above p. 160.
[13] See above pp. 83 and 204.
[14] See above pp. 154 and 157.

could be brought before the suzerain for arbitration. Yet, while this kind of arbitration is well attested in the Ancient Near East documents, arbitration by a third party to whom the disputants were not subordinated is hardly known in these documents.

In managing conflicts, the most crucial instrument was the diplomatic messenger. The available diplomatic correspondence of the Old Babylonian period and the Late Bronze Age reveal an elaborate protocol that was developed in order to regulate the proper exchange of diplomatic messengers, save for the most crucial point: their immunity. While it was acknowledged that to kill a messenger is "not proper", the idea of diplomatic immunity was not yet developed, and diplomatic messengers were vulnerable to maltreatment. The early kind of a diplomatic passport with which the messengers were provided might have reduced to a certain extent the dangers that waited them on their mission, but could not entirely eliminate them.

Finally, while the present study was intended to provide an up-to-date picture of the earliest recorded concepts of international law, this picture, as noted in the introduction to this discourse, can by no means claim to be complete; the more so as there is a steady flow of new Ancient Near Eastern documentation and each day may bring up new information.

BIBLIOGRAPHY

Adams, W.Y., *Nubia: Corridor to Africa*, London: Allen Lane, 1977.

Adcock, Sir F. and Mosely, D.J., *Diplomacy in Ancient Greece*, London: Thames and Hudson, 1975.

Ager, S.L., *Interstate Arbitration in the Greek World, 337–90 BC*, Berkeley, Calif.: California University Press, 1996.

Alp, S., "Die soziale Klasse der NAM.RA-Leute und ihre hethitische Bezeichung", *Jahrbuch für kleinasiatische Forschung* 1, pp. 113–135, 1950–51.

——, *Hethitische Briefe aus Maşat-Höyük*, Ankara: Türk Tarih Kurumu Basimevi, 1991.

Altman, A., "Claim of possession over occupied or conquered territory in the Bible and in the Ancient Near East", *ZAR* 7, pp. 332–352, 2001.

——, "On some Basic Concepts in the Law of People Seeking Refuge and Sustenance in the Ancient Near East", *ZAR* 8, pp. 323–342, 2002.

——, "Rethinking the Hittite System of Subordinate Countries from the Legal Point of View", *JAOS* 123, pp. 741–756, 2003a.

——, "Who Took the Oath on the Vassal Treaty: Only the Vassal King or also the Suzerain?—The Hittite Evidence", *ZAR* 9, pp. 178–184, 2003b.

——, *The Historical Prologue of the Hittite Vassal Treaties. An Inquiry into the Concepts of Hittite Interstate Law*, Ramat-Gan: Bar-Ilan University Press, 2004a.

——, "The Role of the 'Historical Prologue' in the Hittite Vassal Treaties: An Early Experiment in Securing Treaty Compliance", *JHIL* 6/1, pp. 43–63, 2004b.

——, "Provisions for a Case of Conflicting Commitments in 15th Century BCE Treaties", in Y. Sefati et al. (eds.), *"An Experienced Scribe who Neglects Nothing": Ancient Near Eastern Studies in Honor of Prof. J. Klein*, Bethesda, Md: CDL Press, pp. 434–445, 2005a.

——, "Šattiwaza's Declaration Reconsidered", in *Acts of the V. International Congress of Hittitology, Çorum, 2–6 September 2002*, edited by A. Süel, Ankara: Nokta Ofset, pp. 43–48, 2005b.

——, "Hittite imperialism in perspective: the Hittite and the Roman treatment of subordinate states compared", in Wilhelm (ed.) 2008, pp. 377–393, 2008a.

——, "What Kind of Treaty Tradition Do the Sefire Inscriptions Represent?", in *Treasures on Camels' Humps. Historical and Literary Studies from the Ancient Near East Presented to Israel Eph'al*, edited by M. Cogan and D. Kahn, Jerusalem: The Hebrew University Magnes Press, pp. 26–40, 2008b.

Anbar, M., "La 'petite tablette' et la 'grande tablette' ", *NABU* 1991, p. 68, No. 98, 1991.

Arnaund, D. and Salvini, M., "Une letter du roi de Beyrouth au Roi d'Ugarit de l'époque dite 'd'El-Amarna' ", *Studi Micenei ed Egeo-Anatolici* 42, pp. 5–17, 2000.

Artzi, P., "In Search of Just Retribution in Law", in *Occident and Orient. A Tribute to the Memory of A. Scheiber*, edited by R. Dan, Budapest: Akademiai Kiado, pp. 13–20, 1988.

——, "EA 42, The Earliest Known Case of *parşu*, 'Correct International Custom' ", in *"An Experienced Scribe who Neglects Nothing": Ancient Near Eastern Studies in Honor of Prof. J. Klein*, edited by Y. Sefati et al., Bethesda, Md: CDL Press, pp. 462–479, 2005.

Artzi, P., Klein, J. and Elgavish, D., "The Letter of the King of Beirut to the King of Ugarit: A Different Interpretation", in *Shlomo—Studies in Epigraphy, Iconography, History and Archaeology in Honor of Shlomo Moussaieff*, edited by R. Deutsch, Tel Aviv – Jaffa: Archaeological Center Publication, pp. 23–35, 2003.

Austin, J., *The Province of Jurisprudence Determined*, London: J. Murray, 1832.

Bakir, Abd el-M., *Slavery in Pharaonic Egypt* (Supplément aux Annales du service des antiquités de l'Égypt, 18), Cairo: l'Institut francais d'archeologie orientale, 1952.

Balkan, K., *Letter of the King Anum-Hirbi of Mama to King Warshama of Kanish* (Türk Tarih Kurumu Yayinlarindan VII. Seri—No. 31), Ankara: Tūrk Tarih Kurumu Basimevi, 1957.

Bar, J., *Der assyrische Tribut und seine Darstellung: eine Untersuchung zur imperialen Ideologie im neuassyrischen Reich*, Kevelaer: Butzon & Bercker, 1996.

Barré, M.L., *The God-List in the Treaty Between Hannibal and Philip V of Macedonia. A Study in the Light of the Ancient Near Eastern Treaty Tradition*, Baltimore and London: Johns Hopkins University Press, 1983.

Barton, G.A., *The Royal Inscriptions of Sumer and Akkad*, New Haven: Yale University press, 1929.

Bauer, J., "Der vorsargonische Abschnitt der mesopotamischen Geschichte", in J. Bauer, R.K. Englund, and M. Krebernik, *Mesopotamien—Späturuk-Zeit und Frühdynastische Zeit* (Annäherungen 1, edited by Pascal Attinger and Markus Wäfler), Freiburg, Schweiz: Universitätsverlag; Göttingen: Vandenhoeck & Ruprecht, pp. 431–585, 1998.

Bauer, T., *Das Inschriftenwerk Assurbanipals vervollständigt und neu bearbeitet*, Leipzig: J.C. Hinrichs, 1933.

Beal, R.H., *The Organisation of the Hittite Military* (THeth, 20), Heidelberg: C. Winter, 1992.

——, "Hittite Military Rituals", in *Ancient Magic and Ritual Power*, edited by M. Meyer and P. Mirecki, Leiden – New York – Köln: E.J. Brill, pp. 63–76, 1995.

——, "The Ten Year Annals of Great King Muršili II of Ḫatti", in Hallo and Younger 2000, pp. 82–90, 2000.

——, "Hittite Oracles", in *Magic and Divination in the Ancient World*, edited by L. Ciraolo and J. Seidel, Leiden: Brill Styx, pp. 57–81, 2002a.

——, "Gleanings from Hittite Oracle Questions on Religion, Society, Psychology and Decision Making", in *Silvia Anatolica: Anatolian Studies Presented to Maciej Popko on the Occasion of His 65th Birthday*, edited by P. Taracha, Warsaw: Agade, pp. 11–37, 2002b.

Beckman, G., "[Review of] Heinrich Otten, *Die Bronzetafel...*", *Die Welt des Orients* 20/21, pp. 289–294, 1989/90.

——, *Hittite Diplomatic Texts*, edited by H.A. Hoffner, Jr. (Society of Biblical Literature. Writing from the Ancient World Series, 7), 2nd edn., Atlanta, GA, 1999.

——, "International Law in the Second Millennium: Late Bronze Age", in R. Westbrook (ed.) 2003, Vol. 1, pp. 753–774, 2003.

——, "The Anitta Text", in *The Ancient Near East*, edited by M. Chavalas, Oxford: Blackwell, pp. 216–219, 2006a.

——, "Annals of Ḫattušili I", in *The Ancient Near East*, edited by M. Chavalas, Oxford: Blackwell, pp. 219–222, 2006b.

Bederman, D.J., *International Law in Antiquity*, Cambridge: Cambridge University Press, 2001.

Benito, C., "'Enki and Ninmah' and 'Enki and the World Order'", Unpublished Ph.D. Dissertation, University of Pennsylvania, Ann Arbor : University Microfilms, 1969.

Berger, P.-R., *Die neubabylonischen Königsinschriften: Königsinschriften des ausgehenden babylonischen Reiches (625–534 a. Chr.)*, (Alter Orient und Altes Testament 4/1), Neukirchen-Vluyn: Kevelaer, Butzon & Bercker, 1973.

Bezold, C., *Oriental Diplomacy*, London: Luzac and Co., 1893.

Blumenthal, E., Muller, I. and Reineke, W.F., *Urkunden der 18. Dynastie—Übersetzung zu den Heften 5–16*, Berlin: Akademie-Verlag, 1984.

Boese, J., "Zur absoluten Chronology der Akkad-Zeit," *Wiener Zeitschrift für die Kunde des Morgenlandes* 74, pp. 33–55, 1982.

Bordreuil, P. (ed.), *Un bibliothèque au sud de la ville* (Ras Shamra-Ougarit VII), Paris: Éditions Recherche sur les civilisations, 1991.

Borger, R., *Die Inschriften Asarhaddons Königs von Assyrien* (*AfO*, Beiheft 9), Graz: Selbstverlage (reprinted: Osnabrück, Biblio-Verlag 1967), 1956.

——, "Gottesbrief", *RlA* 3, p. 575f, 1957–71.

——, *Beiträge zum Inschriftenwerk Assurbanipals. Die Prismenklassen A, B, C = K, D, E, F, G, H, J und T sowie andere Inschriften, Mit einem Beitrag von A. Fuchs*, Wiesbaden: Harrassowitz Verlag, 1996.

Briant, P., *From Cyrus to Alexander. A History of the Persian Empire* (Translated by P.T. Daniels), Winona Lake, Indiana: Eisenbrauns, 2002.

Brinkman, J.A., *A Political History of Post-Kassite Babylonia 1158–722 B.C.*, Roma: Pontificium Institutum Biblicum, 1968.

——, "Appendix: Mesopotamian Chronology of the Historical Period", in A.L. Oppenheim, *Ancient Mesopotamia—Portrait of a Dead Civilization*, Revised edition compiled by Erica Reiner, Chicago and London: The University of Chicago, pp. 335–348, 1977.

——, *Prelude to Empire: Babylonian Society and Politics, 747–628 B.C.*, Philadelphia: Babylonian Fund, 1984.

——, "Political Covenants, Treaties, and Loyalty Oaths in Babylonia and Between Assyria and Babylonia", in Canfora, Liverani, and Zaccagnini 1990, pp. 81–111, 1990.

Bryce, T., *The Kingdom of the Hittites*, Oxford: Clarendon Press, 1998.

——, *Letters of the Great Kings of the Ancient Near East. The Royal Correspondence of the Late Bronze Age*, London and New York: Routledge, 2003.

Cancik-Kirschbaum, E. Ch., *Die Mittleassyrischen Briefe aus Tall Šēḫ Ḥamad*, Berlin: D. Reimer, 1996.

Canfora, L., Liverani, M., and Zaccagnini, C. (eds.), *I trattati nel mondo antico: Forma, ideologia, funzione*, Rome: "L'ERMA" di Bretschneider, 1990.

Cardascia, G., "Le statut de l'etranger dans la Mesopotamie ancienne", *Recueils de la Societé Jean Bodin*, 9 (Bruxelles), pp. 105–117, 1958.

Carruba, O., "Die Chronologie der hethitischen Texte und die hethitische Geschichte der Grossreichzeit", in *XVII. Deutscher Orientalilstentag vom 21. bis 27. Juli 1968 in Würzburg* (*Zeitschrift der Deutsche Morgenländischen Gesellschaft*, Suppl. 1), edited by: Voigt W., Wiesbaden: F. Steiner, pp. 226–249, 1969.

Çeçen, S. and Hecker, K., "*ina mātīka eblum*. Zu einem Text zum Wegerecht in der Kültepe-Zeit", in *Vom Alten Orient zum Alten Testament: Festschrift für Wolfram Freiherrn von Soden zum 85. Geburtstag am 19. Juni 1993*, edited by M. Dietrich & O. Lorentz, Kevelaer: Butzon & Bercker, pp. 31–41, 1995.

Charpin, D., "Première partie", in D. Charpin et al. *Archives épistolaires de Mari* I/2, ARMT 26/2, Paris: Édition Recherche sur les Civilisations, pp. 7–232, 1988.

——, "Un traité entre Zimrî-Lim de Mari et Ibâl-pî-El II d'Ešnunna", in Charpin and Joannès (eds.) 1991, pp. 139–166, 1991.

——, "Histoire politique du Proche-Orient Amorrite (2002–1595)", in Charpin, Edzard and Stol 2004, pp. 25–480, 2004.

Charpin, D. and Durand J.-M., "La pris du pouvoir par Zimri-Lim", *MARI* 4, pp. 339–342, 1985.

——, "La suzeraineté de l'empereur (sukkalmah) d'Elam sur la Mésopotamie et le 'nationalisme' Amorrite", in *Mésopotamie et Elam, Actes de la XXXVI*[e] *Rencontre Assyriologique International (Gand, 10–14 juillet 1989)*, (Mesopotamian History and Environment Occasional Publications, I), Ghent: University of Ghent, pp. 59–66, 1991.

——, "Aššur avant l'Assyrie", *MARI* 8, pp. 367–392, 1997.

Charpin D. and Joannès, F. (eds.), *Marchands, diplomates et empereurs. Études sur la civilisation mésopotamienne offertes à Paul Garelli*, Paris: Éditions Recherche sur les civilisations, 1991.

——, *La circulation des biens, des personnes et des idées dans le Proche-Orient ancien.* (Actes de la XXXVIIIe Rencontre Assyriologique Internationale, Paris, 8–10 juillet 1991), Paris: Éditions Recherche sur les civilisations, 1992.

Charpin, D., Edzard D.O. and Stol, M., *Mesopotamien—Die altbabylonische Zeit* (Annäherungen 4, edited by Pascal Attinger and Markus Wäfler), Freiburg, Schweiz: Universitätsverlag; Göttingen: Vandenhoeck & Ruprecht, 2004.

Cogan, M., *Imperialism and Religion: Assyria, Judah and Israel in the Eighth and Seventh Centuries B.C.E.*, Missoula, Montana: Society of Biblical Literature and Scholars Press, 1974.

——, "Judah under Assyrian Hegemony: A Reexamination of Imperialism and Religion", *Journal of Biblical Literature* 112, pp. 403–414, 1993.

Cogan, M. and Eph'al, I. (eds.), *Ah, Assyria... Studies in Assyrian History and Ancient Near Eastern Historiography Presented to H. Tadmor* (Scripta Hierosolymitana, XXXIII), Jerusalem: The Magnes Press, The Hebrew University, 1991.

Cohen, R., "All in the Family: Ancient Near East Diplomacy", *International Negotiation* 1, pp. 11–28, 1996a.

——, "On Diplomacy in the Ancient Near East: The Amarna Letters", *Diplomacy & Statecraft* 7, pp. 245–270, 1996b.

Cohen, R. and Westbrook, R. (eds.), *Amarna Diplomacy: The Beginnings of International Relations*, Baltimore and London: The Johns Hopkins University Press, 2000.

Cohen, Y., *Taboos and Prohibitions in Hittite Society. A Study of the Hittite Expression natta āra ('not permitted')*, (THeth, 24), Heidelberg: Carl Winter Universitätsverlag, 2002.

Cook, J.M., *The Persian Empire*, New York: Schocken Books, 1983.

——, "The rise of the Achaemenids and establishment of their empire", in I. Gershevitch (ed.) 1985, pp. 200–291, 1985.

Cooper, J.S., *Reconstructing History from Ancient Inscriptions: The Lagash-Umma Border Conflict*, Malibu, CA.: Undena Publications, 1983a.

——, *The Curse of Agade*, Baltimore and London: The Johns Hopkins University Press, 1983b.

——, *Sumerian and Akkadian Royal Inscriptions*, Vol. I: Presargonic Inscriptions, New Haven, Connecticut: The American Oriental Society, 1986.

Cornelius, F., "Ein hethitischer Hexenprozess", *RIDA* 22, pp. 27–45, 1975.

Dandamaev, M.A., *Slavery in Babylonia: From Nabopolassar to Alexander the Great (626–331 BC)*, translated by Victoria A. Powell, edited by M.A. Powel and D.B. Weisberg, DeKalb, Illinois: Northern Illinois University Press, 1984.

——, *A Political History of the Achaemenid Empire*, Leiden: Brill, 1989.

——, "Neo-Babylonian Society and Economy", *CAH*[2] III/2, pp. 252–275, 1991.

Dandamaev, M.A. and Lukonin, V.G., *The Culture and Institutions of Ancient Iran*, Cambridge: Cambridge University Press, 1989.

Dercksen, J.G., *Old Assyrien Institutions*, Leiden: Nederlands Instituut voor het Nabije Oosten, 2004.

——, "The Assyrian colony at Kanesh", in Wilhelm (ed.) 2008, pp. 109–124, 2008.

Diakonoff, I.M., "Media", in Gershevitch (ed.) 1985, pp. 36–148, 1985.

Dietrich, M. and Loretz, O., "Vor Zeugen beurkundete Übergabe von Alalah und Murar an Jarimlim...", in O. Kaiser (ed.), *Rechts- und Wirtschaftsurkunden. Historisch-chronologische Texte*, (Texte aus der Umwelt des Alten Testaments, I/5), Guetersloh: G. Mohn, pp. 498–501, 1985.

——, "Der Vertrag von Ir-Addu und Niqmepa", in Gordon D. Young, Mark W. Chavalas and Richard E. Averbeck (eds.), *Crossing Boundaries and Linking Horizons. Studies in Honor of Michael C. Astour on his 80th Birthday*, Bethesda, Maryland: CDL Press, 211–242, 1997.

Dietrich, M. et al., *The Cuneiform Alphabetic Texts from Ugarit, Ras Ibn Hani and Other Places*, Münster: Ugarit-Verlag, 1995.

Donbaz, V., "An Old Assyrian Treaty from Kültepe", *JCS* 57, pp. 63–68, 2005.

Douglas, M., *Purity and Danger*, London: Routledge & Kegan Paul, 1966.

Draffkorn, A., "Was King Abba-AN of Yamḫad a Vizier for the King of Ḫattuša?" *JCS* 13, pp. 94–97.

VAN Driel, G., *The Cult of Aššur*, Assen: van Gorcum, 1969.

Driver, G.R., *Aramaic Documents of the Fifth Century B.C.*, abridged and revised edition, Oxford: Oxford University Press, 1965.

Durand, J.-M., "Fragments rejoints pour une histoire élamite", in L. de Meyer et al. (eds.), *Fragmenta Historiae Elamicae. Mélanges offerts à M.-J. Stève*, Paris: Éditions Recherche sur les civilisations, pp. 111–128, 1986.

——, "La Cite-État d'Imâr", *MARI* 6, pp. 39–92, 1990a.

——, "šuke"unum = 'prosternation' ", *NABU* 1990/24, 1990b.

——, "Vie diplomatique et relations internationales", in Durand 1997–2000, Vol. I, pp. 383–639, 1997.

——, *Les documents épistolaires du palais de Mari*, I–III, (LAPO, 16–18), Paris: Les Éditions du Cerf, 1997–2000.

——, *Florilegium marianum* VII. *Le Culte d'Addu d'Alep et l'affaire d'Alahtum* (Mémoires de *NABU* 8), Paris: SEPOA, Societe pour l'etude du Proche-orient ancient, 2002.

Edel, E., *Die ägyptisch-hethitische Korrespondenz aus Boghazköy*, Bd. I. *Umschriften und Übersetzungen*; Band II. *Kommentar*, Opladen: Westdeutscher Verlag, 1994.

——, *Der Vertrag zwischen Ramses II. von Ägypten und Ḫattušili III. von Ḫatti*, Berlin: Gebr. Mann Verlag, 1997.

Edzard, D.O., "Der Vertrag von Ebla mit A-bar-Qa", in P. Fronzaroli (ed.), *Literature and Literary Language at Ebla*, Firenze: Dipartimento di linguistica, Universita di Firenze, pp. 187–217, 1992.

——, *Gudea and His Dynasty* (The Royal Inscriptions of Mesopotamia, Early Period [=RIME], Vol. 3/1), Toronto – Buffalo – London: University of Toronto Press, 1997.

——, "Sumerian Civilization: The Sumerians to the end of the Early Dynastic period", *The New Encyclopaedia Britannica*, 15th edition, Chicago: Encyclopaedia Britannica, Vol. 23, pp. 866–869, 2002a.

——, "Sumer and Akkad from 2350 to 2000 BC", *The New Encyclopaedia Britannica*, 15th edition, Chicago: Encyclopaedia Britannica, Vol. 23, pp. 869–872, 2002b.

Eidem, J., "An Old Assyrian Treaty from Tell Leilan", in Charpin and Joannès 1991, pp. 185–207, 1991.

——, "International Law in the Second Millennium: Middle Bronze Age", in Westbrook (ed.) 2003, pp. 745–752, 2003.

——, "Apum: A Kingdom on the Old Assyrian Route", in Veenhof and Eidem 2008, pp. 265–352, 2008.

——, *The Royal Archives from Tell Leilan 1: Old Babylonian Letters and Treaties from the Lower Town Palace*, New Haven: Yale University Press, Forthcoming.

Eidem, J. and Læssøe, J., *The Shemshara Archives*, 1. *The Letters*, Copenhagen: Kongelige Danske Videnskabernes Selskab, 2001.

Elat, M., "Mesopotamische Kriegsrituale", *Bibliotheca Orientalis* 39, pp. 5–25, 1982.

Elgavish, D., *The Diplomatic Service in the Bible and Ancient Near Eastern Sources*, Jerusalem: The Hebrew University Magnes Press (in Hebrew), 1998.

——, "Did Diplomatic Immunity Exist in the Ancient Near East?" *JHIL* 2, pp. 73–90, 2000.

——, "The Division of Spoils of War in the Bible and in the Ancient Near East", *ZAR* 8, pp. 242–273, 2002.

——, "Extradition of Fugitives in International Relations in the Ancient Near East", in H. Gamoran (ed.), *Jewish Law Association Studies* XIV, *The Jerusalem 2002 Conference Volume*, Binghamton, New York, pp. 33–57, 2003.

——, "Justification for War in the Ancient Near East and in the Bible", *Jewish Law Association Studies* XVIII, pp. 37–69, 2008.

Englund, R.K., "Texts from the Late Uruk Period", in J. Bauer, R.K. Englund, and M. Krebernik, *Mesopotamien—Späturuk-Zeit und Frühdynastische Zeit*, (Annäherungen 1, edited by Pascal Attinger and Markus Wäfler) Freiburg, Schweiz: Universitätsverlag; Göttingen: Vandenhoeck & Ruprecht, pp. 15–233, 1998.

Eph'al, I., "Assyrian Dominion in Palestine", in A. Malamat (ed.), *World History of the Jewish People*, Vol. 4/I: *The Age of the Monarchies: Political History*, Jerusalem: Jewish History Publications, pp. 276–289 (in Hebrew; English Translation: New Brunswick: Rutgers University Press), 1979.

——, *The Ancient Arabs. Nomads on the Borders of the Fertile Crescent 9th–5th Centeries B.C.*, Jerusalem and Leiden: The Hebrew University Magnes Press and E.J. Brill, 1982.
——, "Syria-Palestine under Achaemenid rule", in *CAH*² IV, Chapter 3b, 1988.
——, "Esarḫaddon, Egypt, and Shubria: Politics and Propaganda", *JCS* 57, pp. 99–111, 2005.
——, "Assyrian Imperial Rule in Non-literary Documents Relating to the Territory 'Beyond the River' ", in *Israel and its Land—Inscriptions and History* (*Beer-Sheva* 19), ed. by Zipora Talshir, Beer-Sheva (in Hebrew), Forthcoming.
Eyre, C.J., "Work and Organization of Work in the Old Kingdom", in Powell (ed.) 1987, pp. 5–47, 1987a.
——, "Work and Organization of Work in the New Kingdom", in Powell (ed.) 1987, pp. 167–221, 1987b.
Falkenstein, A., "Zu den Inschriftenfunden der Grabung in Uruk-Warka 1960–1961", *Baghdader Mitteilungen* 2, pp. 1–82, 1963.
Fensham, F.C., "Ordeal by Battle in the Ancient Near East and in the O.T.", *Studi in Onore de Edoardo Volterra*, VI, Milano, pp. 127–135, 1971.
Fisher, H.G., "The Nubian mercenaries of Gebelein during the First Intermediate Period", *Kush* 9, pp. 44–80, 1961.
Fitzmyer, J.A., *The Aramaic Inscriptions of Sefire*, Revised edition, Roma: Editrice Pontificio Instituto Biblico, 1995.
——, "The Inscriptions of Bar-ga'yah and Mati'el from Sefire", in Hallo and Younger (eds.) 2000: pp. 213–217, 2000.
Foster, B.R., *Umma in the Sargonic Period* (Memoirs of the Connecticut Academy of Arts and Sciences, 20), Hamden, Conn.: Published for the Academy by Archon Books, 1982a.
——, *Administration and Use of Institutional Land in Sargonic Sumer*, Copenhagen: Akademisk forlag, 1982b.
——, "The Sargonic Victory Stele from Telloh", *Iraq* 47, pp. 15–30, 1985
——, "Management and Administration in the Sargonic Period", in Liverani (ed.) 1993, pp. 25–39, 1993a.
——, *Before the Muses: An Anthology of Akkadian Literature*, I–II, Bethesda, Md: CDL Press, 1993b.
Frame, G., *Rulers of Babylonia: From the Second Dynasty of Isin to the End of Assyrian Domination (1157–612 BC)*, (The Royal Inscriptions of Mesopotamia, Babylonian Periods 2), Toronto-Buffalo-London: University of Toronto Press, 1995.
Frankena, R., *Briefe aus dem British Museum* (AbB, Heft 2), Leiden: E.J. Brill, 1966.
Frayne, D.R., *Old Babylonian Period (2003–1595 BC)* (The Royal Inscriptions of Mesopotamia, Early Period, Vol. 4 [= RIME 4]), Toronto – Buffalo – London: University of Toronto Press, 1990.
——, *Sargonic and Gutian Periods (2334–2113 BC)* (The Royal Inscriptions of Mesopotamia, Early Period, Vol. 2 [= RIME 2]), Toronto – Buffalo – London: University of Toronto Press, 1993.
——, *Ur III Period (2112–2004 BC)*, (The Royal Inscriptions of Mesopotamia, Early Period, Vol. 3/2 [=RIME 3/2]), Toronto – Buffalo – London: University of Toronto Press, 1997.
——, *Pre-Sargonic Period 2700–2350 BC* (The Royal Inscriptions of Mesopotamia. Early Periods, Vol. 1 [= RIME 1]), Toronto: University of Toronto Press, 2008.
Freydank, H., "Die Rolle der Deportierten im mittelassyrischen Staat", in J. Hermann—I. Sellnow (eds.), *Die Rolle der Volksmassen*, Berlin, pp. 55–63, 1975.
——, "Zur Lage der deportierten Hurriter in Assyrian", *Altorientalische Forschungen* 7 (1980), pp. 89–117, 1980.
Friedrich, J., "Staatsverträge des Ḫatti-Reiches in Hethitischer Sprache I", *MVAeG*, 31/1, 1926.
——, "Staatsverträge des Ḫatti-Reiches in Hethitischer Sprache II", *MVAeG* 34/1, 1930.
Fronzaroli, P., *Archivi Reali di Ebla. Testi.* XIII, Rome: Missione archeologica italiana in Siria, pp. 43–76, 2003.

Frymer-Kensky, T. "The Judicial Ordeal in the Ancient Near East", Ph.D. Dissertation, Yale University, Ann Arbor: University Microfilms, 1977.
Fuchs, A., *Die Inschriften Sargons II. aus Khorsabad*, Göttingen: Cuvillier, 1994.
——, *Die Annalen des Jahres 711 v.Chr* (SAAS VIII), Helsinki: Neo-Assyrian Text Corpus Project, 1998.
Gamper, A., *Gott als Richter in Mesopotamien und im Alten Testament*, Innsbruck: Universitätsverlag Wagner, 1966.
Garelli, P., *Les Assyriens en Cappadoce*, Paris: Depositaire, Librairie A. Maisonneuve, 1963.
——, "The Achievement of Tiglath-pileser III: Novelty or Continuity?", in Cogan and Eph'al (eds.) 1991, pp. 46–51, 1991.
Garelli, P., Charpin, D. and Durand, J.-M., "Rôle des prisonniers et des déporttés à l'epoquue médio-assyrienne", in *Gesellschaft und Kultur im alten Vorderasien*, edited by H. Klengel, Berlin: Akademie-Verlag, pp. 69–76, 1982.
Gelb, I.J., *Glossary of Old Akkadian*, Chicago: University of Chicago Press, 1957.
——, "[Review of] D.J. Wiseman, *The Vassal-Treaties of Esarḫaddon*", *Bibliotheca Orientalis* 19, pp. 159–162, 1962.
——, "Prisoners of War in Early Mesopotamia", *JNES* 32, pp. 70–98, 1973.
Gelb, I.J. and Kienast, B., *Die altakkadischen Königsinschriften des Dritten Jahrtausends V. Chr.* (Freiburger altorientalische Studien, 7) Stuttgart: Franz Steiner Verlag, 1990.
Gelb, I.J. et al., *Earliest Land Tenure Systems in the Ancient Near East: Ancient Kudurrus*, Texts (The Oriental Institute Publication, 104), Chicago: University of Chicago Press, 1991.
Gerardi, Pamela, "Declaring War in Mesopotamia", *AfO* 33, pp. 30–38, 1986.
Gershevitch I. (ed.), *The Cambridge History of Iran*, Vol. 2: *The Median and Achaemenian Periods*, Cambridge: Cambridge University Press, 1985.
Gitin, S. et al. (eds.), *Mediterranean People in Transition: Thirteenth to Early Tenth Centuries BCE*, Jerusalem: The Israel Exploration Society, 1998.
Glassner, J.-J., *Mesopotamian Chronicles*, edited by B.R. Foster (Society of Biblical Literature: Writings from the Ancient World, 19), Atlanta, GA.: Society of Biblical Literature, 2004.
Goedicke, H., *The Report of Wenamun*, Baltimore and London: Johns Hopkins University Press, 1975.
Goetze (Götze), A., "Die Pestgebete des Muršiliš", in *Kleinasiatische Forschungen*, 1, edited by F. Sommer and H. Ehelolf, Weimer 1927–30, pp. 160–251, 1929.
——, *Die Annalen des Muršiliš* (MVAeG 38), Leipzig: J.C. Hinrichs, 1933.
——, *Kizzuwatna and the Problem of Hittite Geography* (Yale Oriental Series, Researches, 22), New Haven, Connecticut: Yale University Press, 1940.
——, "An Old Babylonian Prayer of the Divination Priest", *JCS* 22, pp. 25–29, 1968.
——, "Hittite Rituals, Incantations, and Description of Festivals", in J.B. Pritchard (ed.), *Ancient Near Eastern Texts Relating to the Old Testament*, 3rd edition, Princeton, New Jersey: Princeton University Press, pp. 346–361, 1969.
Grayson, A.K., *Assyrian and Babylonian Chronicles* (Texts from Cuneiform Sources, 5), Locust Valley, New York: J.J. Augustin Publisher, 1975.
——, *Assyrian Rulers of the Third and Second Millennia BC (To 1115 BC)* (The Royal Inscriptions of Mesopotamia, Assyrian Periods Vol. 1), Toronto – Buffalo – London (=RIMA 1): University of Toronto Press, 1987a.
——, "Akkadian Treaties of the Seventh Century B.C.", *JCS* 39: pp. 127–159, 1987b.
——, *Assyrian Rulers of the Early First Millennium B.C.* Vol. I *(1114–859 B.C.)* (The Royal Inscriptions of Mesopotamia, Assyrian Periods Vol. 2), Toronto-Buffalo-London (=RIMA 2): University of Toronto Press, 1991.
——, "Assyrian Rule of Conquered Territory in Ancient Western Asia", in Sasson et al. 1995, Vol. II, pp. 959–968, 1995.

——, *Assyrian Rulers of the Early First Millennium B.C.* Vol. II *(858–745 B.C.)* (The Royal Inscriptions of Mesopotamia, Assyrian Periods Vol. 3), Toronto-Buffalo-London (=RIMA 3): University of Toronto Press, 1996.

Green, J.T., *The Role of the Messenger and Message in the Ancient Near East*, Atlanta, Georgia: Scholars Press, 1989.

Greenfield, J.C., "Asylum at Aleppo: A Note on Sfire III, 4–7", in Cogan and Eph'al (eds.), 1991, pp. 272–278, 1991.

Greengus, S., *Old Babylonian Tablets from Ishchali and Vicinity*, Leiden: Nederlands Historisch-Archaeologisch Instituut te Istanbul, 1979.

——, "[Review of] F.R. Kraus, *Königliche Verfügungen in altbabylonischer Zeit*", *JAOS* 108, pp. 153–157, 1988.

Grélois, J.-P., "Les annales décennales de Mursili II (CTH 61, I)", *Hethitica* 9, 17–145, 1988.

Grewe, W.G., *Fontes Historiae Iuris Gentium*, Vols. I–III, Berlin-New York: Walter de Gruyter, 1995.

——, *The Epochs of International Law*, Translated and revised by Michael Byers. Berlin – New York: Walter de Gruyter, 2000.

Guichard, M., "Zimrî-Lîm à Nagar", *MARI* 8, pp. 329–338, 1997.

——, "Les aspects religieux de la guerre à Mari", *RA* 93, pp. 27–48, 1999.

Günbatti, C., "The River Ordeal in Ancient Anatolia", in W.H. van Soldt et al. (eds.), *Veenhof Anniversary Volume*, Leiden: Nederlands Instituut voor het Nabije Oosten, pp. 151–160, 2001.

——, "Two Treaty Texts Found at Kültepe", in J.G. Dercksen (ed.), *Assyria and Beyond: Studies Presented to Mogens Trolle Larsen*, Leiden: Nederlands Instituut voor het Nabije Oosten, pp. 249–264, 2004.

Gurney, O.R., "Hittite Prayers of Muršili II", *Annals of Archaeology and Anthropology* (issued by the Institute of Archaeology, University of Liverpool) 27, 1947.

Güterbock, H.G., "The Deeds of Šuppiluliuma as Told by his Son, Muršili II", *JCS* 10, pp. 41–68, 75–98, 107–130, 1956.

Haas, V. and Wilhelm, G., *Hurritische und luwische Riten aus Kizzuwatna*, Kevelaer: Butzon & Bercker; Neukirchen-Vluyn: Neukirchener Verlag, 1974.

Hagenbuchner, A., *Die Korrespondenz der Hethiter*, I–II (THeth, 15–16), Heidelberg: Carl Winter Universitätsverlag, 1989.

Hallo, W.W., *Early Mesopotamian Royal Titles: A Philologic and Historical Analysis*, New Haven, Connecticut: American Oriental Society, 1957.

——, "Gutium", in RlA 3, pp. 708–720, 1957–71.

Hallo, W.W. and Jounger, K.L. Jr. (eds.), *The Context of Scripture*, Vol. I: *Canonical Compositions from the Biblical World*, Leiden – Boston – Köln: Brill, 1997.

——, *The Context of Scripture*, Vol. II: *Monumental Inscriptions from the Biblical World*, Leiden – Boston – Köln: Brill, 2000.

Harrak, A., *Assyria and Hanigalbat*, Hildesheim – Zürich – New York: Georg Olms Verlag, 1987.

Heimpel, W., *Letters to the King of Mari*, Winona Lake, Indiana: Eisenbrauns, 2003.

Helck, W., *Urkunden der 18. Dynastie. Übersetzung zu den Heften 17–22*, Berlin: Akademie Verlag, 1961.

——, *Die Beziehungen Ägyptens zu Vorderasien im 3. und 2. Jahrtausend v. Chr.*, 2nd ed. Wiesbaden: Otto Harrassowitz, 1971.

Hess, R.S., "Treaties", in Hallo and Younger (eds.) 2000, pp. 329–332, 2000a.

——, "Land Grant *AT* 456*", in Hallo and Younger (eds.) 2000, pp. 369–370, 2000b.

Higginbotham, C.R., *Egyptianization and Elite Emulation in Ramesside Palestine*, Leiden – Boston – Köln: Brill, 2000.

Hinz, W., "Elams Vertrag mit Narām-Sin von Akkade", ZA 58, pp. 66–96, 1967.

——, "Persia c. 2400–1800 B.C.", *CAH*, I/2 (3rd edn.), Ch. 33, 1971.

Hirsch, H.E., "Die 'Sünde' Lugalzagesis", in G. Wiessner (ed.), *Festschrift für Wilhelm Eilers: Ein Dokument der internationalen Forschung zum 27. September 1966*, Wiesbaden: Otto Harrassowitz, pp. 99–106, 1967.

Hoffner, H.A. Jr., "A Prayer of Muršili II About his Stepmother", *JAOS* 103, pp. 187–192, 1983.
——, "Proclamation of Anitta of Kuššar", in Hallo and Younger (eds.) 1997, pp. 182–184, 1997a.
——, "Deeds of Šuppiluliuma", in Hallo and Younger (eds.) 1997, pp. 185–192, 1997b.
——, *The Laws of the Hittites: A Critical Edition*, Leiden, 1997c.
——, "The Treatment and Long-Term Use of Persons Captured in Battle according to the Maşat Texts", in K.A. Yener and H.A. Hoffner Jr. (eds.), *Recent Developments in Hittite Archaeology and History. Papers in Memory of Hans G. Güterbock*, Winona Lake, Indiana: Eisenbrauns, pp. 61–72, 2002.
——, *Letters from the Hittite Kingdom*, edited by G.M. Beckman (Society of Biblical Literature. Writing from the Ancient World Series, 15), Atlanta, GA: Society of Biblical Literature, 2009.
Hoftijzer, J. and van Soldt, W.H., "Appendix: Texts from Ugarit Pertaining to Seafaring" in Shelley Wachsmann, *Seagoing Ship & Seamanship in the Bronze Age Levant*, College Station: Texas A & M University Press, pp. 333–344, 1998.
van den Hout, Th. P.J., "Apology of Ḫattušili III", in Hallo and Younger (eds.) 1997, pp. 199–204, 1997.
——, "Ordal. B. Bei den Hethitern", *RlA* 10/1–2, pp. 129–130, 2003.
Houwink Ten Cate, P.H.J., "Hittite Royal Prayers", *Numen* 16, pp. 81–98, 1969.
——, "The History of Warfare according to Hittite Sources: The *Annals* of Ḫattušili I (Part II)", *Anatolica* 11, pp. 47–83, 1984.
Hruška, B., *Der Mythenadler Anzu in Literatur und Vorstellung der alten Mesopotamier*, Budapest: Eötvös Loránd Tudományegyetem, Ókori Történeti Tanszékek, 1975.
Hueck, I.J., "The Discipline of the History of International Law—New Trends and Methods on the History of International Law", *JHIL* 3, pp. 194–217, 2001.
Jacobsen, Th., *The Sumerian King List* (Assyriological Studies 11), Chicago: University of Chicago Press, 1939.
——, *The Gimil-Sin Temple and the Palace of Tell Asmar* (Oriental Institute Publication, No. 43), Chicago: University of Chicago Press, 1940.
——, "Mesopotamia", in H. Frankfort et al., *Before Philosophy—An Essay on Speculative Thought in the Ancient Near East*, Harmondsworth: Penguin Books, [originally: *The Intellectual Adventure of Ancient Man*, Chicago, 1946], pp. 137–234, 1949.
——, "Early Political Development in Mesopotamia", *ZA* 52, pp. 91–140 (reprinted in Jacobsen 1970, pp. 132–156, and notes on pp. 366–396), 1957.
——, *Toward the Image of Tammuz and Other Essays on Mesopotamian History and Culture*, edited by W.L. Moran (Harvard Semitic Series, XXI), Cambridge, Massachusetts, 1970.
——, *The Treasures of Darkness*, New Haven, Connecticut: Yale University Press, 1976.
Jankowska, N.B., "Some Problems of the Economy of the Assyrian Empire", in I.M Diakonoff (ed.), *Ancient Mesopotamia: Socio-Economic History*, Moscow: "Nauka" Publishing House, pp. 253–276, 1969.
Joannès, F., "La traité de vassalité d'Atamrum d'Andarig envers Zimri-Lim de Mari", in Charpin and Joannès (eds.) 1991, pp. 167–178, 1991.
Kammenhuber, A., "Historisch-geographische Nachrichten aus der althurrischen Überlieferung, dem Altelamischen und den Inschriften der Könige von Akkad für die Zeit vor dem Einfallder Gutäer (ca. 2200/2136)", in J. Harmatta und G. Komoróczy (eds.), *Wirtschaft und Gesellschaft im alten Vorderasien*, Budapest: Akademiai Kiado, pp. 157–247, 1976.
Kang, Sa-Moon, *Divine War in the Old Testament and in the Ancient Near East*, Berlin – New York: Walter de Gruyter, 1989.
Karavites, P. (Panayiotis), *Promise-Giving and Treaty-Making: Homer and the Near East*, with the collaboration of Th. Warn (Mnemosyne, bibliotheca classica Batava, Suppl. 119), Leiden – New York-Köln: Brill, 1992.

Katz, D., *Gilgamesh and Akka*, Broomall, PA: STYX Publications, 1993.

Kienast, B., "Der Vertrag Ebla-Assur in rechtshistorischer Sicht", in H. Waetzoldt and H. Hauptmann (eds.), *Wirtschaft und Gesellschaft von Ebla*, Heidelberg: Heidelberger Orientverlag, pp. 231–243, 1988.

Kitchen, K.A., *Ramesside Inscriptions, Translated and Annotated Translations*, Vol. I: *Ramesses I, Sethos I and Contemporaries*, Oxford: Blackwell, 1993.

——, Ramesside Inscriptions, *Translated and Annotated Translations*, Vol. II: *Ramesses II, Royal Inscriptions*, Oxford: Blackwell, 1996.

——, *Ramesside Inscriptions—Translated and Annotated: Notes & Comments*, Vol. II: *Ramesses II, Royal Inscriptions*, Oxford: Blackwell, 1999.

——, *Ramesside Inscriptions, Translated and Annotated Translations*, Vol. III: *Ramesses II, his Contemporaries*, Oxford: Blackwell, 2000.

——, *Ramesside Inscriptions, Translated and Annotated Translations*, Vol. IV: *Merenptah and the Late Nineteenth Dynasty*, Oxford: Blackwell, 2003.

Klein, J., "Šulgi and Gilgameš: The Two Brother-Peers", in B.L. Eichler (ed.), *Kramer Anniversary Volume: Cuneiform Studies in Honor of Samuel Noah Kramer* (Alter Orient und Altes Testament, 25), Neukirchen-Vluyn: Kevelaer, Butzon & Bercker, pp. 271–92, 1976.

——, *The Royal Hymns of Shulgi King of Ur: Man's Quest for Immortal Fame* (Transactions of the American Philosophical Society, vol. 71, part 7), Philadelphia: The American Philosophical Society, 1981.

——, "From Gudea to Šulgi: Continuity and Change in Sumerian Literary Tradition", *dumu-e$_2$-dub-ba-a: Studies in Honor of Åke W. Sjöberg*, edited by H. Behrens, D. Loding, and M. Roth, Philadelphia: University Museum, pp. 289–301, 1989.

Klengel, H., *Geschichte Syriens im 2. Jahrtausend v.u.Z.*, Teil 1: *Nordsyrien*, Berlin: Akademie Verlag, 1965.

——, *Syria: 3000 to 300 B.C.*, Berlin: Akademie Verlag, 1992.

——, *Geschichte des hethitischen Reiches*, Leiden: Brill, 1999.

Koch, H., "Elams Vertrag mit dem akkadischen König Narām-Sîn (2260–2223 v. Chr.)", in M. Lichtenstein (ed.), *Texte aus der Umwelt des Alten Testaments*, Neue Folge, Band 2: *Staatsverträge, Herrscherinschriften und andre Documente zur politischen Geschichte*, Gütersloh: G. Mohn, pp. 283–287, 2005.

König, F.W., *Corpus Inscriptionum Elamicarum, I. Die altelamischen Texte. Tafeln*. Hanover (Reprinted: Osnabruek: Biblio, Repr. 1975), 1926.

——, *Die elamischen Königsinschriften* (*AfO*, Beiheft 16), Graz: Selbstverlag, 1965.

Korošec, V., *Hethitische Staatsverträge* (Leipziger rechtswissenschaftliche Studien 60), Leipzig: Verlag von Theodor Weicher, 1931.

——, "Über den nichtparitätischen Charakter des Šunašura-Vertrages [KBo I, 5]", in H. Hunger and H. Hirsch (eds.), 28. *Rencontre Assyriologique International, Wien 1981* [*AfO*, Beiheft 19], Horn, Austria: Verlag F. Berger, pp. 168–172), 1982.

——, "Der Vertrag zwischen Narām-Sin aus Akkad und unbekannten Elamischen Herrscher (MDP, XI, 2–11)", *Razprave, Disertationes* XIV, Academia Scientiarum et Artium Slovenica, Clasis I: Historia et Sociologia, Ljubljana: Slovenska akademija znanosti in umetnosti, 1983.

Kramer, S.N., *The Sumerians*, Chicago: University of Chicago Press, 1963.

——, "The Deluge", in Pritchard (ed.) 1969: pp. 42–44, 1969a.

——, "Lamentation over the Destruction of Ur", in Pritchard (ed.) 1969: pp. 455–463, 1969b.

Kraus, F.R., *Königliche Verfügungen in altbabylonischer Zeit*, Leiden: E.J. Brill, 1984.

Krebernik, M., "Die Texte aus Fāra und Tell Abū Ṣalābīḫ", in J. Bauer, R.K. Englund, and M. Krebernik, *Mesopotamien—Späturuk-Zeit und Frühdynastische Zeit*, (Annäherungen 1, edited by Pascal Attinger and Markus Wäfler), Freiburg, Schweiz: Universitätsverlag; Göttingen: Vandenhoeck & Ruprecht, pp. 237–427, 1998.

Kuhrt, A., *The Ancient Near East c. 3000—330 BC*, Vols. I–II, London and New York: Routledge, 1995.

——, "The Achaemenid Persian empire (*c.* 550–*c.* 330 BCE): continuities, adaptations, transformations", in Susan E. Alcock et al. (eds.), *Empires: Perspectives from Archaeology and History*, Cambridge: Cambridge University Press, pp. 93–123, 2001.

Labat, R., "Assyriologie", *Annuaire du Collège de France*, pp. 259–265, 1960.

Lackenbacher, S., "Lettres et Fragments (Nos. 39–47)", in: P. Bordreuil (ed.), *Une bibliothèque au sud de la ville* (Ras Shamra—Ougarit, VII), Paris: Éditions Recherche sur les civilisations, pp. 83–104, 1991.

Lafont, B., "Messagers et ambassadeurs dans les archives de Mari", in Charpin and Joannès (eds.) 1992, Paris, pp. 167–183, 1992.

——, "Relations internationales, alliances et diplomatie au temps des royaumes Amorrites. Essai de synthèse", in J.-M. Durand & D. Charpin (eds.), *Mari, Ébla et les Hourrites: dix ans de travaux. Actes du colloque international (Paris, mai 1993)*. Deuxième partie, *Amurru* 2, Paris: Éditions Recherche sur les civilisations, pp. 213–328, 2001a.

——, "International Relations in the Ancient Near East: The Birth of a Complete Diplomatic System", *Diplomacy & Statecraft* 12/1, pp. 39–60, 2001b.

Lafont, S., "L'arbitrage en Mésopotamie", *Revue de l'arbitrage* 4, pp. 557–590, 2000.

Lambert, W.G., *Babylonian Wisdom Literature*, Oxford: Clarendon Press, 1960.

——, "Ištarān" in RlA 5, p. 211, 1976–80.

——, "The Treaty of Ebla", in Luigi Cagni (ed.), *Ebla 1975–1985, Dieci anni di studi linguistici e filologici*, Napoli: Istituto universitario orientale, Dipartimento di studi asiatici, pp. 353–364, 1987.

Lanfranchi, G.B., "Esarḫaddon, Assyria and Media", *State Archives of Assyria* Bulletin 12/2, pp. 99–109, 1998.

Lanfranchi, G.B. and Parpola, S., *The Correspondence of Sargon II, Part II: Letters from the Northern and Northeastern Provinces* (SAA V), Helsinki: Neo-Assyrian Text Corpus Project, 1990.

Lanfranchi, G.B. et al., *Continuity of Empires(?): Assyria, Media, Persia*, Padua: S.a.r.g.o.n., 2003.

Langdon, S., *Die neubabylonischen Königsinschriften* (translated by R. Zehnpfund; Vorderasiatische Bibliothek, 4), Leipzig: J.C. Hinrichs, 1912.

Langdon, S. and Gardiner, Alan H., "The Treaty Alliance Between Ḫattušili King of the Hittites, and the Pharaoh Ramesses II of Egypt", *Journal of Egyptian Archaeology* 6, pp. 179–205, 1920.

Laroche, E., "La prière hittite: vocabulaire et typologie", *École pratique des Hautes Études*, V[e] section: Sciences Religieuses, *Annuaire*, tome LXXII, pp. 3–29, 1964/5.

——, *Catalogue des textes hittites*, Paris: Éditions Klincksieck, 1971.

Larsen, M.T., *The Old Assyrian City-State and its Colonies* (Mesopotamia – Copenhagen Studies in Assyriology, 4), Copenhagen: Akademisk Forlag, 1976.

——, "Going to the River", in M.T. Roth (ed.), *Studies presented to Robert D. Biggs, June 4, 2004* (Assyriological Studies 27), Chicago, Ill.: Oriental Institute of the University of Chicago, pp. 173–188, 2007.

Leemans, W.L., "Kidinnu. Un symbole de droit divin babylonien", in M. David et al. (eds.), *Symbolae ad jus et historiam antiquitatis pertinentes Julio Christiano van Oven dedicatae*, Leiden: Brill, pp. 36–61, 1946.

Leichty, E., "Esarḫaddon's 'Letter to the Gods' ", in Cogan and Eph'al (eds.) 1991, Jerusalem, pp. 52–57, 1991.

Lichtheim, M., *Ancient Egyptian Literature. A Book of Readings*, Vol. I, Berkeley: University of California Press, 1975.

——, *Ancient Egyptian Literature*, Vol. II, Berkeley – Los Angeles – London: University of California Press, 1976.

Lie, A.G., *The Inscriptions of Sargon II king of Assyria*, Part I. *The Annals*, Paris: Paul Geuthner, 1929.

Lind, M.C., *Yahweh Is a Worrier: The Theology of Warfare in Ancient Israel*, Scottdale, Penn.: Herald Press, 1980.

Liverani, M., "The Growth of the Assyrian Empire in the Habur / Middle Euphrates Area: A New Paradigm", *State Archives of Assyria Bulletin* 2, pp. 81–98, 1988.
——, "The Medes at Esarḫaddon's Court", *JCS* 47, pp. 57–62, 1995.
——, *International Relations in the Ancient Near East, 1600–1100 BC*, (a revised edition of the book under the name *Prestige and Interest*, Padova 1990), New York: Palgrave, 2001.
Liverani, M. (ed.), *Akkad—The First World Empire: Structure, Ideology, Traditions*, Padova: Sargon Srl, 1993.
Luckenbill, D.D., "Hittite Treaties and Letters", *AJSL* 37, pp. 161–211, 1921.
——, *The Annals of Sennacherib*, Chicago, Ill.: University of Chicago Press, 1924.
Machinist, P.B., "The Epic of Tukulti-Ninurta I", Unpublished Ph.D. Dissertation, Yale University 1978 [Ann Arbor, Michigan, University Microfilms no. 7819473], 1978.
——, "Provincial Governance in Middle Assyria", *Assur* 3/2, pp. 1–37, 1982.
Maeda, T., "'King of Kish' in Pre-Sargonic Sumer", *Orient* (Tokyo) 17, pp. 1–17, 1981.
Malinowski, B., *Crime and Custom in Savage Society*, London: Routledge, 1926.
Martin, W.J., *Tribut und Tributleistungen bei den Assyrern* (Studia Orientalia 8/1), Helsingforsiae: Societas orientalis fennica, 1939.
Masson, O., "A propos d'un ritual hittite pour la lustration d'une Armé", *Revue de l'histoire des religions* 137, pp. 5–25, 1950.
Mayer, G.R., "Zwei neue Kizzuwatna-Verträge", *MDOG* 1, pp. 108–123, 1953.
Mayer, W., *Politik und Kriegskunst der Assyrer*, Münster: Ugarit-Verlag, 1995.
McCarthy, D.J., *Treaty and Covenant*, New edition, Rome: Biblical Institute Press, 1978.
Meier, S.A., *The Messenger in the Ancient Semitic World* (Harvard Semitic Monographs, 45), Atlanta, GA.: Scholars Press, 1988.
Mendenhall, G.E., "Covenant Forms in Israelite Tradition", *The Biblical Archaeology* 17, pp. 50–76, 1954.
Michalowski, P., "The Bride of Simanum", *JAOS* 95, pp. 716–19, 1975.
——, *The Lamentation over the Destruction of Sumer and Ur*, Winona Lake, In.: Eisenbrauns, 1989.
——, *Letters from Early Mesopotamia*, edited by Erica Reiner (Society of Biblical Literature. Writings from the Ancient World, 3), Atlanta, GA.: Scholars Press, 1993.
Michel, C., *Correspondance des marchands de Kanis au début du IIe millénaire avant J.-C.* (LAPO 19), Paris: Cerf, 2001.
Miller, J.L., "Amarna Age Chronology and the Identity of Nibhururuiya in the light of a Newly Reconstructed Hittite Text", *Altorientalische Forschungen* 34/2, pp. 252–293, 2007.
Miller, P.D. Jr., *The Divine Warrior in Early Israel*, Cambridge, Mass.: Harvard University Press, 1973.
Moortgat, A., *The Art of Ancient Mesopotamia*, London: Phaidon, 1969.
DEL Monte, G.F., "Note sui trattati fra Ḫattuša e Kizzuwatna", *Oriens Antiquus* 20, 1981, pp. 203–221, 1981.
——, "I testi amministrativi da Maşat Höyük/Tapika", *Orientis Antiqui Miscellanea* 2, pp. 89–138, 1995.
Moran, W.L., *The Amarna Letters*, Baltimore and London: John Hopkins University Press, 1992.
Moyer, S., "The Concept of Purity among the Hittites", Unpublished Ph.D. Dissertation, Brandeis University (Ann Arbor, Michigan, University Microfilms No. 69–20, 733), 1969.
Munn-Rankin, J.M., "Diplomacy in Western Asia in the Early Second Millennium B.C.", *Iraq* 18, pp. 68–110, 1956.
Neu, E., *Der Anitta Text* (StBoT 18), Wiesbaden: Otto Harrassowitz, 1974.
Neumann, H., "Der Vertrag zwischen Ebla und Abarsal", in M. Lichtenstein (ed.), *Texte aus der Umwelt des Alten Testaments*, Neue Folge, Band 2: *Staatsverträge, Herrscherinschriften und andre Documente zur politischen Geschichte*, Gütersloh: G. Mohn, pp. 2–9, 2005.

Nissinen, M., *Prophets and Prophecy in the Ancient Near East,* with contributions by C.L. Seow and R.K. Ritner, edited by P. Machinist (Writings from the Ancient World, 12), Atlanta, GA.: Society of Biblical Literature, 2003.

Noth, M., "Der historische Hintergrund der Inschriften von Sefire", *Zeitschrift des Deutschen Palaestina-Vereins* 77, pp. 118–172, 1961.

Nougayrol, J., *Le palais royal d'Ugarit,* IV: *Textes accadiens des archives sud* (=PRU IV), Paris: Imprimerie nationale, 1956.

Nougayrol, J. et al., *Ugaritica* V (Mission de Ras Shamra XVI), Paris: Imprimerie nationale, 1968.

Nussbaum A., *A Concise History of the Law of Nations,* Rev. Edition, New York: Macmillan, 1954.

Oded, B., *Mass Deportations and Deportees in the Neo-Assyrian Empire,* Wiesbaden: L. Reichert, 1979.

——, *War, Peace and Empire: Justifications for War in Assyrian Royal Inscriptions,* Wiesbaden: L. Reichert, 1992.

Oettinger, N., *Die militärischen Eide der Hethiter* (StBoT, 22), Wiesbaden: Harrassowitz, 1976.

Oller, G.H., "Messengers and Ambassadors in Ancient Western Asia", in Sasson et al. (eds.) 1995, Vol. III, pp. 1465–1473, 1995.

Olmstead, A.T., *History of Assyria,* New York: C. Scribner's Sons, 1923.

Oppenheim, A.L., "The City of Assur in 714 B.C.", *JNES* 19, pp. 133–147, 1960.

——, *Letters from Mesopotamia,* Chicago and London: University of Chicago Press, 1967.

——, *Ancient Mesopotamia—Portrait of a Dead Civilization,* Revised Edition compiled by Erica Reiner, Chicago and London: University of Chicago Press, 1977.

——, "Neo-Assyrian and Neo-Babylonian Empires", in H.D. Lasswell, D. et al. (eds.), *Propaganda and Communication in World History,* Vol. I, Honolulu: University Press of Hawaii, pp. 111–144, 1979.

Oren, E.D. (ed.), *The Sea Peoples and Their World: A Reassessment,* Philadelphia: The University Museum, University of Pennsylvania, 2000.

Orlin, L.L., *Assyrian Colonies in Cappadocia,* The Hague: Mouton, 1970.

Otten, H., "Ein althethitischer Vertrag mit Kizzuvatna", *JCS* 5, pp. 129–132, 1951.

——, "Die inschriftliche Funde", *MDOG* 86, pp. 59–64, 1953.

——, "Zwei althethitische Belege zu den Ḫapiru (SA.GAZ)", *ZA* 52, pp. 216–223, 1957.

——, "VII. Die Textfunde der Campagnen 1958 und 1959", *MDOG* 93, pp. 75–77, 1962.

——, "Ein hethitischer Vertrag aus dem 15./14. Jahrhundert v. Chr. (KBo XVI 47)", *Istanbuler Mitteilungen* 17, pp. 55–61, 1967.

——, "Das Siegel des hethitischen Großkönigs Taḫurwaili", *MDOG* 103, pp. 59–68, 1971.

——, *Die Apologie Ḫattušilis III.* (StBoT 24), Wiesbaden: Otto Harrassowitz, 1981.

——, *Die Bronzetafel aus Boğazköy—Ein Staatsvertrag Tuthalijas IV.* (StBoT, Beiheft 1), Wiesbaden: Otto Harrassowitz, 1988.

Parker, B.J., "Garrisoning the Empire: Aspects of the Construction and Maintenance of Forts on the Assyrian Frontier", *Iraq* 59, pp. 77–87, 1997.

——, *The Mechanics of Empire. The Northern Frontier of Assyria as a Case Study in Imperial Dynamics,* Helsinki: Neo-Assyrian Text Corpus Project, 2001.

Parpola, S., *The Correspondence of Sargon II,* Part I: *Letters from Assyria and the West* (SAA I), Helsinki: Neo-Assyrian Text Corpus Project, 1987a.

——, "Neo-Assyrian Treaties from the Royal Archives of Nineveh", *JCS* 39: pp. 161–189, 1987b.

——, "International law in the First Millennium", in Westbrook (ed.) 2003, Vol. II, pp. 1047–1066, 2003.

Parpola, S. and Watanabe, Kazuko, *Neo-Assyrian Treaties and Loyalty Oaths* (SAA II), Helsinki: Neo-Assyrian Text Corpus Project, 1988.

Pečírková, J., "The Administrative Organization of the Neo-Assyrian Empire", *Archív Oríentální* 45, pp. 211–228, 1977.

——, "The Administrative Method of Assyrian Imperialism", *Archív Oríentální* 55, pp. 162–175, 1987.

Pettinato, G., *Ebla, A New Look at History*, translated by C.F. Richardson, Baltimore and London: The John Hopkins University Press, 1991.

Pettinato G. and Waetzoldt, H., "Dagan in Ebla und Mesopotamien nach den Texten aus dem 3. Jahrtausend," *Orientalia* 54, pp. 234–256, 1985.

Phillipson, C., *The International Law and Custom of Ancient Greece and Rome*, Vols. I–II, London: Macmillan and co, 1911.

Piepkorn, A.C., *Historical Prism Inscriptions of Assurbanipal* (Assyriological Studies, 5) Chicago, Ill.: The Oriental Institute, University of Chicago Press, 1933.

Pirenne, J., "Le statut de l'etranger dans l'ancienne Egypt", *Recueils de la Societé Jean Bodin*, 9 (Bruxelles), pp. 93–103', 1958.

Pomponio, F., "The Hexapolis of Šuruppak…", in Francesco Pomponio—Giuseppe Visicato, *Early Dynastic Administrative Tablets of Šuruppak*, Instituto Universitario Orientale de Napoli, Dipartimento de Studi Asiatici, Series Major VI, Napoli: Istituto Universitario Oriental di Napoli, pp. 10–20, 1994.

Pongratz-Leisten, Beate, *Herrschaftswissen in Mesopotamien. Formen der Kommunikation zwichen Gott und König im 2. und 1. Jahrttausend v. Chr.*, (SAAS X), Helsinki: Neo-Assyrian Text Corpus Project, 1999.

Postgate, J.N., *Taxation and Conscription in the Assyrian Empire* (Studia Pohl: Series Maior 3), Rome: Biblical Institute Press, 1974.

——, "Ancient Assyria—A Multi-Racial State", *Aram* 1, 1–10, 1989.

——, "The Land of Assur and the yoke of Assur", *World Archaeology* 23/3, pp. 247–263, 1992.

——, "The Assyrian army in Zamua", *Iraq* 62, pp. 89–108, 2000.

Powell, M.A. (ed.), *Labor in the Ancient Near East*, New Haven, Conn.: American Oriental Society, 1987.

Preiser, W., "Zum Völkerrecht der vorklssischen Antike", *Archiv des Volkerrecht* 4/3, pp. 257–288, 1954.

——, "History of the Law of Nations: Basic Questions and Principles", in R. Bernhardt (ed.), *Encyclopedia of Public International Law*, Vol. 7, pp. 126–132, 1984a.

——, "History of the Law of Nations: Ancient Times to 1648", in R. Bernhardt (ed.), *Encyclopedia of Public International Law*, Vol. 7, pp. 132–160, 1984b.

Pritchard, J. (ed.), *The Ancient Near East in Pictures*, Princeton, N.J.: Princeton University Press, 1954.

——, *Ancient Near Eastern Text*, 3rd ed., Princeton, N.J.: Princeton University Press, 1969.

von Rad, G., *Der Heilige Krieg im alten Israel*, 3rd ed., Göttingen: Vandenhoeck & Ruprecht, 1958.

Redford, D.B., *Egypt and Canaan in the New Kingdom* (*Beer-Sheva—Studies by the Department of Bible and Ancient Near East of Ben-Gurion University of the Negev*, Vol. IV; edited by Sh. Aḥituv), Beer-Sheva: Ben-Gurion University of the Negev Press, 1990.

——, *Egypt, Canaan, and Israel in Ancient Times*, Princeton, N.J.: Princeton University Press, 1992.

Reiner, E., *Šurpu* (*AfO*, Beiheft, 11), Graz: Selbstverlag des Herausgebers, 1958.

——, "Akkadian Treaties from Syria and Assyria", in Pritchard (ed.) 1969, pp. 531–541, 1969.

——, *Enūma Anu Enlil, Tablet 63: The Venus Tablet of Ammiṣaduqa*, with collaboration with David Pingree, (Bibliotheca Mesopotamica 2/1), Malibu, Calif.: Undena Publications, 1975.

Renger, J., "Legal Aspects of Sealing in Ancient Mesopotamia", in McGuire Gibson and Robert D. Biggs (eds.), *Seals and Sealing in the Ancient Near East*, Malibu, Calif.: Undena Publications, pp. 75–87, 1977.

Reviv, H., "kidinnu: Observations on Privileges of Mesopotamian Cities", *Journal of Economic and Social History of the Orient* 31, pp. 286–298, 1988.

Reynolds, Frances, *The Babylonian Correspondence of Esarḫaddon and Letters to Assurbanipal and Sin-šarru-iškun from Northern and Central Babylonia* (SAA XVIII), Helsinki: Neo-Assyrian Text Corpus Project, 2003.

Rheinstein, M., "Process and Change in the Cultural Spectrum Coincident with Expansion: Government and Law," in Carl H. Krealing and Robert M. Adams (eds.), *City Invincible: A Symposium on Urbanization and Cultural Development held at the Oriental Institute of the University of Chicago, December 4–7, 1958*, Chicago, Ill.: University of Chicago Press, pp. 405–418, 1960.

Roberts, J.J.M., *The Earliest Semitic Pantheon*, Baltimore and London: The Johns Hopkins University Press, 1972.

Röllig, W., "Heirat, politische", *RlA* 4, pp. 282–87, 1972–75.

De Roos, J., "*KBo* 33–216. A votive text of Tuthališ IV", *Journal of Ancient Civilization* 4, pp. 39–48, 1989.

Rosenne, Sh., "The Influence of Judaism on the Development of International Law", in idem, *An International Law Miscellany*, Dordrecht: Nijhoff, pp. 509–547 (originally appeared in *Nederlands Tijdschrift voor Internationaal Recht* 5 [1958], 119–149), 1993.

Roth, M.T., *Law Collections from Mesopotamia and Asia Minor*, with a contribution by H.A. Hoffner, Jr., edited by P. Michalowski (Society of Biblical Literature, Writing from the Ancient World Series, 6), Atlanta, GA.: Scholars Press, 1995.

Rowton, M.B., "Watercourses and Water Rights in the Official Correspondence from Larsa and Isin", *JCS* 21, pp. 267–274, 1967.

van Rooy, H.F., "The Structure of the Aramaic Treaties of Sefire", *Journal of Semitic Studies* 1, pp. 133–139, 1989.

Saggs, H.W.F., "Historical texts and fragments of Sargon II of Assyria. I. The 'Aššur Charter' ", *Iraq* 37, pp. 11–20, 1975.

——, *The Nimrud Letters, 1952* (Cuneiform texts from Nimrud, V), London: British School of Archaeology in Iraq, 2001.

Sallaberger, W., "Ur III Zeit", in Aage Westenholz and Walther Sallaberger, *Mesopotamien: Akkade-Zeit und Ur III-Zeit*, (Annäherungen 3, edited by Pascal Attinger and Markus Wäfler), Freiburg, Schweiz: Universitätsverlag; Göttingen: Vandenhoeck & Ruprecht, pp. 121–390, 1999.

San Nicolò, M., *Beiträge zur Rechtsgeschichte im Bereiche der keilschriftlichen Rechtsquellen*, Oslo: H. Aschehoug, 1931.

Saporetti, C., "Una deportazione al tempo di Salmanassar I", *Atti della Accademia nazionale dei Lincei*, classe di scienze morali, storiche e filologiche: rendiconti, Ser. 8, 25, Rome: Accademia nazionale dei Lincei, pp. 437–453, 1970.

Sasson, J.M., "Instances of Mobility among Mari Artisans", *Bulletin of the American Schools of Oriental Research* 190, pp. 46–54, 1968.

——, "Yarim-Lim's War Declaration", in J.-M. Durand & J.-R. Kupper (eds.), *Miscellanea Babylonica. Mélanges offerts à Maurice Birot*, Paris: Éditions Recherche sur les civilisations, pp. 237–256, 1985.

——, "Oath-taking formulae", *NABU* 1992, p. 17, No. 21, 1992.

——, "Mari Apocalypticism Revisited", in K. Van Lerberghe and A. Schoors (eds.), *Immigration and Emigration within the Ancient Near East: Festschrift E. Lipiński* (Orientalia Lovaniensia Analecta, 65), Leuven: Uitgeverij Peeters en Departement Orientalistiek, pp. 287–292, 1995.

——, "Scruples: Extradition in the Mari Archives", in *Festschrift für Hermann Hunger, zum 65. Geburtstag gewidmet von seinen Freunden, Kollegen, und Schülern* (*Wiener Zeitschrift für die Kunde des Morgenlandes* 97), Wien: Institut für Orientalistik, pp. 453–473, 2007.

——, "Casus belli in the Mari Archives", *Proceedings of the 52e Rencontre assyriologique internationale, Münster 2006*, Forthcoming.

Sasson, J.M., et al. (eds.), *Civilizations of the Ancient Near East*, Vols. I–IV, New York: Scribner, 1995.

Schaeffer, C.F.-A., *Ugaritica III. Sceaux et cylindres hittites, épée gravée du cartouche de Mineptah, tablettes chypro-minoennes et autres découvertes nouvelles de Ras Shamra* (Mission de Ras Shamra VIII), Paris: Paul Geuthner, 1956.

Scheil, V., *Textes élamites-anzanites, qutrième série* (Mémoires de la Délégation en Perse, XI), Paris: E. Leroux, 1911.

Schmidt, J.D., *Ramesses II: A Chronological Structure for His Reign*, Baltimore and London: The John Hopkins University Press, 1973.

Schwemer, D., "Witchcraft and war: the ritual fragment Ki 1904–10–9, 18 (BM 98989)", *Iraq* 69, pp. 29–42, 2007.

——, "Fremde Götter in Ḫatti. Die hethitische Religion im Spannungsfeld von Synkretismus und Abgrenzung", in Wilhelm (ed.) 2008, pp. 137–157, 2008.

von Schuler, E., *Dienstanweisungen für höhere Hof- und Staatsbeamte* (*AfO*, Beiheft 10), Graz: Selbstverlag des Herausgebers, 1957.

——, *Die Kaškäer: Ein Beitrag zur Ethnographie des alten Kleinasien*, Berlin: Walter de Gruyter, 1965.

de Selincourt, Aubrey, [Translation of] Herodotus, *The Histories*, Harmondsworth: Penguin Books, 1954.

Sethe, K., *Urkunden der 18. Dynastie—Übersetzung zu den Heften 1–4*, Leipzig: J. C. Hinrichs (reprinted, Berlin: Akademie-Verlag 1984), 1914.

Singer, I., "Western Anatolia in the Thirteenth Century B.C. according to the Hittite Sources", *Anatolian Studies* 33, pp. 205–217, 1983.

——, "The Battle of Nihiriya and the End of the Hittite Empire", *ZA* 75, pp. 100–123, 1985.

——, "Hittite Cultural Influence in the Kingdom of Amurru", in Charpin and Joannès (eds.) 1992, pp. 231–234, 1992.

——, " 'The Thousand Gods of Ḫatti'. The Limits of an Expanding Pantheon", *Israel Oriental Studies* 14, pp. 81–102, 1994.

——, "A Political History of Ugarit", in Watson and Wyatt (eds.) 1999, pp. 603–733, 1999.

——, *Hittite Prayers*, edited by H.A. Hoffner, Jr. (Writings from the Ancient World, 11), Atlanta, GA.: Society of Biblical Literature, 2002.

——, "The Kuruštama Revisited", *Šarnikzel—Hethitologische Studien Zum Gedenken an Emil Orgetorix Forrer [19.02.1894–10.01.1986]*, edited by Detlev Groddek & Sylvester Rößle, Dresden: Verlag der TU Dresden, pp. 591–607, 2004.

Smith, S.T., *Askut in Nubia—The Economics and Ideology of Egyptian Imperialism in the Second Millennium B.C.*, London and New York: Kegan Paul International, 1995.

Snell, D.C., *Flight and Freedom in the Ancient Near East*, Leiden-Boston-Köln: Brill, 2001.

von Soden, W., "Die Assyrer und der Krieg", *Iraq* 25, pp. 131–144, 1963.

Sollberger E., "The So-Called Treaty Between Ebla and 'Ashur' ", *Studi Eblaiti*, III/9–10, pp. 129–148, 1980.

Sollberger E. and Kupper, J.R., *Inscriptions royales sumériennes et akkadiennes*, Paris: Éditions du Cerf, 1971.

van Soldt, W.H., "Ordal. A. Mesopotamien" *RlA* 10/1–2, pp. 124–129, 2003.

Sommer, F., *Die Aḫḫijavā-Urkunden*, Abhandlungen der Bayerischen Akademie der Wissenschaften Philosophisch-historische Abteilung, Neue Folge. 6, München: Verlag der Bayerischen Akademie der Wissenschaften, 1932.

Sommerfeld, W., "The Kassites of Ancient Mesopotamia: Origins, Politics, and Culture", in Sasson et al. (eds.) 1995, Vol. II, pp. 917–930, 1995.

Soysal, O., "KUB XXXI 4 + KBo III 41 und 40 (Die Puḫanu-Chronik). Zum Thronstreit Ḫattušilis I.", *Hethitica* 7, pp. 173–253, 1987.

Spalinger, A., "Considerations of the Hittite Treaty between Egypt and Ḫatti", *Studien zur altägyptischen Kulture* 9, pp. 299–358, 1981.

Speiser, E.A., "The Epic of Gilgamesh", in Pritchard (ed.) 1969: pp. 72–99, 1969.

Spigel, J., *The Bible as a Cradle for the Law of Nations*, Tel-Aviv: Self publication (in Hebrew), 1990.

Stadtmüller, G., *Geschichte des Völkerrechts*, Teil I: *Bis sum Wiener Kongreß (1815)*, Hanover, 1951.
Starr, I., *The Rituals of the Diviner*, Malibu: Undena, 1983.
——, *Queries to the Sungod. Divination and Politics in Sargonid Assyria* (SAA IV), Helsinki: Neo-Assyrian Text Corpus Project., 1990.
Stefanini, R., "Studi hittiti, I", *Athenaeum* 40, pp. 3–36, 1962.
Steible, H., *Die altsumerischen Bau- und Weihinschriften*, 2 Vols., Wiesbaden: Franz Steiner Verlag, 1982.
——, *Die neusumerischen Bau- und Weinhinschriften*, 2 Vols. (Freiburger altorientalische Studien, 9: 1–2), Stuttgart: Franz Steiner Verlag, 1991.
Steiner, G., "Gott. D. Nach hethitischen Texten", *RlA* 3, pp. 547– 575, 1957–71.
——, "Der Grenzvertrag zwischen Lagaš und Umma," *Acta Sumerologica, Japan* 8, pp. 219–300, 1986.
Steinkeller, P., "The Administrative and Economic Organization of the Ur III State: The Core and the Periphery", in *The Organization of Power: Aspects of Bureaucracy in the Ancient Near East*, edited by McG. Gibson and R.D. Biggs, Chicago: Oriental Institute of the University of Chicago, pp. 19–41, 1987.
——, "Mesopotamia in the Third Millennium B.C.", in D.N. Freedman et al. (eds.) *The Anchor Bible Dictionary*, Vol. 4, New York: Doubleday, pp. 724–732, 1992.
——, "Early Political Development in Mesopotamia and the Origins of the Sargonic Empire", in Liverani (ed.) 1993, pp. 107–129, 1993.
Stol, M., *Letters from Yale* (*AbB* Heft 9), Leiden: E.J. Brill, 1981.
——, "[Review of] Abraham Malamat, *Mari and the Early Israelite Experience*, Oxford 1989", *Bibliotheca Orientalis* 48, cols. 862–865, 1991.
——, "Wirtschaft und Gesellschaft", in Charpin, Edzard and Stol 2004, pp. 643–975, 2004.
Stolper, M.W., "Part I: Political History", in Elizabeth Carter and Matthew W. Stolper, *Elam: Surveys of Political History and Archaeology*, Berkeley – Los Angeles – London: University of California Press, pp. 3–100, 1984.
Streck, M., *Assurbanipal und die letzten assyrischen Könige bis zum Untergang Niniveh's*, I–III (Vorderasiatische Bibliothek 7), Leipzig: J.C. Hinrichs, 1916.
Strommenger, E.', *5000 Years of the Art of Mesopotamia*, New York, NY.: H.N. Abrams, 1964.
Tadmor, H., "Assyria and the West: The Ninth Century and its Aftermath", in H. Goedicke and J.J.M. Roberts (eds.), *Unity and Diversity*, Baltimore: John Hopkins University Press, pp. 36–48, 1975.
——, "Treaty and Oath in the Ancient Near East: A Historian's Approach", in G.M. Tucker and D.A. Knight (eds.), *Humanizing America's Iconic Book: Society of Biblical Literature Centennial Addresses 1980*, Chico CA,: Scholars Press, pp. 127–152, 1982.
——, *The Inscriptions of Tiglath-pileser III*, Jerusalem: The Israel Academy of Sciences and Humanities, 1994.
Thureau-Dangin, F., *Die sumerischen und akkadischen Königsinschriften*, Leipzig: J.C. Hinrichs, 1907.
——, *Une relation de la huitième campagne de Sargon* (TCL 3), Paris: P. Geuthner, 1912.
Tod, M.N., *International Arbitration amongst the Greeks*, Oxford: Clarendon Press, 1913.
Trigger, B.G., *Nubia under the Pharaohs*, London: Thames and Hudson, 1976.
Vanderhooft, D.S., *The Neo-Babylonian Empire and Babylon in the Later Prophets* (Harvard Semitic Museum Publications 59), Atlanta, GA.: Scholars Press, 1999.
Vanstiphout, H., "Political Ideology in Early Sumer", *Orientalia Lovaniensia Periodica* 1, pp. 7–38, 1970.
——, *Epics of Sumerian Kings: The Matter of Aratta*, edited by Jerrold S. Cooper (Writings from the Ancient World, 20), Atlanta, GA.: Society of Biblical Literature, 2003.
Veenhof, K.R., "Kaniš, kārum. A. Philologisch", *RlA* 5 (1976–1980), pp. 369–378, 1976–80.
Veenhof, K.R. and Eidem, J., *Mesopotamia. The Old Assyrian Period* (Annäherungen 5, edited by Markus Wäfler), Freiburg, Schweiz: Universitätsverlag; Göttingen: Vandenhoeck & Ruprecht, 2008.

Villard, P., "Les liberations de personnel de l'annee du trone de Šamaš", in ARMT 23, pp. 476–505, 1984.
——, "Shamshi-Adad and Sons: The Rise and Fall of an Upper Mesopotamian Empire", in Sasson et al. (eds.), 1995, Vol. II, pp. 873–883, 1995.
Vita, J.-P., "The Society of Ugarit", in Watson and Wyatt (eds.) 1999, pp. 455–498, 1999.
DI Vito, R.A., *Studies in Third Millennium Sumerians and Akkadians Personal Names*, Roma: Editrice Pontificio Istituto Biblico, 1993.
Vogelzang, M., *Bin šar dadmē, Edition and Analysis of the Akkadian Anzu Poem*, Groningen: Styx Publication, 1988.
Ward, W.A. and Joukowsky, Martha S. (eds.), *The Crisis Years: the 12th Century B.C.: From Beyond the Danube to the Tigris*, Dubuque, Iowa: Kendall Hunt, 1992.
Watanabe, Kazuko, *Die ade-Vereidigung anlässlich der Thronfolgeregelung Asarhaddons*, (Baghdader Mitteilungen, Beiheft 3), Berlin: Gebr. Mann, 1987.
——, "Mit Gottessiegeln versehene hethitische Staatsverträge", *Acta Sumerologica* 11, pp. 261–276, 1989.
Waterman, L., *Royal Correspondence of the Assyrian Empire*, Vols. I–II, Ann Arbor: University of Michigan Press, 1931.
Watson, W.G.E., and Wyatt, N. (eds.), *Handbook of Ugaritic Studies*, (Handbuch der Orientalistik, Erste Abteilung, 39), Leiden – Boston – Köln: Brill, 1999.
Weidner, E., *Politische Dokumente aus Kleinasien* (*Boghazköi Studien* 8 & 9), Leipzig: J.C. Hinrichs (reprinted by Georg Olms Verlag, Hildesheim and New York 1970), 1923.
——, "Assyrische Beschreibungen der Kriegs-Reliefs Aššurbânaplis," *AfO* 8, pp. 175–203, 1932–33.
——, "Assyrische Epen über die Kassiten-Kampfe", *AfO* 20, pp. 113–116 + Tf. V, 1963.
Weinfeld, M., "Covenant Terminology in the Ancient Near East and Its Influence on the West", *JAOS* 93, pp. 190–199, 1973.
Wente, E.F. Jr., "The Report of Wenamon", in W.K. Simpson (ed.), *The Literature of Ancient Egypt*, New Haven and London, pp. 141–155, 1972.
Westbrook, R., "International Law in the Amarna Age", in Cohen and Westbrook (eds.) 2000, pp. 28–41, 239–242 (notes), 2000a.
——, "Babylonian Diplomacy in the Amarna Letters", *JAOS* 120, pp. 377–382, 2000b.
——, "Introduction. The Character of Ancient Near Eastern Law, §9: International Law", in Westbrook (ed.) 2003, Vol. 1, pp. 82–86, 2003a.
——, "Old Babylonian Period", in Westbrook (ed.) 2003, Vol. I, pp. 361–430, 2003b.
Westbrook, R. (ed.), *A History of Ancient Near Eastern Law*, I–II, Leiden – Boston: Brill, 2003.
Westenholz, A., "*berūtum, damtum*, and the Old Akkadian KI.GAL: Burial of Dead enemies in Ancient Mesopotamia", *AfO* 23, pp. 27–31, 1970.
——, "The World View of Sargonic Officials. Differences in Mentality between Sumerians and Akkadians", in Mario Liverani (ed.), *Akkad—The First World Empire: Structure, Ideology, Traditions*, Padova: Sargon srl, pp. 157–169, 1993.
——, "The Old Akkadian Period: History and Culture", in Aage Westenholz and Walther Sallaberger, *Mesopotamien: Akkade-Zeit und Ur III-Zeit*, (Annäherungen 3, edited by Pascal Attinger and Markus Wäfler), Freiburg, Schweiz: Universitätsverlag; Göttingen: Vandenhoeck & Ruprecht, pp. 17–117, 1999.
Westenholz, J.G., *Legends of the Kings of Akkade, The Texts*, Winona Lake, Ind.: Eisenbrauns, 1997.
——, "Objects with Messages: Reading Old Akkadian Royal Inscriptions", *Bibliotheca Orientalis* 55, cols. 44–57, 1998.
——, "King by love of Inanna—an image of female empowerment?", *NiN—Journal of Gender Studies in Antiquity*, 1, pp. 75–89, 2000.
Whiting, R.M. Jr., *Old Babylonian Letters from Tell Asmar* (Assyriological Studies 22), Chicago: The Oriental Institute of the University of Chicago, 1987.

——, "Amorite Tribes and Nations of Second-Millennium Western Asia", in Sasson et al. (eds.) 1995, Vol. II, pp. 1231–1242, 1995.

Wilhelm, G., *The Hurrians*, Translated from German by Jennifer Barnes, with a chapter by Diana L. Stein, Warminster, England: Aris & Phillips, 1989.

——, "The Kingdom of Mitanni in Second-Millennium Upper Mesopotamia", in Sasson et al. (eds.) 1995, Vol. II, pp. 1243–1254, 1995.

Wilhelm, G. (ed.), *Ḫattuša-Bogazköy. Das Hethiterreich im Spannungsfeld des Alten Orients. Akten des 6. Internationales Colloquiums der Deutschen Orient-Gesellschaft, Würzburg, 22.–24. März 2006*, Wiesbaden: Harrassowitz, 2008.

Winter, I.J., "After the Battle Is Over: The *Stele of the Vultures* and the Beginning of Historical Narrative in the Art of the Ancient Near East", in Herbert L. Kessler and Marianna Shreve Simpson (eds.), *Pictorial Narrative in Antiquity and the Middle Ages* (Studies in the History of Art, 16), Washington D.C.: National Gallery of Art, pp. 11–32, 1985.

Wiseman, D.J., *The Alalakh Tablets*. London: The British Institute of Archaeology at Ankara, 1953.

——, *The Vassal Treaties of Esarḫaddon*, London: British School of Archaeology in Iraq, 1958a.

——, "Abban and Alalaḫ", *JCS* 12, pp. 124–129, 1958b.

Wright, J.L., "Warfare and Wanton Destruction: A Reexamination of Deuteronomy 20: 19–20 in Relation to Ancient Siegecraft", *Journal of Biblical Literature* 127/3, pp. 423–458, 2008.

Witte, M., et al. (eds.), *Die deuteronomistischen Geschichtes: Redaktions-und religionsgeschichtliche Perspektiven zur "Deuteronomismus"—Discussion in Tora und Vorderen Propheten* (Beiheft zur Zeitschrift für die alttestamentliche Wissenschaft 365), Berlin: De Gruyter, 2006.

Yamada, Sh., *The Construction of the Assyrian Empire*, Leiden – Boston – Köln: Brill, 2000.

Young, T.C., "The consolidation of the empire and its limits of growth under Darius and Xerxes", in *CAH*² IV, pp. 53–111, 1988.

Yuhong, W., *A Political History of Eshnunna, Mari and Assyria During the Old Babylonian Period*, Changchun, China: The Institute for the History of Ancient Civilizations, Northeast Normal University, 1994.

Zaccagnini, C., "The Forms of Alliance and Subjugation in the Near East of the Late Bronze Age", in L. Canfora et al. (eds.) 1990, pp. 37–79, 1990.

Ziskind, J.R., "Aspects of International Law in the Ancient Near East", PhD dissertation, Columbia University (University Microfilm Ann Arbor, Michigan, No. 68–8631), 1967.

INDEX

(Superscript numbers denote footnotes)

A. Sources—According to collections, field numbers, catalog numbers, or publication

B. Designated Texts—according to language and system of writing

Mesopotamian Cuneiform Sources

Hittite

Egyptian

Hebrew Bible

West Semitic

Greek & Roman Sources

C. Treaties and Loyalty Oaths (main discussions)

D. Topics

www.ingramcontent.com/pod-product-compliance
Lightning Source LLC
LaVergne TN
LVHW010657300926
849161LV00005B/1145